Ancient Rhetoric and the New Testament

Ancient Rhetoric and the New Testament

The Influence of Elementary Greek Composition

Mikeal C. Parsons
Michael Wade Martin

BAYLOR UNIVERSITY PRESS

Cover Design by Aaron Cobbs. Jacket layout by *the*BookDesigners.
The cover art is based on wax tablets used by students in ancient Egypt to practice writing (c. 350 AD). Wax tablets of this kind are housed in the Collection of the Leiden Papyrological Institute, Universiteit Leiden.

The Library of Congress has cataloged this book under the ISBN
978-1-4813-0980-6.

Printed in the United States of America on acid-free paper with a minimum of 30 percent post-consumer waste recycled content.

For Carey Newman

In gratitude for his steadfast friendship, unswerving vision, and generous spirit

Contents

Acknowledgments

This book is the result of the assistance of a good many folk. For Mikeal, it represents the result of nearly twenty years of teaching rhetorical criticism in doctoral seminars at Baylor University, focusing especially on the contributions of the progymnasmata. The work of those graduate students is evident on nearly every page, even when the indebtedness is not formally acknowledged, and Mikeal is grateful for what his students have taught him about rhetorical criticism over the years. For Michael, one of those students, this work represents the culmination of rhetorical critical inquiry begun under Mikeal's tutelage and nurtured these many years since under his mentorship. All acknowledgment of Michael's indebtedness thus begins and ends with this treasured relationship. Michael would also be remiss if he did not mention in particular those students (Ron Guzmán, Bryan Nash, Timothy Gibson, and Jonathan Dansby) and colleagues (Jason Whitlark) with whom he has coauthored other rhetorical critical studies, and whose thinking is undoubtedly reflected in the pages of this book.

While the book, in many respects, represents a synthesis of previous work, we hope each chapter also contributes in some small way to a deeper understanding of how these rhetorical exercises shape and are reflected in ancient prose composition, especially in the New Testament writings. We have tried to be generous in citing examples both from the New Testament and from its larger literary environment in order that one may see the connections—and tensions—that exist between rhetorical theory and practice.

Michael wishes to thank his provost, Rod Blackwood; his dean, Jesse Long; his chair, Charles Stephenson; and his fellow faculty members for granting him a sabbatical in the spring of 2017 so that he could pursue this research project full time. Michael also expresses his deep gratitude to Al and Patricia Smith for providing the funds for the sabbatical and their generous patronage of the college that now bears their name. Michael's father, Don Martin; his mother, Lou Stafford;

and son, J. H., have all been a source of great encouragement and love during the course of this work.

Mikeal wants to thank his department chair, W. H. Bellinger Jr., who arranged for a research leave for the spring of 2017. The book was completed during that semester at Harvard Divinity School, where Mikeal and his spouse, Heidi Hornik, served as visiting scholars. Heidi was a great encouragement during the project, even while working on her own beautifully illustrated book on Christian ethics and art. Appreciation is expressed to Matthew Turner, department manager in the Office of Academic Affairs at HDS, for making available the considerable resources of the divinity school and the Andover-Harvard Theological Library. Jason Whitlark read through the entire manuscript, making numerous helpful suggestions. Jeremiah Bailey provided assistance in gathering bibliography. Greg Barnhill trained his eagle eyes on the manuscript, correcting matters of style and format and, more than once, offering substantive suggestions.

Mikeal's relationship with Carey Newman, director of Baylor University Press, spans some thirty years. In 1988, as a new Baylor faculty member, Mikeal participated in Carey's oral defense of his doctoral dissertation. It was clear even then that here was a scholar whose first-rate mind and boundless energy were matched by an indefatigable enthusiasm. Fast forward to 2002–2003, when Mikeal chaired a search for a director for the Baylor University Press, which was publishing fewer than five books per year and was not even a blip on the radar of university presses. This was hardly the fault of past directors. The institution simply did not view the press as integral to the university's mission, and the press' minimal resources reflected this lack of investment. But the Baylor 2012 Initiative changed that, and the provost at the time was committed to raising the profile of the press. A nationwide search ensued and produced several excellent candidates. Still, Carey rose to the top. The story of the meteoric rise of Baylor University Press in the ensuing fifteen years in which academic publishing has generally languished is a remarkable one and due solely to the energies of Carey Newman and the staff he gathered around him. Anyone who knows Carey Newman recognizes that in him intellectual curiosity reacts with entrepreneurial spirit in an unusually potent alchemy. Michael is pleased to join Mikeal in dedicating the book to our friend, Dr. Carey Newman, the "author's editor" par excellence!

Michael W. Martin, Lubbock Christian University
Mikeal C. Parsons, Baylor University

Introduction

> Training in the exercises is absolutely necessary, not only for those who are going to be orators, but also if anyone wishes to practice the art of poets or prose-writers, or any other writers. These things are, in effect, the foundation of every form of discourse.
>
> Theon

The Place of the Progymnasmata in Graeco-Roman Rhetorical Education

Literacy in the ancient Graeco-Roman world was inextricably bound to the theory and practice of rhetoric. It is conventional to speak of a tripartite educational system from Homeric times to its fullest expression in the Hellenistic period and beyond into late antiquity.[1] At the primary level, (mostly) boys and (some) girls, ages roughly seven to eleven and presumably mostly of elite status (with an occasional slave or middling-class individual),[2] learned their alphabets, copied lists and short passages (which they could not read), and learned to write their names, all activities aimed at acquiring some basic literary competence and improving handwriting.[3] At the secondary level, aristocratic boys and (fewer) girls, roughly aged eleven to fifteen, continued to practice handwriting, often copying lists "made up of names of gods, Homeric heroes and even philosophers, [which] also supplied students with cultural knowledge."[4] But now the student began reading, especially Homer and the Greek poets. Study of grammar, noun declensions, inflection (running a sentence or saying through all the cases and numbers), culminated in elementary composition, which might include letters to parents. The third and tertiary level of rhetorical education in the ancient world was populated by an ever-dwindling number of students, now composed almost entirely of the male elite, who were in their mid- to late teens (fifteen to nineteen). The aim now was to prepare orators for declamation and a public life in the court system or politics, or both.[5] The rhetorical handbooks attributed to luminaries such as Cicero and Quintilian were aimed at this last level of declamation.

Until recently, it was thought that these levels were idealized into uniformly discrete and self-contained units (in separate classrooms, if not separate spaces entirely).[6] Raffaella Cribiore and others, working especially with the material remains (tablets, *ostraca*, papyri) of actual classroom activities, have demonstrated a fluidity in what, when, and how students learned.[7] The implementation of the tripartite educational system varied from locale to locale. The school of Libanius in Antioch, for example, ran all three levels of education concurrently, perhaps even in the same classroom. Thus, older students, working in the tertiary stratum, could serve as models for the younger students at the primary and secondary levels, assisting the teacher, and at times even substituting for him (see Libanius, *Ep.* 1408).[8] In many cases, and anachronistically speaking, the result, perhaps prompted as much by necessity as intention, was something of a cross between the proverbial one-room schoolhouse and the Montessori educational philosophy of the mixed-age classroom.

Within this fluid structure, students would encounter the preliminary exercises, the progymnasmata, intended to facilitate the transition between the study of grammar and the engagement of rhetoric proper.[9] Typically, these exercises were associated with the beginning of the tertiary level of education, though it is quite possible that the exercises were introduced at some point during the secondary level, and given what we now know of the fluidity of the educational system, the exact location of the exercises in the system might be viewed as somewhat irrelevant.[10] After all, when the orator Quintilian was asked when a student should be sent to the rhetor, he responded "When he is fit!" (*Inst.* 2.1.7).[11]

The progymnasmata were "handbooks that outlined 'preliminary exercises' designed to introduce students who had completed basic grammar and literary studies to the fundamentals of rhetoric that they would then put to use in composing speeches and prose."[12] As such, these graded series of exercises were probably intended to facilitate the transition from grammar school to the more advanced study of rhetoric.[13] Four of these progymnasmata from the first to fifth centuries CE, have survived.[14] What is important about these writings is that some of the exercises in the progymnasmata are clearly intended to embrace both written and oral forms of communication. The epigraph by Theon at the beginning of this chapter makes that point clear: "Training in the exercises is absolutely necessary, not only for those who are going to be orators, but also if anyone wishes to practice the art of poets or prose-writers, or any other writers. These things are, in effect, the foundation of every form of discourse" (*Prog.* 70.24–30).[15]

Thus, though the rhetorical handbooks and the progymnasmata often address the same topics, the progymnasmata, aimed as they are to equip young students with the building blocks of communication, both written and oral, serve as a kind of filter for the handbooks to sift out what comments might be more appropriate for written communication.

Furthermore, George Kennedy has commented:

> The curriculum described in these works, featuring a series of set exercises of increasing difficulty, was the source of facility in written and oral expression for many persons and training for speech in public life. . . . Not only the secular literature of the Greeks and Romans, but *the writings of early Christians beginning with the gospels* and continuing through the patristic age, and of some Jewish writers as well, *were molded by the habits of thinking and writing learned in schools.*[16]

If the last part of Kennedy's comment is true, and we think that it is, then a thoroughgoing investigation into the rhetorical conventions of the New Testament writers is warranted.[17] It is important to tease out the implications of this fact for understanding the impact of early Christian writings upon their authorial audience, who presumably also knew how to respond appropriately (if unconsciously) to the effects of persuasive rhetoric.

The progymnasmatists are both descriptive and prescriptive. The forms existed long before the textbooks, as did the names for them and practices associated with them. Many are even pan-Mediterranean, existing outside the confines of Greek and Roman literature—so much so that Philo and Josephus believed the Greeks stole all rhetoric generally from Moses! The correspondence between progymnastic theory and Mediterranean practice, then, is not unidirectional or strictly direct.[18] Theory could directly shape practice or vice versa. They undoubtedly had a mutually formative and standardizing effect on one another as we approach the first century CE. And theory and practice together could—directly or indirectly—shape the subsequent practice of later theory. All of that is to say that a New Testament writer could gain familiarity with and competence in a progymnastic form through any number of means (all of which are complementary and not necessarily exclusive of the others—but none of which is requisite for the correspondences we may see). Rhetoric, as they say, was "in the air," and some of the air breathed by early Christian writers may well have been in the schoolrooms of the progymnasmatists. Our accounts of correspondence assume from the beginning the possibility of all of these factors, and the certainty of none.

The Scope and Structure of This Book

The structure, arguments, and comparisons of this book are drawn primarily from the *Progymnasmata* of Aelius Theon of Alexandria (ca. 50–100 CE), the only textbook roughly contemporary to the New Testament writers.[19] We are not, of course, suggesting any kind of literary dependence between the early Christian writers and Theon but rather that Theon's text conveniently represents the kind of rhetorical exercises practiced in the first century, many of which, in fact, had been practiced as early as the first or second centuries BCE.[20] Thus, we assume that most of what Theon says about these rhetorical exercises was not unique to Theon. This assumption is buttressed by occasional appeal to the discussions in the rhetorical handbook tradition, which, while discussing specifically rhetorical speech, have remarkable similarity to Theon's text at a number of points.

The extant Greek manuscripts of Theon preserve twelve chapters; the Armenian versions add another five chapters.[21] The first two chapters consist of a brief preface, summarizing the contents that follow, and a philosophy "On the Education of the Young" that we have already cited. Theon's presentation is unique among the extant progymnasmata in that it is addressed to the teacher and not the students and in its order and numbering of the exercises. Table 1 conveniently summarizes the differences:[22]

Table 1. Order of Treatment of Progymnasmata in Extant Treatises

Exercise	Theon (1st c. CE)	Ps.-Hermogenes (3rd/4th c. CE)	Aphthonius (4th c. CE)	Nicolaus (5th c. CE)
Chreia	1	3	3	3
Maxim	1*	4	4	4
Fable	2	1	1	1
Narrative	3	2	2	2
Refutation	3†	5	5	5
Confirmation	3†	5	6	5
Common-place	4	6	7	6
Ekphrasis	5	10	12	10
Speech-in-character	6	9	11	9
Encomium	7	7	8	7
Invective	7‡	-	9	7
Syncrisis	8	8	10	8
Thesis	9	11	13	11
Law	10	12	14	12

* *Treated as a form of the Chreia.*

† *Refutation and confirmation are discussed by Theon in connection with narrative.*

‡ *Encomium and invective are treated together as parts of one exercise by Theon.*

In this book, we deal extensively with seven of these preliminary exercises, in the order originally preserved by Theon: chreia (chapter 1), fable (chapter 2), narrative (chapter 3), ekphrasis (chapter 4), speech-in-character (chapter 5), encomium (chapter 6), and syncrisis (chapter 7). We will reserve explanation of these exercises for the chapters devoted to an analysis of their theory and practice. At this point, it is important to observe that we have only treated two kinds of exercises:

1. the preliminary exercises common to all four theorists and Quintilian and thus having a fixed place in the curriculum: chreia, fable, narrative (maxim, too—but we have followed Theon in treating it as part of chreia);
2. the "larger and more ambitious exercises" (Quintilian's phrase for those exercises that he says are sometimes taught by rhetors, and sometimes—to his great disapproval—by the *grammatici*; *Inst.* 1.9.6) (a) that are attested by all four Greek theorists (thereby eliminating idiosyncratic or late exercises) and (b) that are in our judgment at least as important to the theory and practice of composition as to that of declamation: ekphrasis, speech-in-character, encomium (we follow Ps.-Hermogenes in including invective within encomium), and syncrisis.

Thus, we have joined Quintilian in leaving common-place, thesis, and introduction of the law for the rhetors (*Inst.* 1.9.1–6).[23] And we have joined Theon in including treatment of refutation and confirmation, but only in connection with narrative, and *not* as an exercise unto itself as we find in the other progymnasmatists. Finally, because we have focused on what the progymnasmata can teach us about ancient compositional practices, we are not dealing with issues typically taken up in the "third-level" handbooks (e.g., Quintilian and *Rhetorica ad Herennium*, inter alia)—namely, figures of speech and thought and the form and function of declamation or speeches.[24]

It is worth pausing, however, to discuss briefly two rhetorical strategies that are not exercises proper but are devices used within one or more exercises and the influence of which can be detected in the New Testament. We will return to these devices as they emerge in our discussion of the exercises.

(1) <u>*Inflection*</u>. Every beginning language student is aware that Greek is a highly inflected language, but, in light of the progymnasmata, the significance of that fact for NT interpretation has not been fully appreciated.[25] Inflecting the main subject or topic (*klisis*) was one of the first exercises taught to beginning students of elementary rhetoric and provided a transition from the study of grammar to the study of rhetoric since the exercise focused on the rhetorical function of inflection.[26] Theon gives a rather full description of how such inflection is to take place in his discussion of chreia and fable and refers back to it in his discussion of narrative (85.29–31). In his chapter on "Fable," Theon asserts:

> Fables should be inflected, like chreia, in different grammatical numbers and oblique cases. . . . The original grammatical construction must not always be maintained as though by some necessary law, but one should introduce some

> things and use a mixture (of constructions); for example, start with one case and change in what follows to another, for this variety is very pleasing. (74.24–35, 74–75; cf. also 101.10–103.2)

Quintilian (*Inst.* 9.1.34) also comments briefly on the use of inflection as a rhetorical device.[27] Following a discussion of the effects of repetition, he suggests: "Other effects may be obtained by the graduation or contrast of clauses, by the elegant inversion of words, by arguments drawn from opposites, asyndeton, paraleipsis, correction, exclamation, meiosis, the employment of a *word in different cases* (in multis casibus), moods and tenses." And again at 9.3.37:

> At times the cases and genders of the words repeated may be varied, as in "Great is the goal of speaking, and great the task, etc."; a similar instance is found in Rutilius, but in a long period. I therefore merely cite the beginnings of the clauses. "Pater hic tuus? Patrem nunc appellas? Patris tui filius es?" ["Is this your father? Do you still call him father? Are you your father's son?"] This figure may also be effected solely by change of cases, a preceding which the Greeks call πολύπτωτον [*polyptōton*].

What Theon calls *klisis*, Quintilian refers to as *polyptōton*; but the phenomenon is the same. Inflection was more than just an ornamental figure of style designed to please the aesthetic tastes of the audience. In fact, Quintilian included inflection in his discussion of figures of thought, a "class of figure, which does not merely depend on the form of the language for its effect, but lends both charm and force to the thought as well" (9.3.28 [Russell, LCL]).[28] The function of inflection was for emphasis (see Quintilian, *Inst.* 9.3.67) and to attract the audience's attention to the subject under discussion (9.3.27). We should not, however, view the use of inflection as a particularly elegant rhetorical device. Rather, inflection was one of the first rhetorical devices practiced by the beginning student of rhetoric, who quickly passed on to more challenging exercises.[29] In fact, Quintilian recognized that inflection and other figures like it "derive something of their charm from their very resemblance to blemishes, just as a trace of bitterness in food will sometimes tickle the palate" (9.3.27 [Russell, LCL]).[30] But its "ordinary" nature might argue for its effectiveness as a rhetorical device in signaling the importance of the inflected term for the understanding of the narrative in which it is couched. Certainly, this seems to be that for which Theon hoped. In one of the chapters on "Listening to What Is Read," preserved only in the Armenian versions, Theon comments: "In listening, the most important thing is to give frank and friendly attention to the speaker. Then the student should recall the subject of the writing, identify the main points and the arrangement, finally recall also the better passages" (*Prog.* 105–106).[31]

Any student of elementary rhetoric then would have been accustomed to inflecting the main topic or subject of a chreia, fable, or narrative, and presumably an ancient audience would have been naturally, almost instinctively, able to identify the main subject by hearing the topic inflected in the various cases of the Greek noun.[32]

(2) *Paraphrase*. This expansion through repetition reflects a well-known rhetorical exercise known as "paraphrase" (*paraphrasis*) in which a writer would "change the form of expression while keeping the thoughts" (Theon, *Prog.* 107). There were four kinds of paraphrase: "variation in syntax, by addition, by subtraction and by substitution" or by any combination of these four (*Prog.* 107–108). In his introduction Theon addresses objections to the practice of paraphrase:

> The argument of opponents is that once something has been well said it cannot be done a second time, but those who say this are far from hitting on what is right. Thought is not moved by any one thing in only one way so as to express the idea that has occurred to it in a similar form, but it is stirred in a number of different ways. (*Prog.* 62)

Furthermore, paraphrase could be undertaken "by a poet of his own thoughts elsewhere or paraphrase by another poet and in the orators and historians, and in brief, all ancient writers seem to have used paraphrase in the best possible way, rephrasing not only their own writings but those of each other" (*Prog.* 62).

Theon gives several examples of paraphrase as restatement, even suggesting the device could be used for clarification: "Thucydides (1.142.1) said, 'in war, opportunities are not abiding,' while Demosthenes (4.37) paraphrased this, 'opportunities for action do not await our sloth and evasions'" (*Prog.* 108). In his discussion of *conversio*, Quintilian advises that students of rhetoric

> should learn to paraphrase Aesop's fables . . . in simple and restrained language and subsequently to set down the paraphrase in writing with the same simplicity of style; they should begin by analyzing each verse, then give its meaning in a different language, and finally proceed to a freer paraphrase in which they will be permitted now to abridge and now to embellish the original, so far as this may be done without losing the poet's meaning. He should also set to write aphorisms, chreiae, and delineations of character, of which the teacher will first give the general scheme, since such themes will be drawn from their reading. In all of these exercises the general idea is the same, but the form differs. (1.9.2–3)[33]

Paraphrase was similar to translation from one language to another, and they are often discussed in relation to each other (cf. Quintilian, *Inst.* 10.5.2–3 on translation, which immediately proceeds a discussion of paraphrase in 10.5.4–11). We will return to the importance of *paraphrasis* for New Testament studies in the subsequent chapters, especially chapter 3 on "Narrative."[34]

The Progymnasmata and Moral Formation: "Homer" or "Moses"?

Finally a word about the ethos culture of rhetoric. According to Raffaella Cribiore, education in the ancient world (not unlike today in many quarters) "was based on the transmission of an established body of knowledge, about which there was wide consensus."[35] The transmission of traditional values included also the formation of the moral character of the students (or audience). Todd Penner has observed:

> We need to appreciate fully the kind of pedagogical environment that is being fostered in this environment. Like most, if not all, educational systems, there is an underlying moral vision being perpetuated, wherein both student and material are being closely drawn together so as to mold the student. It is thus a culture of repetition—of one time great moments from the past repeated over and over again in each new student present. It is also a culture of moral suasion—the patterns that are repeated, as well as the act of repetition itself, contain not only an implied theory of psychological development, but, more to the point, also an appreciation and assessment of events and narratives in fundamentally moral terms—as good and bad, in both literary and rhetorical quality, as well as in terms of the value systems being perpetuated.[36]

Theon of Alexandria confirms this point several times: "Surely the exercise in the form of the khreia (or anecdote) not only creates a certain faculty of speech but also good character [ethos], while we are being exercised in the moral sayings of the wise" (*Prog.* 60.18; see also 71.6; 78.9). In a similar vein, Pseudo-Hermogenes argues for fable as the first of the exercises to be encountered by students because of its value in moral formation: "Fable (*mythos*) is regarded as the first exercise to be assigned to the young because it can bring their minds into harmony for the better. In this way they think to form students while tender" (*Prog.* 1). Thus, beyond acquiring facility in grammar and rhetoric, a fortunate by-product of the rhetorical exercises from the teacher's point of view was the shaping of moral habits that reflected the prevailing cultural values of the day.

The anonymous writer of *Rhetorica ad Herennium* (first century BCE) agreed with this view: "Even if, in public speaking, we have not reached our goal, we shall miss but little of the wholly perfect life" (4.56.69). In the pursuit of the "wholly perfect life," negative character traits—dishonoring parents, betraying friends, greed, and shameful behavior, in general—were to be avoided (4.14.20–4.28.38).[37] On the positive side, support of the state was a common feature of moral exhortation among the rhetoricians (see *Rhet. Her.* 4.8.19). Quintilian likewise agrees with the moral goal of rhetorical education: "I am proposing to educate the perfect orator, who cannot exist except in the person of a good man. We therefore demand of him not only exceptional powers of speech, but all the virtues of character as well" (*Inst.* 1.proem.9 [Rackham, LCL]). For Quintilian, to be a good orator was to be a good man:

> What will he do in an encomium, unless he understands honour and shame? How can he urge a policy unless he has a grasp of expediency? How can he plead in the law courts if he knows nothing about justice? Again, does not oratory also call for courage, since we often have to speak in the face of threats of public disorder, often at the risk of offending the powerful, and sometimes even . . . with armed soldiers all around? So, if it is not a virtue, oratory cannot even be complete. (2.20.8 [Rackham, LCL])[38]

Most, if not all, early Christians who were literate acquired the ability to read and write through rhetorical education in some form or fashion, through which they also learned ethos argumentation (i.e., how to shape the moral character of their audiences).

Despite these laudatory exhortations to virtuous living by the rhetoricians, the moral vision propagated by the Graeco-Roman rhetorical tradition, including the progymnasmatists, was—in modern terms—elitist, racist, and sexist. The ideal was the free male Roman citizen against whom all others were deemed inferior.[39] The New Testament writers at times reflect the mores and ethos passed down, and not infrequently forcibly imposed, by the dominant Roman culture. But there is also evidence that, at times, early Christians resisted this moral vision and invoked the methods and categories of rhetorical argument in order to subvert or overturn them, a rhetorical move of ethos-argumentation that they no doubt learned from the very teachers of grammar and rhetoric whose moral vision they so severely challenge.[40] Their use of rhetoric, in these cases, is aimed at forming the moral character and theological vision of the Christian community, already in the process of being shaped by the Jewish Scriptures. Thus, while ancient Graeco-Roman rhetoric is helpful in discerning the mode and method of early Christian communication, the meaning is thoroughly grounded in those Jewish Scriptures and its interpretive streams, in which they (or most of them) understood Jesus to stand. That is why, simply put, the New Testament writers regularly quote and allude to the Jewish Scriptures in their writings (refracted through a christological lens) and only rarely appeal to "pagan" sources (cf. Acts 17:28). Or to put it differently, "Moses," not "Homer," was the "Bible"—the source of authority—for early Christian faith and practice, even if that faith and practice were communicated through thoroughly Hellenized rhetorical devices.[41] And this is no small matter, since medium and message are inextricably intertwined. Understanding the medium will assist in tracking the message.[42] So we turn now to a primer in theory and practice of the preliminary exercises.

Notes

1 See H. I. Marrou, *A History of Education in Antiquity* (London: Sheed & Ward, 1956).

2 Theresa Morgan, *Literate Education in the Hellenistic and Roman Worlds* (Cambridge: Cambridge University Press, 1998), 150–59, 265–74.

3 Raffaella Cribiore, *Gymnastics of the Mind: Greek Education in Hellenistic and Roman Egypt* (Princeton: Princeton University Press, 2001), 160–84. Ronald F. Hock, "Observing a Teacher of *Progymnasmata*," in *Ancient Education and Early Christianity*, ed. Matthew Ryan Hauge and Andrew W. Pitts (London: Bloomsbury T&T Clark, 2016), 39–40.

4 Hock, "Observing a Teacher of *Progymnasmata*," 41.

5 Cribiore, *Gymnastics of the Mind*, 232–33.

6 Marrou, *Education*, 104; and many others who followed him.

7 Raffaella Cribiore, *Writing, Teachers, and Students in Graeco-Roman Egypt* (Atlanta: Scholars Press, 1996), 173–87; Hock, "Observing a Teacher of *Progymnasmata*," 40.

8 Cribiore, *Gymnastics of the Mind*, 38–42. See also Michael R. Whitenton, "The Place and Scope of Composition and Rhetoric in Greco-Roman Education: A Literature Review," (seminar paper for His 4324: Ancient Rome, Dr. Kenneth R. Jones, instructor, fall 2010). This practice apparently existed despite the fact that some rhetors disapproved of mixed-age learning (Quintilian, *Inst.* 2.2.14).

9 See Sean A. Adams, "Luke and *Progymnasmata*: Rhetorical Handbooks, Rhetorical Sophistication and Genre Selection," *Ancient Education and Early Christianity*, ed. Matthew Ryan Hauge and Andrew W. Pitts (London: Bloomsbury T&T Clark, 2016), 137–63, esp. 139–43.

10 Contra Adams, "Luke and Progymnasmata," 142; and Osvaldo Padilla, "Hellenistic Paideia and Luke's Education: A Critique of Recent Approaches," *NTS* 55 (2009): 416–37. Padilla (417) has "accused" us of assuming that NT authors, specifically Luke, had achieved the "tertiary level of Hellenistic education." Nowhere, however, in our previous writings have either of us claimed that Luke, or any other writer, must have completed all three levels of rhetorical education. We remain agnostic on this question, since, in our view, tertiary rhetorical education focuses primarily on oral declamation, and it would be virtually impossible to be certain about Luke's level of education as a writer beyond the progymnasmata, which, as Padilla himself admits, provides no sure evidence of education beyond the secondary level. Some NT writers may have "graduated," diploma in hand, from the rhetorical schools, but—given what we have said above—that point is not germane to our argument.

11 Cited by Whitenton, "Composition and Rhetoric," 4n16.

12 Willi Braun, *Feasting and Social Rhetoric in Luke 14*, SNTSMS 85 (Cambridge: Cambridge University Press, 1995), 146.

13 Quintilian, in fact, refers to the preliminary exercises as part of the educational curriculum of young boys (*Inst.* 1.9). On the role of rhetoric in the educational curricula of antiquity, in addition to the works by Marrou, Cribiore, and Morgan, already cited, see also S. F. Bonner, *Education in Ancient Rome* (Berkeley: University of California Press, 1977); D. L. Clark, *Rhetoric in Graeco-Roman Education* (New York: Columbia University Press, 1957).

14 In addition to the text of Aelius Theon (cited below), other surviving progymnasmata include those by Ps.-Hermogenes of Tarsus (third/fourth century; critical edition in H. Rabe, ed., *Hermogenes opera*, Rhetores Graeci 10 [Leipzig: Teubner, 1913], 1–27; English trans. in Charles Sears Baldwin, *Medieval Rhetoric and Poetic [to 1400] Interpreted from Representative Works* [New York: Macmillan, 1928], 23–38); Aphthonius of Antioch (fourth century; critical edition in H. Rabe, ed., *Aphthonii progymnasmata*, Rhetores Graeci 10 [Leipzig: Teubner, 1926], 1–51; English translation in Ray E. Nadeau, "The *Progymnasmata* of Aphthonius in Translation," *Speech Monographs* 19 [1952]: 264–85); Nicolaus of Myra (fifth century; critical edition in J. Felten, ed., *Nicolai progymnasmata*, Rhetores Graeci 11 [Leizpig: Teubner,

1913]). English translations of, introductions to, and notes about Theon, Ps.-Hermogenes, Aphthonius, and Nicolaus (along with selections from some others) may be found in George A. Kennedy, trans., *Progymnasmata: Greek Textbooks of Prose Composition and Rhetoric* (Atlanta: Society of Biblical Literature, 2003). A fifth document, a commentary on Aphthonius' *Progymnasmata* attributed to John of Sardis, is available in the Teubner edition, *Ioannis Sardiani commentarium in Aphthonii progymnasmata* (Leipzig: Teubner, 1928), edited by Hugo Rabe.

15 James R. Butts, "The *Progymnasmata* of Theon: A New Text with Translation and Commentary" (Ph.D. diss., Claremont Graduate School, 1986), 181n36, rightly observes: "This statement is clear evidence that T[heon] understood the *progymnasmata* as providing instruction for literary activity ranging far beyond the technical parameters of rhetoric."

16 Kennedy, *Progymnasmata*, v (emphasis added).

17 As recently as 1994, Duane Watson was able to write, "A thorough and balanced assessment of the rhetoric of the Gospels has yet to be written." "Notes on History and Method," in *Rhetorical Criticism of the Bible: A Comprehensive Bibliography with Notes on History and Method*, ed. Duane F. Watson and Alan J. Hauser, BibInt 4 (Leiden: E. J. Brill, 1994), 115.

18 The critical consensus seems to be that early attempts to relate rhetoric to the NT sometimes erred in this regard. Hans Dieter Betz' commentary on Galatians, among others, has been roundly criticized for trying to force the structure of Galatians into the form and species of rhetorical declamation. Others have been reluctant to follow the pioneering work of R. O. P. Taylor (*The Groundwork of the Gospels* [London: Basil Blackwell, 1946]) because the rhetorical tradition represented by Cicero, Quintilian, and others was aimed at training orators for declamation and not on writing narratives. That reading of the handbooks, of course, misses the point that Quintilian, Cicero, and the others generously quote examples from various Greek and Latin epics, histories, poetry, etc. Still, the reluctance is understandable, and the progymnasmata with their explicit aim to enhance all forms of communication, oral and written, are an adequate antidote to this problem. Over the past thirty years, notable and important works on rhetoric, including the progymnasmata, and its relationship to early Christian composition have appeared. Prominent among that literature is the work by Burton Mack and Vernon Robbins; see Burton L. Mack and Vernon K. Robbins, *Patterns of Persuasion in the Gospels* (Sonoma, Calif.: Polebridge, 1989); Burton L. Mack, *Rhetoric and the New Testament*, GBS (Minneapolis: Fortress, 1990); Vernon K. Robbins, *The Tapestry of Early Christian Discourse: Rhetoric, Society, and Ideology* (London: Routledge, 1996); Robbins, *Exploring the Texture of the Texts: A Guide to Socio-rhetorical Interpretation* (Philadelphia: Trinity Press International, 1996); Stanley Porter, ed., *Handbook of Classical Rhetoric in the Hellenistic Period, 330 B.C.–A.D. 400* (Leiden: Brill, 2001). The interest in the chreia tradition has led also to the collection and publication of the chreia exercises of prominent progymnasmata; see Ronald F. Hock and Edward N. O'Neil, *The Chreia in Ancient Rhetoric*, vol. 1, *The Progymnasmata*, SBLTT 27 (Atlanta: Scholars, 1986). Other works are cited in the following chapters. For an assessment of these and other leading scholars in this field, see Troy W. Martin, ed., *Genealogies of New Testament Rhetorical Criticism* (Minneapolis: Fortress, 2014). There are several other useful histories of research into rhetorical analysis and the New Testament, and we see no reason to reproduce that history here, given that our focus is on early Christian compositional practices in light of the progymnasmata and not the secondary literature produced on that topic (though, obviously, we hope the endnotes reflect deep engagement with that literature).

19 Malcolm Heath ("Theon and the History of the Progymnasmata," *GRBS* 43 [2002/2003]: 129–60, esp. 141–58), has proposed a fifth-century CE dating for Theon. Here is no place for a sustained engagement with Heath's argument, but in our view, Heath has underplayed the distinctive structure of Theon, in which chreia is placed first among the exercises, a point recognized by Nicolaus (*Prog.* 18) as well as the history of the transmission of Theon's text,

which "corrects" Theon's order to reflect the dominant tradition (see below). Also, rather than employing the more usual "saying" (*logos*), Theon refers to the chreia as a "statement" (*apophasis*), the term typically used to define a maxim (cf. Aphthonius, *Prog.* 4). Theon, moreover, describes nearly a dozen schemas in his narrative exercise, and so does not reflect the orthodoxy of five established schemas eventually settled upon by the later progymnasmatists. Nor does Theon join the later theorists in dividing narrative by three or four "species"; he has only two. Theon (*Prog.* 115) also uses the term prosopopoeia to cover what the other theorists separate into three distinct terms in this regard. Theon fits with the first-century Quintilian (*Inst.* 9.2.32) who also uses prosopopoeia as an umbrella term (see chapter 6). If Theon's *Progymnasmata* were a fifth-century document, one might expect him to at least explain his choice of prosopopoeia in light of the current tripartite division, as, for example, the other theorists were prone to do when discussing the placement of the chreia exercise. Theon also orders encomiastic topics by the three goods in the style Nicolaus deems the "ancient method." In this regard Theon stands with Cicero and earlier theorists of the centuries BCE, and differentiates himself from theorists of the centuries CE (including even the late first-century Quintilian). The same may be said for Theon's divisions of encomiastic genres and of "things" that may be encomionized: among the later theorists, the divisions are more numerous, and the related discussion more developed. Heath's arguments await a full engagement, but we find that Theon is more at home in the rhetorical milieu of the first century than the fifth; thus, we see no compelling reason to depart from a conventional first-century dating. For other arguments in favor of a first-century date, see Michel Patillon, ed., *Aelius Théon: Progymnasmata* (Paris: Les Belles Lettres, 1997), viii–xvi; and Justin King, "Speech-in-Character, Diatribe, and Romans 3:1-9: Who's Speaking When and Why It Matters" (Ph.D. diss., Baylor University, 2016), 46n3.

20 Butts, "*Progymnasmata* of Theon," 7. Theon himself acknowledges that others had written on the subject of preliminary exercises (1.15–16) and can even refer (1.18) to "traditional exercises" (*ēdē paradedomenois gymnasmasin*).

21 We have used the critical edition of the Greek text (along with a French translation) found in Patillon, *Aelius Théon* (see note 19 above). The Patillon text has replaced Leonard Spengel, ed., *Rhetores Graeci* (Leipzig: Teubner, 1853–1856), 2:59–130, as the standard critical edition. Patillon with the aid of Bolognesi has reconstructed from the Armenian manuscript's five chapters (13–17) missing from the Greek texts. For text and translation of Theon, see also Butts, "*Progymnasmata* of Theon." It should be noted that both Patillon and Butts have rearranged the chapters in Theon to reflect what they believe to be Theon's original order of presentation. They have also inserted "On Refutation and Confirmation," a separate chapter in all extant Greek manuscripts, into the chapter "On the Narrative," again restoring what is believed to be the original order. Hence, when we cite Theon, we have employed the Spengel numbering system (which is still the standard), supplementing it with the page number where the text can be found in the Patillon edition. For a thorough treatment of the author, text, versions, and critical editions, see Patillon, *Aelius Théon*, vii–clvi; also Butts, "*Progymnasmata* of Theon," 7–95. Unless otherwise noted we have used Kennedy's translation, though only after consulting the Greek in Patillon's critical edition.

22 Modified from Kennedy, *Progymnasmata*, viii.

23 A further word of explanation for those exercises omitted is in order. Common-place, or topos, is an important concept in ancient rhetoric and has been usefully explored in relation to the New Testament (see, e.g., James McConnell, *The Topos of Divine Testimony in Luke-Acts* [Eugene, Oreg.: Wipf and Stock, 2014]). Topoi are a kind of cultural thesaurus of conventional scenarios (hence common-place) that the rhetor/writer can easily draw upon when making a particular point (see Parsons' comments on the topos of the evil tyrant in Luke 18 in *Luke*, PCNT [Grand Rapids: Baker Academic, 2015], 280–82). Showing their usefulness in practice, however, requires leaving the progymnasmata behind because the explanations

found there, especially in Theon, are somewhat convoluted and really only tangential to the more substantive and instructive discussions found especially in Cicero's *Topica*. Likewise, the exercises of law and thesis might shed light on the compositional practices of early Christian (or other) writings, especially letters and Hebrews but would require more dependence on the rhetorical handbooks as the primary lens into their argumentation.

24 See our suggestions in the conclusion regarding other rhetorical avenues to pursue including not only figures of speech and thought and rhetorical speeches, but also questions of structure and argumentation. On figures in the New Testament, see, e.g. Keith Reich, *Figuring Jesus: The Power of Rhetorical Figures of Speech in the Gospel of Luke*, BibInt 107 (Leiden: Brill, 2011). The literature on rhetorical speeches is voluminous, even on speeches in Acts alone. See, e.g., George Kennedy, "The Speeches in Acts," in *New Testament Interpretation through Rhetorical Criticism* (Chapel Hill: University of North Carolina Press, 1984), 114–40. See also Clifton C. Black II, "The Rhetorical Form of the Hellenistic Jewish and Early Christian Sermon: A Response to Lawrence Wills," *HTR* 81 (1988): 1–18; Jerome Neyrey, "The Forensic Defense Speech and Paul's Trial Speeches in Acts 22–26: Form and Function," in *Luke-Acts: New Perspectives from the Society of Biblical Literature Seminar*, ed. C. H. Talbert (New York: Crossroad, 1984), 210–24; Philip E. Satterthwaite, "Acts against the Background of Classical Rhetoric," in *The Book of Acts in Its Ancient Literary Setting*, ed. Bruce W. Winter and Andrew D. Clarke, vol. 1 of *The Book of Acts in Its First Century Setting*, ed. Bruce W. Winter (Grand Rapids: Eerdmans, 1993), 337–79; Marion L. Soards, "The Speeches in Acts in Relation to Other Pertinent Ancient Literature," *ETL* 70 (1994): 65–90; Soards, *The Speeches in Acts: Their Content, Context, and Concerns* (Louisville: Westminster John Knox, 1994); F. Veltman, "The Defense Speeches of Paul in Acts," in *Perspectives on Luke-Acts*, ed. C. H. Talbert, Perspectives in Religions Studies Special Studies Series 5 (Macon, Ga.: Mercer University, 1978), 243–56; D. F. Watson, "Paul's Speech to the Ephesian Elders (Acts 20.17–38): Epideictic Rhetoric of Farewell," in *Persuasive Artistry: Studies in New Testament Rhetoric in Honor of George A. Kennedy*, ed. D. F. Watson, JSNTSup 50 (Sheffield: Sheffield Academic, 1990), 184–208; Bruce Winter, "The Importance of the *Captatio Benevolentiae* in the Speeches of Tertullus and Paul in Acts 24:1-21," *JTS* 42 (1991): 505–31; Winter, "Official Proceedings and the Forensic Speeches in Acts 24–26," in *Acts in Its Ancient Literary Setting*, ed. Winter and Clarke, 305–36; D. Zweck, "The *Exordium* of the Areopagus Speech, Acts 17.22, 23," *NTS* (1989): 94–103; Derek Hogan, "Paul's Defense: A Comparison of the Forensic Speeches in Acts, *Callirhoe*, and *Leucippe and Clitophon*," *PRSt* 29 (2002): 73–87.

25 On the occurrence of inflection in Latin poetry (with some reference to Greek literature as well), see Jeffrey Wills, *Repetition in Latin Poetry: Figures of Allusion* (Oxford: Clarendon, 1996), esp. part 2 on "Polyptoton," 188–268.

26 Nicolaus (*Prog.* 4.18–19) suggests that more advanced students could skip the exercise of grammatical inflection and move on to elaborating, condensing, refuting, or confirming.

27 Aristotle had also commented briefly on *ptōsis*, as he called it (cf. *Poetics*, 20.10; *Art of Rhetoric* 1.7.27; 2.23.2; and esp. 3.9.9), but he used the term generally to refer to similar forms of words whether nouns, verbs, adjectives, or adverbs. See also *Rhet. Her.* 4.22.30–31, which like Quintilian views *polyptōton* as a form of paronomasia.

28 The Latin text reads: ". . . genus, quod non tantum in ratione positum est loquendi, sed ipsi sensibus cum gratiam tum etiam vires accommodat."

29 Nicolaus, *Prog.* 4.18–19, e.g., suggests that more advanced students could skip the exercise of grammatical inflection and move on to elaborating, condensing, refuting, or confirming.

30 The author of *Rhetorica ad Herennium*, who also cautions that *polyptōton* is to be used sparingly, considers *polyptōton* to be merely an ornament of style, more appropriate for entertainment (or at best epideictic speech) than for juridical speech and is less charitable than Quintilian about its aesthetic value (see *Rhet. Her.* 4.22.32).

31 At this point, we are relying on Kennedy's English translation (50) of Patillon's French translation of the Armenian version of a lost Greek text. As such, as Kennedy rightly observes, these sections "would be of dubious value for detailed interpretation." Nonetheless, our general conclusion seems warranted. At the least, the practice of inflection deserves further reflection both as it was practiced in the ancient world and as it may have been employed in the NT writings.

32 For examples of inflection in parables, see ch. 2 on fable.

33 Further on paraphrase, see Heinrich Lausberg, *Handbook of Literary Rhetoric: A Foundation for Literary Study* (Leiden: Brill, 1998), 1099–121. There are many other examples of paraphrase in ancient literature not noted in the rhetorical tradition. Suetonius cites *paraphrasis* as among the exercises employed since the beginning of rhetoric (*Gramm.* 4). It was also known by other names: the elder Seneca referenced Virgil's *metaphrasis* of a passage in Homer that may have seemed unduly "fabulous" (*Suas.* 1.12; cf. *Od.* 9.481–82; *Aen.* 10.128; 8.691–92; cited in Timothy A. Brookins, "Luke's Use of Mark as παράφρασις: Its Effects on Characterization in the 'Healing of Blind Bartimaeus' Pericope (Mark 10:46-52/Luke 18:35-43)," *JSNT* 34 (2011): 70–89, here 73. Brookins (74) concludes, "The name was less important than the essential skill." See also P. J. Parsons' discussion of a third-century CE paraphrase of the first twenty-one lines of the *Iliad* in "A School-Book from the Sayce Collection," in *ZPE* 6 (1970): 133–49; cf. also Morgan, *Literate Education in the Hellenistic and Roman Worlds*, 202–26. In the background of all this, there is the Platonic distinction between words (appearance or form) and the subject itself (substance or content; cf. Phaedrus); cf. Brookins, "Luke's Use of Mark," 72n6.

34 For examples of the use of the rhetorical device in understanding the reception of Jesus material in the book of James, see John S. Kloppenborg, "The Reception of the Jesus Traditions in James," in *The Catholic Epistles and the Tradition*, ed. J. Schlosser (Leuven: Leuven University Press, 2004), 94–141, esp. 117–41. As an example of dealing with double and triple tradition material in the Synoptic Gospels, see Brookins, "Luke's Use of Mark" (n. 33 above).

35 Cribiore, *Gymnastics of the Mind*, 8.

36 Todd Penner, "Reconfiguring the Rhetorical Study of Acts: Reflections on the Method in and Learning of a Progymnastic Poetics," *PRSt* 30 (2003): 425–39, here 433. Elsewhere Penner claims: "A progymnastic poetics thus causes us to think much more seriously about *ethos* argumentation than we are wont to do" (438). See also Craig Gibson, "Better Living through Prose Composition? Moral and Compositional Pedagogy in Ancient Greek and Roman Progymnasmata," *Rhetorica* 32 (2014): 1–30; R. Webb, "The Progymnasmata as Practice," in *Education in Greek and Roman Antiquity*, ed. Y. L. Too (Leiden: Brill, 2001), 289–316.

37 On the goal of moral formation in the progymnasmata and rhetorical handbooks, see Amanda Brobst-Renaud, "The Elder Brother's Quandary and the Rich Man's Fate: Ancient Characterization, Rhetoric, and Moral Formation in Luke's Parables" (Ph.D. diss., Baylor University, 2018), ch. 2.

38 Likewise, Plutarch notes that "the Good creates a stir of activity towards itself, and implants at once in the spectator an active impulse; it does not form his character by ideal representation alone; but through the investigation of its work furnishes him with a dominant purpose. For such reasons I have decided to persevere in my writing of Lives" (Plutarch, *Per.* 2 [Perrin, LCL]). On Quintilian's discussion of the qualities of the teacher of rhetoric in *The Orator's Education*, see Brobst-Renaud, "Elder Brother's Quandary," ch. 2.

39 Maud Gleason, *Making Men: Sophists and Self-Presentation in Ancient Rome* (Princeton: Princeton University Press, 1995).

40 See James R. Harrison, "The Seven Sages, the Delphic Canon and Ethical Education in Antiquity," in *Ancient Education and Early Christianity*, ed. Matthew Ryan Hauge and Andrew W. Pitts (London: Bloomsbury T&T Clark, 2016), 71–86, esp. 85–86; Mikeal C. Parsons,

Body and Character in Luke and Acts: The Subversion of Physiognomy in Early Christianity (Waco: Baylor University Press, 2010), 123–42.

41 See Catherine Hezer, "The Torah versus Homer: Jewish and Greco-Roman Education in Late Roman Palestine," in *Ancient Education and Early Christianity*, ed. Matthew Ryan Hauge and Andrew W. Pitts (London: Bloomsbury T&T Clark, 2016), 5–24; on Jewish education in antiquity, see also Catherine Hezer, *Jewish Literacy in Roman Palestine*, WUNT 81 (Tübingen: Mohr Siebeck, 2001).

42 The above paragraphs should make clear that we find efforts merely to label rhetorical devices as a necessary but not sufficient condition for interpreting the message(s) of the NT writings. The preliminary exercises, in that regard, provide only a preliminary step in the interpretive process.

I

Chreia

Revealing Essentials through Word and Deed

> *What is the chreia?*
> A concise reminiscence associated with some character.
>
> *Why is the chreia a "reminiscence"?*
> Because it is remembered so that it may be recited.
>
> *Why "concise"?*
> Because often, once it has been expanded, it becomes a narrative or something else.
>
> *Why "with a character"?*
> Because often without a character a concise reminiscence is a maxim or something else.
>
> *Why is it called a "chreia"?*
> Because of its being useful, not because the other exercises do not have this quality, but because of its excellence, the name is a proper one instead of a common one.[1]

The chreia was widespread in antiquity. Some estimates put the number of chreia from antiquity in excess of one thousand.[2] Their popularity has continued into the modern period, at least in the form of scholarly analysis. Unlike many of the exercises in the progymnasmata, the classroom exercise on chreia has garnered much attention by New Testament scholars, especially over the past thirty-five years owing to the pioneering work of Ronald Hock and Edward O'Neil under the auspices of the Hellenistic Texts Seminar sponsored by the Claremont Institute for Antiquity and Christianity and the Society of Biblical Literature Pronouncement Stories Seminar under the leadership particularly of Vernon Robbins.[3]

Theory

Chreia Definition(s)

Theon asserts "a chreia is a brief saying or action making a point, attributed to some specified person or something corresponding to a person" (*Prog.* 96). Later progymnasmata have similar but not identical definitions. Aphthonius, for example, defines a chreia as a "brief recollection, referring to some person in a pointed way" (*Prog.* 23). That this recollection (or "reminiscence," *apomnēnomeuma*) can take the form of word or deed is made clear by Pseudo-Hermogenes: "A chreia is a recollection of a saying or action or both, with a pointed meaning, usually for the sake of something useful" (*Prog.* 6). Nicolaus is even more precise: "A chreia is a pointed and concise saying or action, attributed to some specific person, reported for the correction of some things in life" (*Prog.* 19). Thus, a chreia shares certain features in common with the extant progymnasmata:

(1) The chreia is *concise*; typically, chreia consist of only one (at times, complex) sentence, though it can be more than a single sentence (as in a question-and-answer chreia; see below).[4]

(2) Distinct from the maxim, which seems to function as a general proverb, the chreia is typically *attributed to a specific character.* Usually the character is a specific person, but occasionally a chreia may be attributed to a group of persons or a representative of a group—for example, "A Laconian, when someone asked him where the Cacedaimonians set the limits of their land, showed his spear" (Theon, *Prog.* 99).[5]

(3) A third characteristic, *aptness,* may apply to the suitability of the chreia for the situation at hand, or it may refer to the aptness of the chreia in disclosing something about the essence of the character to whom the chreia is attributed. Hermogenes and Nicolaus (above) seem to be referring to a "well-aimed" quality of the statement (or action), while Aphthonius (see above) seems to speak of the aptness of the attribution.[6] Kennedy's translation of Theon ("a brief saying or action making a point") would fit the former category, although the prepositional phrase *met' eustochias* ("making a point") is placed between "brief saying or action" and "attributed to some specific person" and could modify either noun phrase or, conceivably, even both.[7]

Each progymnasmata approaches the classroom exercise of chreia in other, distinctive ways. Only Theon treats chreia as the first of the classroom exercises, reasoning that it "is short and easily remembered" (*Prog.* 6).[8] Nicolaus recognizes that "there are some who assign it [chreia] before both fable and narrative" but attributes the sequence to the rationale that the chreia exercise "should be put first since it shows the way to good and avoidance of evil" (*Prog.* 18). Also, rather than using the more usual "saying" (*logos*), Theon refers to the chreia as a "statement" (*apophasis*), the term typically used to define a maxim (cf.

Aphthonius, *Prog.* 4). Since Theon, unlike the other progymnasmatists, does not include a separate chapter on maxims, this gesture toward the maxim allows him to indicate the close relationship between the two forms.[9] Aphthonius has the shortest definition of chreia (only nine words in Greek), but he does include an etymology, indicating it is so-called because it is "useful" (*chreiōdēs*). Nicolaus clarifies that while chreia are useful, it is not because "the other progymnasmata do not fulfill some use, but either because it has been especially honored with this common name as characteristic, in the way that Homer is called 'the poet' and Demosthenes 'the orator,' or because originally someone made use of it primarily from some circumstance and need" (*Prog.* 20; cf. Theon, *Prog.* 97). Nicolaus observes that some theorists claim "chreias are transmitted because of some utility and some only because of their charm" (*Prog.* 21), though he finds that even those that appear designed only for pleasantry "seem to contain good advice" and thus some utility (*Prog.* 21).[10]

Chreia Classifications

All the extant progymnasmata list the principal classifications of the chreia: there are sayings chreias, action chreias, and mixed chreias, which consist of both sayings and action (Theon, *Prog.* 97; Ps.-Hermogenes, *Prog.* 6; Aphthonius, *Prog.* 23; Nicolaus, *Prog.* 20). The following epithet attributed to Isocrates, very popular in antiquity, is an example of a sayings chreia: "The root of education is bitter but the fruits are sweet" (Aphthonius, *Prog.* 23; cf. Ps.-Hermogenes, *Prog.* 7; Libanius, *Prog.* 8.82–97). Theon gives the following as an example of a chreia of action: "When Diogenes the Cynic philosopher saw a boy eating fancy food, he beat his pedagogue with his staff" (*Prog.* 98–99; cf. Nicolaus, *Prog.* 20; Libanius, *Prog.* 1.2).[11] Pseudo-Hermogenes cites a similar chreia to illustrate a mixed chreia that contains both an action and a saying: "Diogenes, on seeing an undisciplined youth, beat his pedagogue and said, 'Why did you teach him such things?'" (*Prog.* 6; cf. Aphthonius, *Prog.* 23).[12] Theon's understanding of a mixed chreia differs from that of Nicolaus. For Theon, the verbal aspect of a mixed chreia can occur in the circumstances that prompt the action. So under mixed chreias, Theon cites this chreia: "A Laconian, when someone asked him where the Lacedaimonians set the limits of their land, showed his spear" (*Prog.* 99). The fact that the Laconian's action of displaying his spear was prompted by a verbal question, for Theon, qualifies the chreia as "mixed"—that is, with both actional and verbal features. For Nicolaus, a similar chreia is a mixed chreia only because the Laconian not only shows his spear but also speaks, "When a Laconian was asked where the walls of Sparta were, holding up his spear, he said, 'There'" (*Prog.* 20). Pseudo-Hermogenes shares Nicolaus' view that a mixed chreia "requires both an action and a saying of the character."[13]

Aphthonius includes only these principal classifications, and Pseudo-Hermogenes and Nicolaus allude to further categories, but only Theon subdivides the categories of chreia into a rather complex system of classification. Theon divides the sayings chreia into two subcategories. There is the unprompted, declarative statement (*apophantikon*) and the responsive statement (*apokritikon*). The declarative statement is typically introduced with a finite verb and without reference to a specific situation.[14] Theon's example is this: "Isocrates the sophist used to say that those of his students with natural ability were children of gods" (*Prog.* 97). The responsive sayings chreia is typically introduced by a participle of seeing:[15] "Diogenes, the Cynic philosopher, seeing a rich young man who was uneducated, said 'He is dirt plated with silver'" (*Prog.* 97).

Theon further divides the responsive chreia into four subdivisions. Three are statements in response to questions, ranging from a simple yes or no to additional information to advice or something beyond an answer to the question. For many modern interpreters "these distinctions seem too finely drawn," despite the fact that Theon gives examples.[16] The fourth subcategory is a chreia made in response to a remark or statement rather than a question.[17] Beyond these four subdivisions is another type or species of sayings chreia, the double chreia, which is "one having statements by two persons where either statement makes a chreia by one person." Theon gives this example: "Alexander, the king of Macedon, stood over Diogenes when he was sleeping and said, 'A man who is a counselor should not sleep all night,' and Diogenes responded, 'A man to whom the people have been entrusted and who has many cares'" (*Prog.* 98).[18]

With regard to the category of sayings chreia, Theon states that they can be expressed in a variety of ways, which he lists (with examples): gnomic sayings, logical demonstrations, a jest or joke, a syllogism, an enthymeme, an example, a prayer or wish, a sign or symbolic expression, a figure or trope, a double entendre or ambiguity, a change of subject or metalepsis, or any combination of two or more of these expressions (*Prog.* 99–100).[19] Some ancient theorists were less than convinced of the pedagogical usefulness of listing various categories of chreia. Pseudo-Hermogenes, for example, says, "Much is said by the ancients about different kinds of chreia, (for example,) that some of them are declarative, some interrogative, some investigative. But now let us come to the point, and this is the elaboration (*exergasia*)" (*Prog.* 7).

Theon proposes that there are two subcategories of actional chreia: active and passive, which function as their names suggest. The protagonist is the main actor in an active chreia of action: "When Diogenes the Cynic philosopher saw a boy eating fancy food, he beat his pedagogue with his staff" (*Prog.* 98–99). The protagonist is acted upon in a passive chreia of action: "Didymon the flute-player, on being convicted of adultery, was hanged by his namesake" (*Prog.* 99).[20] None of the theorists proposes further subdivisions for mixed chreia.

Chreia Manipulation

The ancient theorists do not agree on what the elaboration or manipulation of chreias consists of. Again, Theon stands alone in his understanding. He ends his chapter on chreia with instructions on how to "practice" or manipulate chreias through eight separate exercises: "restatement, grammatical inflection, comment, and contradiction, and we expand and compress the chreia, and in addition (at a later stage in study) we refute and confirm" (*Prog.* 101). The practice of expanding and condensing chreia is especially significant. Theon cites a brief chreia: "Epaminondas, dying childless, said to his friends, 'I leave two daughters, the victory at Leuctra and that at Mantinea'" (*Prog.* 103–104). He then shows how the chreia can be expanded by adding to the information about its speaker and circumstances.

> Epaminadas, the general of the Thebans, was, you should know, a great man in peacetime, but when war with Lacedaimonians came to his fatherland he demonstrated many shining deeds of greatness. When serving at Boeotarch at Leuctra, he defeated the enemy; and conducting a campaign and contending on behalf of his country, he died at Mantinea. When he had been wounded and his life was coming to an end, while his friends were bewailing many things, including that he was dying childless, breaking into a smile, he said, "Cease your weeping, my friends, for I have left you two immortal daughters: two victories of my country over Lacedaimonians, one at Leuctra, the elder, the younger just begotten by me at Mantinea." (*Prog.* 104)[21]

This complicates the understanding that the sayings of Jesus typically circulated as independent sayings that were later couched in a narrative setting, which eventually was expanded into more elaborate contexts.[22] It is certainly possible that some dominical sayings were transmitted that way but not necessarily the case. For one trained in the rhetorical tradition of expanding and condensing chreia, it is possible that the opposite scenario occurred, namely that a chreia in a longer context was condensed.[23] From the evidence of Theon and the progymnasmata, it is impossible to determine a priori the directional flow of transmission.

For Pseudo-Hermogenes, on the other hand, chreia elaboration consists of a single exercise, including an encomium of the speaker (or actor) of the chreia, a paraphrase, the cause, contrast, comparison, example, judgment (optional), and exhortation (*Prog.* 8). Chreia elaboration for Nicolaus is very similar to that of Pseudo-Hermogenes and consists of (1) praise, (2) paraphrase, (3) statement of probability and truth, (4) judgment, and (5) exhortation (optional) (*Prog.* 24).[24] Chreia elaboration reaches its standard form in Aphthonius and is the basis for most later commentators who try to emulate him.[25]

Following a brief definition of chreia and a simple classification of sayings, actional and mixed chreias, Aphthonius advises that one "should elaborate it [the chreia] with the following headings: praise, paraphrase, cause, contrary, comparison, example, testimony of the ancients, brief epilogue" (*Prog.* 23). He then gives the following example:[26]

A Verbal Chreia (Prog. 23–25)	
Isocrates said, "The Root of Education is Bitter but the Fruits are Sweet"	
Praise	It is right to admire Isocrates for his art; he made its name most illustrious, and in his practice he showed how great the art was and proclaims its greatness, rather than having been himself proclaimed by it. Now it would take a long time to go through all the benefits he has brought to human life, whether in proposing laws to kings or in advising private individuals, but (we can note) his wise teaching about education.
Paraphrase	One who longs for education, he is saying, begins with toils, but yet the toils end in an advantage. The wisdom of these words we shall admire in what follows.
Cause	Those who long for education attach themselves to educational leaders, whom it is frightening to approach and very stupid to abandon. Fear comes on boys both when they are there and when they are about to go to school. Next after the teachers come the pedagogues, fearful to see and more dreadful when they beat the boys. Fright anticipates discovery, and punishment follows fright; they go looking for the boys' mistakes but regard the boys' successes as their own doing. Fathers are more strict than pedagogues, dictating the routes to be followed, demanding boys go straight to school, and showing suspicion of the market place. And if there is need to punish, fathers ignore their natural feelings. But the boy who has experienced these things, when he comes to manhood wears a crown of virtue.
Contrary	If, on the other hand, out of fear of these things someone were to flee from teachers, run away from parents, and shun pedagogues, he is completely deprived of training in speech and has lost ability in speech with his loss of fear. All of these considerations influenced Isocrates' thought in calling the root of education bitter.
Comparison	Just as those who work the earth cast the seeds in the ground with toil but reap the fruits with greater pleasure, in the same way those exchanging toil for education have by toil acquired future renown.
Example	Look, I ask you, at the life of Demosthenes, which was the most filled with labor of any orator but became the most glorious of all. He showed such an abundance of zeal that he took the ornament from his head, because he thought the ornament that comes from virtue was the best; and he expended in toils what others lavished on pleasures.

Testimony	Thus, one should admire Hesiod's saying [cf. *Works and Days* 289–292] that the road of virtue is rough, but the height is easy, the same philosophy as found in the saying of Isocrates; for what Hesiod indicated by a "road" is what Isocrates called a "root," both expressing one thought, but with different words.
Epilogue	Looking at all this, one should admire Isocrates for his wise and beautiful speculation about education.

This lengthy elaboration "more clearly demonstrates to teacher and student alike what the elaboration of a chreia ought to look like."[27]

Examples from Ancient Literature

There are multitudes of chreias preserved in writings from antiquity, particularly those attributed to philosophers acknowledged as founders of philosophical schools.[28] There are also extant exercises and commentaries involving the inflection and elaboration of chreia within the rhetorical tradition.[29] Many of the examples that follow are found both in the rhetorical tradition and outside it. For example, Lucian's *Demonax* alone has over fifty chreia attributed to Demonax, a philosopher and Lucian's teacher.[30] Diogenes Laertius' *Lives* contain many sayings attributed to the philosophers whose lives he presents.[31]

Sayings Chreia

Declarative. Diogenes Laertius attributes the following declarative statement to the Cynic philosopher Diogenes: "the love of money is the mother-city of every evil" (*Lives* 6.50).[32]

"Isocrates said that education's root is bitter, its fruit is sweet" (Stobaeus 2.31.29).[33]

"[Socrates] used to say that he knew nothing except just the fact of his ignorance" (Diogenes Laertius, *Lives* 2.32).

"For R Eliezer used to say, 'There is a time to shorten [one's prayers] and a time to lengthen [them]' " (Mekhilta Ishmael Vayassa 1).[34]

Responsive (to an action). "Damonidas the gymnastic teacher whose feet were deformed when his shoes had been stolen, said: 'May they fit the thief' " (Plutarch, *De aud. poet.* 18D).[35]

Diogenes the Cynic philosopher, on seeing a youth who was the son of an adulterer throwing stones into the crowd, said: "Stop, boy! You may unwittingly hit your father" (Diogenes Laertius, *Lives* 6.62).

Responsive (to a question). When Demonax was nearly a hundred years old and death was apparently imminent, a man asked him, " 'Isn't it shameful that the body of such a man should be exposed as food for birds and dogs?' [Demonax] replied: 'I see nothing unusual in this, if even in death I am going to be useful to some living things'" (Lucian, *Demon.* 66.5–7). This chreia reveals something of the essence of Demonax that Lucian was trying to present: it demonstrated Demonax's good humor,[36] which he kept until the end of his life (65.7–8); his humility, for which the Athenians revered him (67.1–3); and his freedom from fear, even of death (19.4–20.7; cf. also 35.1–6 and 5.1–3).[37]

"Isocrates the rhetor, when a boy was being enrolled with him and when the one who was enrolling him asked what the boy needed, said, 'A new tablet and a new stylus' " (Maximus Planudes 2.18.18–21). Theon also cites this chreia as an example of a chreia presented as an ambiguity since "it is ambiguous whether he means a tablet 'and a mind' (*kai nou*) and a pencil 'and a mind' or a new (*kainou*) tablet and new pencil" (*Prog.* 100).

"When he [Aristippus] had made some money by teaching, Socrates asked him, 'Where did you get so much?' to which he replied, 'Where you got so little' (Diogenes Laertius, *Lives* 2.80).

<u>*Responsive (to a statement)*</u>. "Once the Sidonian sophist was distinguishing himself in Athens and voicing his own praise to the effect that he had examined all philosophy. . . . 'If ever Aristotle calls me to the Lyceum, I shall attend; if Plato calls me to the Academy, I shall arrive; if Zeno calls, I shall spend my time in the Poecile [great hall]; if Pythagoras calls, I shall keep silence.' Demonax arose in the midst of the audience and said, calling him by name, 'Pythagoras is calling you'" (Lucian, *Demon.* 1.1–4).

To one who boasted that he belonged to a great city his [Aristotle's] reply was, "That is not the point to consider, but who it is that is worthy of a great country" (Diogenes Laertius, *Lives* 5.19).

"To one reproaching him [Diogenes] for entering unclean places he said, 'The sun, also, enters the privies but is not defiled'" (Diogenes Laertius, *Lives* 6.63). This saying typifies the kind of subversion often associated with chreia (especially of the Cynic variety). Here Diogenes had been criticized for entering unclean places (such as brothels). Rather than deny the charge, he appeals to an analogy of nature to confound the criticism. "The shift to another order of discourse is a typical ploy of Cynic chreia. It isolates an assumption fundamental to the reasons behind the challenge, and then points to another set of circumstances in which the logic of the reasons does not fit."[38]

"They showed Jesus a gold coin and said to him, 'Caesar's men demand taxes from us.' He said to them, 'Give Caesar what belongs to Caesar, give God what belongs to God, and give me what is mine' " (Gos. Thom. 100).

Actional Chreia

Quintilian reports an actional chreia attributed to Crates: "Crates, when he saw an uneducated boy, struck his paedagogus" (*Inst.* 1.9.5).[39]

Also from Quintilian: "Milo used to carry the bull which he had grown accustomed to carry as a calf" (1.9.5). Milo was a legendary Olympic athlete whose fame for strength was widespread (Herodotus 3.137; Diodorus Siculus 12.9; Pausanias 6.1.5–8).[40]

"Diogenes the Cynic used to seek a man with a lighted lamp by day" (Diomedes 1.310.22–23; cf. Diogenes Laertius, *Lives* 6.1). This actional chreia depicts Diogenes looking for an honest man and reflects his well-known characterization as a pessimist.[41]

"One time Sabta of Ulan hired his donkey to a gentile woman. When she reached the edge of the territory, she said to him, 'Wait until I enter the temple of the territory's idol.' When she came out, he said to her, 'Wait for me until I enter and do as you have done.' She said to him, 'Is it possible that you, a Jew, [will enter and serve the idol]?' He entered, [uncovered himself], and wiped himself on the nose of Peor. Then all the gentiles laughed and said, 'No man has served [Peor] like this before' " (*Sifre Num.* 13.1).[42]

Mixed Chreia

In Xenophon's *Hellenica* (fifth to fourth century BCE) we find an example of a mixed chreia involving both a saying and an action of a certain Theramenes: "And when, being compelled to die, he [Theramenes] had drunk the hemlock, they said that he threw out the last drops, like a man playing kattabos, and exclaimed: 'Here's to the health of my beloved Critias [who had condemned him]'" (2.3.56).

"Plato had defined a human being as an animal, biped and featherless, and was applauded. Diogenes plucked a fowl and brought it into the lecture-room with the words, 'Here is Plato's human being'" (Diogenes Laertius, *Lives* 6.40).

Lucian records a mixed chreia attributed to Demonax: "Now when a natural philosopher was discussing the antipodes, [Demonax] made him stand up and led him to a well. He pointed to the reflection in the water and asked, 'Are you speaking about antipodes such as these?'" (*Demon.* 22.1–4).[43] Both the action and the saying are integral to the story's meaning.

On another occasion, Demonax "saw a certain pompous person who prided himself on the width of the purple stripe on his garment, [Demonax] leaned over to his ear and, taking hold of his garment, pointed out to him, 'A sheep wore this before you and he was nevertheless (just) a sheep" (*Demon.* 1.1–5). In this mixed chreia, the action of taking hold of the garment provides the referent for the demonstrative pronoun "this," and the act of (presumably) whispering into the person's ear contributes to Demonax's characterization as a gentle person (cf. 9.7–8).[44]

Chreia Elaboration

A pattern of elaboration similar to that of Aphthonius is found in the anonymous rhetorical handbook *Rhetorica ad Herennium* (first century BCE).[45] There the author discusses "refining" (*expolitio*) a topic (4.43.54) in seven parts: (1) statement of the theme; (2) the reason; (3) paraphrase (with or without the reason); (4) the contrary or opposite; (5) a comparison; (6) an example; and (7) conclusion (4.43.56). He then illustrates the pattern of elaboration, using the following example:[46]

Theme	The wise man will, on the republic's behalf, shun no peril,
Reason	because it may often happen that if a man has been loath to perish for his country it will be necessary for him to perish with her. Further, since it is from our country that we receive all our advantages, no disadvantage incurred on her behalf is to be regarded as severe.
Paraphrase (with reason)	I say, then, that they who flee from the peril to be undergone on behalf of the republic act foolishly, for they cannot avoid the disadvantages, and are found guilty of ingratitude towards the state.
Contrary	But on the other hand they who, with peril to themselves, confront the perils of the fatherland, are to be considered wise, since they render to their country the homage due her, and prefer to die for many of their fellow citizens instead of with them. For it is extremely unjust to give back to nature, when she compels, the life you have received from nature, and not to give to your country, when she calls for it, the life you have preserved thanks to your country; and when you can die for fatherland with the greatest manliness and honour, to prefer to live in disgrace and cowardice; and when you are willing to face danger for friends and parents and your other kin, to refuse to run the risk for the republic, which embraces all these and that most holy name of fatherland as well.
Comparison	He who in a voyage prefers his own to his vessel's security, deserves contempt. No less blameworthy is he who in a crisis of the republic consults his own in preference to the common safety. For from the wreck of a ship many of those on board escape unharmed, but from the wreck of the fatherland no one can swim to safety.

Example	It is this that, in my opinion, Decius well understood, who is said to have devoted himself to death, and, in order to save his legions, to have plunged in the midst of the enemy. He gave up his life, but did not throw it away; for at the cost of a very cheap good he redeemed a sure good, of a small good the greatest good. He gave his life, and received his country in exchange. He lost his life, and gained glory, which transmitted with highest praise, shines more and more every day as time goes on.
Conclusion	But if reason has shown and illustration confirmed that it is fitting to confront danger in defence of the republic, they are to be esteemed wise who do not shrink from any peril when the security of the fatherland is at stake. (4.44.57 [Caplan, LCL])

Elaborated chreia can also fill what is lacking. The following rabbinic story contains an elementary elaboration presented as a question and answer and moving from a statement to analogy, in order to demonstrate that a wise person (in contrast to an "understanding" one) practices what he preaches and applies his wisdom to his own circumstances.

> Yose points out that rabbis (rich men), who carry out their knowledge in all aspects of everyday life, are superior to pagan philosophers (poor men), who teach but have no overall theory of proper day-to-day behavior, such as is represented by rabbinic law. (*Sifre Deut.* 13)[47]

Examples from the New Testament

Sayings Chreia

Declarative chreia. There are a number of declarative chreia attributed to Jesus in the Gospels that fit the expectations of a chreia in aptly disclosing something about Jesus' character. These declarative statements are not in response to any particular statement or question or action.

> Now after John was arrested, Jesus came to Galilee, proclaiming the good news of God, and saying, "The time is fulfilled, and the kingdom of God has come near; repent, and believe in the good news." (Mark 1:1-15)[48]

> Then he called the crowd to him and said to them, "Listen and understand: it is not what goes into the mouth that defiles a person, but it is what comes out of the mouth that defiles." (Matt 15:10-11)

This saying is presented in Matthew as a declarative statement, although the audience will recognize the connection to the complaint of the Pharisees and scribes that Jesus' disciples do not wash their hands before they eat (Matt 15:1; cf. also Mark 7).

Responsive Chreia

Likewise, there are numerous responsive chreia that serve as Jesus' rejoinder to his interlocutors' actions, questions, or statements:

Responsive (to an action). "As Jesus passed along the Sea of Galilee, he saw Simon and his brother Andrew casting a net into the sea—for they were fishermen. And Jesus said to them, 'Follow me and I will make you fish for people' " (Mark 1:16-17).

Responsive (to a question). "Jesus went through one town and village after another, teaching as he made his way to Jerusalem. Someone asked him, 'Lord, will only a few be saved?' He said to them, 'Strive to enter through the narrow door; for many, I tell you, will try to enter and will not be able'" (Luke 13:22-24).

Responsive (to a statement). "Now when Jesus saw great crowds around him, he gave orders to go over to the other side. A scribe then approached and said, 'Teacher, I will follow you wherever you go.' And Jesus said to him, 'Foxes have holes, and birds of the air have nests; but the Son of Man has nowhere to lay his head'" (Matt 8:18-20).

Actional Chreia

In all four gospels, Jesus' feeding of the five thousand functions as an actional chreia (cf. Matt 14:13-21; Mark 6:30-44; Luke 10:10-17; John 6:1-14).[49] Consider the relevant portion of the Lukan version:[50]

> For there were about five thousand men. And he said to his disciples, "Make them sit down in groups of about fifty each." They did so and made them all sit down. And taking the five loaves and the two fish, he looked up to heaven, and blessed and broke them, and gave them to the disciples to set before the crowd. And all ate and were filled. What was left over was gathered up, twelve baskets of broken pieces. (Luke 10:14-17)

This chreia of action is appropriate to the character of Jesus, especially in Luke in which Jesus is depicted as "going to a meal, at a meal, or coming from a meal" and is himself depicted as "food for the world" (2:7).[51] In Luke, this chreia of action serves to link three scenes (feeding of the five thousand, Last Supper, supper at Emmaus). "The feeding of the five thousand is the climax of Jesus' Galilean ministry, just as the Last Supper is the climax of his Jerusalem ministry, and the meal at Emmaus is the climax of his post-resurrection appearances."[52] That the scene is memorable because of Jesus' actions is underscored by the declaration by the Emmaus travelers to the disciples that Jesus was "made known to them in the breaking of the bread" (24:35) and becomes shorthand for the Eucharist in the Acts of the Apostles (cf. Acts 2:42).

Mixed Chreia

In Matthew's passion narrative, Pilate engages in a mixed chreia whose action combines with his words to proclaim emphatically his disengagement from the proceedings associated with the "trial" of Jesus:

> So when Pilate saw that he could do nothing, but rather that a riot was beginning, he took some water and washed his hands before the crowd, saying, "I am innocent of this man's blood; see to it yourselves." (Matt 27:24)[53]

The so-called cleansing of the temple episode in the gospels functions as a mixed chreia, with both the prophetic action of overturning the money changers' tables (cf. 1 Kgs 11:29-31; 2 Kgs 2; Jer 7:1-8:3; 19:1-15; 26; Ezek 5:1-17; etc.) and a prophetic word of judgment. The story occurs in all four canonical gospels (Mark 11:15-17//Matt 21:12-17//Luke 19:5-8//John 2:13-22), but each version has its own distinctive function in its particular context.

Consider Mark's story:

> Then they came to Jerusalem. And he entered the temple and began to drive out those who were selling and those who were buying in the temple, and he overturned the tables of the money changers and the seats of those who sold doves; and he would not allow anyone to carry anything through the temple. He was teaching and saying, "Is it not written, 'My house shall be called a house of prayer for all the nations'? But you have made it a den of robbers." (Mark 11:15-17)

Mark's version (with its violent actions, addition of "all the nations," and framing narrative of the cursing of the fig tree) is harsher and suggests that Jesus' actions symbolize a cursing of the temple, which failed in its mission to be a place of multinational and ethnically inclusive prayer, and has rather been co-opted as a nationalist stronghold (interpreting *lēstēs* as political insurrectionists).[54]

Compared to Mark 11:15-17, Luke's version of the cleansing of the temple is brief (sixty-five Greek words in Mark compared to twenty-five in Luke).[55] The reference to Jesus entering the city is omitted, as are the violent details of the cleansing (cf. Mark 11:15). The prohibition by Jesus disallowing anyone to carry vessels through the temple (Mark 11:16), as well as the end of the citation from Isaiah 56:7 ("for all the nations"; cf. Mark 11:17a) are deleted. The latter omission may reflect Luke's view that the temple, now destroyed by the time of Luke's writing, can play no part in the Gentile mission. Finally, the story of Jesus cursing the fig tree, which frames the temple incident in Mark (11:12-14, 20-25), is likewise deleted.[56] Luke's version, however, still maintains some teeth in its critique by depicting Jesus as expelling (*ekballō*) the money changers. This is the word used for exorcisms in Luke (9:40, 49; 11:14–15,

18–20; 13:32), making the money changers comparable to "unclean spirits who profane the holy place."[57] Like Mark, Luke's Jesus combines Isaiah 56:7 ("my house shall be a house of prayer") with Jeremiah 7:11 ("but you have made it a den of thieves") to level his prophetic critique against the institution. Such intra-Jewish criticism of the financial dealings of the temple were not unknown: those at Qumran viewed such practices as a defilement of the temple (CD 6.15-16; 4QpHab 9.1-7); later rabbinic Judaism, however, was uncompromising in its support of money changers providing the necesssary coinage for the annual temple tax (*m. Šeqal.* 1:3).

John's version stands at the outset of the Fourth Gospel and not only helps create first impressions of Jesus for the audience of the Fourth Gospel but also sets the stage for the ongoing conflict between Jesus and the religious authorities as it unfolds. All four versions of the temple incident present Jesus' chreia as *apocritic* or responsive. In the Synoptic Gospels, Jesus' words and actions respond to the actions of the money changers, as does Jesus' action in John. But the verbal response of the Johannine Jesus is twofold. His first words are in response to those selling doves in the temple, "Take these things out of here! Stop making my Father's house a marketplace!" (John 2:16b), but there is a second chreia, this one as part of a question and answer with "the Jews" who ask, "What sign can you show us for doing this?" (2:18). Jesus responds, "Destroy this temple, and in three days I will raise it up" (2:19).[58] In this regard, the Johannine Jesus returns to the theme of the temple's destruction, rather than its cleansing, a theme first raised in Mark's account.[59]

Chreia Expansion/Condensation

In Matthew we read the following story about Jesus blessing the children:

> Then little children were being brought to him in order that he might lay his hands on them and pray. The disciples spoke sternly to those who brought them; but Jesus said, "Let the little children come to me, and do not stop them; for it is to such as these that the kingdom of heaven belongs." And he laid his hands on them and went on his way. (Matt 19:13-15)

Mark has a longer version of this same pericope:

> People were bringing little children to him in order that he might touch them; and the disciples spoke sternly to them. But when Jesus saw this, he was indignant and said to them, "Let the little children come to me; do not stop them; for it is to such as these that the kingdom of God belongs. Truly I tell you, whoever does not receive the kingdom of God as a little child will never enter it." And he took them up in his arms, laid his hands on them, and blessed them. (Mark 10:13-16)

Both versions would be classified as mixed chreia, since they contain a saying attributed to Jesus ("Let the little children come to me, and do not stop them; for it is to such as these that the kingdom of heaven/God belongs") and an action ("he laid his hands on them" or "he took them up in his arms, laid his hands on them, and blessed them"). Further, both versions present the chreia as "responsive" to the disciples' rebuke of those bringing children to Jesus.

Assuming Markan priority, and given what we now know about compositional practices surrounding the chreia, it is entirely possible that Matthew has condensed the chreia. Commentators have proposed different reasons for Matthew's preference for a condensed version of the chreia.[60]

On the other hand, assuming the minority view of Matthean priority, Mark's version seems to expand Matthew's text in ways reminiscent of Theon's expanded version of Epaminandas' chreia (see above).[61] Both introduce the speaker's response with emotion: Epaminandas smiles; Jesus is indignant. Both contain a paraphrase of the chreia: in Theon, the longer version speaks of two victories of "my country" over Lacedaimonians; Mark gives a negative restatement: "Whoever does not receive the kingdom of God as a little child will never enter it." Further, the "action" of the protagonist is expanded. Epaminadas is described as "wounded and his life was coming to an end." In Mark, Jesus not only laid hands on the children: he took them into his arms and blessed them.[62]

Enthymemic Chreia

Mark uses the form of an enthymemic chreia in Mark 2:27-28 to conclude his story about grain plucked in the grain field.[63] According to Theon an enthymeme occurs when the chreia is presented as an incomplete syllogism in need of an additional proposition (*Prog.* 100). This phenomenon has been dubbed an "elliptic enthymeme."[64] Theon lists the enthymeme as one way to express a chreia and cites the following example: "Socrates the philosopher, when a certain Apollodorus said that the Athenians had condemned him to death unjustly, laughed and said, 'Do you wish they had done so justly?' It is necessary for us to add a proposition that it is better to be condemned unjustly than justly, which seems to have been omitted in the chreia, but is potentially clear" (*Prog.* 99–100). We find that Mark 2:27-28 also follows this pattern of the "elliptic enthymeme":

Major premise	The Sabbath was made for humans (27a)
Opposing corollary	not humans for the Sabbath (27b)
Conclusion	So the Son of Man is Lord of the Sabbath (28)

The missing premise here is something like, "I am no ordinary human, but a figure like the Son of Man, who came to serve and not to be served, and through that service will express my authority and lordship" (cf. Mark 1:41-45). As such, Jesus is more than the beneficiary of the Sabbath, he is also its lord, and he has the authority to allow his disciples to break the Sabbath.[65] The appropriate response to the story by Jesus' followers is not to insist on the right and freedom to do something on the grounds of human autonomy (Sabbath is made for humans) but rather to submit wholly to the lordship of Christ. The follower is not called to be lord of the Sabbath; that role is reserved exclusively for Christ. Of course, not everyone will be convinced by the Markan Jesus' reinterpretation of the Sabbath and its demand on Jesus' devotees, a point proven by the religious leaders' skepticism expressed in the very next story, another controversy about Sabbath observance (Mark 3:1-6).

Luke presents a series of three chreia in 9:57-62 in which Jesus offers replies to would-be disciples. The first two (9:57-60) are found also in Matt 8:18-22; the third statement (9:61-62), a responsive chreia, is unique to Luke: "I will follow you Lord, but first allow me to say goodbye to those in my household. But Jesus said to him, 'Nobody who has put his hand to the plow and looks back is fit for the kingdom of God'" (9:61). Missing in this excuse is any sense of urgency ("I will follow you anywhere!"; "let me first bury my father"); rather, the request is simply to return home to say good-bye to family (as Elijah did; cf. 1 Kgs 19:19-21). Jesus' response functions to provide a rationale for why the would-be disciple must leave the dead and cannot return to his family ("Nobody who has put his hand to the plow and looks back is fit for the kingdom of God"). Luke has elaborated the chreias "let the dead bury the dead" and "(you) preach the kingdom" into the form of an elliptic enthymeme.[66] The logic of the Lukan Jesus can be reconstructed as follows:[67]

First premise	No one who puts his hand to the plow and looks back is fit for the kingdom of God.
(Missing) Second premise	You wish to be fit for the kingdom of God.
Conclusion	Therefore, leave the dead to bury the dead, and go, proclaim the kingdom of God. (Luke 9:61-62)

Furthermore, the new chreia is a gnomic saying in form (Theon, *Prog.* 99)—that is, it attributes to Jesus a saying that would have been rather well known in the ancient Mediterranean world. For example, in Hesiod's *Works and Days*, a plowman is described as one "who attends to his work and drives a straight furrow and no longer gapes after his comrades, but keeps his mind on his work" (443; cf. Pliny, *Nat.* 18.19.49). In other words, to look back from the plow (whether to family living or dead) was to risk cutting a crooked or shallow furrow and thus ruining the work altogether! There is no place for looking back or even trying to look in two directions at once (being "two-faced"); rather, would-be disciples must be single-minded in purpose, setting their faces like Jesus on the task at hand.

Chreia Elaboration

Luke 10:17-24 is woven around another "apocritic chreia" (cf. Theon, *Prog.* 98; see above) in which Jesus responds to a statement by his disciples (10:17) with the report of a vision in the form of a chreia (10:18)—an "elaborated chreia," which preserves a memorable, if mysterious, saying of Jesus (10:18).[68] The chreia is elaborated to illuminate its meaning along the lines laid out in the *Progymnasmata* (brief praise, anecdote, rationale, contrast, comparison, example, citation of authority, conclusion; cf. Ps.-Hermogenes, *Prog.* 7–8; Aphthonius, *Prog.* 8), although there is no reason to expect that in practice such elaboration would follow the form and content strictly. The elaborated chreia in Luke contains the following elements:[69]

Introduction	Lord . . . (10:17)
Chreia	I saw Satan falling . . . (10:18)
Rationale	I have given you authority (10:19)
Opposite	Nevertheless do not rejoice (10:20)
Example	He rejoiced in the Holy Spirit . . . (10:21)
Authority	All things have been given . . . (10:22)
Conclusion	Blessed are the eyes . . . (10:23-24)

The first section (10:17-20) has no parallels in the synoptic tradition (though cf. Mark 10:19 and 16:18). The unit begins with the disciples' return. Their joy recalls the joy associated with God's anticipated action in the annunciation (1:14; 2:10) and foreshadows the disciples' joy after the resurrection (24:52): "The seventy[-two] returned with joy, saying, 'Lord, even the demons are subject to us in your name'" (10:17).[70] Although the introduction is missing any *explicit* praise of Jesus (typical of an elaborated chreia), it does include *implicit* encomiastic language: Jesus is referred to as "Lord," strengthening the identification of Jesus (with God) as "Lord of the harvest" (10:2), and the power of Jesus' name is acknowledged (10:17b; cf. Acts 3:6; 4:10, 17-18, 30; 5:40; 9:27). The commission of the seventy(-two) contained no explicit command to perform exorcisms (10:1-2), but the authorial audience could easily accommodate the subjection of demons under the general command to heal as part of the proclamation of the kingdom of God (cf. 4:40-41; 9:1).

Jesus responds with a sayings chreia: "Then he said to them, 'I watched Satan falling from heaven like lightning'" (10:18). The interpretation of the chreia is much debated.[71] Some take it as a metaphorical description—that is, a "symbolic way of summing up the effects of the disciples' mission."[72] Others see it as a "prophetic vision" but disagree on the timing and the content of the vision. Some view it as a vision of the primeval fall of Satan (cf. L.A.E. 11–14; 2 En. 29:3-6) witnessed by the preexistent Christ (a view common among patristic writers, e.g., Jerome, *Comm. Isa.* 73, and followed by some older commentators, e.g., Kittel, *TDNT* 4:130n220). Others see it as a vision of Satan's fall witnessed by Jesus at some point in his earthly ministry (whether temptation or baptism).[73] Still others see Satan's fall as an event associated with the mission of the seventy(-two).[74] Most likely, Jesus is reporting a vision of the eschatological future (such as one finds in Amos 8:1-3; Jer 1:13-19; Ezek 2:9-10) that has been foreshadowed by the mission of the seventy(-two).[75] In the Old Testament, Satan played the role of God's (and humanity's) adversary in the heavenly council (Job 1:6-12; 2:1-7; Zech 3:1-2), and the fall of Satan reflects the apocalyptic texts of Second Temple Judaism (Sib. Or. 3.796–807; 11QMelch 13f.; 1 En. 83:4) and early Christianity (John 12:27-33; Rom 16:20; Col 2:15; Rev 12:7-10; 20:3-10) in which Satan and the powers of darkness are defeated by God in an end-time cosmic battle.[76] Quite possibly, the Lukan Jesus saw in the fall of the Babylonian king (Isa 14:11-15 and allusion in 10:15) a connection to the fall of Satan: the fall of earthly powers and principalities foreshadows the downfall of Satan and his minions (cf. Acts 12). In his vision, Jesus' mission is tied to God's "coming triumph over the rule of Satan."[77]

The chreia is followed by its *rationale*: the mission of the seventy(-two) is a harbinger of the cosmic battle between God and Satan not because of the disciples' own power but because Christ has empowered them: "I have given you the authority to walk on snakes and scorpions, and over all the power of the Enemy" (10:19a). Through Christ the disciples have the authority to tread on "snakes and scorpions," which are well known symbols for the sources of evil (Gen 3:14; Num 21:6-9; Sir 21:2; Pss 58:4; 140:3). The two are paired in Deut 8:15 as a vivid reminder of the dangerous wasteland through which God had led his people (cf. also Luke 11:11-12). The reference to "walk on" may echo Psalm (LXX) 90:13 ("you shall tread on the asp"), and the identification of the combination of the snake and scorpion as a symbol of evil gains further traction in *Testament of Levi*'s rewriting of that same psalm: "And Beliar shall be bound by him [God] and he [God] shall give *power to his children to tread upon the evil spirits*" (T. Levi 18:12). That the downfall of Satan is anticipated, but not ultimately fulfilled, by the mission of the seventy(-two) is underscored by the use of the future tense at the end of the rationale: "and nothing will by any means harm you!" (10:19b). Through the complex of events that leads to Jesus' exaltation in Luke, Satan will be defeated decisively. In some Christian apocalyptic texts, however, Satan's fall may also hint at some temporary period in which he wreaks havoc (Rev 12:7-12; among Jewish texts, see possibly T. Sol. 20:17). Jesus also hints at this eschatological havoc in Luke 21:12-27 and reassures his followers that "not a hair of your head will perish" (21:18).[78] Jesus' words here also provide assurance that this victory over Satan will happen—indeed, has already begun to happen—and the reference to Satan's fall (Luke 10:18) anticipates an event destined to occur when Jesus is raised to God's right hand.

The elaboration of the chreia continues with a *statement of contrast* intended to clarify what the disciples should rejoice over (and what they should not): "However, do not rejoice in this, that the spirits are subject to you, but rejoice that your names have been written in heaven" (10:20). It is clear from what precedes that the disciples have no reason to rejoice over the fact that the spirits are subject to them since their dominion over the spirits is due exclusively to the authority of the Lord who has sent them. Rather, they should rejoice over the fact that their names have been written in the "heavenly registry."[79] In the face of impending eschatological woes, they should take consolation that the source of their joy is their status in heaven, which they owe to God, and not their success over the spirits![80]

Next in the elaborated chreia, the Lukan Jesus provides an *example* of how and why the the disciples should rejoice: "At that very time he was overjoyed in the Holy Spirit and said, 'I acknowledge to you, Father, Lord of heaven and of earth, that you concealed these things from the wise and intelligent and revealed them to little children'" (10:21a). Jesus is "overjoyed" in the Spirit and offers a prayer of thanksgiving to God who is "Father" and "Lord of heaven and earth," who has chosen, in his sovereignty, to reveal "these things" (Satan's fall and the ultimate protection of God's people) not to the wise and intelligent but to the "little children" (*nēpiois;* literally, "babies"; cf. Matt 21:16). Clearly, the disciples' source of joy is not in their own abilities and power to perform miracles but in the fact that they, as "babes," are the beneficiaries of God's revelation to them (cf. LXX Pss 18:8; 114:6; 118:130). The disciples and Jesus are not the only ones who rejoice that this insight into God's sovereign character has been revealed to them: "Yes, Father, because (doing it) this way was pleasing to you" (10:21b).

In a further elaboration, Jesus turns from praising God as Father and Lord to discussing his own authority and the source of it: "Everything has been given to me by my Father; and no one knows who the Son is except the Father, and who the Father is except the Son and the one to whom the Son wishes to reveal (him)" (10:22). This intimate relational language is unusual for Luke (and the Synoptics; but cf. Luke 20:41-44; 22:69-70) and more typical of the Fourth Gospel (cf. 3:35; 7:29; 10:14-15; 13:3; 17:2, 25, 29).[81] The high christology reflected here "grants to the Son the authority to dispense the authority of the Father."[82]

The *conclusion* to the elaborated chreia begins with a beatitude: "Then he turned to the disciples and said privately, 'Blessed are the eyes that see what you are seeing'" (10:23). Jesus places emphasis on eyewitness, a theme found at the beginning and end of Luke's narrative (1:2; 24:31, 48). Jesus underscores the privileged place the disciples have in seeing and hearing this revelation from God through the son by claiming, "For I tell you, many prophets and kings wanted to see what you are seeing and did not see it, and to hear what you are hearing and did not hear it" (10:24).

Not all elaborated chreia follow the pattern of Aphthonius. Remember that Theon said that "elaboration is language that adds what is lacking in thought or expression." Luke has also supplied what is "lacking" in his elaboration of the Markan chreia found in Mark 1:16-18.[83]

> Once while Jesus was standing beside the lake of Gennesaret, and the crowd was pressing in on him to hear the word of God, he saw two boats there at the shore of the lake; the fishermen had gone out of them and were washing their nets. He got into one of the boats, the one belonging to Simon, and asked him to put out a little way from the shore. Then he sat down and taught the crowds from the boat. When he had finished speaking, he said to Simon, "Put out into the deep water and let down your nets for a catch." Simon answered, "Master, we have worked all night long but have caught nothing. Yet if you say so, I will let down the nets." When they had done this, they caught so many fish that their nets were beginning to break. So they signaled their partners in the other boat to come and help them. And they came and filled both boats, so that they began to sink. But when Simon Peter saw it, he fell down at Jesus' knees, saying, "Go away from me, Lord, for I am a sinful man!" For he and all who were with him were amazed at the catch of fish that they had taken; and so also were James and John, sons of Zebedee, who were partners with Simon. Then Jesus said to Simon, "Do not be afraid; from now on you will be catching people." (5:1-10)

The image of "people-fishing" was ambivalent, sometimes containing negative connotations in the ancient world.[84] The Jewish Scriptures frequently depict Israel as the target of their enemy's people-fishing activity, an activity often linked to divine judgment (Amos 4:2; Hab 1:14-15; Jer 16:6). In ancient philosophical thought, the image was used of duplicitous philosophers who seek to deceive others to their own ends (cf. Plato, *Soph.* 222A) or who are themselves caught on the hook baited with material wealth (Lucian, *Pisc.*). By elaborating the Markan chreia to include the setting of the crowds gathering to hear Jesus proclaim "the word of God," Luke removes any potential misunderstanding related to the metaphor of people-fishing.[85] The disciples are called and commissioned to participate in Jesus' people-fishing mission, and this mission, as Luke makes clear in Luke 4, is a mission of release and redemption, not one of deception and destruction. Its ultimate success is intimated and foreshadowed by the "great catch" that strains the nets (5:6). The mission of Jesus and his followers is confirmed and elaborated by the miraculous catch, and it leads to an elevation in the identity of Jesus from "master" to "Lord" not only for Simon (5:5, 8) but also for James and John, whom Simon had beckoned for help (5:7) and who join Simon in leaving everything and following Jesus (5:11), as well as the authorial audience who in the process of hearing the story are also challenged to take up this mission.

Elaborated Maxim

The focus of this chapter has been on the chreia exercise, since Theon treats maxims not in a separate chapter but rather as a species of chreia (unlike the other theorists). Theon does distinguish the maxim from the chreia: (1) chreias are always attributed to a character, maxims are not; (2) chreias can state universals or particulars, maxims are always universal; (3) chreias can be for "pleasantry" and not just utility, maxims are "always about something"; (4) chreias can be actions or sayings, maxims are always sayings (*Prog.* 97). All the examples of chreia in the New Testament are drawn from the Gospels (and are most often attributed to Jesus). There are, however, several examples in nonnarrative New Testament writings. Below we consider an example from James 2:17-26.[86]

Simple statement	So faith by itself, if it has no works, is dead. (2:17)
Statement of the cause	But someone will say, "You have faith and I have works." (2:18a)
Contrast	Show me your faith apart from your works, and I by my works will show you my faith. (2:18b)
Comparison	You believe that God is one; you do well. Even the demons believe—and shudder. Do you want to be shown, you shallow man, that faith apart from works is barren? (2:19-20)
Example	Was not Abraham our father justified by works, when he offered his son Isaac upon the altar? You see that faith was active along with his works, and faith was completed by works. (2:21-22)
Testimony	And the scripture was fulfilled which says, "Abraham believed God, and it was reckoned to him as righteousness"; and he was called the friend of God. (2:23)
Judgment	You see that a man is justified by works and not by faith alone. (2:24)
Example (2)	And in the same way was not also Rahab the harlot justified by works when she received the messengers and sent them out another way? (2:25)
Conclusion	For as the body apart from the spirit is dead, so faith apart from works is dead. (2:26)

James' pattern of argument echoes the pattern for a maxim advocated by Aphthonius (*Prog.* 26–27). The only slight variation is that James offers a second example (Rahab) to support his point. The testimony comes in the form of an explicit citation of Genesis 15:6. Thus, the passage is a tight rhetorical unit that flows in a progressive and, in light of rhetorical compositional techniques, logical fashion.[87] Lying in the background, of course, is Paul's claim that no one is justified by works (Gal 2:16; Rom 4:5). Nowhere in Paul's letters does he claim that Christian good works are useless; in fact, in Galatians 5:6 he seems to suggest the opposite. By couching the argument as an elaborated maxim that pits faith against works ("faith by itself, if it has no works, is dead"), and not a specific refutation of a chreia attributed to Paul, James is able to imply that the "maxim" is not directly aimed against Paul (whom otherwise he might have cited) but a refutation of an "opinion that deforms his [Paul's] doctrine of justification by faith alone."[88]

Conclusion

Chreias of all varieties were stock conventions in ancient compositional practices. Familiarity with their forms and functions can inform our reading of the New Testament, especially the Gospels in their final form. The elaboration and expansion (and condensation) of chreias also contribute to our understanding of the transmission of Jesus material from the oral period into literary contexts, even if that contribution is to complicate our understanding of that process. Writers (and speakers) found chreias (sayings, actional, and mixed) a convenient way to disclose the character of the speaker/protagonist they sought to present. We ignore those conventions at our own exegetical peril.

Notes

1 This remarkable catechism on chreia is from a small third-century CE scrap of papyrus found in Oxyrhynchus. Apparently, the format reflects a question and answer exercise that may have been employed by the pedagogue when teaching about chreia. The translation comes from Ronald F. Hock and Edward N. O'Neil, trans. and eds., *The Chreia and Ancient Rhetoric: Classroom Exercises*, WGRW 2 (Atlanta: Society of Biblical Literature, 2002), 97.

2 Henry A. Fischel, "Studies in Cynicism and the Ancient Near East: The Transformation of a Chria," in *Religions in Antiquity: Essays in Memory of E. R. Goodenough*, ed. Jacob Neusner (Leiden: Brill, 1968), 374.

3 The work by Ronald F. Hock and Edward O'Neil has significantly advanced our understanding of the form and function of the chreia in ancient theory and practice; see Ronald F. Hock and Edward N. O'Neil, trans. and eds., *The Chreia in Ancient Rhetoric*, vol. 1, *The Progymnasmata*, SBLTT 27 (Atlanta: Scholars Press, 1986); Hock and O'Neil, *Classroom Exercises*; Ronald F. Hock, trans. and eds., *The Chreia and Ancient Rhetoric: Commentaries on Aphthonius' Progymnasmata*, WGRW 31 (Atlanta: Society of Biblical Literature, 2012). Also important is the work by Burton L. Mack and Vernon K. Robbins, *Patterns of Persuasion in the Gospels* (Sonoma, Calif.: Polebridge Press, 1989).

4 Hock and O'Neil, *Progymnasmata*, 24.
5 See chreias 43–45 in Hock and O'Neil, *Progymnasmata*, 327–29.
6 Hock and O'Neil, *Progymnasmata*, 25.
7 Hock and O'Neil, *Progymnasmata*, 24, e.g., think the prepositional phrase modifies the specified character. On the various ways to understand "aptness" or "suitability," see Vernon K. Robbins, "The Chreia," in *Greco-Roman Literature and the New Testament: Selected Forms and Genres*, ed. David E. Aune (Atlanta: Scholars Press, 1988), 2n5. As evidence that "aptness" can apply both to the suitability of the saying/action for the circumstances and also as pointed disclosure of some characteristic quality of the attributed person, Robbins cites chreias 26 and 52 in Hock and O'Neil, *Progymnasmata*, 316, 333–34.
8 George Kennedy, trans., *Progymnasmata: Greek Textbooks of Prose Composition and Rhetoric* (Atlanta: Society of Biblical Literature, 2003), 8n25, states that the Greek text of Theon places chreia after myth and narrative to align Theon with the other handbooks. Apparently, the original order, which places chreia first, is found in the Armenian version and followed by Kennedy.
9 Hock and O'Neil, *Progymnasmata*, 67. Theon distinguishes the maxim from the chreia: (1) chreias are always attributed to a character, maxims are not; (2) chreias can state universals or particulars, maxims are always universal; (3) chreias can be for "pleasantry" and not just utility; maxims are "always about something"; (4) chreias can be actions or sayings, maxims are always sayings (*Prog.* 97). One could argue that chreias, which are distinctive of a particular individual (or group), become proverbial maxims when they successfully penetrate the ethos, thought, and practice of a community, even if they never completely lose their original attribution. As noted in the introduction, we do not include a separate chapter on maxims, since the chreia has been the focus of most NT scholarship in the area of ancient rhetoric; we do, however, provide one example of an elaborated maxim. See also Rollin Ramsmaran, *Liberating Words: Paul's Use of Rhetorical Maxims in 1 Corinthians 1–10* (Valley Forge, Pa.: Trinity Press International, 1996); Anders Eriksson, "Elaboration of Argument in 1 Cor 15:20-34," *Svensk exegetisk årsbok* 64 (1999): 101–14; J. D. Hester, "The Use and Influence of Rhetoric in Galatians 2:1-14," *ThZ* 42 (1986): 386–408.
10 Hock and O'Neil, *Progymnasmata*, 27, view the chreia's usefulness for living as yet another characteristic of the chreia, but given Nicolaus' observation that all the exercises have a certain utility, it does not seem prudent to include this feature as particularly distinctive of the chreia, despite the etymology of its nomenclature.
11 Hock and O'Neil, *Progymnasmata*, 315–16, list this as chreia 25.
12 Hock and O'Neil, *Progymnasmata*, 316, list this as chreia 26 and note that it is closely related to the previous chreia (chreia 25). Chreia 26 "is the most popular in our collection, appearing fourteen times in nine authors, although surprisingly, it seems not to occur outside the rhetorical tradition. . . . In eight instances it is used to illustrate a mixed chreia."
13 Hock and O'Neil, *Progymnasmata*, 28. Ps.-Hermogenes' examples of an action chreia and a mixed chreia clarify this distinction. Actional chreia—"Diogenes, on seeing an undisciplined youth, beat his pedagogue"; mixed chreia—"Diogenes, on seeing an undisciplined youth, beat his pedagogue and said, 'Why did you teach him such things?'" (Ps.-Hermogenes, *Prog.* 6). Based on his example of actional and mixed chreias, it is reasonable to assume that Aphthonius shares this understanding with Ps.-Hermogenes and Nicolaus (cf. Aphthonius, *Prog.* 23). In this chapter we will follow the majority view of Nicolaus and Ps.-Hermogenes.
14 Hock and O'Neil, *Progymnasmata*, 28.
15 Hock and O'Neil, *Progymnasmata*, 28. Cf. also Robbins, "Chreia," 4.
16 Hock and O'Neil, *Progymnasmata*, 29. They suggest combining the first two subdivisions into one, a question calling for answer and keeping the third variation as a question that demands

an explanation. Despite Theon's oversubtleties, Robbins observes that the subcategories "help us to see a range of possibilities in the speech in a chreia" ("The Chreia," 5).

17 Hock and O'Neil (*Progymnasmata*, 30) find this category is "not drawn finely enough," amounting to "little more than a miscellaneous category for non-interrogative responsive chreiai." For our purposes, and since Theon stands alone in these further subdivisions, in the examples section we are content to deal with actional chreia and sayings chreia in the form of declarative and responsive.

18 Here Alexander quotes from *Iliad* 2.24, and Diogenes cites the next line in *Iliad* 2.25. Diogenes' point is that he is not a ruler and thus does not have the same obligation as Alexander. Athenaeus (10.457e) reports that this practice of quoting two lines of a poem in which the second person attempts to outdo the first was a popular form of repartee called *gastrologia*, which was played at symposia (cited by Hock and O'Neil, *Progymnasmata*, 315); see also Epictetus, *Discourses* 3.22.90–92. On Diogenes' parodic use of Homer see M. D. Usher, "Diogenes' Doggerel: Chreia and Quotation in Cynic Performance," *Classical Journal* 104 (2009): 207–23.

19 Theon's examples of these formal categories "illustrate how formalized the sayings of chreiai are and how thoroughly reflective of literary practice the categories are" (Hock and O'Neil, *Progymnasmata*, 35). Other ancient theorists were less convinced of the usefulness of listing these categories. We will not explore those categories here, but will reference them where relevant in the examples section below. For more on these presentations of chreias, see Hock and O'Neil, *Progymnasmata*, 32–35; Robbins, "Chreia," 13–16.

20 "Hung by his name" is a pun on the name Didymon, which means twins. Didymus was hung by "the twins"—that is, his testicles—a punishment, according to Theon, fitting the crime of adultery (cf. Kennedy, *Progymnasmata*, 17n71). Hock and O'Neil, *Progymnasmata*, 32, note the distinction between active and passive chreia of action is "purely theoretical," since "passive chreia do not appear outside these textbooks." Robbins, "Chreia," 9, however, cites Mark 1:12-13, in which the Spirit drives Jesus into the wilderness to be tempted by Satan as a passive chreia of action.

21 We will return to this chreia in the section on NT examples.

22 Rudolf Bultmann, *The History of the Synoptic Tradition*, 2d ed., trans. John Marsh (Oxford: Blackwell, 1968), 4–5, 61–69, 145–50, 368–71.

23 See the example of Matt 19:13-15 and Mark 10:13-16 below.

24 Nicolaus further notes, "After probability some put comparison which is part of probability" (*Prog.* 24).

25 Hock and O'Neil, *Progymnasmata*, 35; cf. Hock, *Commentaries on Aphthonius' Progymnasmata*. Aphthonius' place of prominence among the ancient theorists was mostly due to the fact that he provided model exercises in his textbook, such as the one that follows in the text above (see Hock and O'Neil, *Progymnasmata*, 211–16).

26 Ps.-Hermogenes (*Prog.* 7–8) uses the same chreia by Isocrates and elaborates along the lines outlined below. Libanius also elaborates this same chreia.

27 Hock and O'Neil, *Progymnasmata*, 217.

28 Burton L. Mack, *Anecdotes and Arguments: The Chreia in Antiquity and Early Christianity* (Claremont, Calif.: Institute for Antiquity and Christianity, 1987), 5.

29 See esp. Hock and O'Neil, *Classroom Exercises*; and Hock, *Commentaries on Aphthonius' Progymnasmata*.

30 Marion C. Moeser, *The Anecdote in Mark, the Classical World and the Rabbis* (London: Sheffield Academic, 2002), 89. The examples below taken from the Demonax are cited in Moeser.

31 Jan Fredrik Kindstrand, "Diogenes Laertius and the 'Chreia' Tradition," *Elenchos* 7 (1986): 217–43.

32 Chreia 10 in Hock and O'Neil, *Progymnasmata*, 307. They point out that some form of this chreia is attributed to a variety of persons (Bion, Bias, Democritus, and Demetrius of Phalerum).

They further note (307) that "this variation of attribution is hardly surprising, given the gnomic character of the saying" and cite 1 Tim 6:10 ("the love of money is the root of all evil") as a variation on the theme; however, there the saying is unattributed and would be better classified as a maxim.

33 This is one of the most quoted chreias in antiquity, both within and without the rhetorical tradition, although the attribution varies (cf. Hock and O'Neil, *Progymnasmata*, 325).

34 This chreia is placed within a context that could also be construed as a responsive chreia; see Alan J. Avery-Peck, "Rhetorical Argumentation in Early Rabbinic Pronouncement Stories," *Sem* 64 (1993): 60.

35 This chreia, with different attributions, is also found in the progymnasmata tradition, as well as Athenaeus 8.338a and *Gnom. Vat.* 28; cf. Hock and O'Neil, *Progymnasmata*, 310.

36 On Demonax's sense of humor, see R. Bracht Branham, "Authorizing Humor: Lucian's Demonax and Cynic Rhetoric," *Sem* 64 (1993): 33–48.

37 Moeser, *Anecdote in Mark*, 99.

38 Mack, *Anecdotes and Arguments*, 8.

39 This chreia is similar to those where the action of beating the pedagogue is prompted by a youth misbehaving or acting as a glutton; see Hock and O'Neil, *Progymnasmata*, 309.

40 This example is cited as chreia 47 in Hock and O'Neil, *Progymnasmata*, 330. Hock and O'Neil (330) also cite this chreia as the source for Petronius' jest about the prostitute Quartilla, about whom it is said that as a girl she had sex with boys and as she grew older gradually graduated to grown men (cf. Petronius, *Satyr.* 25).

41 See Hock and O'Neil, *Progymnasmata*, 321.

42 Cited by Avery-Peck, "Rhetorical Argumentation," 51. Avery-Peck also observes that this chreia of action is expressed with wit, one of the categories of presentation that Theon lists (*Prog.* 99): "By commending Sabta, the gentiles themselves admit to the irrational character of idol-worship" (51). See this article for other examples drawn from rabbinic literature.

43 Moeser, *Anecdote in Mark*, 94, explains that antipodes are "persons dwelling at a directly opposite point on the globe of the earth."

44 Moeser, *Anecdote in Mark*, 95.

45 See Moeser, *Anecdote in Mark*, 85–86. On *Rhetorica ad Herennium*, see Patrick Sinclair, "The Sententia in *Rhetorica ad Herennium*: A Study in the Sociology of Rhetoric," *AJP* 114, no. 4 (1993): 561–80.

46 Burton L. Mack has identified chreia elaboration as a rhetorical strategy employed by Philo of Alexandria. Mack examines Philo's treatment of Gen 4:2 in *De sacrificiis* 1–10 and concludes that the pattern of argumentation there follows almost exactly the chreia elaboration as described by Hermogenes. See "Decoding the Scripture: Philo and the Rules of Rhetoric," in *Nourished with Peace: Studies in Hellenistic Judaism in Memory of Samuel Sandmel*, ed. Frederick E. Greenspahn, Earle Hilgert, and Burton L. Mack (Chico, Calif.: Scholars Press, 1984), 81–115.

47 Avery-Peck, "Rhetorical Argumentation," 59.

48 For more on chreias in Mark, see Jerome H. Neyrey, "Questions, Chreiai, and Challenges to Honor: The Interface of Rhetoric and Culture in Mark's Gospel," *CBQ* 60 (1998): 657–81.

49 Some might take the feeding of the five thousand as "mixed" chreia, since Jesus' blessing of the bread presumably involved words, but since the words are not reported in any of the versions, the focus is clearly on the revelatory nature of the action (cf. the Last Supper scene, in which the actions are accompanied by direct discourse by Jesus [e.g., "This my blood" / "This is my body"], clearly marking the passage as a mixed chreia).

50 We might also consider Luke 9 as an example of partial elaboration along the lines of Aphthonius or Ps.-Hermogenes (see above pp. 21–23). While there is no reason to expect prose writers (like Luke) to follow this formula mechanistically, one sees in Luke 9:10-17 the rationale for

the *chreia* of action (the day is ending and the crowds have nothing to eat), a statement of the contrary (the disciples initially oppose Jesus' proposal to provide hospitality), analogy (echoes of OT miraculous provision—see below), and authority (Jesus' authority comes from God, as indicated by his lifting his eyes toward heaven). On Luke 12, see Thomas Stegman, "Reading Luke 12:13-34 as an Elaboration of a Chreia: How Hermogenes of Tarsus Sheds Light on Luke's Gospel," *NovT* 49 (2007): 328–52.

51 See Robert J. Karris, *Luke: Artist and Theologian: Luke's Passion Account as Literature* (New York: Paulist, 1985), 47.

52 Arthur A. Just, *Luke: 9:51–24:53* (St. Louis: Concordia, 1997), 156–57.

53 The following verse (Matt 27:25), taken together with Pilate's statement, forms a double chreia, which Theon defines as "having statements by two persons where either statement makes a chreia by one person" (*Prog.* 98): "Then the people as a whole answered, 'His blood be on us and on our children!'" This chreia is attributed to a group (cf. the chreia attributed to a representative of the Laconians, cited above on p. 19: "A Laconian, when someone asked him where the Lacedaimonians set the limits of their land, showed his spear" [Theon, *Prog.* 99]), and holds a singularly tragic place in Jewish-Christian relations; cf. Catherine Sider, "'His Blood Be upon Us': Innocent Blood and the Death of Jesus in Matthew," *CBQ* 70 (2008): 82–100.

54 C. K. Barrett, "The House of Prayer and the Den of Thieves," in *Jesus und Paulus: Festschrift für Werner Georg Kümmel zum 70sten Geburtstag*, ed. E. Earle Ellis and Erich Grässer (Göttingen: Vandenhoeck & Ruprecht, 1975), 13–20.

55 Thus it may be taken as another example of chreia compression (see below).

56 Joseph A. Fitzmyer, *The Gospel according to Luke*, AB 28–28A (Garden City, N.Y.: Doubleday, 1981–1985), 2:1261.

57 Luke Timothy Johnson, *The Literary Function of Possessions in Luke-Acts*, SBLDS 39 (Missoula, Mont.: Scholars Press, 1977), 299.

58 Interestingly, in Matt 26:61 and Mark 14:58 Jesus is accused (apparently falsely) of uttering this saying, but it is never actually attributed to him in those two Gospels.

59 William M. Wright IV, *Rhetoric and Theology: Figural Reading of John 9* (Berlin: Walter de Gruyter, 2009), 156–66, has identified John 9:1-7 as a mixed, apocritic chreia in response to a question raised by the disciples ("Who sinned . . . ?").

60 W. D. Davies and Dale C. Allison explain: "On the theory of Markan priority, Matthew omitted the verse [Mk 10.15] because he already used a variant in 18.3" (*A Critical and Exegetical Commentary on the Gospel according to Saint Matthew*, 3 vols., ICC [Edinburgh: T&T Clark, 1997], 3:31). Likewise, Adela Collins asserts, "Matthew found the saying to be out of place in this narrative and moved it to his version of the controversy about greatness (18:1-5)" (*Mark: A Commentary*, Hermeneia [Minneapolis: Fortress, 2007], 473). Robert H. Gundry thinks Matthew deletes the reference to Jesus' indignation at the disciples as part of his overall more positive view of the disciples (*Matthew: A Commentary on His Handbook for a Mixed Church under Persecution*, 2d ed. [Grand Rapids: Eerdmans, 1994], 384).

61 Davies and Allison suggest, "On the theory of Matthean priority, either Mark or Luke moved Mt 18.3 into the pericope on children for thematic reasons" (*Critical and Exegetical Commentary on Matthew*, 3:31). And further, "Although we do not accept the Griesbach hypothesis, it must be admitted that Mk 10:15 does appear to be a secondary insertion . . . a fact consistent with the theory of Matthean priority" (3:31n4). In this scenario, Mark would have moved Matt 18:3 to this point in the story and further expanded the chreia along the lines outlined above.

62 On this passage, see Vernon Robbins, "Pronouncement Stories and Jesus' Blessing of the Children: A Rhetorical Approach," *Sem* 29 (1983): 42–74.

63 Sharyn Dowd, *Reading Mark: A Literary and Theological Commentary on the Second Gospel* (Macon, Ga.: Smyth & Helwys, 2000), 26–27; Mikeal C. Parsons, "Mark 2:23-28," *Int* 59 (2005): 57–60.

64 Manfred Kraus, "Theories and Practice of the Enthymeme in the First Centuries B.C.E. and C.E.," in *Rhetorical Argumentation in Biblical Texts: Essays from the Lund 2000 Conference*, ed. Anders Eriksson, Thomas H. Olbricht, and Walter Übelacker (Harrisburg, Pa.: Trinity Press International, 2002), 95–11, esp. 109–11. Theon's definition of the enthymeme reflects a shift in the understanding of its form and function. Theon's contemporary, Quintilian, in summarizing previous definitions of the enthymeme (which go as far back as Aristotle, *Rhet.* 1.2.8), offers no fewer than five meanings (*Inst.* 5.10.1–3). While he mentions the "incomplete syllogism," Quintilian favors a rhetorical definition that draws on "consequences" or "incompatibles" (Kraus, "Theories and Practice of the Enthymeme," 96–97; on syllogistic contraries, see also *Rhet. Her.* 4.25–26; for a NT example, see Rom 2:21-23). According to Kraus (99–100), for Quintilian, the enthymeme is the result of three factors: (1) The enthymeme "is the rhetorical counterpart to philosophy's deductive syllogism." (2) It "pays respect to the socio-cultural background of its audience. It proceeds not from scientific axioms, but from preconceived opinions shared by the audience or a majority of them. As a consequence, it generally does not attain absolute truth, but still convincing plausibility," leaving "the audience something to think or infer themselves." (3) "An enthymeme will be expressed in a short, pungent, and witty manner, employing strong and powerful figures of speech, of which antithesis is only one." Reflecting on the diversity of opinions in antiquity regarding the definition of an enthymeme, Kraus concludes: "In different periods, however, others of these factors predominated, which at least partly accounts for the complex and manifold history of the term" (100). It is important to remember this "complex history" when reviewing Theon's univocal understanding of the function of a chreia within the framework of the elliptic enthymeme. See also David E. Aune, "The Use and Abuse of the Enthymeme in New Testament Scholarship," *NTS* 49 (2003): 299–320.

65 Robert H. Gundry, *Mark: A Commentary on His Apology for the Cross* (Grand Rapids: Eerdmans, 1993), 144.

66 See note 64. For other examples of chreias within the framework of an elliptic enthymeme, see Seneca the Younger, *Letters to Lucilius* 95.33; 1 Cor 11:29-30, cited by Kraus, "Theories and Practice of the Enthymeme," 110.

67 Mack and Robbins, *Patterns of Persuasion*, 80.

68 On this example, see Mikeal C. Parsons, *Acts*, PCNT (Grand Rapids: Baker Academic, 2012), 175–78.

69 Edith M. Humphrey, *And I Turned to See the Voice: The Rhetoric of Vision in the New Testament* (Grand Rapids: Baker Academic, 2007), 105.

70 Cf. R. Alan Culpepper, "Luke," in *The New Interpreter's Bible* (Nashville: Abingdon, 1995), 9:223.

71 For much of what follows, see Simon Gathercole, "Jesus' Eschatological Vision of the Fall of Satan: Luke 10,18 Reconsidered," *ZNW* 94 (2003): 145–58.

72 Fitzmyer, *Luke*, 2:860; cf. I. Howard Marshall, *The Gospel of Luke: A Commentary on the Greek Text* (Grand Rapids: Eerdmans, 1978), 429.

73 Temptation: Norval Geldenhuys, *Commentary on the Gospel of Luke* (Grand Rapids: Eerdmans, 1951); baptism: Joel Marcus, "Jesus' Baptismal Vision," *NTS* 41 (1995): 512–21.

74 Frederick W. Danker, *Jesus and the New Age: A Commentary on St. Luke's Gospel* (Philadelphia: Fortress, 1988), 217; Darrell L. Bock, *Luke*, 2 vols., BECNT (Grand Rapids: Baker Academic, 1994–1996), 2:1007.

75 John Nolland, *Luke*, 3 vols., WBC (Dallas: Word, 1989–1993), 2:454.

76 Susan R. Garrett, *The Demise of the Devil: Magic and the Demonic in Luke's Writings* (Minneapolis: Fortress, 1989), 51–53.

77 Nolland, *Luke*, 2:564.

78 Cf. Gathercole, "Jesus' Eschatological Vision," 159.

79 Fitzmyer, *Luke*, 2:860.

80 David E. Garland, *Luke* (Grand Rapids: Zondervan, 2011), 429.
81 Bock calls this verse a "bolt out of the Johannine blue" (*Luke*, 2:1011).
82 Culpepper, "Luke," 225.
83 Peter Reynolds, "Miracle and Mission in Luke: A Rhetorical Analysis of Luke 5:1-11" (Ph.D. diss., Baylor University, 2016).
84 Wilhelm Wuellner, *The Meaning of "Fishers of Men"* (Philadelphia: Westminster, 1967).
85 Reynolds, "Miracle and Mission in Luke."
86 We draw on and modify the work of Jean Nöel Aletti, "James 2,14-26: The Arrangement and Its Meaning," *Bib* 95 (2014): 88–101.
87 Thus, commentators who argue for a tripartite division force an unwarranted disjointedness on the pericope; cf. H. Frankemölle, *Der Brief des Jakobus* (Gütersloh: Gütersloher Verlagshaus, 1994), 420–78.
88 Aletti, "James 2, 14-26," 97. Aletti goes on to conclude that "the chosen form of argumentation allows for combatting an erroneous opinion without polemicizing against the one (Paul) who is probably being used by those defending it to recommend it" (97).

2

Fable

Telling the Truth through Fiction

An Ethical Fable of the Cicadas and Ants,
Exhorting the Young to Toil

> It was the height of summer and the cicada were offering up their shrill song, but it occurred to the ants to toil and collect the harvest from which they would be fed in the winter. When the winter came on, the ants fed on what they had laboriously collected, but the pleasure of the cicadas ended in want. Similarly, youth that does not wish to toil fares badly in old age.
>
> Aphthonius

Though second in Theon's progymnasmata, the fable exercise appears first in all other extant progymnasmata from antiquity because of its formative aims. Quintilian explains that it naturally "follows on directly from (the pupils') nurses' stories" (*Inst.* 1.9.2 [Russell, LCL]), and Pseudo-Hermogenes, that it may "form students while still tender" and "bring their minds into harmony for the better" (*Prog.* 1).[1] This concern for character formation is reflected, too, in Aphthonius' model fable above, with its moral tailored to youth.

The fable exercise also taught literary skills considered foundational to prose composition and oratory. In a general sense, the exercise served as a primer in narrative writing. Theon says that a student who has "expressed a fable well" will not only "compose a history well" but also excel at writing "what is called the narration" in declamation of a speech (*Prog.* 60). More specifically, though, the exercise taught a form, the Graeco-Roman *mythos*, that was nothing less than an essential building block of Hellenistic composition. One finds the form in every manner of Hellenistic writing, everything from prose philosophical treatises and histories to epic poetry. The form appears, too, as one of the major species of exemplum, or inductive argument, commonly used in speeches—thus its place among the *progymnasmata*, or exercises *preliminary to* declamation.

Theory

In general, the fable exercise falls in two parts. The first introduces the genre, and the second, a series of exercises encouraging its manipulation by students in a variety of ways. In attending to both aspects of the exercise, modern readers may gain insight both into the genre as it was understood by the educated of the ancient world and into the ancient literary practices that shaped its transmission in various forms.

The Genre of Fable

Theon defines the *mythos,* or what we call "fable," as a "fictitious story/statement that gives an image of truth" (*Prog.* 72). He clarifies that he has in mind short tales like those of Aesop that illustrate some moral or principle. Theon's definition, which classicist Ben Edward Perry judges to be "perfect and complete," reflects three essential and commonly attested elements:[2]

(1) *In calling it "fictitious" (or, literally, "false"), Theon is not merely saying that it is "made up"; rather, he is invoking rhetorical theory's larger taxonomy of proofs and locating the fable within it.* Generally speaking, rhetoricians divided proofs into two main classes, the deductive argument or enthymeme, and the inductive argument, or exemplum. The latter—often referred to in English as an "example," but better thought of as an "analogy" or "paradigm" since the inference it draws is from a pattern rather than a single instance or model[3]—was divided into two broad classes, the fictitious and the historical. Though variously defined in the handbooks, the fable is consistently located in the fictional class of paradigm as one of its major species. Thus, the word "fictitious" in Theon's definition serves as a subtle reminder to young students of the fable's place in declamation as a particularly type of *analogy,* and of the fable exercise's role as a preparation for declamation.

(2) *Theon calls the fable a* logos, *which may be translated "story" but may also signify more broadly a "statement" or "saying."*[4] Unlike our English word "fable," which denotes a very specific kind of story, all the other Greek and Latin terms the theorists commonly use for the genre (*mythos, ainos, fabella, fabula*) can mean not only "story" but also "word," "saying," "statement," or "speech"—and can have in view utterances that abbreviate the action even within a single sentence.[5] Indeed, Theon's explications of some of the terms actually tend to frame them in this wider sense. The ancients use *mythos,* he says, because *mytheisthai* for them meant "to speak." And they use *ainos* "because it also provides some *parainesis* ('advice')" (*Prog.* 73). Theon's discussion thus sets the parameters for the genre more broadly than English terms like "fable" or even "tale" might suggest. As Perry observes, the "story" Theon has in view "may be contained in no more than a single short

sentence"—and that "when it happens to be very short it is indistinguishable from what we call a proverb, and what the ancient Semitic writers called a 'likeness' (Aram. *mathla*, Heb. *mashal*, Ar. *mathal*, likewise Armen. *Arak*)."[6]

(3) *Theon says that the "story/saying" in view "images truth." This is the element that distinguishes the Aesopic* logos *from other fictional analogies*. Its purpose is to illustrate some moral, principle, idea, or piece of practical wisdom. As Theon puts it, "the whole point is useful instruction" (*Prog.* 73–74).

In addition to these essential elements, the theorists also describe common subject matter of the fable and put forward various classifications of subtypes based upon that subject matter. Aphthonius, for example, attests a distinction commonly drawn between "animal fables" and "human fables": "Some fables are rational, some ethical, some mixed; rational when a human being is imagined as doing something, ethical when representing the character of irrational animal, mixed when made up of both irrational and rational" (*Prog.* 21). Nicolaus mentions this distinction and adds that there are also fables that feature gods, as in "Hera's Homelife with Zeus" (*Prog.* 7). Theon, not with a little disdain, mentions the animal/human division along with another commonly drawn between realistic and unrealistic fables: "Those who say that some involve mute beasts, others human beings, some are impossible, others capable of being true, seem to me to make a silly distinction. All the specific features are found in all those mentioned" (*Prog.* 73). Interestingly, the tradition Theon attests represents a correction of Aristotle's *Rhetorica*, which incorrectly limits the Aesopic *logos* to "unrealistic" fiction (see ancient examples below of the realistic type) and assigns another word, *parabolē*, to the "realistic" class of fictional paradigms (*Rhet.* 2.20.2–8). The Theonic stream stands at odds, too, with a third attested in Apsines' *Rhetorica*, which lets the term *parabolē* stand for the entire class of fictional analogies and makes no mention at all of the Aesopic *logos* (Apsines, *Rhet.* 6.1).[7]

The theorists describe as well various types of morals or "truths imaged" by the story. Theon acknowledges that some morals are stated and that others are left unstated—though he makes clear that his exercise concerns the former type only, which because of its moral was more useful in declamation.[8] Among those stated, the theorists attest two kinds: the *promythion*, which was found at the beginning of the fable; and the *epimythion*, which was found at the end. Nicolaus also attests a late and idiosyncratic—but descriptively accurate—threefold division of the *epimythion*: (1) the "paradigmatic" type, which frames the fable explicitly as an example ("This fable teaches us to do or not to do some particular thing"; *Prog.* 10); (2) the "enthymematic" type, which arrives at its application indirectly through a deduction ("One not doing this particular thing deserves criticism"; *Prog.* 10); and (3) the "prosphonetic" type, which addresses a person directly with the fable's counsel ("And you, my boy, keep away from this or that"; *Prog.* 10).

Theorists frequently comment, too, on the fable's ideal style, which they find modeled in classical literature. Nicolaus summarizes the consensus well, stating, "As a general rule, one should employ language that is rather simple and deviates little from that used in ordinary conversation" (*Prog.* 11). Comparing fables to chreia, Theon states, "In fables the style should be simpler and natural, and in so far as possible artless and clear" (*Prog.* 74). Pseudo-Hermogenes and Nicolaus both commend, as well, an absence of "periodic" sentences—that is, the balanced, poetic prose statements described by Aristotle and others as having a beginning, middle, and end, and thus a concentric form.[9]

The Fable Exercises

In addition to introducing the genre, the theorists taught students how to manipulate fables in various ways so as to gain a compositional mastery of the form. Among the various practices attested are the following:

(1) *Memorization*. The first part of "stating the fable," the goal of this exercise was to imprint on young minds the very best examples of the genre from classical literature. Theon, in particular, emphasizes the importance of this task for learning the simple style of the classical examples.

(2) *Oral recitation*. Once a fable was memorized, students would recite it orally to the class. The exercise, commended by Quintilian, served as a form of early preparation for declamation.

(3) *Written recitation*. Students would also attempt to write the parable from memory using, as best they could, the exact words of the classical original. If oral recitation was preparation for declamation, this practice was preparation for literary composition.

(4) *Paraphrase*. Quintilian attests an incremental process. Students would first divide the fable into individual phrases or sentences and then restate each, one at a time, with phrasing of their own creation. Then they would move on to the "bolder" forms of paraphrase entailed in the exercises described below (*Inst.* 1.9.2–3). Theon, who discusses and illustrates paraphrase in several contexts (*Prog.* 62–64; 107–110), notes that the goal was to preserve the "idea" or "imagination" (*phantasia*) of the original while recasting the wording in good style.

(5) *Inflection*. After stating the fable in original and paraphrased forms, students would then advance to recasting it "in different grammatical numbers and oblique cases" (Theon, *Prog.* 74). The goal was stylistic, in part. As Theon explains, "variety is very pleasing" (*Prog.* 74). Inflection was also a means of laying emphasis on a subject (Quintilian, *Inst.* 9.3.66–67) and calling hearers' attention to it (9.3.27).[10] Theon commends giving "special attention to the accusative cases, because that is the way the ancients told most of those myths" (*Prog.* 74). In illustration of the exercise, Theon cites "the myth by Phaedo the Socratic in

his (dialogue) *Zopyr* (Phaedo, frag. 11),"[11] which begins with an accusative subject and transitions thereafter to the nominative.

(6) *Weaving into narrative*. In imitation of the classics, which generally feature fables embedded in larger narratives, students would practice incorporating fables into their own narrative contexts. The exercise entailed placing the narrative in front of the fable and, alternatively, after it. More importantly, the student was required to relate the fable and its moral in some way to the narrative. Theon gives the following illustration, which draws multiple allegorical points of contact between fable and narrative: "Having imagined that a camel who longed for horns was deprived even of his ears, after stating this first, we go on to the narrative as follows: 'Croesus the Lydian seems to me to have suffered something similar to this camel,' followed by the whole story about him" (*Prog.* 75). According to the "whole story," Croesus (= the camel) in his thirst for Cappadocia (= horns) ended up losing his own kingdom (= his ears).[12]

(7) *Expansion and compression*. Students were also encouraged both to lengthen and to shorten the fable. Prescribed methods included adding or deleting dialogue and description. In illustration of the technique, Pseudo-Hermogenes offers two versions of a fable about apes, one with and another without dialogue and a few additional details.

(8) *Providing conclusions*. As an exercise in composition, students were challenged to make up conclusions for fables. Interestingly, part of the exercise entailed supplying multiple conclusions for the same fable. The practice suggests that ancients saw the fable genre as polyvalent in meaning and therefore flexible in its application.

(9) *Providing fables*. Students similarly were given a conclusion and told to supply a fable appropriate for it, either from the many they had encountered in classical literature, or one of their own or their peers' original composition. The exercise also entailed gathering multiple fables around a single moral.

(10) *Refutation and confirmation*. This final exercise, an entrée into declamation, entailed delivering a speech critiquing (refuting or confirming) another's declamation of a fable *as a rhetorical argument*: "One should refute by showing that what he says is implausible and not beneficial, and one should confirm in the opposite way" (Theon, *Prog.* 76). Students would essentially bring forward arguments affirming or denying the fable and its asserted claims on the basis of standard criteria: "the unclear, the implausible, the inappropriate, the deficient, the redundant, the unfamiliar, the inconsistent, the disordered, the inexpedient, the unlike, the false" (Theon, *Prog.* 76). Theon illustrates each of these in greater detail, defining and illustrating how to correct, for example, a redundancy or an inconsistency. From the list of criteria and their illustrations, one gains insight into editorial standards specific to the fable that, because of their ubiquity in Hellenistic education, most certainly shaped its oral and written transmission as a genre.

Examples from Ancient Literature

Examples of fables from the ancient Mediterranean world are preserved in a number of sources. Some of the oldest are found embedded in a variety of genres from classical literature.[13] These are the examples the progymnasmata generally point to as models for young students to memorize, state, and manipulate in various ways. Some, such as the fable of the Lion's Cub in Aeschylus' *Agamemnon* (told to illustrate what Helen's coming to Troy meant for the Trojans), are poetic works with meter that is lost in translation:[14]

> Even so a man reared in his house a lion's whelp, robbed of its mother's milk yet still desiring the breast. Gentle it was in the prelude of its life, kindly to children, and a delight to the old. Much did it get, held in arms like a nursling child, with its bright eye turned toward his hand, and fawning under compulsion of its belly's need.
>
> But brought to full growth by time it showed forth the nature it hid from its parents. Unbidden, in requital for its fostering, it prepared a feast with ruinous slaughter of the flocks; so that the house was defiled with blood, and they that dwelt therein could not control their anguish, and great was the carnage far and wide. A priest of ruin, by ordinance of God, was it reared in the house.
>
> At first, methinks, there came to Ilium the spirit of unruffled calm, a delicate ornament of wealth, a darter of soft glances from the eye, love's flower that stingeth the heart. Then, swerving from her course, she made her marriage end in ruth, sped on to the children of Priam under escort of Zeus, the warder of host and guest, blasting with ruin by her sojourn and her companionship, a fiend whose bridal was fraught with tears. (Aeschylus, *Agamemnon* 716–749 [Smyth, LCL])

Others, such as Socrates' notorious story of the Dog, are written in ordinary prose:[15]

> "Then why not tell them the story of the dog?" asked Socrates. "It is said that when beasts could talk, a sheep said to her master: 'It is strange that you give us sheep nothing but what we get from the land, though we supply you with wool and lamb and cheese, and yet you share your own food with your dog, who supplies you with none of these things.' The dog heard this, and said: 'Of course he does. Do not I keep you from being stolen by thieves, and carried off by wolves? Why, but for my protection you couldn't even feed for fear of being killed.' And so, they say, the sheep admitted the dog's claim to preference. Do you then tell these women that you are their watch-dog and keeper, and it is due to you that they live and work in safety and comfort, with none to harm them." (Xenophon, *Memorabilia* 2.7.13–14 [Marchant, LCL])

Because fables were co-opted by orators for use in declamation as a kind of inductive proof, one also finds them embedded in speeches. Quintilian (*Inst.* 5.11.17–18) cites as an example of this usage Cicero's *Pro Milone*:

> And so, Gentlemen, it is not without reason that even in their fictions accomplished poets have narrated how *one, who, to avenge a father, had slain a mother, who, though the human vote was divided, acquitted by a sentence that proceeded not merely from a divine being, but from the wisest of the goddesses.* If the Twelve Tables enacted that a thief by night might be slain with impunity in any circumstances, and a thief by day if he defended himself with a weapon, who is there who can hold that punishment should follow *any* act of slaying, whatever its circumstances, seeing, as he does, that at times the laws themselves hold out to us a sword for the slaying of a fellow-creature? (*Pro Milone* 9 [Watts, LCL], citing Aeschylus, *Eumenides,* where Athena's vote acquits Orestes)

The majority of fables from antiquity, however, are preserved in ancient collections. Originally, these were organized as repositories for writers and orators to draw upon for use in other compositions. In the early first century CE, however, collections began to appear that regarded the fable as an art form unto itself, worthy of appreciation.[16] Though the former kind of collection is not extant, several of the latter kind, most notably *Babrius, Phaedrus,* and *Aesopica,* preserve examples such as the following:

DISARMED BY LOVE

> A lion, overcome with love for a young girl, asked for her in marriage from her father. Without showing any ill will or underlying hostility the old man answered: "I give my consent to the marriage, and I give it gladly. Who would refuse kinship with a mighty ruler and lion? But the hearts of young maidens and children are timorous. Think with what huge claws you confront us, what formidable teeth! How would any young maiden dare to embrace you unafraid? How could she even look at you and not cry out? Consider this carefully, if you are bent on marriage. Don't be a wild beast any more, but make yourself a gentle bridegroom." Borne aloft on wings of hope and trusting that the girl would be given, the lion had his teeth extracted and his claws cut out with a surgeon's knife. Then he showed himself to his prospective father-in-law and claimed the bride. At once everyone in the household fell to mauling him, some with clubs, others with stones. And there he lay helpless, dying like a pig, having learned from the shrewd device of a wily old man that there can be no joining in love of mankind with lions or of lions with men.
>
> [A man injures himself without knowing it, when he strives to partake of something that nature has denied him.] (*Babrius* 98 [Perry, LCL])

ON THE FORTUNES OF MEN

> When a certain man was complaining about his ill fortune, Aesop invented the following story to comfort him.
>
> A ship had been badly tossed about by fierce storms so that its passengers were in tears and fear of death, when suddenly the weather changed and took on

a serene aspect; the ship began to ride safely, borne along by favourable winds, which raised the spirits of the sailors to an excessive pitch of joy. Hereupon the pilot, made wise by danger in the past, remarked: "One must be cautious in rejoicing and slow to complain, for the whole of life is a blend of grief and joy." (*Phaedrus*, 4.18)

WHEN THE BEAR GETS HUNGRY

Hunger sharpens the wits of living creatures

Whenever the bear's food supply in the woods gives out, he runs to a rocky shore and, clinging to a rock, lets down his hairy legs little by little into the water; then as soon as some crabs have caught hold amid the shaggy hairs, he jumps back on to the land, shakes out his booty from the sea, and enjoys, clever fellow, the dainties he has collected from all sides.

So, you see, hunger sharpens the wits even of the dull-witted. (Perotti's Appendix 22)

One finds fables, too, in the Hebrew Bible. Classicist B. E. Perry speaks of the fable as a "Graeco-Semitic" category common to Western Asia and Greece, derived from the same Semitic origins, and characterized by the same narrative structure and metaphorical function prescribed by Theon. Perry cites as an example of the Hebrew "fable" Nathan's prophetic parable of the Ewe Lamb (2 Sam 12:1-6), but many others could be cited as well.[17] The story, intended as a rebuke of David for arranging Uriah's murder and taking his wife, Bathsheba, has obvious allegorical relevance to the king's situation:

But the thing that David had done displeased the Lord, and the Lord sent Nathan to David. He came to him, and said to him, "There were two men in a certain city, the one rich and the other poor. The rich man had very many flocks and herds; but the poor man had nothing but one little ewe lamb, which he had bought. He brought it up, and it grew up with him and with his children; it used to eat of his meager fare, and drink from his cup, and lie in his bosom, and it was like a daughter to him. Now there came a traveler to the rich man, and he was loath to take one of his own flock or herd to prepare for the wayfarer who had come to him, but he took the poor man's lamb, and prepared that for the guest who had come to him." Then David's anger was greatly kindled against the man. He said to Nathan, "As the Lord lives, the man who has done this deserves to die; he shall restore the lamb fourfold, because he did this thing, and because he had no pity." (2 Sam 12:1-6)

Also belonging to the Semitic side of Perry's "Graeco-Semitic" genre are rabbinic parables such as that in *Deuteronomy Rabbah* 2:24:[18]

Another explanation [of] "Thou wilt return to the Lord thy God" (Deuteronomy 4:30). It is like the son of a king who took to evil ways. The king sent a tutor to

> him who appealed to him saying: "Repent my son." But the son sent him back to his father [with a message], "How can I have the effrontery to return? I am ashamed to come before you." Thereupon his father sent back word: "My son, is a son ever ashamed to return to his father? And is it not to your father that you will be returning?" Even so the Holy One, blessed be He, sent Jeremiah to Israel when they sinned, and said to him, "Go, say to my children: 'Return.'"

One may observe from the fables above and other extant occurrences a general conformity to Theon's three-part definition of the genre.

(1) *All are fictional paradigms.* That is, they make their point by way of analogy through invented, and not historical, accounts. One does find a few fables in the *Phaedrus* that feature historical figures as their main subjects—for example, "Caesar to a Flunkey" (*Phaedrus* 2.5), "Aesop and the Farmer" (*Phaedrus,* 3.3), and "Socrates to His Friends" (*Phaedrus* 3.9)—but even these are highly exceptional and, in any case, likely fictions.

(2) *Despite their diversity, all are* logoi*—that is, "stories" or brief, story-like "sayings."* To be certain, the category is broader than our English word "fable" may suggest. As Perry observes, the sources attest "a very wide range of stories and brief statements which differ from each other multifariously";[19] e.g., "a fairy tale (*Märchen*), an aetiological nature-myth, an animal story exhibiting the cleverness or the stupidity of this or that animal, or a series of amusing actions, a novella, like the story of the widow in Phaedrus (App. 15), a myth about the gods, a debate between two rivals (*Streitgedicht*), or an exposition of the circumstances in which a sententious or a witty remark was made."[20] The category also includes brief, proverb-like utterances that abbreviate the action: "Someone told a story to an ass and he wiggled his ears" (Zenobius 5.42); "The fool learned after the event" (*Iliad* 17.32); "The prudent man was slow-moving, but he overtook the swift-footed man in the pursuit, Kyrnos, by the righteous decree of the immortal gods" (Theognis 329–330).[21] Perry limits the genre to past-tense narrations, which he regards as an essential feature of "story" (his translation of *logos*), but even this constriction fails to hold. One encounters, for example, present-tense narrations of action such as "Coddled to Death" (*Babrius* 35) and "When the Bear Gets Hungry" (Perrotti's Appendix 22) that are better described as "similitudes" or "analogies" than "stories."

(3) *All "give an image of truth," and often in the form of an explicitly stated moral.* Here again, the diversity of metaphorical truths imaged in fable is greater than the English word "moral" may suggest. As Perry observes, the truth in view is "not always a moral or ethical principle, as is often supposed"—that, in fact, a "majority [of fables] . . . do not teach moral truths, strictly speaking, but rather matters of worldly wisdom and shrewdness."[22] Perry further notes that the moral is frequently "personal in its application" (see, e.g., *Phaedrus* 4.18 and 2 Sam 12:1-6 above), especially when "the primary aim . . . is not instructive but satirical or in the nature of personal denunciation," or when the fable "consist[s] mainly in a jest or a clever

bit of repartee."[23] Mary Ann Beavis has noted that the moral may be religious in nature, as in *Babrius* 20: "Pray to the gods only when you are doing something to help yourself. Otherwise your prayers will be useless."[24] One may observe, too, that when the moral is addressed to specific persons, or is embedded in narrative contexts, it frequently displays multiple allegorical points of contact with the situation in view, as in several of the examples cited above (see, e.g., Aeschylus, *Agamemnon* 716–749; Xenophon, *Memorabilia* 2.7.13–14; *Phaedrus*, 4.18; and 2 Sam 12:1-6). Furthermore, while the fables of the first-century collections sometimes appear to be secondary and poorly matched with the story in view, the embedded examples typically feature morals that fit the context well and are no less original than the stories and settings to which they are attached.

From these and other examples one notes, too, a range of formal features and literary practices associated with the fable genre in the progymnasmata:

(1) *All classes of fable by subject are represented.* One finds the three major categories mentioned by the theorists: (a) the "ethical" fable featuring animals (e.g., story of the Dog, Xenophon, *Memorabilia* 2.7.13–14; story of the Lion and the Hares, Plato, *Pol.* 3.8.2; and the parable of the Eagles and the Vine, Ezek 17:2-10); (b) the "rational" fable featuring humans ("The Middle Aged Man with Two Mistresses," *Babrius*, 22; "Brother and Sister," *Phaedrus* 3.8; parable of the Two Brothers, 2 Sam 14:4-7); and (c) the "mixed" type mentioned by Aphthonius ("The Shepherd and the She-Goat," Perotti's Appendix 24; fable of the Lion's Cub, Aeschylus, *Agamemnon* 716–749; and parable of the Ewe Lamb, 2 Sam 12:1-6). There are also examples, as Nicolaus says, of fables featuring gods ("Hermes on Sale," *Babrius*, 30; "Aphrodite and the Slave Girl," *Babrius*, 10). One also observes fables that defy the progymnastic categories: for example, fables devoted to plants and trees ("The Fir Tree and the Bramble," *Babrius* 64; and parable of the Tree, Judg 9:8-15) and to inanimate objects ("The Boasting Lamp," *Babrius*, 114; parable of the Seething Pot, Ezek 24:2-5).

(2) *Both the "realistic" and "unrealistic" classes of fable are represented.* There are fantastic kinds of fables where animals talk and act like humans ("The Goat and the Goatherd," *Babrius* 3), where the wind and sun engage in contests ("The North Wind and the Sun," *Babrius* 18), and where trees and plants arrange marriages (fable of the Thistle and Cedar, 2 Kgs 14:8-10). There are also realistic stories from ordinary life that altogether lack the element of fantasy—what Aristotle calls "parable" but what the progymnasmata consider realistic "fable" ("The Butchers and the Ape," *Babrius* 44; "On the Fortunes of Men," *Phaedrus*, 4.18; and parable of the Ewe Lamb, 2 Sam 12:1-6).[25]

(3) *The kind of "moralizing" described in the progymnasmata is apparent.* Some fables leave the moral unstated (*Babrius* 1, 2, 3), while others state it explicitly (*Babrius* 4, 5), just as Theon observes. Among the latter type, some state the moral at the beginning in the form of a *promythion* (*Phaedrus* 1.8, 9), and others at the end

in the form of an *epimythion*, whether in the voice of the narrator (*Phaedrus* 1.1) or as a line of final dialogue by a character in the story (*Phaedrus* 1.2). The progymnastic practice of attaching multiple morals to a single fable is also occasionally witnessed (*Phaedrus* 4.11).[26] One finds, too, all three genres of *epimythia* attested by Nicolaus: (a) the paradigmatic, which frames the fable as an example—"This parable was composed to fit those persons who invent false charges by which to oppress the innocent" (*Phaedrus* 1.1); (b) the enthymematic, which arrives at its application indirectly through a deductive argument or "enthymeme"—"If the Twelve Tables enacted that a thief by night might be slain with impunity in any circumstances, and a thief by day if he defended himself with a weapon, who is there who can hold that punishment should follow *any* act of slaying, whatever its circumstances, seeing, as he does, that at times the laws themselves hold out to us a sword for the slaying of a fellow-creature?" (Cicero, *Pro Milone* 9 [Watts, LCL]);[27] and (c) the prosphonetic, which addresses a person directly with the fable's counsel: "Likewise you, citizens of Athens," said Aesop, "must bear the evil that you have, lest a greater one befall you" (*Phaedrus* 1.2).

(4) *In style, all the prose examples are simple and conversational.* In keeping with progymnastic instruction, extant prose fables altogether lack the balanced structure of periodic prose. They are, as Theon prescribes, artless, natural, and clear. The poetic examples, too, though displaying the purposeful artistry of meter, nonetheless have the character of simple, clear, and otherwise natural storytelling.

(5) *The kind of inflection practiced in the progymnasmata is evident in some examples.* Several fables, mostly those embedded in classical literature, employ the accusative subject + infinitive construction commended by Theon (e.g., Cyrus' fable of the Flute-Player, Herodotus 1.141, which employs the construction throughout). There are also fables where the intentional use of different oblique cases and grammatical numbers is evident. For example, "The Heterogeneous Dogs" (*Babrius*, 85) opens with three clauses, each beginning with the word "dog" in Greek—and each changing from one oblique case and number to another. A literal translation conveys the progression:

> With dogs [*dative plural*] a state of war and with wolves arose
>
> A dog [*nominative singular*] of Achaea was chosen,
>
> Of dogs [*genitive plural*], for the state, a general to be.

While such case variation was considered characteristic of good style, it also served, as we have said, as a practical means of laying emphasis on the main subject—in this case, on the dogs as the main characters of the story. The same effect is seen in "Disarmed by Love" (*Babrius* 98), where variation of case lays emphasis on the "lion" as the main subject of the fable. The first two occurrences of the word, both at the beginning of the fable, are in the nominative singular and dative singular, respectively. The remaining two occurrences, both in the final line of the story, are in the genitive plural and accusative plural, respectively. Thus, in just four occurrences, the writer cycles through the four major cases and both common numbers.

(6) *The progymnastic skill of weaving fable into narrative is evident in most of the embedded examples.* This is true for most (if not all) classical Greek and Hebrew examples, as well as the occasional collected fable (e.g., *Phaedrus* 4.18 above). In all these cases, the fable is put forward as a fictional reflection of characters or events from the attached narrative, imaging it usually through multiple allegorical points of contact. Thus, in the parable of the Ewe Lamb cited above, the wealthy man who steals the beloved ewe from the poor man is intended to image David, who has stolen Bathsheba from Uriah. Or consider, for example, Cyrus' fable of the Flute-player:

> As soon as the Lydians had been subdued by the Persians, the Ionians and Aeolians sent messengers to Cyrus, offering to be his subjects on the same terms as those which they had under Croesus. Having heard what they proposed, Cyrus told them a story (*logos*). Once, he said, there was a flute-player who saw fishes in the sea and played upon his flute, thinking that so they would come out on to the land. Being disappointed of his hope, he took a net and gathered in and drew out a great multitude of the fishes; and seeing them leaping, "You had best," said he, "cease from your dancing now; you would not come out and dance then, when I played to you." The reason why Cyrus told the story to the Ionians, who were ready to obey him when the victory was won, had before refused when he sent a message asking them to revolt from Croesus. So he answered them in his anger. (Herodotus 1.141 [Godley, LCL]; cf. *Aes.* 11a)

In this fable, the flute-player's rebuke of the fish for dancing only when caught is intended to image Cyrus' own rebuke of the Ionians for responding belatedly to the terms he had earlier offered. From these and similar examples, it is clear that the meaning of the fable is dependent upon the narrative context it is intended to reflect.

(7) *Paraphrase and expansion/contraction are evident among different versions of the same fable.* One sees these practices underlying, for example, two different versions of the same fable: "The Goat and the Goatherd" (*Babrius* 3) and "The Shepherd and the She-Goat" (Perotti's Appendix 24). In these fables, which have no direct literary relationship, there are almost no verbal correspondences. There is, however, despite the variances in wording and length, a common *phantasia* or "imagination." Both tell the story of the herd's breaking of the animal's horn, his entreaty of the animal not to tell the master, and the animal's response that the broken horn would shout out the truth. Thus, the kind of transmission processes that shaped these fables, one in which wording is intentionally changed but meaning is preserved, very much corresponds to that described by Theon in his discussion of paraphrase.

Examples from the New Testament

In the New Testament, we find the fable genre represented as a form commonly used in Jesus' preaching, and with a designation associated with various classes of fable—the *parabolē*, or "parable."[28] The following examples illustrate the form, which is limited to the Gospels.[29]

THE PARABLE OF THE SEED

He began to teach them many things in parables, and in his teaching he said to them: "Listen! A sower went out to sow. And as he sowed, some seed fell on the path, and the birds came and ate it up. Other seed fell on rocky ground, where it did not have much soil, and it sprang up quickly, since it had no depth of soil. And when the sun rose, it was scorched; and since it had no root, it withered away. Other seed fell among thorns, and the thorns grew up and choked it, and it yielded no grain. Other seed fell into good soil and brought forth grain, growing up and increasing and yielding thirty and sixty and a hundredfold." And he said, "Let anyone with ears to hear listen!"

When he was alone, those who were around him along with the twelve asked him about the parables. And he said to them, "To you has been given the secret of the kingdom of God, but for those outside, everything comes in parables; in order that 'they may indeed look, but not perceive, and may indeed listen, but not understand; so that they may not turn again and be forgiven.'" And he said to them, "Do you not understand this parable? Then how will you understand all the parables? The sower sows the word. These are the ones on the path where the word is sown: when they hear, Satan immediately comes and takes away the word that is sown in them. And these are the ones sown on rocky ground: when they hear the word, they immediately receive it with joy. But they have no root, and endure only for a while; then, when trouble or persecution arises on account of the word, immediately they fall away. And others are those sown among the thorns: these are the ones who hear the word, but the cares of the world, and the lure of wealth, and the desire for other things come in and choke the word, and it yields nothing. And these are the ones sown on the good soil: they hear the word and accept it and bear fruit, thirty and sixty and a hundredfold." (Mark 4:2-20)

THE PARABLE OF THE WICKED TENANTS

"Listen to another parable. There was a landowner who planted a vineyard, put a fence around it, dug a wine press in it, and built a watchtower. Then he leased it to tenants and went to another country. When the harvest time had come, he sent his slaves to the tenants to collect his produce. But the tenants seized his slaves and beat one, killed another, and stoned another. Again he sent other slaves, more than the first; and they treated them in the same way. Finally he sent his son to them, saying, 'They will respect my son.' But when the tenants saw the son, they said to themselves, 'This is the heir; come, let us kill him and get his inheritance.' So they seized him, threw him out of the vineyard, and killed him. Now when the owner of the vineyard comes, what will he do to those tenants?"

They said to him, "He will put those wretches to a miserable death, and lease the vineyard to other tenants who will give him the produce at the harvest time."

Jesus said to them, "Have you never read in the scriptures: 'The stone that the builders rejected has become the cornerstone; this was the Lord's doing, and it is amazing in our eyes'? Therefore I tell you, the kingdom of God will be taken away from you and given to a people that produces the fruits of the kingdom. The one who falls on this stone will be broken to pieces; and it will crush anyone on whom it falls." When the chief priests and the Pharisees heard his parables, they realized that he was speaking about them. They wanted to arrest him, but they feared the crowds, because they regarded him as a prophet. (Matt 21:33-46)

THE PARABLE OF THE LOST SHEEP

Now all the tax collectors and sinners were coming near to listen to him. And the Pharisees and the scribes were grumbling and saying, "This fellow welcomes sinners and eats with them." So he told them this parable: "Which one of you, having a hundred sheep and losing one of them, does not leave the ninety-nine in the wilderness and go after the one that is lost until he finds it? When he has found it, he lays it on his shoulders and rejoices. And when he comes home, he calls together his friends and neighbors, saying to them, 'Rejoice with me, for I have found my sheep that was lost.' Just so, I tell you, there will be more joy in heaven over one sinner who repents than over ninety-nine righteous persons who need no repentance." (Luke 15:1-7)

THE PARABLE OF THE GOOD SAMARITAN

Just then a lawyer stood up to test Jesus. "Teacher," he said, "what must I do to inherit eternal life?"

He said to him, "What is written in the law? What do you read there?"

He answered, "You shall love the Lord your God with all your heart, and with all your soul, and with all your strength, and with all your mind; and your neighbor as yourself."

And he said to him, "You have given the right answer; do this, and you will live."

But wanting to justify himself, he asked Jesus, "And who is my neighbor?"

Jesus replied, "A man was going down from Jerusalem to Jericho, and fell into the hands of robbers, who stripped him, beat him, and went away, leaving him half dead. Now by chance a priest was going down that road; and when he saw him, he passed by on the other side. So likewise a Levite, when he came to the place and saw him, passed by on the other side. But a Samaritan while traveling came near him; and when he saw him, he was moved with pity. He went to him and bandaged his wounds, having poured oil and wine on them. Then he put him on his own animal, brought him to an inn, and took care of him. The next day he took out two denarii, gave them to the innkeeper, and said, 'Take care of him; and when I come back, I will repay you whatever more you spend.'

Which of these three, do you think, was a neighbor to the man who fell into the hands of the robbers?"

He said, "The one who showed him mercy."

Jesus said to him, "Go and do likewise." (Luke 10:25-37)

That parables such as these are, in fact, *mythoi* is far from a settled matter. The identification, first suggested by Adolf Jülicher in the first modern study of parables,[30] and affirmed in recent years by others,[31] has never gained wide assent.[32] The reasons alleged, however, have typically reflected an understanding of the genre that is too narrow and that could be easily broadened by a quick reading of Perry's introduction, to say nothing of the extant examples themselves in their great variety.

In any case, from these and similar examples, it is clear that the parables of Jesus (like fables from antiquity generally) display a remarkable conformity to Theon's tripartite definition of the *mythos* genre. First, they are fictional and not historical paradigms. That is, they draw their analogy not from past occurrences but through "invented" action. Second, they are *logoi*. Most are "stories" in the modern sense of the past tense narrations with plot. Others are story-like "analogies" still within the range of *logos'* meaning, including present tense narrations of action (e.g., the parable of the Lost Coin above) and proverb-like sayings that abbreviate the action and thereby test the bounds of the genre (e.g., "Physician, heal yourself!" [Luke 4:23]; cf. the Aesopic fable of the same name, *Babrius* 120). Third, they without exception "give an image of truth"—and usually in the form of an explicitly stated moral. The diversity of truths imaged in Jesus' parables, moreover, falls within the broad range of imaging on display in ancient examples (and is particularly in line in its religious content with the prophetic fables of the Hebrew Bible).[33] One finds everything from ethical instruction (the Good Samaritan, Luke 10:25-37) and reflection on shrewdness (the Dishonest Manager, Luke 16:1-13) to religious teaching (the Persistent Widow, Luke 18:1-8) and personal denunciation (the Pharisee and the Tax Collector, Luke 18:9-14), just as in other fables from antiquity.

One sees in these parables, too, the same literary features and practices we identified earlier in examples of fable from the ancient world.

(1) *They feature the same kinds of subjects and thus fall into the same theoretical classifications.*[34] The vast majority are what the theorists call "rational" fables in that they feature humans as the main subjects—for example, the parable of the Good Samaritan (Luke 10:30-37) and the parable of the Wicked Tenants (Mark 12:1-11; Matt 21:33-46; Luke 20:9-18). Though not often counted as a parable, the saying on the Ravens (Luke 12:24) is a rare example in Jesus' preaching of the "ethical" class of fable devoted to animals. There are also occasional examples of the "mixed" class—for example, the parable of the Lost Sheep (Matt 18:12-4; Luke

15:3-7). Jesus also tells parables devoted to plants (the parable of the Mustard Seed, Mark 4:30-32; Matt 13:31-32; Luke 13:18-19), trees (the parable of the Fig Tree, Mark 13:28-32; Matt 24:32-36; Luke 21:29-33), inanimate objects (the parable of the Leaven, Matt 13:33; Luke 13:20-21), and divinities (the parable of the Rich Man and Lazarus, Luke 16:19-31).

(2) *They may be classed, as well, by their realism.*[35] Interestingly, Jesus only tells what Theon calls the fable "capable of being true." He is never depicted engaging in the unrealistic class of fiction wherein animals talk and seasons are anthropomorphic. Perhaps this is one of the underlying reasons Jesus' "fables" are consistently referred to in Greek with the term *parabolē*, and not *logos*. As we have seen, though Theon correctly understood the Aesopic corpus to encompass both realistic and unrealistic fictional paradigms, some like Aristotle incorrectly defined it as strictly unrealistic and thus designated another term, *parabolē*, for all realistic fictional analogy. Though problematic, Aristotle's use of *parabolē* nevertheless thus corresponds perfectly to its use in the New Testament.[36]

(3) *They display the same formal range of "moralizing" described in the progymnasmata and evident in extant fable composition.* One finds parables where the moral is both stated (Matt 25:14-30) and unstated (Mark 4:30-32). Some morals take the form of a *promythion* (Luke 18:9), others an *epimythion* (Matt 25:13). With the latter type, some are stated in the voice of the narrator or fable teller (Matt 20:6), and others as a final line of dialogue by a character in the story or analogy (Luke 15:32). One finds, too, all three types of morals described by Nicolaus: (a) the paradigmatic, which frames the fable explicitly as an example ("Then Jesus told them a parable about their need to pray always and not to lose heart," Luke 18:1); (b) the *enthymematic*, which arrives at its application indirectly through an enthymeme or deductive argument ("Whoever is faithful in a very little is faithful also in much; and whoever is dishonest in a very little is dishonest also in much," Luke 16:10);[37] and (c) the *prosphonetic*, which addresses a person directly with the fable's counsel ("Truly I say to you, the tax collectors and the harlots go into the kingdom of God before you," Matt 21:28). One finds, as well, individual parables with multiple morals—for example, the parable of the Persistent Widow (Luke 18:1-8): (a) "Then Jesus told them a parable about their need to pray always and not to lose heart" (Luke 18:1); (b) "And yet, when the Son of Man comes, will he find faith on earth?" (Luke 18:8).[38] One also finds multiple parables organized, as progymnastic theory prescribes, around the same general moral or didactic theme—for example, the parables of the Lost Coin, the Lost Sheep, and the Lost/Prodigal Son in Luke 15, or the three parables of the Seed in Mark 4.

(4) *They display the same simple, conversational style seen in extant prose fables.* Though Jesus is often portrayed preaching and praying in more elevated periodic prose (see, e.g., the Sermon on the Mount and, specifically, the Lord's Prayer in

Matt 5–7),[39] his parables altogether lack periodic form. Rather, they are artless, natural, and clear in style, just as the theorists prescribe.

(5) *They occasionally display the same kind of inflection prescribed in the progymnasmata and occasionally witnessed in extant fables.* One finds, for example, the emphasis prescribed by Theon on the accusative case in the first parable of the Seed in Mark 4:2-20. Thus, "the word," the central concern of the parable, occurs eight times—once in the nominative case, and the remaining seven in the accusative. (The repetition is so heavy-handed that Matthew and Luke both reduce the number of occurrences in their versions.) One also finds the kind of variation of case and number prescribed by the theorists. In the same parable, pronominal references to the seed (which images "the word") vary between the nominative and the accusative cases, and between the singular and the plural. (Both Matthew and Luke "repair" the variation in number: Matthew by making them all plural, and Luke by making them all singular).

Similarly, in the parable of the Ravens of Luke 12:24, pronominal references to the "ravens" progress with each line through all the common oblique cases.

> Consider the ravens:
>
> they [*implied nominative subject*] neither sow nor reap,
>
> they [*dative object*] have neither storehouse nor barn,
>
> and yet God feeds them [*accusative object*].
>
> Of how much more value are you than the birds [*genitive object*]!

Perhaps the most remarkable display of inflection, however, is seen in the parable of the Lost/Prodigal Son, where the word "Father" occurs twelve times and in all five cases: nominative (15:20, 22, 27, 28), genitive (15:17), dative (15:12, 29), accusative (15:18, 20), and also the rare (for Luke) vocative (15:12, 18, 21).[40]

(6) *They are frequently woven into narrative in the manner prescribed in the progymnasmata and evident in most classical Greek and Hebrew fables.*[41] The parables of Jesus are often embedded in narrative contexts, and when this occurs, the parable fictionally images the reality of the narrative context, reflecting it through multiple allegorical points of contact. Thus, in the parable of the Two Sons, the belatedly faithful son is framed by the narrative introduction as an image of the prostitutes and tax collectors, and the belatedly disobedient son, of the chief priests and elders. Similarly, in the parable of the Lost/Prodigal Son (which shares the narrative introduction of Luke 15:1-2 with the parables of the Lost Sheep and Lost Coin), the prodigal son is made to image the sinners and tax collectors with whom Jesus eats; and the older brother, the Pharisees and scribes who begrudge Jesus for eating with such people. This allegorizing dynamic, evident in a majority of Jesus' parables, is precisely the allegorizing dynamic that attends "weaving" as

Theon teaches it (the fable of the Camel). Further, it is the dynamic seen in virtually all embedded examples from antiquity (the parable of the Ewe Lamb and the fable of the Flute-Player).

(7) *They undergo the same kind of paraphrase and expansion/contraction evident in the theory and practice of fable transmission.* One only has to compare the parables that appear in the multiple gospels (e.g., the parable of the Sower/Seed) to see these specific practices at work. Though space prohibits a fuller investigation, one can also see the principles of confirmation and refutation guiding these practices. Redundancies are frequently eliminated, ambiguous matters are often clarified, and inconsistencies resolved. Such changes reflect the fable-specific editorial practices learned in schools all around the Mediterranean.

From this collective evidence, then, it is clear that the parables of Jesus belong to the fable genre. Such a conclusion does not contradict the claims of those who associate the parable with various ancient Hebrew or rabbinic parables but incorporates those claims into a more holistic perspective: New Testament parables, Hebrew parables, and rabbinic parables *all* belong to the Semitic side of what classicist B. E. Perry, independent of biblical scholarship, deemed a *Graeco-Semitic* genre, the ancient Mediterranean fable.

On the other hand, such a conclusion does challenge an alternative perspective in New Testament scholarship that hypothesizes concerning an original "form" of Jesus' parables that is very different from the final form represented in the New Testament. According to this view—and we may only speak in generalities in an introductory survey such as this—the true (historical) form of Jesus' parables is one without introductory or concluding morals, without narrative contexts, free of all allegorical points of contact with social situations, free of religious content, free of personal or prophetic denunciation, and/or expressing a secular, existential, and world-shattering truth so profound as to defy expression.[42] That is, it is a form free of all that is at home in the Graeco-Semitic fable—and one, ultimately, with a purpose far different from the fable with its practical aim of "useful instruction" (to cite Theon's description). Such a thesis requires first that Jesus preached a form of a parable for which there was no genre parallel in the ancient Mediterranean world generally or Jewish religious culture specifically—a scenario that not only removes Jesus from history but also that genre theory calls into question given its tenant that all communication is necessarily genre bound and cannot occur without reference to established genres.[43] This perspective requires, moreover, that the early church and the evangelists in transmitting Jesus' parables greatly distorted the original form through the slow haphazard accretion of morals, contexts, allegory, groupings, religious content, prophetic denunciation, and the like, and yet somehow made them collectively something more coherent and recognizable than they were before, a Jewish fable. Ockham's razor commends the simpler and more obvious conclusion: that Jesus—like other Jewish prophets and rabbis before and after him—preached in the form of the Graeco-Semitic fable and that the evangelists, after a half century or so of ecclesial transmission, represent his preaching more or less in its original form.

This is not to say that every specific moral, grouping, narrative context, allegory, religious claim, or prophetic utterance that the evangelists record is "original." To the contrary, if we view the parables from their imagined original form(s) through to their final form(s) and at every point in between as fables, we expect that the kinds of editorial practices taught in connection with fables in the ancient world apply, so that morals, narrative contexts, and the stories themselves very likely underwent all manner of literary manipulation, and with varying literary skill and faithfulness to the original(s). But it is to say that the evangelists do represent the *general* form of Jesus' parables accurately—that Jesus did in fact tell parable-fables with the *kinds* of morals, groupings, narrative contexts, allegory, religious content, and personal denunciation remembered by the evangelists.

This conclusion, in turn, has serious implications for the more than century-old scholarly goal of "reconstructing" the original form of Jesus' parables and interpreting accordingly. If morals, groupings, narrative contexts, allegory, religious content, prophetic denunciation, and the like are not distortions of the true form of Jesus' parable preaching but rather characteristic of it, then the restoration of the original form is not so straightforward as simply removing them, as scholars through the centuries have proposed. The excision even of a suspiciously secondary moral, for example, does not necessarily get us any closer to "the original" and may in fact take us one editorial step further from it, as it is entirely possible the parable may have had a different moral, multiple morals, different morals on different occasions, or the like, rather than no moral at all. Certainly, a number of scholarly "rules" concerning the original form of parables—for example, that contexts are "always" assumed to be "secondary" inventions,[44] or that "interpretive conclusions are always secondary"[45]—if applied to other fables from antiquity would result, ironically, in their effacement rather than their "restoration."

Similar implications attend the closely related scholarly agenda of reconstructing the "original words" of individual parables and on that basis finding "original" meanings obscured in the canonical forms. Because this work begins with the tailoring of individual parables to a hypothesized original generic form free of standard fable elements, it is already problematic for the reasons just mentioned. Additionally, though, what we know of the editorial processes that shaped fables calls into question the viability of such reconstructive aims. First, because fables were conceived as adaptable to a variety of morals and a variety of social situations, the very concept of a single "original" text is quite possibly a mirage. Jesus himself very well may have preached the same parable-fables in a variety of settings in the course of his ministry, and in support of a variety of morals or applications, or sometimes (though not necessarily) with no stated moral at all. That the evangelists remember him doing so certainly should not be dismissed with prejudice; the memory is in keeping with what we know of the genre. Furthermore, virtually every conceivable editorial practice commended for fables had an opposite practice that was likewise commended, so that alleged "editorial tendencies" identified by scholars and ascribed to the transmission process (e.g., expansion and elaboration) can only be viewed with suspicion and cannot be used as a reliable guide in the selection of more "original" wording from among multiple versions.[46] Editors were also encouraged in the "refutation" of fables to identify and remove redundancies, contradictions, and other similar flaws—thus these cannot be simplistically treated as marks of secondary, editorial distortion and removed in the pursuit of "simple" originality, as they often are in biblical scholarship;[47] indeed, they are as likely marks of originality, and their absence, as likely marks of the kind of editorial correction taught and practiced in the schools. Last and perhaps most important, because progymnastic theory prescribed the intentional *abandonment* of original wording of a fable, and often wholesale, through paraphrase, inflection, expansion, contraction, and editorial refutation, the "authentic words of Jesus," even in the unlikely event they are present, simply cannot be identified or reconstructed with any confidence, much less made a central source of meaning in parable interpretation. All arguments pointing to "original" wording are as likely, given this state of affairs, to take us back to a distant paraphrase multiple versions removed from the original(s)—or worse, to a modern effacement that never before existed in history—as to Jesus' words themselves. On the other hand, because progymnastic theory prescribed the intentional *preservation* of the fable's *phantasia* in all forms of paraphrase, and because this is the only thing we find preserved with certainty in multiple versions of extant fables much further removed from one another both literarily and temporally than those in the Gospels (e.g., "The Goat and the Goatherd," *Babrius* 3; and "The Shepherd and the She-Goat," Perotti's Appendix 24), it is the only element we can with any reasonable hope expect to have been preserved in Jesus' parables. In short, if there is anything "authentic" preserved in the parables of Jesus, it is the essential imagination or idea of the original(s).

All of this is to suggest that biblical scholarship is in need of a new paradigm of interpretation, one that attends to the parables in their final form as fables, with all the ancient cultural expectations associated with the genre, and that ultimately finds meaning in their *phantasia*.[48] Such an approach does not abandon concern for the historical Jesus but rather operates with awareness concerning what ancient writers and editors did and did not seek to preserve in the transmission of the genre.

We may illustrate the method we are proposing with reference to the parable of the Lost Sheep, which occurs in two canonical forms (Matt 18:10-14; Luke 15:4-7).[49] An older paradigm of parable research begins its inquiry with the removal of the narrative contexts that introduce these versions.[50] In Matthew, the narrative context portrays Jesus telling the parable with a child still in his arms—a provocative image given that children (unlike in modern society) were regarded as nonpersons of the most marginal status.[51] The chapter begins with Jesus' summons to welcome children as models of kingdom "least-ness" and emissaries of his own presence:

> At that time the disciples came to Jesus and asked, "Who is the greatest in the kingdom of heaven?" He called a child, whom he put among them, and said, "Truly I tell you, unless you change and become like children, you will never enter the kingdom of heaven. Whoever becomes humble like this child is the greatest in the kingdom of heaven. Whoever welcomes one such child in my name welcomes me." (Matt 18:1-5)

Then with the child still in his arms, Jesus begins the parable a few sentences later with reference to children:

> Take care that you do not despise one of these little ones; for, I tell you, in heaven their angels continually see the face of my Father in heaven. What do you think? If a shepherd has a hundred sheep, and one of them has gone astray, does he not leave the ninety-nine on the mountains and go in search of the one that went astray? And if he finds it, truly I tell you, he rejoices over it more than over the ninety-nine that never went astray. So it is not the will of your Father in heaven that one of these little ones should be lost. (18:10-14)

In Luke, the narrative context depicts Jesus telling the parable while welcoming sinners and tax collectors—again, persons of marginal status in Jewish society—and while being criticized for it by religious authorities. The opening sentences tie the controversy causally to the telling of the parable story:

> *Now all the tax collectors and sinners were coming near to listen to him. And the Pharisees and the scribes were grumbling and saying, "This fellow welcomes sinners and eats with them." So he told them this parable:* "Which one of you, having a hundred sheep and losing one of them, does not leave the ninety-nine in the wilderness and go after the one that is lost until he finds it? When he has found it, he lays it on his shoulders and rejoices. And when he comes home, he calls together his friends and neighbors, saying to them, 'Rejoice with me, for I have found my sheep that was lost.' Just so, I tell you, there will be more joy in heaven over one sinner who repents than over ninety-nine righteous persons who need no repentance." (Luke 15:1-7)

Having excised these introductory contexts, scholarship of the kind we are describing then removes all allegorical points of contact between the parable story and these contexts, any religious content related to the social situations introduced in those contexts, all personal and prophetic denunciation related to those situations, and all morals drawn from the story (whether they have reference to those situations, as morals like contexts are judged secondary as a rule).

Thus in the Matthean account, the lost and valued sheep is no longer read as an image of the marginal, disenfranchised child who is valued and reclaimed by the divine love born by Jesus or his followers. Religious themes such as the identification of the shepherd's will with the Father's are discarded. The prophetic privileging of the "least of these"—in this case, imaged by the greater joy over the lost sheep than the ninety-nine—is set aside as distortion. And the *epimythion*, which summarizes the meaning of the story as told on this occasion for the child still in Jesus' arms and others like him, is summarily excised not only because of its connections to the narrative context but also as a (supposed) formal distortion of the genre itself.

Similarly in the Lukan account, with the narrative context removed, the lost sheep is no longer read as an allegory for the marginal, disenfranchised sinner or tax collector, nor the ninety-nine for the religious community from which the sheep has been separated with prejudice. Religious themes—God's love for sinners, God's desire for their repentance, God's joy over their reclamation by the community of faith—are regarded as distractions from the true, singular, original meaning. Prophetic critique is named as distortion and ignored: here, the rejection of the religious authorities' inhospitality as at odds with the will of heaven, and the simultaneous affirmation of God's greater joy for the reclaimed sinner than "righteous persons who need no repentance"—an allusion aimed (with no small measure of cheekiness) at the judgmental authorities. The *epithymion*, too, which summarizes the story's meaning for the "sinners" at the center of the controversy, is eliminated as a resource for interpretation. So also are the two subsequent "lost" parables—those of the Lost Coin and the Lost Son—that, together with this parable, make up a three-parable collection addressing the controversy over Jesus' hospitality to religious outcasts. These remaining parables, which address the same themes in the same way, and with *epithymioi* that restate the general thesis, are also excised as distortions of the true form and meaning of the "original" parable.

Left with nothing but a decontextualized and somewhat altered core story which it regards as a close approximation of the singular "original" underlying both versions, scholarship of the kind we are describing then speculates as to the story's singular, original meaning. Though the theories are as varied as the scholars proposing them, they generally lack Jewish religious notes and prophetic themes and tend toward the philosophical: for example, that the parable (and others like it) images the self's existential "experience of God's advent."[52]

By way of comparison, the kind of reading suggested by the present analysis—one that recognizes these parables as fables—shares with scholarship of the kind we just described a healthy skepticism about the Matthean and Lukan versions representing in their final form "the authentic words of Jesus." Indeed, as we have said, what we know of the editorial theory and practice surrounding the transmission of fables would invite an even more robust skepticism in this regard. There is a strong likelihood that we only have distant paraphrases of paraphrases, and in any case, we have no basis for recognizing or objectively reconstructing Jesus' original words even if they by some chance are still buried within these versions, much less making them the crux of interpretation.

On the other hand, a reading of these parables as fables looks upon all that the reconstructive method discards in these two versions as, in fact, of great historical and interpretive value—not because of any likely historicity of each individual item, but rather because of their collective and unified testimony to the only aspect of the story that fable transmission sought to preserve, and thus the only aspect with any reasonable claim to originality or centrality in interpretation: the *phantasia*. Both versions, if allowed to speak as they have been transmitted, attest a common, essential "idea" or "imagination," inviting hearers to experience the shepherd's joy over a lost sheep, and as an analogy (or a "fictitious paradigm," to use the language of rhetorical theory) for the sheer joy that attends welcoming the valued and heretofore marginalized outcast. Indeed, the story invites hearers to experience *greater* joy over the lone outcast reclaimed—whether child, sinner, or traitor—than over the collective enfranchised majority, and thus is a reflection in microcosm of the larger prophetic theme of Jesus' preaching (as it is remembered, at least, by the evangelists) concerning the "last becoming first" and "the least of these" being afforded highest honor in the kingdom of God. Such prophetic use of the fable is in keeping, too, with the Jewish fable tradition and is particularly reminiscent of Nathan, who also employed a "mixed" fable concerning a sheep and its owner as a way of evoking sympathy for the disenfranchised—and when it would otherwise not likely have been forthcoming.

In sum, to read the parables of Jesus in this fashion—as *fables*—is to listen for the *ipsissima vox Jesu* (the very voice of Jesus) rather than the *ipsissima verba* (the very words) as the thing of value preserved in the Gospel accounts. In the case of the parable of the Lost Sheep (and many others like it), that voice is remembered for speaking prophetically on behalf of the marginal, and in settings where religious opponents and followers alike actively engaged in excluding rather than welcoming. Modern reconstructions that recast that voice with secular, existentialist shades are simply, by ancient standards, bad paraphrases.

Notes

1 For the following discussion see the fable exercises of Theon (*Prog.* 72–78), Ps.-Hermogenes (*Prog.* 1–4), Aphthonius (*Prog.* 21), and Nicolaus (*Prog.* 6–11); cf. also Quintilian, *Inst.* 1.9.1–3.

2 Ben Edward Perry, *Babrius and Phaedrus* (Cambridge, Mass.: Harvard University Press, 1965), xx. Theon's definition is repeated verbatim in Aphthonius, and nearly verbatim in Nicolaus. Ps.-Hermogenes, who never defines fable, nonetheless says it is both "fictitious" and "in all cases . . . useful for some aspect of life."

3 See Edward P. J. Corbett and Robert J. Connors, *Classical Rhetoric for the Modern Student*, 4th ed. (New York: Oxford University Press, 1998), 145–46.

4 Cf. Kennedy's various renderings of the word in the theorists' definitions: "a fictitious *story* giving an image of truth" (Theon, *Prog.* 72); "a fictive *statement*, imaging truth" (Aphthonius, *Prog.* 21); "false *speech* . . . imaging truth" (Nicolaus, *Prog.* 6).

5 The Latin terms *fabella* and *fabula* do primarily signify "story" but nonetheless can mean "anecdote" and "talk, conversation," respectively.

6 Perry, *Babrius and Phaedrus*, xx. Quintilian, though distinguishing the two, notes the similarity: "Close to this [fable] is the genre of *paroimia* ('proverb'), a sort of abbreviated fable understood allegorically: 'Not my load, he says: the ox takes the panniers'" (*Inst.* 5.11.20; cf. Cicero, *Att.* 5.15.3).

7 Oddly enough, though, *Apsines* limits the *parabolē* class to fictional paradigms featuring inanimate things or irrational animals and has no category at all for fictional paradigms featuring humans. Thus, Apsines' *parabolē* is virtually the opposite of Aristotles' *parabolē* and, together with it, covers the span of fictional paradigms—i.e., what the progymnasmata call "fable."

8 Aphthonius states, "Fable (*mythos*) originated with poets but has come to be used also by orators for the sake of the moral" (*Prog.* 21).

9 See the discussion of periodic prose in Aristotle, *Rhet.* 3.9.1–10.

10 See Mikeal C. Parsons, "Luke and the Progymnasmata: A Preliminary Investigation into the Preliminary Exercises," in *Contextualizing Acts: Lukan Narrative and Greco-Roman Discourse*, ed. Todd Penner and Caroline Vander Stichele, SBLSS 20 (Atlanta: Scholars Press, 2004), 43–63.

11 In *Socratis et Socraticorum reliquiae*, vol. 1, ed. Gabriele Giannantoni (Napoli: Bibliopolis, 1990); cf. Diogenes Laetius 2.105, as noted by Kennedy, *Progymnasmata*, 25n96.

12 Herodotus 1.71–91; so Kennedy, *Progymnasmata*, 25n97.

13 Perry, *Babrius and Phaedrus*, xii–xiii.

14 Cf. also Hesiod, *Works and Days*, 202–212; Aeschylus, *Myrmidons* frag. 139; Sophocles, *Ajax* 1142–1158; Aristophanes, *Wasps* 1400–1408; *Birds* 470–476.

15 Cf. also Plato, [Alc. *maj.*] 1.117–127; *Pol.* 3.8.2; *Phaed.* 60B–D; Aristotle, *Mete.* 2.3.10–18.

16 See the brief history outlined in Perry, *Babrius and Phaedrus*, i–xix.

17 See, e.g., the occurrences collected by Craig A. Evans, "Parables in Early Judaism," in *The Challenge of Jesus' Parables*, ed. Richard N. Longenecker (Grand Rapids: Eerdmans, 2000), 51–75: the parable of the Ewe Lamb (2 Sam 12:1-6); the parable of the Tree (Judg 9:8-15); the parable of the Two Brothers (2 Sam 14:4-7); the parable of the Escaped Prisoner (1 Kgs 20:38-43); the fable of the Thistle and Cedar (2 Kgs 14:8-10); Isaiah's song/parable of the Vineyard (Isa 5:1-7); the riddle/parable of the Eagles and the Vine (Ezek 17:2-10); the parable of the Lioness (Ezek 19:1-9); the parable of the Vine (Ezek 19:10-14); the parable of the Seething Pot (Ezek 24:2-5); the parable of the Fruitful Tree (4Q302a, also referred to as 4Qpap parable); and the parable of the Lame Man and the Blind Man (Epiphanius, *Panarion* 64.70.5–17, citing *Apocryphon of Ezekiel* [= frag. 1]). Evans distinguishes "parables" and "fables" by realism, a distinction that goes back, as we have said, to Aristotle. Measured by Theon's definition and the constituency of ancient fable collections, however, all of Evan's examples are fables.

18 For this, other examples, and related analysis, see Harvey K. McArthur and Robert M. Johnston, *They Also Taught in Parables* (Grand Rapids: Zondervan, 1990); David Stern, "The Rabbinic Parable: From Rhetoric to Poetics," in *The Society of Biblical Literature 1986 Seminar Papers*, SBLSPS 25 (Atlanta: Scholars Press, 1986), 631–43; idem, "Jesus' Parables from the Perspective of Rabbinic Literature: The Example of the Wicked Husbandman," in *Parable and Story in Judaism and Christianity*, ed. Clemens Thoma and Michael Wyschogrod (Mahwah, N.J.:

Paulist Press, 1989), 42–82; and idem, *Parables and Midrash* (Cambridge, Mass.: Harvard University Press, 1991).

19 Perry, *Babrius and Phaedrus*, xxii.

20 Perry, *Babrius and Phaedrus*, xxii–xxiii.

21 For theses examples and others, see Perry, *Babrius and Phaedrus*, xxxi.

22 Perry, *Babrius and Phaedrus*, xxi–xxii.

23 Perry, *Babrius and Phaedrus*, xxii.

24 Mary Ann Beavis, "Parable and Fable," *CBQ* 52 (1990): 473–98.

25 In the names that he assigns to the Jewish examples, Craig Evans ("Parables in Early Judaism," 51–75) distinguishes between the realistic and unrealistic stories respectively with the terms "parable" and "fable" respectively. Though we have kept Evans' names, we observe that that the progymnasmata rightly would regard all of these as "fables."

26 Noted by Beavis, "Parable and Fable," 473–98, esp. 482.

27 This moral takes the form of comparison from the greater to the lesser, a commonly prescribed enthymeme in the handbooks (see, e.g., Aristotle, *Rhet.* 2.23.4–6; Cicero, *Top.* 4.23; Theon, *Prog.* 108; Quintilian, *Inst.* 5.11.8–10).

28 As we have seen, Aristotle uses the term *parabolē* for what later theorists call the realistic class of fable, and Apsines, by contrast, for what other theorists would deem animal or ethical fables.

29 Unless otherwise indicated, translations are from the NRSV with modifications.

30 Adolf Jülicher, *Die Gleichnisreden Jesu*, 2 vols. (Tübingen: J.C.B. Mohr, 1888–1899).

31 Beavis, "Parable and Fable," 473–98; Parsons, "Luke and the Progymnasmata," 43–63; cf. Lane C. McGaughy, "Pagan Hellenistic Literature: The Babrian Fables," in *Society of Biblical Literature 1977 Seminar Papers*, SBLSPS 11 (Missoula, Mont.: Scholars Press, 1977), 205–14 ("the closest parallels to parables in pagan Hellenistic literature," 205).

32 Reasons alleged include: (1) Jesus' parables are realistic stories about humans, but fables are unrealistic tales about animals (so T. W. Manson, *The Teaching of Jesus: Studies in Form and Content* [Cambridge: Cambridge University Press, 1931], 57–58; Madeline Boucher, *The Mysterious Parable: A Literary Study*, CQMS 6 [Washington, D.C.: Catholic Biblical Association of America, 1977], 3); but see Perry, *Babrius and Phaedrus*, xxii–xxiii; Beavis, "Parable and Fable," 473–98; and the several realistic examples cited above; (2) Jesus' parables have religious morals, but fables have prudential lessons (so Boucher, *The Mysterious Parable*, 3); but see Perry, *Babrius and Phaedrus*, xxi–xxii, on the diversity of fable moralizing; and Beavis, "Parable and Fable," 473–98, on religious moralizing in fables (e.g., *Babrius* 20); (3) fables, unlike Jesus' parables, are written primarily for entertainment and secondarily for wise counsel that is usually witty or satirical (so Klyne Snodgrass, *Stories with Intent: A Comprehensive Guide to the Parables of Jesus* [Grand Rapids: Eerdmans, 2008], 49); but see Perry, *Babrius and Phaedrus*, xxii–xxiii, and the diverse examples above and in extant collections; (4) fables, unlike Jesus' parables, are "told for their own interest and [do] not serve a larger narrative or a specific context" (so Snodgrass, *Stories with Intent*, 49); but see Perry, *Babrius and Phaedrus*, xii–xiii, and the several embedded examples, Greek and Hebrew, cited above.

33 Contra Snodgrass, *Stories with Intent*, 49.

34 Contra Manson, *Teaching of Jesus*, 57–58; Boucher, *Mysterious Parable*, 3.

35 Contra Manson, *Teaching of Jesus*, 57–58; Boucher, *Mysterious Parable*, 3, who distinguishes the realism of Jesus' parables from the unrealism of fable.

36 Undoubtedly, the use of the Greek *parabolē* to translate the Hebrew *mashal* in the Old Testament is a major reason for the continued use of *parabolē* for the form in the New Testament, as many interpreters have noted. But the Aristotelian view of *parabolē* as a broad class of all realistic fictional analogy may very well account for that translation choice, which has sometimes puzzled interpreters.

37 This moral takes the form of a comparison from the lesser to the greater—a commonly prescribed enthymeme in rhetorical handbooks (see, e.g., Aristotle, *Rhet.* 2.23.4–6; Cicero, *Top.* 4.23; Theon, *Prog.* 108; Quintilian, *Inst.* 5.11.8–10).

38 Noted by Beavis, "Parable and Fable," 473–98.

39 See Michael W. Martin, "The Poetry of the Lord's Prayer: A Study in Poetic Device," *JBL* 134 (2015): 347–72.

40 So Parsons, "Luke and the Progymnasmata," 43–63.

41 Contra Snodgrass, *Stories with Intent*, 49, who mistakenly claims this feature is absent in fable.

42 The perspective that has its origins with Joachim Jeremias (*The Parables of Jesus*, rev. ed., trans. S. H. Hooke [New York: Charles Scribner's Sons, 1962]) and C. H. Dodd (*Parables of the Kingdom*, rev. ed. [New York: Scribner, 1961; originally published 1935]), and is represented in more recent years by the Jesus Seminar (Funk, Scott, and Butts, *Parables of Jesus*).

43 See, e.g., E. D. Hirsch Jr., *Validity in Interpretation* (New Haven: Yale University Press, 1967), 76; cf. Kenton L. Sparks, "Genre Criticism," in *Methods for Exodus*, ed. Thomas B. Dozeman, MBI (New York: Cambridge University Press, 2010), 55–60.

44 Funk, Scott, and Butts, *Parables of Jesus*, 18.

45 Funk, Scott, and Butts, *Parables of Jesus*, 18; cf. Jeremias, *Parables of Jesus*, 103–13.

46 See, too, on this point E. P. Sanders, *The Tendencies of the Synoptic Tradition*, SNTSMS 9 (New York: Cambridge University Press, 1969); cf. Mark Goodacre, *Thomas and the Gospels: The Case for Thomas' Familiarity with the Synoptics* (Grand Rapids: Eerdmans, 2012), 148–50.

47 See, e.g., J. D. Crossan, "Seed Parables of Jesus," *JBL* 92 (1973): 244–66; cf. the criticisms of Simon Gathercole, *The Composition of the Gospel of Thomas: Original Language and Influences*, SNTSMS 151 (New York: Cambridge University Press, 2012), 132–33.

48 Such an approach not only more closely approximates the reception of the authorial audience of the Gospels but mirrors the manner in which modern classicists read all other fables.

49 A version likely derivative of these two is also found in the Gos. Thom. 107.

50 Here again we are speaking generally of a method with roots in Jeremias and Dodd and continuing with the Jesus Seminar. For the following, see esp. Funk, Scott, and Butts, *Parables of Jesus*, 38; cf. 1–23.

51 See Thomas Wiedemann, *Adults and Children in the Roman Empire* (New Haven: Yale University Press, 1989).

52 John Dominic Crossan, *In Parables: The Challenge of the Historical Jesus* (Sonoma, Calif.: Polebridge, 1992), 38–39.

3

Narrative

Persuading through Patterns of Storytelling

A Dramatic Narrative Concerning the Rose

> Let anyone who admires the rose for its beauty consider Aphrodite's wound. The goddess was in love with Adonis and Ares in turn was in love with her, and the goddess was to Adonis what Ares was to her: a god was in love with a goddess and a goddess was pursuing a mortal. The emotion was the same even if the species was different. Struck with jealousy, Ares wanted to do away with Adonis, thinking the death of Adonis would be the end of the love. Ares attacks Adonis. Learning what had been done, the goddess hurried to the rescue, and in her haste, falling on a rose, she stumbled among the thorns and pierces the bottom of her foot. The blood from the wound dripped on the rose and changed its color to the now familiar appearance; the rose, originally having been white, changed to the appearance it how has.
>
> Aphthonius

The narrative exercise, as the name suggests, consisted of training for the composition of all forms of narrative exposition.[1] According to Theon's introductory comments for teachers, the exercise provided preparation on the one hand for written narrative composition such as history and on the other hand for composition of the narrative portions of orations.

> One who has expressed a narration and fable in a fine and varied way will also compose a history well and what is specifically called "narrative" in hypotheses—historical writing is nothing other than a combination of narrations—and one who can refute or confirm these is not far behind those speaking hypotheses. (Theon, *Prog.* 60)

The exercise also prepared young students to write both fictional and nonfictional narrative, or what Theon calls narrative of the "mythical" and the "factual" sort, respectively (*Prog.* 66). Thus, the exercise served as nothing less than foundational training in everything from creative writing and composition to historiography and declamation, and as such, it reveals much about both the narratives deriving from the ancient Mediterranean world and the diverse culture that shaped them.

Theory

Both in the progymnasmata and the handbooks of rhetoric, the theorists regularly define "narrative" as "language descriptive of" or "exposition" concerning "things that have happened or as though they have happened" (see Theon, *Prog.* 78; Ps.-Hermogenes, *Prog.* 4; Aphthonius, *Prog.* 22; Nicolaus, *Prog.* 11; cf. Cicero, *Inv.* 27; Anon. Seg. 49; Apsines, *Rhet.* 3.1). The definition is most certainly shaped with a view to a student's eventual graduation to declamation, which required the narration of events in the interest of a case—and not necessarily in the interest of the truth. The definition shows that narrative's aim is *verisimilitude*, not accuracy. As George Kennedy observes, "A narrative does not need to be factually true. John of Sardis (pp. 15–16, ed. Rabe . . .) points out that there are many things in the orators that are not true but are regarded as true on the basis of the reputation of the persons who report them."[2] Indeed, verisimilitude is the characteristic that distinguishes narrative from fable, which is by contrast commonly fantastic or unrealistic. This distinction suggests that the modern word "narrative" is too broad for the category envisioned by the theorists. "Realistic narrative" is more apt.

All progymnastic theorists aside from Theon describe major "species" of narrative. These may be seen, however, as derivative of the same fact/fiction and oral/written polarities attested by Theon. Aphthonius (*Prog.* 22) divides all narrative into the dramatic (fictional written composition), the historical (factual written composition), and the political (all oral composition). Preparation for the latter, of course, was the point of the narrative exercise as a *pro*gymnasma—that is, an exercise *preliminary to* declamation. Students needed to learn how to compose the major narrative materials of a speech: narrative portions of arguments, narrative proofs based on example, narrative in epilogue, and most important, the second part of the speech that immediately followed the *exordium* and preceded the *argumentatio*, the *narratio*.[3]

Pseudo-Hermogenes (*Prog.* 4) and Nicolaus (*Prog.* 12) attest the same three classes as Aphthonius but add the mythical (devoted to gods and heroes and mythical animals) as a category of written narrative distinct from both history and drama. Nicolaus' definition suggests the category occupied a liminal space between fact and fiction: "Mythical are those not worthy of unquestioned belief and having a suspicion of falsehood, like stories about the Cyclopses and Centaurs."

More important to progymnastic theory of narrative is the distinction the theorists draw between "the elements" of the story and the "schemas" of discourse. The former concern the subject matter of the narrative, the components of the tale itself. The latter concern the modes of narration a narrator may use to tell the story. In dividing narrative in this manner, the progymnasmata anticipate the same distinction Russian formalists, French structuralists, and other modern literary theorists draw between "story" and "discourse."[4] Then and now, the distinction is most basic to an understanding of a narrative's "anatomy."

Elements of Narrative

Theon succinctly describes what all theorists agree are the essential components of a story: "Elements of narration are six: the *person*, whether that be one or many; and the *action* done by the person; and the *place* where the action was done; and the *time* at which it was done; and the *manner* of the action; and sixth, the *cause* of these things" (*Prog.* 78). The six topoi correspond to the full range of questions any exposition of events might answer: who? what? where? when? how? and why?

Theon's exercise further divides each of these elements in ways that were characteristic of Hellenistic education (78–79):[5]

Person	origin, nature, training, disposition, age, fortune, morality, action, speech, manner of death, and what followed death
Action	great or small, dangerous or not dangerous, possible or impossible, easy or difficult, necessary or unnecessary, advantageous or not advantageous, just or unjust, honorable or dishonorable
Time	what has gone by, what is present, what is going to be; what was first or second or so on; what is appropriate to life in our time, what in ancient times; in all cases, the dates people have set in public or private life; then whether in winter or spring, summer or autumn, during the night or by day, whether the action took place during a meeting of the assembly or during a procession or festival; and whether at weddings or a reception of friends or in time of grief or any such circumstance of life
Place	size, distance, near a city or town, whether the place was sacred or unhallowed, owned or someone else's, deserted or inhabited, strong or insecure, flat or mountainous, dry or wet, barren or wooded, and all similar things
Manner	unwillingly: ignorance, accident, necessity willingly: by force, in secret, by deceit
Cause	to acquire good things, for the sake of escape from an evil, from friendship, because of a wife, for children, out of the passions: anger, love, hate, envy, pity, inebriation, and things like these

Though some of Theon's subelements may be idiosyncratic, his list of subelements belonging to "person" corresponds generally to most topical divisions of personhood taught elsewhere in the progymnasmata, and especially in the encomium and invective exercises. Though we will survey these in greater detail later, the most common among them are worth noting here: origin, birth, upbringing, training, deeds, death, and events after death. Such topoi served as the essential components of characterization in ancient narrative.

We may view the elements of narrative as roughly corresponding to the basic components of "story" in modern narratology, which is interested in describing how the interaction of events (i.e., actions and happenings) and existents (i.e., characters and items of setting) interact to form the narrative content.[6] Whereas modern literary critical theory is designed primarily for *criticism*, progymnastic theory was more concerned with *composition*. That is, young students undergoing the narrative exercise learned the elements primarily for the purpose of discovering and ordering narrative materials of all kinds in the creative writing process, and only secondarily for the purpose of critical engagement of narrative (and especially declamatory narratives in political debate). Further, whereas modern literary critical theory through its anatomy of narrative reflects contemporary, Western ways of apprehending the world, progymnastic theory is a reflection of Graeco-Roman culture. Its particular ways of construing personhood, ordering social space, constructing public time, and the like may be glimpsed in the divisions and subdivisions of the list above.

Schemas of Narrative

In addition to discussing the essential components or "elements" of a narrative's story, the progymnasmata also reflect on the various modes of discourse, or "schemas," a writer or speaker may use to narrate a story. Whereas with "elements" the interaction of characters, events, setting, time, and the like is in view, with "schemas" the interaction of the author/narrator with the audience/narratee is in view.

A majority of theorists attest five schemas, each with particular functions, as well as particular suitability for different kinds of narrative.

(1) *Direct discourse, wherein "the whole account, or most of it, keeps the nominative case."* "Medea [nominative] was a daughter of Aeetes. She betrayed the Golden Fleece" (Ps.-Hermogenes, *Prog.* 5). According to Pseudo-Hermogenes and Nicolaus, direct discourse is especially suitable for historical narrative because of its clarity.[7]

(2) *Oblique declarative discourse, which narrates via the oblique cases (genitive, dative, accusative, vocative).* "The story is that Medea [accusative], daughter of Aeetes, was infatuated with Jason" (Ps.-Hermogenes, *Prog.* 5). Pseudo-Hermogenes and Nicolaus prescribe oblique narration for practical oratory (Ps.-Hermogenes: "trials"; Nicolaus: "arguments and refutation"). Theon, however, associates inflection

with fictional narrative (he cites as an example "the myth by Phaedo the Socratic" in his [dialogue] *Zopyr* [Phaedo, frag. 11]). Quintilian notes that inflection through multiple cases can be used to emphasize a subject (*Inst.* 9.3.66–67) and call hearers' attention to it (*Inst.* 9.3.27).[8]

(3) Interrogation. "What dreadful thing did Medea not do? Was she not infatuated with Jason, and did she not betray the Golden Fleece, and did she not kill her brother Apsyrtus?" (Ps.-Hermogenes, *Prog.* 5). The theorists assign this schema, too, to practical oratory (Ps.-Hermogenes: "dialectical debate"; Nicolaus: "arguments and refutations").

(4) Comparison. "Medea, the daughter of Aeetes, instead of showing self-control, fell in love; and instead of guarding the Golden Fleece, betrayed it; and instead of saving her brother Apsyrtus, murdered him" (Ps.-Hermogenes, *Prog.* 5). Nicolaus, the only theorist to comment further on the schema, says comparison is useful "where occasion allows." Elsewhere in the progymnasmata, however, and particularly the syncrisis exercise, comparison is prescribed for the "amplification" or heightening of praise and blame—precisely the function of the schema in the example above.

(5) *Asyndeton, or the absence of conjunctions within sentences.* "Medea, the daughter of Aeetes, was infatuated with Jason, betrayed the Golden Fleece, murdered her brother Apsyrtus" (Ps.-Hermogenes, *Prog.* 5). Quintilian notes that the figure can be used not only with individual clauses but also with individual words (*Inst.* 9.3.50). Quintilian notes the power of the figure as a summative and emphatic device, saying it is useful "when we are particularly insistent on something because our points are thus driven home one at a time and also, as it were, made more numerous" (*Inst.* 9.3.50 [Russell, LCL]). The usefulness of the schema as an "emotive" concluding device is noted, too, by Pseudo-Hermogenes and Nicolaus, who prescribe it for epilogues. Aristotle observes that asyndeta "are rightly disapproved in written speech" but are commonly used in public debate by rhetoricians because "they lend themselves to acting" (*Rhet.* 3.12.2 [Freese, LCL]).[9] Quintilian states that asyndeton is particularly at home in letters (*Inst.* 9.4.19–21).

Related to the discussion of schemas, because it also concerns discourse between author and audience, is the theorists' discussion of the "virtues" of narrative. In short, the theorists say that a narrative should aim for brevity, clarity, and credibility. Schemas are occasionally associated with these virtues (e.g., in the assertion that direct discourse yields clarity), though not in any systematic way. The potential tension, too, between certain virtues (e.g., brevity and clarity) is often noted. Certainly, young students would be critiqued on the basis of whether their narrative compositions effectively displayed brevity, clarity, and credibility.

With progymnastic theory of narrative we have the makings of an ancient literary theory not unlike modern narratological models, albeit with a sensitivity to theoretical categories and divisions specific to ancient Mediterranean literature.

We may liken progymnastic narrative theory, for example, to Seymour Chatman's influential contemporary model, which also distinguishes between story and discourse, and represent it like Chatman's in diagram form:[10]

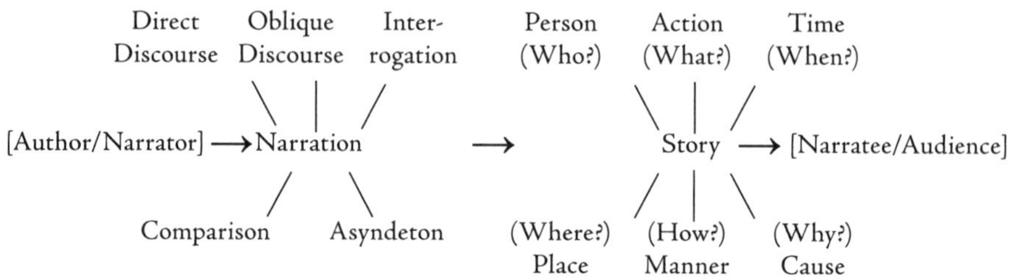

Editorial Exercises

In addition to learning the schemas and elements of narrative, students were required to practice writing, editing, and critiquing narrative using a set of established exercises. Theon's instructions (*Prog.* 85–93), for example, are illustrative. He recommends stating the narrative, changing the inflection to oblique cases, interweaving it with other material, compressing it, then expanding it. He also advises adjusting *narrative* time relative to *story* time, so that a story's beginning (B), middle (M), and end (E) are narrated by the student in all five alternative orders: MBE, EMB, MEB, EBM, BEM.[11] He prescribes altering, too, the discursive "expression" of the story rather than its order. All these exercises, it should be noted, are dependent upon the theoretical distinction between story and discourse and entail the manipulation of discourse without altering story elements.

Last, Theon requires students to practice "refutation and confirmation" of narratives (*Prog.* 93–96). (Other theorists teach such manipulation in a separate exercise by that title.) This was a specific kind of literary criticism wherein the hearer affirmed and/or challenged the quality of a narrative on the basis of a number of criteria. These criteria included the same used to critique fable, but with the addition of "the false" and the "impossible" (criteria inappropriate for fable, which is openly fictional and under no obligation to realism). In order, the criteria were

1. unclear;
2. impossible;
3. incredible;
4. false;
5. something omitted or too much added;
6. contradictory;
7. order of headings inappropriate;
8. inappropriate;

9. not beneficial; and
10. arguments from elements—person, action, place, time, manner, cause.

One can imagine how the examination of both extant and original narratives alike in light of such criteria served to sharpen students in both their compositional and literary critical skills.

Examples from Ancient Literature

Examples of Graeco-Roman, Jewish, and Christian narrative, both oral and written and in every manner of genre imaginable, survive from antiquity. In oral composition, the "political" species of narrative is widely represented, especially in the form of the *narrationes* of speeches (e.g., Cicero, *Rosc. Amer.* 15–34; Demosthenes 34.6–21; 54.3–5; Josephus, *Ant.* 15.130–134; 136a; *B.J.* 5.378–389, 390–391, 394, 395–398). Narrative materials appear, as well, in letters that were written or edited with a view to publication or intended to be read aloud for gathered audiences (Cicero, *Letter* 301.1; 2 Macc 1:7-9, 11-161; 1 Clem. 1:2–6:4; Mart. Pol. 2:1–22:1).

Countless examples of written narrative exist, too, and in all three species attested in the progymnasmata: (1) the "dramatic" (e.g., novels such as Apuleius' *Golden Ass*, the *Alexander Romance*, Judith, and *Joseph and Aseneth*); (2) the "mythical" (e.g., "about those in the underworld" [Theon, *Prog.* 66] in *Phaedo* 107d–108c, *Gorgias* 523a–524a, and Plato's *Republic* 10.614a–621b, or similarly, apocalypses from the Jewish and Christian tradition such as 3 Baruch, *Apocalypse of Abraham*, Shepherd of Hermas, and *Apocalypse of Peter*); and (3) the "historical" (e.g., biographies such as Plutarch's *Themistocles*, Philo's *Life of Moses*, and Pontius' *Life of Cyprian*, and histories such as Thucydides' *History of the Peloponnesian War*, Josephus' *Jewish Antiquities*, and Eusebius' *Ecclesiastical History*).[12] Within this broad spectrum of narrative in the ancient world, a general correspondence to progymnastic theory of narrative is evident—one owing, no doubt, to both the descriptive and prescriptive relationship of progymnastic theory to actual practice.

Elements of Narrative

In all species of ancient Mediterranean narrative, one regularly encounters the "elements of narrative" as the essential components of storytelling. In most cases, ascertaining with any certainty their intentional address is difficult, as good writers inevitably answer such questions as who, what, where, when, how, and why. Nevertheless, analysis in the light of the elements is useful in that it highlights culturally conditioned ways of subdividing personhood, time, space, and the like (see especially the subelements of Theon). Also, it is natural to organize narrative materials via such divisions and subdivisions—an instinct formalized and inculcated in Hellenistic education. Hence, analysis may shed light on the use of elements as search and compositional headings.

Clearly the theorists view them as serving such purpose in composition. In Aphthonius' model dramatic narrative concerning the rose, one witnesses the key sentence of the narrative moving in a somewhat pedantic manner befitting a classroom through all six elements. The sentence describes the action that led to the white rose turning blood red according to the myth:

Cause	Learning what had been done [Ares had attacked Adonis]
Person	the goddess
Time	hurried to the rescue, and in her haste,
Manner	falling on a rose,
Place	she stumbled among the thorns
Action	and pierced the bottom of her foot. (*Prog.* 22)

Similarly, Theon's analysis of Thucydides' arrangement makes clear his assumption that the historian has used certain elements as a major organizational feature—albeit with mixed results. Following Dionysius of Halicarnassus (*Thuc.* 9),[13] Theon complains that Thucydides' decision to divide his history by winters and summers (subelements of time) has the consequence of spreading events (another element) across multiple sections, so that subject matter is narrated piecemeal.[14] The discussion, in essence, is a critique of a particular use of elements as headings in narrative, and it conditions the modern reader to see elements employed for such purposes generally. Thus, for example, in addition to the elements Theon highlights, one notices Thucydides' invocation of elements other than "events" as headings within the major seasonal divisions—for example, "causes" (1.23.6) of the war, in 1.24–1.66, which are themselves organized by place (Epidamnus, 1.24–55; Potidaea, 1.56–66); and "speeches" given at the gathering of the Peloponnesian League at Lacedaemon (the speech of the Corinthians, 1.68–1.71; the speech of the Athenians, 1.73–78; the speech of Archidamus, 1.80–85; the speech of Sthenelaidas, 1.86).

Other historical writings of antiquity display similar organizational strategies. In the introduction to the *Jewish War*, Josephus frames his history as concerned primarily with the element of actions: "I will prosecute the actions of both parties [Romans and Jews] with accuracy" (1.9; cf. *Ant.* 1.4).[15] The history's seven books are organized, accordingly, around actions: from Antiochus Epiphanes' capture of Jerusalem down to the death of the last Sicarii.[16] Canonized Jewish history in Hebrew sometimes displays similar organization around actions (e.g., Joshua); more often, though, it is organized around persons and, specifically, the reigns of judges and kings (e.g., Judges, Kings, and Chronicles).

In Christian historiography, Eusebius of Caesarea in the introduction to his *Ecclesiastical History* (1.19) explicitly invokes several elements of narration in laying out the conceptual plan of his work.[17] He plans, he says, to narrate the church's history in terms of persons (he lists bishops, teachers, heretics, Jews, Gentiles [pagans], and martyrs), "times" (from the "dispensation" of Christ's reign down to present times, and as measured by the reigns of Roman emperors), and "events" related to these.

Several histories, too, are framed in their prefaces as comparative projects that set out to show the greatness of *ethnos* ("race" or "nation"—a subelement of origin, which itself is a subelement of person) in comparison to others—again, a strategy of organization centered around elements of narrative—for example, Polybius' *Histories* (Romans vs. the Persians, the Lacedaemonians, and the Macedonians); Dionysius of Halicarnassus (Romans vs. Assyrians, Medes, Persians, Macedonians, Greeks); Livy's *History of Rome* (Romans vs. all nations); Appian's *Foreign Wars* (Romans vs. Assyrians, Medes, Persians, Greeks); Josephus' *Jewish Antiquities* (Jews vs. Romans). Biographical narrative also sometimes pursues a similar strategy—for example, Plutarch's *Parallel Lives* (Greeks vs. Romans)[18]. So, too, does nonhistorical narrative sometimes—for example, Homer's *Iliad* (Greeks vs. Trojans).

In dramatic narrative, one finds biographical novels that are organized via the elements of personhood—and that sometimes, even, invoke them by name. For example, the *Aesop Romance*, a novel devoted to the great fabulist, Aesop, may be sketched beginning to end using common divisions of personhood, and with notation of the elements named:[19]

The *Aesop Romance*	
Origin	His "origin": Ammorius, a town in Phrygia (though some say he is Thracian, others Samian) (1)
Nature	
Body	". . . his Person deformed, to the highest degree: Flat-nos'd, hunch-back'd, blobber-lipp'd; a long misshapen Head; his Body crooked all over . . ." (1)
Mind	"Excellency of Mind" (1)
Age	"As to the age he lived in . . . it was when Croesus governed *Lydia*." Discussion ensues. (1)
Fortune	"It was Aesop's Fortune to be sent to Ephesus, in company with other slaves to be sold." The tale ensues. (2)
Action and speech	Stories about Aesop, along with his fables and sayings (3–18)

Death	The conspiracy of the magistrates at Delphos; his arrest, trial (falsely accused), and execution (thrown headlong from a rock down a precipice) (19)
Events after death	Delphians experience famine and pestilence. (19)
	Oracle says they are to atone for Aesop's death. (19)
	Delphians erect pyramid to Aesop's honor. (19 [L'Estrange])

Other novels such the *Alexander Romance* and *The Story of Apollonius, King of Tyre* may be sketched with equal if not greater detail via the elements of personhood.[20]

In political narrative (i.e., narrative in speeches), the use of elements as conceptual or organizational features is widely attested. In King Herod's speech in Josephus' *Jewish Antiquities* (15.127–146)—one of several deliberative speeches embedded in Josephus' works (*Ant.* 4.177–193; *B.J.* 4.162–192; 5.376–419; 6.99–110; 7.323–388)—one finds an opening narrative displaying the unjust "deeds" (*Ant.* 15.137) of the Arabs.[21] The narrative's deliberative thesis invokes a Theonic sub-topos of deeds, "just or unjust": "This war is a just one on our side, and that on this account it is a war of necessity, and occasioned by the injustice of our adversaries" (*Ant.* 15.129). Similarly, in Josephus' own speech as recorded in *B.J.* 5.376–419, Josephus narrates several historical examples under the heading "deeds of God," wherein God—and not Jewish armies—defeated the enemy. The narration, intended to support the deliberative thesis that the Jewish people should not send their armies against the Romans, is subdivided by person and place: Abraham and Sarai in Egypt (379–381), the fathers in Egypt (382–383), the fathers in the time of Assyria (384–388), and the captives in Babylon (389). A second narration (390–398) then narrates as negative examples the failed deeds of Jews who decided to fight the enemy with armies. It again is subdivided by person and place: Zedekiah versus Babylon (391–393); "our fathers" versus Antiochus Epiphanes and Greece (394); and the "impious inhabitants" of Palestine versus Rome (395–398). Such composition reflects the use of elements in a speech's *narratio* precisely as it was taught in the progymnasmata.

Cicero provides another example of political narrative organized by elements. In his speech in defense of Sextus Roscius the Younger, Cicero begins the main body of the oration with a *narratio* of the alleged crime—the murder of the elder Sextus Roscius—per the conventions of judicial arrangement.[22] This *narratio* is structured via the subelements of personhood (see esp. Cicero's lists, *Inv.* 1.34–36; 2.177–178; cf. 2.159–165; *Part. or.* 74–75), which function as headings for the entire piece:

CICERO, THE *NARRATIO* OF *PRO SEXTO ROSCIO AMERINO* (15–34)	
Name	Sextus Roscius (15)
City	America (15)
Race, descent, fortune	Chief man of town, neighboring region (15)
Friendships	With Metelli, Servilli, and Scipios (15)
Deeds	His defense of the nobles (16)
Death	The conspiracy of Magnus, Capito, and Sulla, and his murder (17–18)
Events after death	Communication of death among conspirators (19–20)
	The proscription of Roscius and confiscation of property (21–22)
	The removal of the son from Roscius' estate (23)
	The decree of the Decurions against the injustice (24–28)
	The plot to accuse the son of parricide (28–29)
Epilogue and comparison	Comparison with evil deeds of Fimbria (30–34)

One sees the elements at work within this speech as structural features, too, in the brief description of Caeilia (27), who took the younger Roscius in when he was robbed of his home:

Familial origin	The sister of Nepos
	The daughter of Balearicus (whose name I mention with respect)
Friendship	A friend of the (murdered) Sextus Roscius
Reputation	General opinion: in her survives the "traces of the old sense of duty"
Deeds	She extends hospitality to dispossessed son, Sextus Roscius
Virtues	"courage, loyalty, and vigilance"

In Gorgias' *Encomium of Helen*, one finds the famous Sophist orator naming what Hellenistic education would later standardize as elements of narration. Gorgias passes over several intentionally, focusing specifically on cause as the focus of his apology:

> *Who* it was, and *why* and *how* he sailed away, taking Helen as his love, I shall not say. To tell the knowing what they know already shows the right but brings no delight. Having passed over the time then in my speech now, I shall go on to

> the beginning of my future speech, and I shall set forth the *causes* which made it likely that Helen's voyage to Troy should take place. For either it was by the will of Fate and the wishes of the Gods and the votes of Necessity that she did what she did, or by force reduced or by words seduced. (*Encomium of Helen* 5 [Dillon and Gergel])[23]

Last, biography, the historical genre wholly devoted to personhood, naturally uses the divisions of personhood as a major organizational feature. We may illustrate the matter for the present with reference to the Tacitus' *Life of Julius Agricola*,[24] Philo's *Life of Moses*,[25] and Athanasius' *Life of Antony*.[26] Each of the these ancient Mediterranean bioi may be sketched in terms of various divisions or topoi of personhood found in Hellenistic education.[27]

Tacitus, *Life of Julius Agricola*	
Prologue	(1.1–3.3)
Origin	
Geography	"the ancient and illustrious Roman colony of Forum Julii"
Family	"each of his grandfathers was a 'Procurator of Caesar,' a noble equestrian office"
	father Julius "reached the rank of Senator and was noted for his interest in rhetoric and philosophy"
	mother Julia Porocilla "a woman of rare virtue" (4.1–2)
Upbringing/ training	"brought up under her [his mother's] loving care"
	"passed his boyhood and youth in the pursuit of liberal accomplishments"
	"was shielded from the snares of sinners not merely by his own good and upright nature but because from the outset of his childhood the home and the guide of his studies was Massilia, a blend and happy combination of Greek refinement and provincial simplicity"
	Tacitus tells how he was prevented from overindulging his love of philosophy, so that he "achieved the rarest of feats: he was a student, yet preserved a sense of proportion." (4.2–3)
	description of "his apprenticeship to war" in Britain under Suetonius Paulinus (5)
Office/deeds	"From the field he passed on to the city to take up office."
	Large body of the biography devoted to his career (6–42)

Death	"No one was glad about the death—or forgetful." (43.1) Rumored to be by poison; Tacitus adduces no firm evidence. He does observe that the palace sent chief freedmen and its own physicians "with a regularity unusual for a prince who visits by deputy, whether this was interest of espionage." (43.2–3) Notes that Domitian "did show an appearance of grief" and that "his hate was now no longer anxious" (43.3)
Dates of birth and death	"Agricola was born on 13 June, in the third consulship of Gaius Caesar; he died in his fifty-fourth year on 23 August, in the consulship of Collega and Priscinus." (44.1–2)
Nature	
Body	"Should posterity desire to learn his mere appearance, he was well-proportioned rather than imposing. There was no violence in his face; its dominant expression was benign." (44.2–3)
Mind	"You could easily credit him with goodness, and be glad to think him great." (44.3)
Age	As for the man himself, though snatched away in the prime of mid-career, he lived to a ripe old age measured by renown. The true blessings of life which lie in character he had fulfilled. (44.3)
Fortune	"What more could fortune have added to one who had been consul and had worn the decorations of triumph. He did not boast of excessive riches but was possessed of an ample fortune. With daughter and wife surviving him, he may even pass for happy to have escaped what was to come with his position unimpaired, his reputation brilliant, his friends and kin safe." (44.3–4)
Events after death	Escaped Domitian's tyranny The grief and tribute of his son, daughter, and wife; the laying to rest Tacitus wishes he may rest in peace "if there is any habitation for the spirits of the just." Suggests family's reverence, thankfulness, imitation, strength serve as tribute Allows for an image of bronze or marble to be made, but prefers the immaterial image of Agricola's soul as lasting tribute (44.5–46.4 [Hutton/Warmington, LCL])

Philo, *Life of Moses*	
Prologue	(1.1–4)
Origin	Race: Chaldean
	Place of birth: Egypt
	Father and mother: "best of their contemporaries" (1.5–7)
Birth, nature (body), nurture	Saved from royally sanctioned infanticide; nurtured on Hebrew mother's milk; beautiful in form (1.8–19)
Training, nature (mind)	Advancement from prodigy to philosopher; contemporaries unsure if mind is divine, human, or a mixture of both (1.20–31)
Deeds/office	Deeds as king (1.32–334)
	Deeds as legislator (2.1–65)
	Deeds as high priest (2.66–198)
	Deeds as Prophet (2.187–287)
Death	Spirit falls on him, and he prophesies concerning his death (2.288–291a)
Events after death	Also prophesies concerning his (non)burial, his unseen "monument of special dignity," and the nation's mourning for a month (2.291b)
Athanasius, *Life of Antony*	
Origin	By descent an Egyptian
	"his parents were of a good family," wealthy, and Christian (1a)
Upbringing/ training	Brought up by his parents
	When grown and arrived in boyhood, "could not endure to learn letters"; instead undergoes a kind of training for monasticism; avoids associations with other boys; like Jacob (Gen 25:27), lived as a "plain man at home"
	Attended Lord's house with parents; wasn't idle, didn't despise parents; was obedient both to father and mother; attentive to what he read
	Brought up in moderate wealth; did not bother parents about luxury; did not take pleasure from luxury; content with what he had and did not seek more (1b)
	Age 18–20 parents die, sells possessions and gives to the poor (2)
	"Training himself with patience" as there were no monasteries, no monks in the desert, but only those who practiced the discipline in solitude near the village

Upbringing/ training (cont.)	Learns monastic practices from an old man who lived as hermit in the next village
	Goes to places outside the village; seeks good men, imitates in virtue, perfecting his discipline (3–4)
	His first battle with Satan, as "a youth" (5–6)
Deeds	The large body of the biography devoted to his deeds (7–88)
Death	Prophesies his approaching death to the monks in the outer mountain, preaches concerning monasticism (89); preaches against Egyptian practice of placing dead bodies in houses, and for burial of bodies (90); preaches and makes provisions for after his death (91); dies (92a)
What follows death	Followers bury body, meager belongings distributed according to wishes (92b); summary of life; his renown throughout the world (93)
Epilogue	(94)

In addition to shedding light on the macrostructure of narrative units, analysis in the light of "narrative elements" may highlight the culture-specific ways individual elements are habitually ordered and presented in ancient narrative. Theon's subelements are especially helpful in this regard. Theon prepares the modern reader, for example, to experience assemblies, processions, and festivals as *temporal* settings; or to encounter public *space* as divided between the sacred and unhallowed or ordered primarily by ownership; or to estimate a person's honor by their familial stock, education, wealth, and the like. Reflection on each subelement may thus lend greater texture to any reading of an ancient text.

Though space does not permit an exhaustive survey of every subelement, we may illustrate the matter with reference to the first subelement (origin) of the first element (person) in Theon's list. In the various divisions of personhood taught in progymnasmata and other textbooks, the element of origin is among the most commonly attested—so it offers us a potentially fruitful avenue of investigation.[28] It appears even in the shortest list of headings belonging to personhood, that of Aphthonius (origin, upbringing, deeds, and comparison; *Prog.* 36). In virtually all lists it is prescribed as the first topos to be considered—and so it appears to have had a fixed place in Hellenistic education. As a search heading, it has reference most broadly to the origin story of a person. This generally includes both geographical origins, including city, province, and homeland, as well as familial origins, including parents, ancestors, tribe, and race.[29] For some theorists it likely included, as well, the matter of one's birth, and any marvelous events or phenomena in connection with it—though for others, birth was a related but ultimately distinct heading.[30] Reflected in the element of origin (and other divisions of personhood), too, is a static and somewhat deterministic vision of personhood wherein character or ethos is generally determined by one's "stock." One may see this perspective at work somehow in virtually every example discussed below. The topos was used in Hellenistic education, too, to reinforce stereotypes, positive or negative, about places, ethnicities, families, social classes, and the like—though certainly these stereotypes could be subverted, depending on the author's purposes.

In extant ancient narrative, one sees the topos of origin invoked everywhere in accordance with progymnastic theory—that is, as the first topos, via the divisions of geography and family, and as a quick demarcator of identity and honor in the characterization of persons. In the genre of historical narrative, Dionysius is illustrative. He introduces himself—and remains known to this day—in terms of his origin: "I, the author, am Dionysius of Halicarnassus, the son of Alexander" (*Ant. rom.* 1.8.4 [Cary, LCL]).[31] Then he tells the story of the Romans first in terms of their origin: "There are some who affirm that the Aborigines, from whom the Romans have their origin [*genos*], were natives of Italy, a stock which came into being spontaneously" (1.8.4 [Cary, LCL, with modification]); and again: "But the most learned of the Roman historians, among whom is Porcius Cato, who compiled with the greatest care the 'origins' [*genealogies*] of the Italian cities, Gaius Sempronius and a great many others say that they were Greeks, part of those who once dwelt in Achaia . . ." (1.10.3 [Cary, LCL]). He similarly introduces individual figures in terms of their origin, often with the simple epithet "Name of X" (with X being a place or parent of origin—a staple of Graeco-Roman historiography, and literature in general), and sometimes in more elaborate accounts—for example:

> But if what they say is true, the Aborigines can be a colony of no other people but of those who are now called Arcadians; for these were the first of all the Greeks to cross the Ionian Gulf, under the leadership of Oenotrus, the son of Lycaon [lit., 'Oenotrus of Lycaon'], and to settle in Italy. This Oenotrus was the fifth from Aezeius and Phoroneus, who were the first kings in the Peloponnesus. For Niobê was the daughter of Phoroneus, and the Pelasgus was the son of Niobê and Zeus, it is said; Lycaon was the son of Aezeius, and Deïanira and Pelasgus were the parents of another Lycaon, whose son Oenotrus was born seventeen generations before the Trojan expedition. (*Ant. rom.* 1.11.1–2 [Cary, LCL])

And again:

> Now let me also show the origin [*genos*] of the Oenotrian race, offering as my witness another of the early historians, Pherecydes of Athens, who was a genealogist inferior to none. He thus expresses himself concerning the kings of Arcadia: "Of Pelasgus and Deïanira was born Lycaon; this man married Cyllenê, a Naiad nymph, after whom Mount Cyllenê is named." Then, having given an account of their children and of the places each of them inhabited, he mentions Oenotrus and Peucetîus, in these words: "And Oenotrus, after whom are named

> the Oenotrians who live in Italy, and Peucetius, after whom are named the Peucetians who live on the Ionian Gulf." Such, then, are the accounts given by the ancient poets and writers of legends concerning the places of abode and the origin [*genos*] of the Oenotrians. (1.12.1–2 [Cary, LCL])

Such interest in geographical and familial origins, whether of nations, tribes, or individuals, and as the first word on such subjects, is not limited to Dionysius but is characteristic of Greek and Roman historiography generally.

Josephus illustrates the same principle in Jewish historiography. Having modeled his *Jewish Antiquities* on Dionysius' work, he similarly begins with an account of the Jewish nation's origins. Naturally, he begins with discussion of Moses as both the founding "legislator" of the nation and his primary historical source. Then, on the basis of Moses' account (Josephus assumes Mosaic authorship of Genesis), Josephus roots the national story in the creation narrative, thereby framing the God of the Jewish people as the origin of all things, the nation included. Like Dionysius, Josephus also commonly introduces persons via their origin, often invoking the topos even by name: "In this city lived one Abinadab, by birth [*genos*] a Levite, and who was greatly commended for his righteous and religious course of life; so they brought the ark to his house . . ." (*Ant.* 6.18); "Now, Acme was a Jew by birth [*genos*], and a servant to Julia, Caesar's wife, and did this out of her friendship for Antipater, as having been corrupted by him with a large present of money, to assist in his pernicious designs against his father and his aunt" (*Ant.* 17.141); "Costobarus was an Idumean by birth [*genos*], and one of principal dignity among them, and one whose ancestors had been priests to the Koze, whom the Idumeans had [formerly] esteemed as a god" (*Ant.* 15.253); "Now, there were two men, Asineus and Anileus, of the city of Neerda by birth [*genos*], and brothers to one another. They were destitute of a father; and their mother had them to learn the art of weaving curtains, it not being esteemed disgrace among them for men to be weavers of cloth" (*Ant.* 18.134). And like Dionysius, he occasionally offers more extended accounts of origin in the form of genealogy. Counting Moses the greatest of the "Hebrews," Josephus cites Moses' genealogy as the first cause: ". . . and he was, by the confession of all, according to God's prediction, as well for his greatness of mind as for his contempt of difficulties, the best of all the Hebrews; for Abraham was his ancestor, of the seventh generation. For Moses was the son of Amram, who was the son of Caath, whose father Levi was the son of Jacob, who was the son of Isaac, who was the son of Abraham" (*Ant.* 2.229).

Eusebius of Caesarea attests a similar set of practices in Christian historiography. His *Ecclesiastical History* takes up its subject first by examining its Christianity's origins with Christ:

> My work will begin, as I have said, with the dispensation of the Saviour Christ—which is loftier and greater than human conception—and with a discussion

> of his divinity. For it is necessary, inasmuch as we derive even our name from Christ, for one who proposes to write a history of the Church to begin with the very origin of Christ's dispensation, a dispensation more divine than many think. (*Eccl. hist.* 1.8–9 [*NPNF*² 1:82])

And in telling the story of Christ, he naturally begins with his origins:

> No language is sufficient to express the origin and the worth, the being and the nature of Christ. Wherefore also the divine Spirit says in the prophecies, "Who shall declare his generation?" For none knows the Father except the Son, neither can any one know the Son adequately except the Father alone who has begotten him. (2.2 [*NPNF*² 1:115])

Such interest in origin as the first indicator of character is not limited to historiographical narrative. In the *Iliad*, which displays a mixture of the dramatic and mythical narrative, most characters, whether human or divine, are introduced first in terms of familial origin and regularly referred to throughout the narrative in such terms (i.e., as in "X [son] of Y").[32] Thus, the work begins in introduction of one of its main characters with the line: "The wrath sing, goddess, of Achilles son of Peleus" (*Il.* 1.1 [Murray/Wyatt, LCL]). Gods, too, are characterized first in terms of origin. Thus, the poet introduces Apollo with the line: "Who then of the gods was it that brought these two together to contend? The son of Leto and Zeus" (*Il.* 1.8–9 [Murray/Wyatt, LCL]). Achilles says concerning Athene: "Why have you come this time, daughter of Zeus, who bears the aegis?" (*Il.* 1.202 [Murray/Wyatt, LCL]); and Hera of Zeus: "Most dread son of Cronos, what a word you have said!" (*Il.* 1.552 [Murray/Wyatt, LCL]). More sustained reflections on origin as an indication of character are common, as when Apollo urges Aeneas to battle against Achilles on the basis of the former's divine ancestry:

> But come, warrior, pray yourself also to the gods who are for ever; for men say that you were born of Aphrodite, daughter of Zeus, while he is sprung from a lesser goddess [Thetis]. For your mother is daughter of Zeus, and his of the old man of the sea [Nereus]. But carry straight against him your stubborn bronze, and do not let him turn you back with words of contempt and threats. (*Il.* 20.104–105 [Murray/Wyatt, LCL])

In dramatic novels, we find that protagonists are frequently introduced via the topos of origin. The *Aesopic Romance*, we have seen, begins its story with explicit reflection first on Aesop's "origin" [*genos*], noting both his town (Ammorius) and homeland (Phrygia) in the opening lines. The Jewish novel Susanna similarly introduces its namesake in terms of her praiseworthy familial origin along with a few other topoi such as beauty, piety, and training: "He married the daughter of Hilkiah, named Susanna, a very beautiful woman and one who feared the Lord.

Her parents were righteous, and had trained their daughter according to the law of Moses" (Sus 1:2-3).[33]

Some novels give extended treatment of the origin. After a brief proem, Longus' *Daphnis and Chloe* opens with a laudatory description of the main character's geographical origins, before proceeding to other topics of personhood in a fairly traditional order:

> There's a city in Lesbos called Mytilene, a big and beautiful one, divided by canals through which the sea flows gently, and decorated with bridges of white, polished stone. You would think you were looking at an island, not a city. About twenty miles from this city of Mytilene a rich man had an estate, a very fine property. There were hills covered with game, plains rich in wheat, slopes with many vines, pastures stocked with sheep, and the soft sand of a long beach, washed by the sea. (*Daphnis and Chloe* 1.1 [Gill])[34]

In political narrative, we have seen how Cicero begins the *narratio* of *Pro Sexto Roscio Amerino* (15–34) with a sketch of Sextus Roscius via a full set of topics, starting with name and origin: "Sextus Roscius, my client's father, was a citizen of the free town of America; by birth, descent, and fortune he was easily the chief man . . ." (15 [Freese, LCL]). He follows the same procedure, too, in the brief description of Caeilia (though he focuses on familial rather than geographical origin): ". . . my client took refuge in Rome, and betook himself to Caecilia, the sister of Nepos, the daughter of Balearicus (whose name I mention with respect), formerly an intimate friend of his father . . ." (27 [Freese, LCL]). Such identification by family or place of origin is common in narrative sections of oratory—for example, in Demosthenes' speech *Against Lacritus*:[35] "I myself, men of the jury, had not the slightest acquaintance with these men; but Thrasymedes, the son of Diophantus, that well-known Sphettian,[36] and Melanopus, his brother, are friends of mine, and we are on the most intimate terms possible" (35.6 [Murray, LCL]).

In no genre of ancient narrative, however, is origin a more important indicator of character than in biography. Typically, the genre begins with the topos and often addresses it in terms of both geography and generation. Diogenes Laertius typically does so in a short sentence or two at the beginning of his biographies—for example, "Socrates was the son of Sophroniscus, a sculptor, and of Phaenarete, a midwife, as we read in the *Theaetetus* of Plato" (*Lives* 2.18 [Hicks, LCL]); "Xenephon, the son of Gryllus, was a citizen of Athens and belonged to the deme Erchia" (*Lives* 2.48 [Hicks, LCL]); "Aristippus was by birth [*genos*] a citizen of Cyrene and, as Aeschines informs us, was drawn to Athens by the fame of Socrates" (*Lives* 2.65 [Hicks, LCL]).[37] So too Philostratus in his bios: "According to his admirers, Pythagorus of Samos was not really an Ionian, but was born as Euphorbus at Troy" (*Apollonius of Tyana* 1.1 [Jones, LCL]).[38]

Just as often, however, one finds more extensive accounts at the beginning of a bios. Suetonius, for example, begins his biography *Divus Augustus*, stating, "There are many indications that the Octavian family was in days of old a distinguished one at Velitrae . . ." (2.1 [Rolfe, LCL]).[39] He then goes on to describe the family, with special attention to its accomplishments and honors (2.1–2); provides a genealogy tracing Augustus' ancestors down through his grandfather and citing their honors (2.2); and gives special attention to Augustus' father: "His father Gaius Octavius was from the beginning of his life a man of wealth and repute, and I cannot but wonder that some have said that he too was a moneychanger . . ." (*Aug.* 3.1 [Rolfe, LCL]). An apologetic account follows, thereafter, of the father's distinctions (2.3). Last, there are materials devoted to Suetonius' siblings, Ancharia and Atia, and some related associations, and a defense of false disparagement of Augustus via origins (2.4).

Similarly, Plutarch's *Themistocles* begins, "In the case of Themistocles, his family [*genos*] was too obscure to further his reputation. His father was Neocles,—no very conspicuous man,—a Phrearrhian by deme, of the tribe Leontis; and on his mother's side he was an alien" (1.1 [Perrin, LCL]).[40] Plutarch then notes how Themistocles used to take "well-born youths" outside the gates to a gymnasium frequented by aliens and named after Heracles—also of illegitimate birth—and so "is thought to have removed the distinction between aliens and legitimates" (2.2 [Perrin, LCL]). Plutarch does note, however, that Themistocles "was connected with the family of the Lycomidae, as evidenced by his restoration of that family's shrine at his own cost" (1.3 [Perrin, LCL]).

In Jewish biography, we find the Josephus' autobiographical *Life*, which begins, "My family [*genos*] is no ignoble one, tracing its descent far back to priestly ancestors" (1.1 [Thackeray, LCL]).[41] Josephus then gives an account of his ancestors' priestly distinctions, noting that on his mother's side he is "of royal blood" and mentioning her ancestor Asamonaeus (from whom the Maccabees, or "Hasmonaeans," are named). Josephus also provides a genealogy running from his "great-grandfather's grandfather" down to himself and his own sons, and with notations of distinctions throughout. Josephus' conclusion to the section speaks to the importance of origin for estimations of ethos in the ancient world: "With such a pedigree, which I cite as I find it recorded in the public registers, I can take leave of the would-be detractors of my family" (2.1 [Thackeray, LCL]).

Similarly, Philo's *Life of Moses* after an opening *exordium* proceeds to the first topos by name: "I will begin with what is necessarily the right place to being. Moses was by race [*genos*] a Chaldean, but was born and reared in Egypt, as his ancestors had migrated thither" (2.5 [Colson, LCL]). Philo describes Egypt in praiseworthy terms (2.5–7), then considers Moses' parents: "He had for his father and mother the best of their contemporaries, members of the same tribe, though with them mutual affection was a stronger tie than family affection" (2.6–7

[Colson, LCL]). Lastly, Philo comments on Moses' ancestry: "He was seventh in descent from the first settler, who became the founder of the whole Jewish nation" (2.6–7 [Colson, LCL]).

In Christian biography, we find similar materials at the front of the narrative. Possidius' *Life of St. Augustine* after a brief proem begins, "Augustine was born in the African province, in the city of Tagaste of honorable Christian parents of curial rank" (1.1 [Weiskotten]).[42] Pontius' *Life of Cyprian* handles the topos of origin innovatively, subverting traditional ethnic or familial standards. After the prologue, Pontius asks where he should begin the story of Cyprian's life and settles on spiritual equivalents of origin and birth: "the beginning of his faith" and his "heavenly birth" (1 [*ANF* 5:267]).

Such examples suffice to show how a single subelement of narration was conventionally handled in the literature of the Graeco-Roman world. If origin is any indication, an anatomy of ancient Mediterranean narrative could be developed that gives special attention to recurring cultural patterns native to each of the major elements and their subdivisions, thereby illuminating greatly the modern reception of ancient texts.

Schemas of Narrative

One also sees employed across the great spectrum of ancient Mediterranean literature all five schemas of narrative prescribed by the theorists, and often (though certainly not always) in connection with the purposes or species of narrative for which they are prescribed.

(1) Direct discourse, the most common of schemas, occurs in all manner of literature and may be considered the default narrative schema of every genre. Pseudo-Hermogenes and Nicolaus prescribe it for historical writing because it has the virtue of clarity, and indeed, it is regularly employed in Graeco-Roman historiography (e.g., Thucydides, *History of the Peloponnesian War* 1.1: "Thucydides [*nominative*], an Athenian [*nominative*], wrote the history of the war waged by the Peloponnesians and the Athenians against one another"). Progymnastic theory on the matter, however, is at odds with the common practice among historians of employing the high literary style of oblique declarative discourse. Frequently one witnesses the intentional variation of cases other than the nominative in historical writings (e.g., Diodorus Siculus, *Bib. hist.* 1.1; Dionysius of Halicarnassus, *Ant. rom.* 1.1; Dio Cassius, *Hist. rom.* 1.1–2; Josephus, *B.J.* 1.1–2; *Ant.* 1.1; Eusebius, *Hist. eccl.* 1.1).

(2) Oblique declarative discourse is frequently employed, as the theorists prescribe, in declamatory "trials" and "arguments and refutations." A good example is seen in Herod's *narratio* of Arab treachery in the deliberative "commander speech" as related by Josephus.[43] There Herod employs the accusative in place

of the nominative: "And what occasion [*accusative*] is there for me to mention many instances [*accusative*] of such procedures of theirs? When they [*accusative*] were in danger [*accusative*] of losing their own government of themselves, and of being slaves to Cleopatra, what others were they that freed them from that fear?" (*Ant.* 15.131; cf. *Ant.* 4.177; *B.J.* 4.177; 6.103–104).

(3) Interrogation, the schema the theorists associate especially with dialectical debate, arguments, and refutations, is in fact commonly found in narrative sections of oratory and other public literature that is argumentative in nature. For example, 1 Clement, narrating historical examples of the faithful persecuted at the hands of the unfaithful, states in dialectical fashion, "For what shall we say, brothers? Was Daniel cast into the lions' den by those who feared God? Or were Ananias, Azarias, and Misael shut up in the fiery furnace by those who participated in the magnificent and glorious worship of the most High? This could never be! Who then did these things?" (1 Clem. 46.6–7; cf. Cicero, *Rosc. Amer.* 29–30, 32, 34; Josephus, *B.J.* 4.166–167; 5.376–377, 380–384, 387–388; 6.110; 7.361, 364, 369, 375–376, 378, 384).

(4) Comparison, prescribed especially for heightening praise or blame, is exemplified in the *narratio* of Josephus' speech in *Jewish War* 5.376–419. In the speech, Josephus argues against taking arms against Rome and cites a series of examples from Israel's history where either relying on God's deliverance succeeded or fighting against enemies failed. In the following example, which belongs to the latter type, Josephus points to the blameworthy Zedekiah as an analogy to the even worse present-day governors, thereby heightening blame for the latter:

> For example, when the king of Babylon besieged this very city, and our King Zedekiah fought against him, contrary to what predictions were made to him by Jeremiah the prophet, he was at once taken prisoner, and saw the city and the temple demolished. Yet how much greater was the moderation of that king, than is that of your present governors, and that of the people then under him, than is that of yours at this time!
>
> For when Jeremiah cried out aloud, how very angry God was at them, because of their transgressions, and told them they should be taken prisoners, unless they would surrender their city, neither did the king nor the people put him to death; but for you, (to pass over what you have done within the city, which I am not able to describe as your wickedness deserves,) you abuse me, and throw missiles at me, who only exhort you to save yourselves, as being provoked when you are put in mind of your sins, and cannot bear the very mention of those crimes, which you every day perpetrate. (*B.J.* 5.391–393; cf. Cicero, *Rosc. Amer.* 33–34; Josephus, *B.J.* 6.102; 7.342)

(5) Asyndeton occurs frequently, especially in oratory, and for reasons the theorists prescribe: for its emotive effect and especially for driving home points in a summative fashion. Cicero provides a good example of the schema in the

narratio of *Pro Sexto Roscio Amerino*, where, after narrating the crimes against Sextus Roscius, he lists them in an emotive summation as atrocities witnessed by the Decurions: "They saw many sorrowful incidents occurring at the same time; the cruel murder of Sextus Roscius, a most prosperous fellow-citizen; the scandalous poverty of his son, to whom that impious robber had not even left, out of so rich an inheritance, the right of way to the family burying-place; the infamous purchase of the property, seizure, theft, robbery, donations" (*Rosc. Amer.* 24; cf. 29–30; *Letter to Diognetus* 5.5–17). The piece is illustrative of both forms of asyndeton mentioned by Quintilian (*Inst.* 9.3.50), that with clauses and that with individual words.

Editorial Practices

Last, one witnesses in cases where the use of source material may be studied the same kinds of editorial practices prescribed in the progymnasmata for narrative. Ronald Mellor, for example, in his examination of Livy's use of Polybius as a source for the Hannibalic War (20–30) and Rome's conquest in the East (31–45), observes a diverse range of techniques used by the historian.[44] "Most commonly Livy abridges Polybius to give the story a more rapid narrative flow. . . . On occasion, Livy follows the Polybian account word by word, especially where technical or military details are involved. In other cases, Livy recasts the material to add dramatic or rhetorical flavor to the narrative."[45] Also "there are occasions when he re-orders the Polybian narrative or inserts chauvinistic material from the Roman annalists" and when he has "found and added" material.[46] Similarly, Christopher Pelling, in a study of Plutarch's adaptation of his source material, summarizes the biographer's editorial techniques: "The effect has usually been to abbreviate his source-material, or at least to arrange it in as simple and elegant a manner as possible, avoiding duplications, side-tracks, or distracting explanations. The opposite technique is also visible: the *expansion* of inadequate material, normally by the fabrication of circumstantial detail."[47] In these accounts, one sees nearly the full range of editorial practices prescribed for narrative in the progymnasmata: word-for-word restating, interweaving with other materials, compression, expansion, altering the discursive expression, and "refutation" by a variety of stylistic criteria.[48]

Examples from the New Testament

Narrative materials recur throughout the New Testament and in most of the same forms mentioned by the theorists and attested in the Mediterranean milieu. The "political" or oral species of narrative occurs within the one certain declamation included in the New Testament canon, Hebrews (see, e.g., Heb 1:5-14), as well as within conventionally arranged speeches embedded within other species of narrative (e.g., in Paul's speech before the Jerusalem mob in Acts 22). Similar kinds of narrative material occur, too, as embedded features of the New Testament's many public letters (e.g., the exemplum of Abraham in Rom 4). "Historical" narration is also well represented, in the form of both biography (Matthew, Mark, Luke, and John) and historiography (Acts). "Mythical" narration devoted primarily to the realm of the divine, meanwhile, constitutes the primary mode of exposition in the New Testament's one apocalypse (Revelation)—but, of course, is also represented as a form embedded within "historical" and "political" narrative, just as in other such narrative in Mediterranean milieus. Apart from Jesus' realistic parables, which may be seen as belonging to the overlapping area of realistic fable and fictional narrative, there is little if any "dramatic" narrative in the New Testament.

Elements of Narrative

As in the Mediterranean milieu, one finds in the New Testament the elements of narration represented everywhere as the essential constituent aspects of the story in view. Here again, though ascertaining intentionality or consciousness of use is sometimes difficult, one nevertheless sees the same recurring use of elements in conceptual or structural organization.

In Acts, the only history included in the canon, elements are key to organization much as they are in the histories surveyed above. Commentators often note how Jesus' words at the beginning of the narrative, "and you will be my witnesses in Jerusalem, in all Judea and Samaria, and to the ends of the earth" (1:8b), function as an introductory sketch of the narrative that follows. That narrative is commonly outlined, too, in terms of this introductory sketch (e.g., *in Jerusalem*, chs. 2–7; *in all Judea and Samaria*, chs. 3–12; *to the ends of the earth*, chs. 13–28). Theon's subelements lend further insight into this geographical sketch. Theon's division of "sacred or hallowed" may be used to chart the essential progression in Acts from Jerusalem, the epicenter of holy space, to increasingly less hallowed locales (Israel, beyond Israel) in what amounts to an eschatological subversion of holiness maps like that seen in *m. Kelim* 1:6-9.[49]

The narrative materials of speeches within Acts, too, can be outlined in terms of the elements of narrative. A good test case, because it allows for comparison of multiple occurrences, is the form on display in the recurring vision scenes narrated in the speeches of Peter and Paul. In rhetorical terms, these are narrative arguments belonging to the inartificial class of proofs and, specifically, "divine testimony" or "oracles." Such narrative materials are specifically mentioned by Nicolaus as the kind of narrative oratory the narrative progymnasma prepares students to write (*Prog.* 15–16). The essential outline of these proofs may be expressed in terms of the six major elements of narrative:

Peter's Vision (Acts 11:5-10)	
Place	Joppa
Time	while praying
Manner	via trance and vision (11:5)
Action	commands Peter to rise, kill, and eat (11:7)
Person	the Lord (11:8)
Cause	"What God has made clean, you must not call profane" (11:9)
Paul's Damascus Road Vision (Acts 22:6-10)	
Place	near Damascus
Time	about noon (22:6)
Manner	via light/voice from heaven (22:6-7)
Person	Jesus of Nazareth (22:8)
Action	commands Paul to go to Damascus
Cause	"there you will be told everything that has been assigned to you" (22:10)
Paul's Jerusalem Vision (Acts 22:17-21)	
Place	Jerusalem, the temple
Time	while praying (22:17)
Manner	via trance, vision (22:17-18)
Person	Jesus (22:18)
Action	commands Paul to depart Jerusalem (22:18, 21)
Cause	"because they will not accept your testimony about me" (22:18)
	"for I will send you far away to the Gentiles" (22:21)

Narrative proofs such as these fall within entire speeches, too, that reflect organization by elements of narration. A good example is the "defense" (judicial speech) Paul gives to the gathered Jerusalem mob in Acts 22. The materials immediately preceding the speech serve to frame it as an oration concerned primarily with the elements of person (who) and (criminal) action (what). The military tribune, upon arresting Paul, inquired as to "who he was and what he had done" (21:33). But as "some in the crowd shouted one thing and others another," the tribune was not able to "learn the facts" (21:34). Thus, he posed his own theory to Paul directly, expressed in terms of who and what: "Aren't you the Egyptian who recently stirred up a revolt and led the four thousand assassins out into the wilderness?" (21:38). In response, Paul identifies himself (who) via the subelements of ethnic and geographic origins—"I am a Jew, from Tarsus in Cilicia, a citizen of no obscure city"—and asks to address the crowd in his defense (what; 21:39).

The speech, accordingly, is built entirely around these two elements. The speech is, beginning to end, narrative in form. Invoked throughout in proof or justification of Paul's actions, however, are what rhetorical theory calls inartificial proofs: witnesses (22:5a), legal documents (22:5b), and divine testimonies in the form of a vision/oracle (22:6-11), oracle (22:12-16), and another vision/oracle (22:17-21). In terms of ancient arrangement, then, the speech employs "disjointed" *narratio* and *argumentatio*, wherein narrative exposition is interspersed with related proofs (rather than introduced in two distinct sections).[50]

After a brief exordium (22:1), Paul first identifies himself (who) via several elements or topoi of personhood, and in a traditional order:

Person	
Origin	A Jew born in Tarsus in Cilicia
Upbringing	Brought up in this city at the feet of Gamaliel
Training	Educated strictly according to our ancestral law
Deeds	Being zealous for God
Comparison	Just as all of you are today (22:3)

Then he narrates his actions. Though a "defense," Paul ironically admits his crime and invokes witnesses in proof of it. He says he "persecuted this Way up to the point of death by binding both men and women and putting them in prison, as *the high priest and the whole council of elders can testify*." The sentence (in Greek) continues the admission, however, with the invocation of *letters* from these same witnesses that legally (if not morally) authorized his actions, sending him on his way to Damascus.

Thereafter, the defense proper is made by appeal to three *divine testimonies*, each legitimizing Paul's actions (and delegitimizing his accusers'—the first two implicitly, the last explicitly):

Divine Testimony	Commanded Action
Vision on the Damascus road (22:6-11)	"Go to Damascus" (22:10)
Ananias' healing and oracle (22:12-16)	"Get up, be baptized, and have your sins washed away, calling on his name" (22:16)
Vision in the temple	"Hurry and get out of Jerusalem quickly, because they will not accept your testimony about me" (22:18)
	"Go, for I will send you far away to the Gentiles" (22:21)

Another example of a disjointed *narratio* of actions interspersed with proof is seen in Peter's speech to "Israelites" in Acts 3:12-26. After a brief exordium (3:12), Peter embarks in a short *narratio* (3:13-16) of his addressees' crimes against Jesus and of the healing they have just witnessed. In each case, he cites witnesses in proof of the deeds he narrates:

Narrated actions	The God of Abraham, the God of Isaac, and the God of Jacob, the God of our ancestors has glorified his servant Jesus, whom you handed over and rejected in the presence of Pilate, though he had decided to release him. But you rejected the Holy and Righteous One and asked to have a murderer given to you, and you killed the Author of life, whom God raised from the dead.
Inartificial proof—witnesses	To this we are witnesses.
Narrated action	And by faith in his name, his name itself has made this man strong,
Inartificial proof—witnesses	whom you see and know;
Narrated action	and the faith that is through Jesus has given him this perfect health
Inartificial proof—witnesses	in the presence of all of you. (3:13-16)

The *narratio* gives way to a deliberative *argumentatio* urging the listeners to repent (3:16-25). In the opening line of this section, Peter looks back on the crimes narrated and says, "And now, brothers, I know that you acted in ignorance, as did also your rulers" (3:17). "Ignorance" is a sub-topos of *manner* and, more specifically, *unwilling action*. Criminal action done out of ignorance, by accident, or out of necessity—the three sub-topoi of *unwilling manner*—could potentially be excused legally.[51] By invoking the sub-topos of ignorance in the transition to the deliberative appeal, Peter frames the recipients' actions as not willfully criminal, thereby establishing the justice of the opportunity they are afforded—namely, to repent and escape judgment.

The use of elements to structure narrative in speeches is also seen in Hebrews. The first narrative unit of the speech (1:5-14), for example, is an exposition of Jesus' greatness in comparison with the angels. The section may be outlined in terms of common subelements of personhood—which helps to clarify the much-debated matter of where *narratio* and other parts of arrangement are located in the speech.[52]

Origin	Jesus is "begotten" as the "Son" of the "Father" on the day of his enthronement—the angels are not. (1:5)
Birth	Jesus is the "firstborn" in the coming world and worshipped by angels as such. (1:6)
Pursuits	The angels are "servants," but Jesus is the "anointed" whose "throne is forever" because he loved righteousness. (1:7-9)
Death	Jesus will have unending dominion in the coming world because he "remains," in contrast to the angels whose dominion will "perish." (1:10-12)
Events after death	Jesus, not the angels, is exalted to God's right hand until all his enemies are subjected to him in the future. (1:13-14)

Because the unit comes immediately after the exordium of the speech (1:1-4), and immediately before deliberative proof in the form of comparison and witnesses (2:1-4), it falls in the expected place of *narratio*. The structural use of the elements of narrative seems to confirm, then, what location implies—that the unit constitutes *narratio* within the arrangement of the speech.[53]

The Gospels, too, like other biographies in the ancient Mediterranean world, follow the elements of personhood as a general narrative outline. In the study that definitively located the Gospels in the bios genre, Richard A. Burridge argues that a major "internal" feature that situates the four gospels within the spectrum of biographical writing is the topical outline they share with other ancient Mediterranean biographies. Burridge analyzes the content of the Synoptic Gospels, and later the Fourth Gospel, under the following headings: ancestry, birth, boyhood and education, great deeds, virtues, death and consequences.[54] Burridge notes that such topical content is typical of the bios genre generally, and so is further evidence for reading the Gospels as biographies. We concur and would observe additionally that such topical content corresponds perfectly to the divisions of personhood taught not only in the narrative but also in the encomium, invective, and syncrisis progymnasmata.[55] As narrative devoted to personhood, it is structured just as Hellenistic training in prose composition prescribed.[56]

It is possible, too, that narrative materials within New Testament letters have been shaped by the elements of narrative, given their ubiquity in Hellenistic education. Consider, for example, the introduction to Paul's story of his visit to Jerusalem in Galatians 2, which efficiently touches on each of the six elements as well as Aphthonius' model exercise:

Time	Then after fourteen years
Place	I went up again to Jerusalem
Person	with Barnabas, taking Titus along with me.
Cause	I went up in response to a revelation.
Action	Then I laid before them the gospel that I proclaim among the Gentiles,
Manner	but did so privately to those of reputation . . . (2:1-2)

In addition to these larger patterns of organization governed by multiple elements, one also encounters recurring, culture-specific patterns in the handling of individual elements and subelements. Here again, we may illustrate the matter with regard to the first subelement in Theon's list, the topos of origin. As in the Mediterranean milieu, we find that origin in the New Testament is commonly treated as the first topos in characterization, via the divisions of geography and family, and as an indicator of honor and identity in characterization.

The *narrationes* of speeches within Acts, for example, commonly begin their sketches of personhood with origin. In Peter's speech on Pentecost, the apostle identifies Jesus as "Jesus of Nazareth" (2:22), before giving a laudatory account of his deeds, death, and events after his death (2:22-24). Paul, too, begins with his own origins in sketches of his own life: "I am a Jew, born in Tarsus in Cilicia" (22:3); "My life from youth from my beginning among my race and in Jerusalem is known by all the Jews" (26:4).

The *narratio* of Hebrews 1:5-14 similarly begins with origin and birth as we have seen: "For to which of the angels did God ever say, 'You are my Son; today I have begotten you'? Or again, 'I will be his Father, and he will be my Son'? And again, when he brings the firstborn into the world, he says, 'Let all God's angels worship him'" (1:5-6).

Narrative sketches of persons in letters, too, often take up the topic first. In Philippians 3:5, Paul begins an encomiastic sketch of his Jewish credentials that begins with origin: "circumcised on the eighth day, a member of the people of Israel, of the tribe of Benjamin, a Hebrew born of Hebrews."[57]

The most sustained treatments origin, however, are found in the New Testament's four biographies, the Gospels. At the opening of each, we find the same kinds of materials as seen in biography in the ancient Mediterranean milieu.

In the Gospel of Mark, the first words of narration concerning Jesus briefly identify his geographical origins in terms of town and province: "In those days Jesus came from Nazareth of Galilee . . ." (Mark 1:9). Then the next few sentences narrate the story of his baptism (1:9-11), in which a voice from heaven climactically reveals Jesus' familial origins as a son of God ("You are my son, whom I love . . .").

Matthew's account, which uses Mark as a source, expands the Markan treatment. The opening line of the Gospel of Matthew names the topos at hand: "an account of the origin/birth (*genesis*) of Jesus the Messiah, the son of David, the son of Abraham." The Gospel then proceeds to trace a paternal genealogy from Abraham to Jesus (reminiscent of genealogies in the milieu; e.g., Suetonius, *Div. Aug.* 2.1; Josephus, *Life* 2.1), with the final line naming both parents but only explicitly tying Jesus to Mary by birth (Matt 1:16). With the genealogy complete, treatment of the topos continues: "Now the origin/birth (*genesis*) of Jesus the Messiah took place in this way" (1:18). The next four units may be seen as accounts of "origin" centered around prophecies invoked at the conclusion of each unit. The first unit (1:18-25) clarifies Jesus' divine familial origins by the virgin Mary in fulfillment of Isaiah 7:14: " 'Look, the virgin shall conceive and bear a son, and they shall name him Emmanuel,' which means, 'God with us.' " Units two through four (2:1-6; 2:7-15; 2:16-23) are accounts of Jesus' geographical origins, each telling the stories of marvelous occurrences surrounding Jesus' origins and accounting for his derivation, respectively, from Bethlehem, Egypt, and Nazareth of Galilee. Each unit closes with the prophecy fulfilled with regard to each place: "And you, Bethlehem, in the land of Judah, are by no means least among the rulers of Judah; for from you shall come a ruler who is to shepherd my people Israel" (2:6); "Out of Egypt I have called my son" (2:15); "He will be called a Nazorean" (2:23). Finally, the account of Jesus' baptism by John (3:1-17) completes the Matthean "account of the origin of Jesus." As in Mark, here a voice declares Jesus' divine origins as the son of God: "This is my Son, the Beloved, with whom I am well pleased" (3:17). The quotation continues the pattern of a unit devoted to origin (in this case, 3:1-17) ending with an oracle that speaks to the topos.

In Luke, the evangelist promises in the prologue to present an account that is rhetorically "in order" (*kathexēs*; Luke 1:3) and, accordingly, begins his story with the first topos.[58] Luke 1:1–4:13 may be seen as treatment of Jesus' origins and training (and in comparison with the origin and training of John the Baptist—see the chapter devoted to syncrisis). Standard materials belonging to the former are seen everywhere in this section. The opening words devoted to Jesus (1:26-27) name his home province (Galilee), city (Nazareth), presumable father (Joseph), and ancestors (house of David), and precisely in the order that Aphthonius commends (homeland, city, father, and ancestors). An account follows of his miraculous birth, complete with accompanying visions and oracles.

In John the materials of the prologue (1:1-18) are devoted to Jesus' origins as the eternal "Word" in heaven "with God" and as "God" before all creation—and his entrance into the world as such. The section establishes the basis for continued reflection on the theme throughout the rest of the Gospel:

> Nathanael said to him, "Can anything good *come out of Nazareth?*" (John 1:46)
>
> Then the Jews began to complain about him because he said, "I am the bread that *came down from heaven.*" They were saying, "Is not this Jesus, *the son of Joseph, whose father and mother we know?* How can he now say, 'I *have come down from heaven*'?" (6:41-42)
>
> Yet we know *where this man is from;* but when the Messiah comes, no one will know *where he is from.* Then Jesus cried out as he was teaching in the temple, "You know me, and you know *where I am from.* I have not come on my own. But the one who sent me is true, and you do not know him. I know him, because I am *from him,* and he sent me." (7:27-29)
>
> Others said, "This is the Messiah." But some asked, "Surely the Messiah does not *come from Galilee,* does he? Has not the scripture said that the Messiah is descended *from David and comes from Bethlehem,* the village where David lived?" (7:41-42)
>
> They replied, "Surely you are not also from Galilee, are you? Search and you will see that no prophet is to *arise from Galilee.*" (7:52)
>
> Jesus answered, "Even if I testify on my own behalf, my testimony is valid because I know *where I have come from* and where I am going, but you do not know *where I come from* or where I am going." (8:14)
>
> We know that God has spoken to Moses, but as for this man, we do not know *where he comes from.* (9:29)
>
> If this man were not *from God,* he could do nothing. (9:33)

One sees in these sentences contrasting perspectives on both the geographical and the familial origins of Jesus. Whereas insider perspective knows Jesus to derive from heaven/above and from the Father/God, outsider perspective knows only of Jesus' derivations from Nazareth/Galilee and his father and mother.[59]

In sum, one sees from these examples how a single subelement, origin, has left its stamp on a variety of genres in the New Testament, and in ways reflective of the culture's usual treatment of the topos.

Schemas of Narrative

The same schemas seen in the larger Mediterranean literary milieu are evident in New Testament narrative, as well, and these are often (though not always) matched with species of writing in accordance with progymnastic instruction:

(1) <u>Direct discourse</u>, or narration primarily using the nominative case, is frequently seen within "historical" narratives, per progymnastic instruction: e.g.,

"John [*nominative*] the baptizer [*nominative*] appeared in the wilderness, proclaiming [*nominative*] a baptism of repentance for the forgiveness of sins" (Mark 1:4; cf. Matt 1:1-16; 1:17a; Luke 13:1; John 1:1-5). As in the larger Mediterranean milieu, it is also true that historical narrative in the New Testament commonly adopts indirect discourse for its high literary style and pleasing variety. A good example is the proem of Luke, where the writer avoids the nominative in the main clause, employs all oblique cases, and even uses a construction—"it seemed good to me"—commended by Theon for indirect discourse (*Prog.* 102): ". . . it seemed good to me [*dative*] as well, having investigated [*dative*] everything [*dative*] carefully from the beginning, to write it out for you [*dative*] in consecutive order, most excellent [*vocative*] Theophilus [*vocative*], so that you might know the exact truth [*accusative*] about the things [*genitive*] you have been taught" (Luke 1:3-4; cf. Mark 1:29a; Matt 1:18b; 8:14; Luke 4:40; John 13:2). As a rule, Mark, Matthew, and John prefer the simple nominative subject constructions of direct discourse, while Luke tends to vary the cases more and mix in oblique declarative constructions frequently (see, e.g., Luke 3:1-2; cf. Mark 1:2; Matt 3:1; John 1:19-20; or Luke 3:21-22; cf. Mark 1:9; Matt 3:13-14; John 1:29).

(2) <u>*Oblique declarative discourse*</u>, prescribed by the theorists for narration for oratory (Ps.-Hermogenes: "trials"; Nicolaus: "arguments and refutations"), is found mixed accordingly throughout the *narratio* of Paul's speeches in Acts. A good example is Paul's defense in Acts 22:1-21, where Paul deftly moves beyond simple statements with nominative sentences to those featuring genitive and dative participial phrases and infinitival phrases with accusative subjects. At one point, Paul is represented using a common oblique construction ("And it happened to X") prescribed by Theon (*Prog.* 102) and running through subjects in all oblique cases: "And it happened to me [*dative*] that upon returning [*dative*] to Jerusalem, while I [*genitive*] was praying [*genitive*] in the temple, that I [*accusative*] fell into a trance" (Acts 22:17). Such attributed style contributes to the characterization of Paul in Acts as a trained orator. The opening *narratio* of Hebrews (1:5-14) similarly employs the high oblique declarative style per convention, varying both case and number throughout:

> For to which [*dative singular*] of the angels [*genitive plural*] did he ever say? (1:5)
> And to the angels [*accusative plural*] he says (1:7)
> And to which [*accusative singular*] of the angels [*genitive plural*] has he ever said? (1:13)
> Are not all [*nominative plural*] ministering spirits [*accusative plural*] . . . (1:14-15)

The clear use here of oblique declarative, together with additional schemas of narration (see below) provides additional evidence that the passage functions as *narratio* in the arrangement of the speech.[60]

(3) <u>*Interrogation*</u>, the schema where *narratio* occurs in question-and-answer form, is ideally suited for oratory and other similar persuasive discourse (Ps.-Hermogenes: dialectical debate; Nicolaus: arguments and refutations). The example of narrative just cited from Hebrews is a good example, in that it conducts its exposition from beginning to end in question-and-answer form. The passage thus combines multiple schemas in accordance with Theonic doctrine (oblique declarative, interrogative—also comparison [see below]). Paul's speeches in Acts also employ the device on occasion—for example, "Why is it thought incredible by any of you that God raises the dead?" (Act 26:8; cf. Acts 23:3). Also, as in the larger Mediterranean milieu, the schema occurs in argumentative written discourse intended for public reading. Paul, for example, employs it regularly in his letters in connection with exempla and other arguments: e.g., "What then are we to say was gained by Abraham, our ancestor according to the flesh? . . . For what does the scripture say? . . . Is this blessedness, then, pronounced only on the circumcised, or also on the uncircumcised? . . . How then was it reckoned to him? Was it before or after he had been circumcised?" (Rom 4:1, 3, 9, 10; cf. James 2:1-4; Heb 7:11).[61]

(4) <u>*Comparison*</u> is frequently employed in the New Testament as a mode of narration, and with the conventional aim of amplification of praise or blame. For example, Paul employs the schema in Romans in obvious amplification of Christ's gift: "But the free gift is not like the trespass. For if the many died through the one man's trespass, much more surely have the grace of God and the free gift in the grace of the one man, Jesus Christ, abounded for the many. And the free gift is not like the effect of the one man's sin. For the judgment following one trespass brought condemnation, but the free gift following many trespasses brings justification" (Rom 5:12-20; cf. Acts 24:12-16; Heb 3:1-6; 5:1-10; 7:1–10:18; 12:18-24).[62]

(5) <u>*Asyndeton*</u>, the schema in which all conjunctions are omitted for stylistic effect, occurs commonly in the New Testament, and often in the kind of contexts prescribed by the theorists.[63] In Hebrews 11, for example, the writer employs asyndeton for its concluding tenor, and for emphasis' sake, at the end of his famous parade of faithful exemplars: "And what more should I say? For time would fail me to tell of Gideon, Barak, Samson, Jephthah, of David and Samuel and the prophets—who through faith conquered kingdoms, administered justice, obtained promises, shut the mouths of lions, quenched raging fire, escaped the edge of the sword, won strength out of weakness, became mighty in war, put foreign armies to flight" (Heb 11:32-34). The passage features both kinds of asyndeton mentioned by Quintilian (*Inst.* 9.3.50), both with individual words (Gideon, Barak, Samson, etc.) and with clauses ("conquered kingdoms, administered justice, obtained promises . . ."). The passage certainly functions as a conclusion, per progymnastic recommendation, and as Quintilian prescribes, "When we are particularly insistent on something because our points are thus driven home one at a time and also, as it

were, made more numerous" (*Inst.* 9.3.50 [Russell, LCL]). It also displays a certain flair for the dramatic and so accords with Aristotle's observation that asyndeta are at home in oratory since "they lend themselves to acting" (*Rhet.* 3.12.2 [Freese, LCL]). Asyndeton is certainly at home, too, in the letters of the New Testament (cf. Quintilian's comments in *Inst.* 9.4.19–21 on the device's suitability for letter writing). Paul, for example, employs the device per progymnastic theory in a variety of conclusions: as epilogues to individual units (Rom 7:24; 11:33; 1 Cor 7:11b; Phil 4:18b), in concluding salutations (Rom 16:3; 1 Cor 16:19-20; 2 Cor 13:12; Phil 4:21-22; 1 Thess 5:26-27; Phlm 15), and in comments concluding entire letters (Rom 16:20; 1 Cor 16:21-24; 2 Cor 13:13; Gal 6:18; Phil 4:23; 1 Thess 5:28; Phlm 15).[64]

Editorial Practices

Last, one sees in cases where the use of New Testament materials as sources has been studied the same kinds of editorial practices taught in the schools and observed in the larger Mediterranean literary milieu. The classic, but sometimes overlooked, study in this regard remains E. P. Sanders' *The Tendencies of the Synoptic Tradition.*[65] In this study Sanders examines certain "laws" that New Testament scholarship at the time considered (and sometimes still considers) operative in the editing of source materials: that "later tradition" (i.e., edited material) is always marked by increasing length, increasing detail, decreasing Semitism, use of direct discourse, and conflation. What Sanders shows is that none of these tendencies holds—that in each case both the tendency and its opposite are widely observable in the history of transmission.

Such results are fully in keeping with, and anticipated by, progymnastic theory as it pertains to the editing of narrative. Hellenistic education, as we have seen, systematized and inculcated the very sets of opposite practices Sanders observes and documents: expansion and contraction, addition and omission, editing for clarity's sake (a motivation for decreasing Semitism) and for plausibility's sake (a motivation for increasing Semitism), recasting in direct discourse and in indirect discourse. Such results also accord with actual editorial practice in the ancient world. Classicists, as we have observed, have documented these same kinds of opposite editorial changes in their own literature. Thus, it is remarkable that a current generation of biblical scholars continues to operate with the kinds of outdated notions about unidirectional editorial "tendencies" that Sanders debunks, and to publish portraits of Jesus found not in any extant ancient text but rather in texts "reconstructed" by scholars largely on the basis of conviction about those debunked "tendencies."[66] At best, such efforts amount to well-intentioned but flawed historiography; and at worst, to the illiberal effacement of ancient artifacts in the name of modern religious ideology.

Conclusion

As the highest form of training Hellenistic education provided for narrative composition, the narrative progymnasmata are an important resource for ancient Mediterranean narratology. One encounters in these exercises culture-specific methods of composing and ordering the story world of a narrative (the "elements of narrative"), as well as established modes of narrating a story (the "schemas of narrative"). One also encounters ancient standards of criticism employed in the reception and editing of ancient narrative. Thus, the exercises illuminate the full experience of ancient Mediterranean story "telling"—everything from the composition and editing of stories to their transmission and reception—and so are invaluable for the study of all ancient Mediterranean narratives, including the New Testament.

Notes

1 For the following discussion see the narrative exercises of Theon (*Prog.* 78–96), Ps.-Hermogenes (*Prog.* 4–6), Aphthonius (*Prog.* 22), and Nicolaus (*Prog.* 11–17); cf. Quintilian, *Inst.* 1.9.6.
2 George A. Kennedy, *Progymnasmata: Greek Textbooks of Prose Composition and Rhetoric* (Atlanta: Society of Biblical Literature, 2003), 28n103.
3 These are Nicolaus' examples of the kinds of narrative materials one finds in a speech (*Prog.* 15).
4 See Seymour Chatman, *Story and Discourse Narrative Structure in Fiction and Film* (Ithaca, N.Y.: Cornell University Press, 1978), 1–42.
5 E.g., Theon's divisions of person are the same general divisions taught in the encomium, invective, and syncrisis progymnasmata (see the discussion in the chapters devoted to these), and in rhetorical handbooks' instruction concerning epideictic (Quintilian, *Inst.* 3.7.10–25) and *argumentatio* (Quintilian, *Inst.* 5.10.23). The divisions of action similarly correspond to headings for deliberative oratory (Quintilian, *Inst.* 3.8.22–35).
6 Chatman, *Story and Discourse*, 1–42.
7 Citations here and below concerning schemas are from Ps.-Hermogenes, *Prog.* 5–6, and Nicolaus, *Prog.* 16.
8 So Mikeal C. Parsons, "Luke and the Progymnasmata: A Preliminary Investigation into the Preliminary Exercises," in *Contextualizing Acts: Lukan Narrative and Greco-Roman Discourse*, ed. Todd Penner and Caroline Vander Stichele, SBLSS 20 (Atlanta: Scholars Press, 2004), 43–63.
9 David Aune, "Asyndeton," *WDNT*, 66–67.
10 Cf. Chatman's diagram in *Story and Discourse*, 267.
11 In this regard he anticipates modern critical distinctions between the two; see, e.g., Chatman, *Story and Discourse*, 63–67.
12 The distinction between history, drama, and mythos was hardly clear in the ancient world and should be imagined as spectral in nature. Histories and biographies often include what the theorists describe as mythical materials devoted to the gods. Histories and biographies also frequently dramatize events and, especially, speeches and dialogue. Novels and other dramas, meanwhile, often feature as main subjects historical figures, and just as often include mythical materials devoted to gods.
13 So Kennedy, *Progymnasmata*, 30n109.

14 On Thucydides' *History of the Peloponnesian War*, see Charles Forster Smith, *Thucydides: History of the Peloponnesian War*, LCL (Cambridge, Mass.: Harvard University Press, 2003), 1:vii–xxiii.

15 Except where otherwise indicated, here and below we have followed William Whiston's translation in *The Works of Josephus: Complete and Unabridged* (Nashville: Thomas Nelson, 1998).

16 Cf. H. St. J. Thackeray, *Josephus*, LCL (Cambridge, Mass.: Harvard University Press, 2004), 2:vii–xxxi.

17 On Eusebius' *Ecclesiastical History*, see the introduction of Kirsopp Lake, *Eusebius: The Ecclesiastical History*, LCL (Cambridge, Mass.: Harvard University Press, 1998), 1:vii–lvi.

18 For further discussion of the phenomenon, see the chapter on syncrisis.

19 Translations and references are from Simon Stern, ed., *The Life and Fables of Aesop: A Selection from the Version of Sir Roger L'Estrange* (New York: Taplinger, 1970).

20 On these two works as novels, see B. P. Reardon, ed., *Collected Ancient Greek Novels* (Berkeley: University of California Press, 2008), ix–xix. On the topical structure of the latter, see Michael W. Martin, "Progymnastic Topic Lists: A Compositional Template for Luke and Other *Bioi*," *NTS* 54 (2008): 18–41.

21 On the *Jewish Antiquities*, see H. St. J. Thackeray, *Josephus*, LCL (Cambridge, Mass.: Harvard University Press, 2001), 5:vii–xix.

22 *Pro Sexto Roscio Amerino*, one of the early speeches of Cicero, displays the arrangement commonly prescribed in the schools (in contrast to later speeches, which Cicero typically orders with greater license). On the speech generally, see John Henry Caplan, *Cicero*, LCL (Cambridge, Mass.: Harvard University Press, 2000), 6:112–21.

23 On Gorgias of Leontini and the sophists, see John Dillon and Tania Gergel, trans., *The Greek Sophists* (New York: Penguin, 2003), ix–xxiii, 43–97.

24 On *Agricola*, see the introduction by E. H. Warmington in *Tacitus*, LCL (Cambridge, Mass.: Harvard University Press, 2006), 1:3–24.

25 On Philo's *Life of Moses*, see F. H. Colson, *Philo*, LCL (Cambridge, Mass.: Harvard University Press, 2004), 6:vii–xx, 274–75.

26 On the *Life of Antony*, see Robert C. Gregg, *Athanasius: The Life of Antony and Letter to Marcellinus* (Mahway, N.J.: Paulist Press, 1980), 1–28.

27 Such organization is illuminated further by the rhetorical handbooks' teaching on encomium, and treatises devoted entirely to encomium, as the bios genre grew out of the encomium genre and took its essential structure from it. For further discussion, see Martin, "Progymnastic Topic Lists," 18–41; Michael W. Martin and Bryan A. Nash, "Philippians 2:6-11 as Subversive *Hymnos*: A Study in the Light of Ancient Rhetorical Design," *JTS* 66 (2008): 90–138.

28 See, again, the lists in Martin, "Progymnastic Topic Lists," 18–41.

29 Cf. Jerome H. Neyrey, "Encomium versus Vituperation: Contrasting Portraits in the Jesus in the Fourth Gospel," *JBL* 126 (2007): 529–52, following Aphthonius' subdivisions of origin (36).

30 Neyrey, "Encomium versus Vituperation," 529–52.

31 On the *Roman Antiquities*, see Earnest Cary, *Dionysius of Halicarnassus*, LCL (Cambridge, Mass.: Harvard University Press, 2001), 1:vii–xlviii.

32 On the *Iliad*, see William F. Wyatt, *Homer: Iliad*, LCL (Cambridge, Mass.: Harvard University Press, 1999), 1:1–9.

33 On Susanna, see Lawrence M. Wills, ed. and trans., *Ancient Jewish Novels: An Anthology* (Oxford: Oxford University Press, 2002), 51–54.

34 On *Daphnis and Chloe*, see Christopher Gill, "Longus: Daphnis and Chloe," in *Collected Ancient Greek Novels*, ed. B. P. Reardon (Berkeley: University of California Press, 2008), 285–88.

35 On *narratio* in this particular speech, see Michael de Brauw, "The Parts of the Speech," in *A Companion to Greek Rhetoric*, ed. Ian Worthington (Malden, Mass.: Blackwell, 2007), 187–202, esp. 190–94; on Demosthenes and this speech generally, see A. T. Murray, *Demosthenes*,

LCL (Cambridge, Mass.: Harvard University Press, 1936), 4:vii–ix, 276–77; cf. J. H. Vince, *Demosthenes*, LCL (Cambridge, Mass.: Harvard University Press, 2004), 1:xi–xxiiii.

36 As Murray observes, "Sphettus was a deme of the tribe of Acamantis" (*Demosthenes*, 4:281 n. a).

37 On Diogenes Laertius, see the introduction by Herbert S. Long in *Diogenes Laertius: Lives of Eminent Philosophers*, trans. R. D. Hicks, LCL (Cambridge, Mass.: Harvard University Press, 2006), 1:xi–xxvi.

38 On Philostratus' *Apollonius of Tyana*, see Christopher P. Jones, *Philostratus: The Life of Apollonius of Tyana*, LCL (Cambridge, Mass.: Harvard University Press, 2005), 1:1–30.

39 On Suetonius and *Divus Augustus*, see the introduction by K. R. Bradley in *Suetonius: Lives of the Caesars*, trans. J. C. Rolfe, LCL (Cambridge, Mass.: Harvard University Press, 1998), 1:1–34.

40 On Plutarch's *Parallel Lives*, see Bernadotte Perrin, *Plutarch: Lives*, LCL (Cambridge, Mass.: Harvard University Press, 2005), 1:vii–xxi.

41 On Josephus' treatment of his origins, see Jerome H. Neyrey, "Josephus' *Vita* and the Encomium: A Native Model of Personality," *JSJ* 25 (1994): 177–206; cf. Michael W. Martin, "Progymnastic Topic Lists," 18–41. On the *Vita* in general, see H. St. J. Thackeray, *Josephus*, LCL (Cambridge, Mass.: Harvard University Press, 2008), 1:vii–xx.

42 Herbert T. Weiskotten, ed. and trans., *Sancti Augustini vita scripta a Possidio episcope*, rev. ed. (Princeton: Princeton University Press, 1919).

43 On the arrangement of the speech and its use of *narratio*, see Jan Willem van Henten, "Commonplaces in Herod's Commander Speech in Josephus' *A.J.* 15.127–146," in *Josephus and Jewish History in Flavian Rome and Beyond*, ed. Joseph Sievers and Gaia Lembi, SJSJ (Leiden: Brill, 2005), 183–206, esp. 186–89.

44 Ronald Mellor, *The Roman Historians* (New York: Routledge, 1999), 67–68; see also T. J. Luce, *Livy: The Composition of His History* (Princeton: Princeton University Press, 1977), xxvi.

45 Mellor, *Roman Historians*, 67.

46 Mellor, *Roman Historians*, 68.

47 Christopher Pelling, *Plutarch and History: Eighteen Studies* (London: Duckworth; Swansea: Classical Press of Wales, 2002), 94; emphasis in original.

48 Katherine M. Stott's summation of the practices observed in these studies could as easily be a summation of the school practices: "In utilizing a particular account, historians were not averse to copying their source virtually word for word; however, they could also 'omit, expand, abridge and change' material when it suited their purposes" (*Why Did They Write This Way? Reflections on References to Written Documents in the Hebrew Bible and Ancient Literature* [New York: T&T Clark, 2008], 34).

49 The passage in view frames Jerusalem as more holy than Israel, and Israel as more holy than space beyond. Cf. David W. Pau who observes the three geographical stages in terms of the New Exodus: salvation in Jerusalem, the reunification/constitution of Israel (= in *all* Judea and Samaria), and the inclusion of the nations (*Acts and the Isaianic New Exodus*, WUNT 2/130 [Tübingen: Mohr Siebeck, 2000], 95).

50 Disjointed *narratio* is widely attested in theory (Aristotle, *Rhet.* 3.16.1–2, 11; *Rhet. Alex.* 31; Cicero, *Inv.* 1.30; Quintilian, *Inst.* 4.2.101; 4.2.82; Anon. Seg. 32–3) and in practice (noting his own use, Quintilian, *Inst.* 4.2.86; noting Cicero's in *Pro Cluentio*, Quintilian *Inst.* 4.2.85; noting Dionysius of Halicarnassus' use in *De Isaeo*, and Demosthenes' in *Pro Phormione* and *Contra Lacritum*, Michael de Brauw, "The Parts of the Speech," 190, 193–94). For these references and a fuller discussion, see Michael W. Martin and Jason A. Whitlark, *Inventing Hebrews: Design and Purpose in Ancient Rhetoric* (Cambridge: Cambridge University Press, forthcoming in 2018), ch. 6.

51 Paul, e.g., cites ignorance in defense of his violation of the law in Acts 23:1-5.

52 On this debate, see Martin and Whitlark, *Inventing Hebrews*, ch. 1.

53 See Martin and Whitlark, *Inventing Hebrews*, chs. 5 and 6, who argue that Hebrews, in fact, consists of five units of alternating *narratio* and *argumentatio* in what the theorists call "disjointed" structure.

54 Richard A. Burridge, *What Are the Gospels: A Comparison with Graeco-Roman Biography*, 2d ed. (Grand Rapids: Eerdmans, 2004), 200–202, 24–25.

55 On the latter exercises, see the corresponding chapters in this volume.

56 Cf. Philip L. Shuler, "The Genre(s) of the Gospels," in *Interrelations of the Gospels*, ed. David Laird Dungan (Louvain: Leuven University Press, 1990), 459–83; idem, *A Genre for the Gospels: The Biographical Character of Matthew* (Philadelphia: Fortress, 1982), 53–56, 92–98; Martin, "Progymnastic Topic Lists," 18–41; Mikeal C. Parsons, *Luke*, PCNT (Grand Rapids: Baker, 2015), 13–16. Burridge briefly raises the possibility of influence but demurs, saying, "Such lists are designed for school use in rhetorical and encomiastic exercises, rather than for writing, and they are later than most of our works" (*What Are the Gospels*, 200). But on both points, Burridge is simply incorrect: the lists have origins as old as Plato, as the exercises themselves acknowledge (see Nicolaus, *Prog.* 50); and the exercises in which those lists appear were designed as preparation for both declamation *and writing*—and the narrative exercise especially so (see Theon, *Prog.* 60)—hence the subtitle in George A. Kennedy's translation, *Progymnasmata: Greek Textbooks of Prose Composition and Rhetoric*. Indeed, the narrative exercise was the one place in the entire course of Hellenistic education where students were *most directly prepared* for prose narrative composition such as biography.

57 Cf. Bryan A. Nash, "Philippians 3:4-11 as Subversive Encomium," *Stone-Campbell Journal* 19 (2016): 85–94.

58 Cf. the discussion in Parsons, *Luke*, 24–31.

59 Neyrey, "Encomium versus Vituperation," 529–52, esp. 540.

60 The primary evidence being its place in the outline of the speech after the exordium (1:1-4) and before *argumentatio* (i.e., thesis and proof in the form of deliberative comparison; 2:1-4), and its auxiliary function in service to the *argumentatio*; see the discussion in Martin and Whitlark, *Inventing Hebrews*, ch. 6.

61 Interrogation (or "enquiry" according to Theon's divisions) here is used as the theorists suggest, for "arguments and refutations." Specifically, the schema is used to narrate a historical example—one of the two main forms of arguments taught in the handbooks, and one of the specific forms of narrative Nicolaus says the progymnasma is designed to teach.

62 The Theonic figure of negation is also employed in this example (i.e., "the free gift is *not like* . . .").

63 For a fuller discussion and numerous examples, see Aune, "Asyndeton," 66–67.

64 So Aune, "Asyndeton," 66–67; following Eberhard W. Güting and David L. Mealand, *Asyndeton in Paul: A Text-Critical and Stylistical Enquiry into Pauline Style* (Lewiston, Idaho: Edwyn Mellen, 1998), 10–23. See the latter for a full discussion of the device in Paul.

65 E. P. Sanders, *The Tendencies of the Synoptic Tradition*, SNTSMS 9 (New York: Cambridge University Press, 1969).

66 The Jesus Seminar employs such a modus operandi: see, e.g., Robert W. Funk, Bernard Brandon Scott, and James R. Butts, *The Parables of Jesus: Red Letter Edition: The Jesus Seminar* (Sonoma, Calif.: Polebridge, 1988); Robert W. Funk, Row W. Hoover, and the Jesus Seminar, *The Five Gospels: The Search for the Authentic Words of Jesus* (New York: Polebridge, 1993). For similar criticisms as these on the basis of Sanders' study, see Mark Goodacre, *Thomas and the Gospels: The Case for Thomas' Familiarity with the Synoptics* (Grand Rapids: Eerdmans, 2012), 143–50.

4

Ekphrasis

Writing for Ears and *Eyes*

> Ecphrasis (*ekphrasis*) is descriptive language, bringing what is portrayed clearly before the sight.
>
> Theon

Theory

Definition

There is remarkable agreement among the theorists in terms of the definition of *ekphrasis*. This conformity is due in part to the fact that other versions were lost during the transmission of the exercises over the centuries.[1] The later theorists agree with Theon (see epithet above) that ekphrasis is vivid language intended for the eyes and not just the ears. Pseudo-Hermogenes echoes Theon: "Ecphrasis (*ekphrasis*) is descriptive speech, as they say, vivid (*enargēs*) and bringing what is being shown before the eyes" (*Prog.* 22; cf. Aphthonius, *Prog.* 46; Nicolaus, *Prog.* 68). Unfortunately, this definition does not penetrate deeply into the functions and purposes of ekphrasis: "As textbooks, they lack the background of oral explanation, practice and example which would have complemented them in antiquity." Rather, "the most important thing that students learned by working through the *Progymnasmata* was not rules as such but a set of practices and skills that could be put to use in (or transferred to) the composition of full-scale speeches or other types of composition."[2]

This brief and rather vague definition stands in sharp contrast to definitions proffered by classicists and others from the early to mid-twentieth century whose definition focused on content and limited the term to extended literary descriptions of visual artifacts, such as murals or buildings or shields. Pride of place belongs to Homer's description of Achilles' shield (*Il.* 18.478–608) as the earliest example of a literary description of a visual artifact. Homer describes in detail the fashioning of the shield by Hephaestus. The ekphrasis begins:

> First fashioned he a shield, great and sturdy, adorning it cunningly in every part, and round about it set a bright rim, threefold and glittering, and therefrom made fast a silver baldric. Five were the layers of the shield itself; and on it he wrought many curious devices with cunning skill.
>
> Therein he wrought the earth, therein the heavens therein the sea, and the unwearied sun, and the moon at the full, and therein all the constellations wherewith heaven is crowned—the Pleiades, and the Hyades and the mighty Orion, and the Bear. (*Il.* 18.478–483)[3]

Along similar lines is the lengthy description of the shield of Aeneas in Virgil's *Aeneid* 8.626–728, in which Virgil is likely self-consciously imitating Homer. Virgil begins his ekphrasis of Vulcan's fashioning of the shield with these words:

> There [on the shield] the Lord of Fire, well-versed in the seers and aware of the age to come, had worked Italian affairs and the triumphs of the Romans, there [too] the whole family that would spring from Ascanius and their wars fought in order. He had also worked the mother wolf, stretched out in the green cave of Mars; around her teats hung the twin boys, playing and without fear licked their mother. (*Aen.* 8.626–633)[4]

For those (modern) scholars who viewed the shield of Achilles (or Aeneas) as the standard by which to judge other descriptions' qualifications to be categorized as ekphrases, there is little in the New Testament in terms of length and detail that would convince them that this device was part of the early Christian repertoire. One exception to this observation might be the description of the new Jerusalem in Revelation 21:9-21.

> Then one of the seven angels . . . carried me away to a great, high mountain and showed me the holy city Jerusalem coming down out of heaven from God. It has the glory of God and a radiance like a very rare jewel, like jasper, clear as crystal. It has a great, high wall with twelve gates, and at the gates twelve angels, and on the gates are inscribed the names of the twelve tribes of the Israelites; on the east three gates, on the north three gates, on the south three gates, and on the west three gates. And the wall of the city has twelve foundations, and on them are the twelve names of the twelve apostles of the Lamb. The angel who talked to me had a measuring rod of gold to measure the city and its gates and walls. The city lies foursquare, its length the same as its width; and he measured the city with his rod, fifteen hundred miles; its length and width and height are equal. He also measured its wall, one hundred forty-four cubits by human measurement, which the angel was using. The wall is built of jasper, while the city is pure gold, clear as glass. The foundations of the wall of the city are adorned with every jewel; the first was jasper, the second sapphire, the third agate, the fourth emerald, the fifth onyx, the sixth carnelian, the seventh chrysolite, the eighth beryl, the ninth topaz, the tenth chrysoprase, the eleventh jacinth, the

> twelfth amethyst. And the twelve gates are twelve pearls, each of the gates is a single pearl, and the street of the city is pure gold, transparent as glass.

Still, this rather lengthy ekphrasis in Revelation is the exception that proves the rule.

The ancient understanding of ekphrasis attends to the *impact* of the description on the audience, placing the event or object or person before their eyes and inviting their participation.[5] We see this in the language used in the *Progymnasmata* to define ekphrasis. For Theon ekphrasis is *logos periēgēmatikos*, which Kennedy (45) translates as "descriptive language." The term has connotations of a guide showing sights (like Pausanias leading the reader around Greece in his travelogue, *Description of Greece*).[6] Nicolaus changes the term to *aphegēmatikos*, which Kennedy (166) translates as "*bringing* what is described clearly before the eyes." According to Webb, the context of "bringing" or "leading" before the eye suggests the spectators in a theater in which "the dramatist . . . literally produces characters and actions on stage, placing them before the eyes of the audience."[7] In both cases, the emphasis is on the experience of the audience who is guided around the subject or experiences the drama as a spectator.

Thus, the *Progymnasmata* do not require that the term *ekphrasis* be limited to extended descriptions of visual artifacts. While Theon does reference the shield of Achilles (cited above) as an example of an ekphrasis of an object (in this case, an implement of battle), other examples Theon cites are exceptionally brief, and it is not until Nicolaus that we have "statues and pictures" included among possible ekphrastic subjects (*Prog.* 69). As an example of an ekphrasis of a person, he cites the descriptions of Eurybates in Homer's *Odyssey* 19.246 as "round shouldered, swarthy-skinned, wooly-haired" and Thersites in the *Iliad* 2.217–218 as "bandy-legged, lame in one foot, and his two shoulders stooped over his chest" (*Prog.* 118). Similarly brief are the descriptions Theon cites from Herodotus of the Egyptian ibis (2.76), hippopotami (2.71), and crocodiles (2.68). Thus, the student is taught to use vivid language in describing persons, places, and events, and the length of such descriptions was apparently of lesser concern to the ancients than to modern scholars. Nonetheless, in cases where the vivid language is limited to a phrase, or even a word, it may be better to speak of it as reflecting an "ekphrastic" perspective (rather than an example of a full-blown ekphrasis).[8] Thus, the exercise in ekphrasis allows for transference of skills in a variety of ways and in multiple contexts, and, as with other exercises, we need not expect rigid "rules" to be followed slavishly in composition.

Despite the similarities in the definition for ekphrasis among the progymnasmatists, variation did exist regarding the placement of the exercise on ekphrasis or description. Theon places ekphrasis fifth (of ten exercises) after topos or commonplace and before ethopoeia (also called prosopopoeia by some), while Pseudo-Hermogenes, Aphthonius, and Nicolaus place it after ethopoeia/prosopopoeia as either tenth of twelve (Ps.-Hermogenes and Nicolaus) or twelfth of fourteen (Aphthonius).[9] Its placement in these latter three writers indicates that they judged ekphrasis one of the more difficult exercises for the beginning student to master.

Ekphrastic Subjects

The emphasis on impact rather than content among the progymnasmata puts the list of "subjects" appropriate for ekphrastic description in a different light. On the one hand, there is some variation in what constitutes a proper subject for an ekphrasis. Theon observes, "There is ecphrasis of persons and events and places and periods of time" (*Prog.* 118; cf. Ps.-Hermogenes, *Prog.* 22; Aphthonius, *Prog.* 46).[10] Later, Nicolaus added festivals (*Prog.* 68) and statues and paintings (*Prog.* 69) to the list of subjects. On the other hand, variation in the list of ekphrastic subjects are inconsequential since the four categories that Theon lists—persons, places, times, and events—are Theon's same four "elements of narration." They constitute "the 'who, what, when, and where' of the ancient rhetorical schools"; in other words, person, place, time, and event are "rhetorician-speak for 'practically everything'" (see table 5.1).[11] The relationship between ekphrasis and the other exercises (especially narrative) was so close that Pseudo-Hermogenes reports that "some of the more exact teachers do not make ecphrasis an exercise, on the ground that it has already been included in fable and narrative and common-place and encomium" (*Prog.* 23).[12]

Table 5.1. Comparison of Ekphrastic Subjects with Parts of Narration in Progymnasmata

Author	Subjects for ekphrasis	Parts of Narration
Theon	Events, persons, places, times, *tropoi*	Person, event, place, time, manner (*tropos*), cause
Ps.-Hermogenes	Persons, events, places, states of affairs, times	
Aphthonius	Persons, events, seasons, places, mute animals and plants	Person, event, place, time, manner (*tropos*), cause
Nicolaus	Places, seasons, persons, festivals, events, paintings and statues	Person, event, place, time, manner (*tropos*), cause

Furthermore,[13] the "fact that the entries on *ekphrasis* in the progymnasmata vary, and that the list of ekphrastic subjects increases from one handbook to the next, shows that ekphrasis has never been established to be a static and stable convention. Therefore, a capacious rather than purist approach to identifying the form and function of ekphrasis seems most appropriate" (see table 5.2).[14] We turn now to a brief discussion of the form and function of ekphrasis in ancient rhetorical theory.[15]

Table 5.2. Ekphrastic Subjects in the Progymnasmata

Author	Topic	Theon	Ps.-Hermogenes	Aphthonius	Nicolaus
Homer, *Od.* 19.246	Person	X		X	
Homer, *Il.* 2.217–218	Person	X	X		
Homer, *Il.* 18.478–615	Object: shield	X			
Herodotus 2.68–76	Animals	X			
Thucydides 1.46	Place: harbor			X	
Thucydides 2.2–5	Mixed	X			
Thucydides 3.21	Object: wall	X			
Thucydides 4.100	Object: siege engine	X			
Thucydides 3.22	Event: night battle	X	X		
Thucydides 7.44	Event: night battle	X	X	X	
Ctesias, frag. 688	Flag	X			
Aphthonius, *Prog.* 47–49	Shrine (own)			X	
Demosthenes 19.65	Suffering				X

Formal Elements of Ekphrasis

Theon lists the following virtues of an ekphrasis: "most of all, clarity and a vivid impression of all-but-seeing what is described; next one . . . should make the style reflect the subject" (*Prog.* 119). These "virtues" are essentially formal elements of "traits" typical of most ekphrasis.[16] We will treat each of these traits, beginning with style (*lezis*), then clarity (*sapheneia*), and finally, what is arguably the most important feature of ekphrasis, vividness (*enargeia*).[17]

(1) Style. Theon says that "style should reflect the subject, so that if what it describes is colorful, the word choice should be colorful, but if it is rough or frightening or something like that, features of the style should not strike a discordant note with the nature of the subject" (*Prog.* 119–120). Likewise, Pseudo-Hermogenes writes that "the word choice ought to correspond to the subject. If

the subject is flowery, let the style be so too; if the subject is dry, let the style be similar" (*Prog.* 23). Nicolaus connects style with emotional response: "We need a varied style in it [ekphrasis]; for the kind of expression we use should fit the proposed subject, whether we make it sweet or render happenings tragic or impart some other emotion" (*Prog.* 70–71). Nicolaus cites the example of Demosthenes' description of suffering at Phocis after a battle. That text reads:

> Not long ago, when we were traveling to Delphi, necessity compelled us to look upon all those things [the aftermath of battle]—homes razed to the ground, walls stripped away, a countryside bereft of its youth; only women, a few children, and pitiable old men. No one was able to express in words the evils that exist in that country today. (Demosthenes, *Fals. leg.* 19.65)

The language Demosthenes uses is heavy with misery; he and his companions are of "necessity compelled" to observe the ravages of war, concluding that the suffering they observed was beyond words. The style of Demosthenes stands in sharp contrast, for example, to Clitophon's erotic description of his garden in Achilles Tatius' novel.[18]

> It [the garden] was in fact a grove of very pleasant aspect . . . Protected with the columns stood a populous assembly of trees. A network of sturdy branches interlaced to form an intricate pattern wherein petals gently embraced their neighbours, leaves wound round other leaves, and fruits rubbed softly on other fruits. Thus far the world of plants knows intercourse.
>
> Ivy and bindweed raveled their way around some of the massy trunks: the bindweed clung to the plane tree by a soft reticulation of tendrils, while the ivy spiraled intimately among the pine boughs. This symbiosis provided support for the ivy and ivy wreaths of honor for the tree. . . .
>
> The flowers of various colors displayed their beauty in turn—violet, narcissus, rose—the earth's dyed stuffs. The calyx of the rose has the same contour as that of the narcissus—a natural drinking cup. . . . The violet's calyx is nowhere to be seen; its color is like that of sunlight flashing on a still sea. (1.15 [Winkler, *CAGN* 186–87])

Gone is Demosthenes' morbid language, appropriate to an ekphrasis of postwar suffering; rather, with Clitophon we now have the erotic description of a garden as a "world of plants" that "knows intercourse." A later author of a Byzantine progymnasmata suggested using words with gutturals and aspirates (e.g., kappa, gamma, and chi) in an ekphrasis describing a battle and specifically suggested using terms such as *smaragē, klangē, chremetismos, kraugē*.[19] Fitting style to substance was not always an easy task, and at least one Byzantine scholiast wryly complained: "I suppose one ought to grunt (*grulizein*) when talking about piglets."[20] Allowing, even encouraging, style to fit the subject matter, even if it produces "flowery" language, reflects in the progymasmata a flexibility not always found among ancient rhetoricians.[21]

(2) Clarity. Having already discussed clarity as one of the three virtues (along with conciseness and plausibility of narrative; Theon, *Prog.* 79), Theon perhaps felt little need to say more about it in the exercise on ekphrasis other than that it is a virtue. According to Theon, clarity is achieved mostly through avoiding long digressions, poetic or coined words, as well as archaisms, foreign words, and homonyms (for all of which he gives specific examples; *Prog.* 81; cf. also Longinus, *Subl.* 3.1). For Theon, style and clarity are intimately connected. Together, clarity and style are necessary for the hearer "to imagine or see in the mind's eye something described"; "one needs clear and unambiguous language."[22]

(3) Vividness. By far, the most important trait or formal element of ekphrasis is "vividness" (*enargeia*); each of the progymnasmata uses a form of the word *enargeia* in its definition.[23] In fact, "vividness" may be said to be what distinguishes "plain" narration from ekphrasis. Nicolaus claims: "'Clearly' [*enargos*] is added because in this way it most differs from narration; the latter gives a plain exposition of actions, the former tries to make the hearers into spectators" (*Prog.* 68). To illustrate the distinction between narrative and ekphrasis, Nicolaus gives this example:

> It [ekphrasis] differs from narration in that the latter examines things as a whole, the former in part; for example, it belongs to a narration to say "The Athenians and Peloponnesians fought a war," and to ecphrasis to say that each side made this and that preparation and sued this manner of arms. (*Prog.* 68–69)

While the definition of "vividness" is here *in nuce* in the *Progymnasmata*, for a fuller explanation of "vividness" and the function(s) of ekphrasis one must turn to the rhetorical handbooks.

The Function(s) of Ekphrasis

Enargeia, phantasia, and the "enslavement" of the audience. In book 8 of his *Institutio oratoria*, Quintilian remarks on the virtue of vivid speech in a juridical context. *Enargeia* has the goal of "setting forth our facts in such a striking manner that they seem to be placed before our eyes as vividly as though they were taking place in our actual presence" (8.3.62 [Russell, LCL]).[24] Later, Quintilian distinguishes (in a way reminiscent of Nicolaus) between narratives that give a "brief statement" of events that "penetrates the emotions less" and those that employ vividness (*enargeia*) that will "open up things which were included within a single phrase" (8.3.67).[25] He then gives the stock example of the sacking of a city to illustrate his point.

> There will come into view flames racing through houses and temples, the crash of falling roofs, the single sound made up of many cries, the blind flight of some, others clinging to their dear ones in a last embrace, shrieks of children and

> women, the old men whom an unkind fate has allowed to live to see this day; then will come the pillage of property, secular and sacred, the frenzied activity of plunderers carrying off their booty and going back for more, the prisoners driven in chains before their captors, the mother who tries to keep her child with her, and the victors fighting one another wherever the spoils are richer. (*Inst.* 8.3.67–69 [Russell, LCL])[26]

Elsewhere in book 4, Quintilian discusses vividness (*enargeia*) in his remarks on narration ("statement of facts"), from which one may deduce that Quintilian thought of *enargeia* as a "quality to be added to various types of discourse."[27] *Enargeia* is used to create powerful mental images (*phantasiai*) in the audience to elicit an emotional response: "The images of absent things are presented to the mind in such a way that we actually see them with our eyes and have them physically present to us. Whoever has mastery of them will have the most powerful effect on the emotions" (6.2.29–30 [Russell, LCL]). "Quintilian's explanation of the role of *phantasia* in both the creation and the reception of vivid language helps to explain why it was reasonable for him and other ancient theoreticians to speak of language's ability to 'make visible' its subject matter."[28] The orator or writer uses words to help the audience see what the author sees. The impact of language on the imagination could not, according to ancient rhetoricians, be overestimated. Longinus claims that "rhetorical visualization" (*rhetorikē phantasia*) not only persuades the listener: "It enslaves him" (*Subl.* 15.9). Such was the power of words that Plutarch advised that the young should be given earplugs to safeguard them against harmful and inappropriate speech (*De aud.* [*Mor.* 37F–38B]).[29] Plutarch also counseled that "the most powerful historian is he who . . . makes his narration like a painting. . . . He [in this case, Thucydides] is desperately keen to make the listener a viewer and to produce in those who read about events the vivid emotions of amazement and confusion that were experienced by those who saw them" (*Mor.* 347A). Ekphrasis was animated by vividness, clarity, and style in the service of phantasia, and phantasia was "a rhetorical weapon to get around the censor of the intellect" and persuade the audience to adopt the speaker's point of view or, in its most extreme and provocative expression, to "enslave" the audience through an emotionally evocative and compelling visual re-presentation that makes the listener into a participant/spectator.[30]

Ekphrasis and moral judgment. There is one other area where the theory and practice of ekphrasis in antiquity were in tension with each other. In his chapter on ekphrasis, Theon compares topos and ekphrasis. The two share in common a concern for generalities and are less concerned with particulars. He distinguishes between them by claiming that topos includes one's own judgment, "saying something is good or bad," while "in ecphrasis there is only a plain description of the subject" (Theon, *Prog.* 119).[31] Here as elsewhere, Theon is not consistent. For example, as we have seen, Theon encouraged the student to use language that reflects the subject described. "Colorful" subjects demand a colorful word choice; likewise, rough or frightening subjects require a style that "does not strike a discordant note with the nature of the subject" (*Prog.* 119). In either case, however, whether the subject is "colorful" or "frightening" is a judgment on the writer's part. Theon's examples of ekphrasis "clearly include particulars (Thersites, the shield of Achilles, etc.), and in literature ecphrasis regularly includes subjective remarks on the beauty, greatness, or terror of what is described. In describing ecphrasis as not concerned with particulars he is probably thinking of descriptions of a storm, earthquake, spring, etc."[32]

That moral choice or judgment may be an aspect of ekphrasis is especially true in the case of ekphrases of persons (but not limited to them). Many times the description of the person is intended to convey a judgment on the person's character, that is, the physical description of the person can reflect his or her moral character in the form of praise or criticism.[33] In these instances, ekphrasis is a rhetorical technique in service (or in some cases, in subversion) of physiognomy, a popular pseudoscience in antiquity.[34]

For example, in his handbook on oratory, Cicero claims that "everything rests with face, and the face in turn is under the power of the eyes. . . . And the eyes are the index of the emotions. . . . No one can achieve the same end with eyes closed" (*De or.* 3.221–222). Elsewhere Cicero maintains that nature "has so formed his [human] features as to portray therein the character that lies hidden deep within him; for not only do the eyes declare with exceeding clarity the innermost feelings of our hearts, but also the countenance, as we Romans call it, which can be found in no other living being, save man, reveals the character" (*Leg.* 1.9.26). Thus, descriptions of persons were often pressed into service of encomiastic praise or, more often, as a strategy of invective to criticize or condemn the person or character. We will see this aspect of ekphrasis in a number of the examples from ancient literature cited below.

Examples from Ancient Literature

The focus of ekphrasis in ancient rhetoric was the impact it produced on the audience. As such, as we have noted, "practically anything" might be the subject of an ekphrasis; the topics were certainly not limited to visual artifacts, or even to persons, places, events, or times. Still, persons, places, and events provide a convenient way of organizing examples of ekphrasis in the literary environs of the New Testament writers.

Persons/Animate Characters

As already noted, "persons" as an ekphrastic category was rather elastic and, for Theon, could refer to the ibis, hippopotamus, or crocodile. We include here, then, both humans and animals that were the subjects of ekphrases.[35] In almost all the cases, the physical description aids the audience in gaining a deeper understanding of the narrator's viewpoint on the person's moral character or the person's role in the unfolding plot.[36]

Graeco-Roman

Thersites. An early instance of ekphrasis of persons is found in the Homeric line that Theon quotes about Thersites: "He was bandy-legged, lame in one foot, and his two shoulders stooped over his chest" (Theon, *Prog.* 118.13–15).[37] The physical description of Thersites couples with his actions in Homer to portray him as a negative character. We see this clearly when we compare Homer's description with later physiognomic theory. The physiognomic handbooks reflect traditional physiognomic conventions that have evolved over several centuries. It is not surprising to see evidence of physiognomy in practice well before the time of the appearance of the handbooks themselves, as we observe here in Homer. In a symbiotic relationship, the earlier usage helped create the conventions, and the conventions helped shape and interpret the usage.[38]

Thus, the ekphrasis of Thersites fits well into the physiognomic conventions later recorded in Pseudo-Aristotle.[39] Homer describes Thersites as the "most shameful man" (*aischistos anēr*) ever to come to Ilios and then offers the physical description cited as an ekphrasis by Theon, as evidence of that judgment: "he was bandy-legged and lame in the one foot, and his two shoulders were rounded, stooping together over his chest [and in a passage not quoted by Theon] and above them his head was pointed, and a scant stubble grew thereon" (*Il.* 2.216–219).

The later physiognomic handbooks confirm Homer's negative assessment. According to Pseudo-Aristotle, those whose "shoulders are driven into the chest are of evil disposition" (810b). "Pointed" heads are a sign of the "shameless" or "impudent" (812a).[40] "Roundedness" is, according to Adamantius, a sign of the "stupidly wicked" (1.425.4). Finally, Pseudo-Aristotle's comments about feet are likewise illuminating: "Those who have small, narrow, poorly-jointed feet, are . . . weak in character" (810a). Thersites is the only nonelite mentioned by name in Homer's *Iliad*. And, in Homer's ekphrastic language, Thersites is characterized, from head to foot, as an evil, shameless, and weak man, indeed the "most shameful man" ever to come to Ilios, a negative characterization fulfilled in the immediate episode (where Thersites chides Achilles, Odysseus, and Agamemnon only to be upbraided by Odysseus) and confirmed by later physiognomic canons.[41]

Thersites is mentioned a couple of times in the progymnasmata, once more by Theon (*Prog.* 112), and once by Libanius (ex. 4, encomium of Thersites, *Prog.* 8.4.1–19). Theon understands that Thersites is hardly a noble or laudatory character, a point made clear later in his discussion of synkrises (comparisons), where he makes the following observation: "Let it be specified that syncrises are not comparisons of things having a great difference between them; for someone wondering whether Achilles or Thersites was braver was laughable" (*Prog.* 112).[42] It is reasonable to conclude that at least part of Theon's negative judgment about Thersites is due to his (im)moral character, implied by his physical appearance and borne out in the subsequent narrative. Thus, Theon, despite his protests that ekphrasis is not concerned with matters of "moral judgment," combines ekphrasis with the basic physiognomic premise that outward physical appearance is a clue to inward moral character and, by choice of example, encourages his reader to accept it, too. Even Libanius' encomium on Thersites is, in a sense, to display Libanius' rhetorical prowess, not necessarily to extol the "virtues" of Thersites. In other words, he has chosen the "extreme case" to try and praise one about whom "Homer has spoken badly." Thus, the encomium may say less about divided opinion in antiquity about how to view Thersites and more about Libanius' abilities.

Silvia's stag. In book 7 of Virgil's *Aeneid* is the story of a domesticated stag that has been tracked and shot by Iulus; the event initiates the conflict between the Trojans and the indigenous population of Italy. The ekphrasis of the stag is the only physical description of an animal throughout Virgil's writings.[43]

> There was a stag of wondrous beauty and mighty antlers, which, torn from its mother's breast, the sons of Tyrrhus nurtured, and Tyrrhus, their sire, controller of the royal herds and charged with care of pastures near and far. Their sister Silvia had trained it to obey, and with constant love she adorned it, twining its horns with soft garlands, combing the wild thing's coat, and bathing it in the crystal spring. Tame to handling and accustomed to food from its master, it roved the woods, and of its own accord went home again to the well-known door, however late the night. (*Aen.* 7.483–495 [Fairclough, LCL])

Virgil's ekphrasis of Silvia's stag presents a metamorphosis of a stag who is forcibly taken from its mother and is gradually "civilized," a domestication symbolized by the combing, bathing, and feeding that are part of the daily rounds of human existence.[44] The "civilized" stag stands in sharp contrast to Aeneas who

> shouts that his victim [Turnus] must be torn from him. He is not, and Aeneas kills. Had Turnus been snatched away—that is, had Aeneas practiced the paternal, civilizing role, practiced the *clementia* his father suggests to him in the Underworld, and spared his humbled antagonist—we would have quite a different epic, with Silvia and all she stands for in triumph at the end. But that was not Virgil's intent.[45]

The ekphrasis of Silvia's stag, far more than a "moment of respite," serves as a synecdoche for the plot of Virgil's larger narrative.

Jewish

4Q186. A priestly interest in unblemished bodies is detectable in postbiblical Judaism, especially at Qumran. Consider first these passages from Qumran 4Q186:

> 3 [. . .] a man of [. . .] 4 [. . .] secrets. 5 And his thighs are long and slender, and the toes of his feet are 6 slender and long. And he is in the second position. 7 His spirit has six (parts) in the house of light and three in the pit of 8 darkness. And this is the sign in which he was born: the foot of Taurus. He will be poor. And his animal is the bull. (1 II, 3–8)

> His eyes are of a colour between black and stripy. His beard is 2 . . . [. . .] and frizzy. The sound of his voice is simple. His teeth 3 are sharp and well aligned. He is neither tall 4 nor short, and like that from his birth. Then the fingers of his hands are slender 5 and long. His thighs are smooth and the soles of his feet 6 [. . .] are even. His spirit 7 has eight (parts) [in the house of light] in second position, and one 8 [in the house of darkness . . .] And the sign in which he was born is 9 [. . .] And his animal is [. . .] 10 [. . .] this [. . .] 11 [. . .] . . . [. . .]. (2 I, 1–11)[46]

This text is better described as a physiognomy than a horoscope.[47] These texts combine physiognomy and astrology in an effort to predict a person's character and perhaps also destiny. In doing so, the physical description bears resemblance to an ekphrasis. Not all the elements are drawn from physiognomic or astrological symbolism. The "house of light," for example, is contrasted with the "pit of darkness" and has a "strongly sectarian meaning, which is related . . . to some of the central theological ideas of the Qumran community."[48] Likewise, the use of a nine-point scale to assess the degree to which a person is ruled by the cosmic forces of "light/good" and "darkness/evil" appears to be sectarian.[49] The number nine, however, does not seem to have any special astrological or physiognomic significance, but it does mean that no one can have equal parts of light and evil: "One is either predominantly good or predominantly bad."[50]

Nonetheless, there are two significant features about these passages that are shaped by physiognomic concerns. First, the description "appears to be based on the whole body from head to toe."[51] This is also the method of ekphrasis (cf. Aphthonius, *Prog.* 12.1). Some of the observations fit what we know of Greek physiognomy: interest in moderation (eyes between dark and striped), symmetry (neither tall nor short), and unaffected voice and gesture ("simple" voice). The text also draws on a kind of "zoological method"; here the person who is in the "house of light" has as his animal a bull. Importantly, most of the description is available from observation, meaning that the person being examined does not have to cooperate or even be aware of the examination.[52] Further, Josephus drew parallels between the Essenes and the Pythagoreans ("those we call Essenes, a group which employs the same daily regime as was revealed to the Greeks by Pythagoras"; *Ant.* 15.371), making the intriguing suggestion that physiognomy was used in evaluating candidates for entrance into the community, much like the Pythagoreans.[53]

<u>*Testament of Naphtali*</u>. The use of ekphrasis to illustrate the inner coherence between body and spirit is also found in the *Testaments of the Twelve Patriarchs*, a second-century BCE Jewish document (with some later Christian interpolations).[54] In the *Testament of Naphtali*, we have perhaps the fullest expression of what the translator has termed "psychophysiology":[55]

> For just as a potter knows the pot, how much it holds, and brings clay for it accordingly, so also the Lord forms the body in correspondence to the spirit, and instills the spirit corresponding to the power of the body. And from one to the other there is no discrepancy, not so much as a third of a hair, for all the creation of the Most High was according to height, measure, and standard. And just as the potter knows the use of each vessel and to what it is suited, so also the Lord knows the body to what extent it will persist in goodness, and when it will be dominated by evil. . . . As a person's strength, so also is his work; as is his mind, so also is his skill. As is his plan, so also is his achievement; as is his heart, so is his speech; as is his eye, so also is his sleep; as is his soul, so also is his thought . . . for God made all things good in their order: the five senses in the head; to the head he attached the neck, in addition to the hair for the enhancement of appearance; then the heart for prudence; the belly for excretion from the stomach; the windpipe for health; the liver for anger; the gallbladder for bitterness; the spleen for laughter; the kidneys for craftiness; the loins for power . . . and so on. (2:2-9 [Kee])

Here, then, the author makes explicit that this inner coherence between outer appearances and inner character and between internal organs and human behavior are divine gifts bestowed by God, who functions in this text as the master potter (perhaps even the master physiognomist!) and who knows the correspondence between body and spirit because he created it.

<u>*Josephus*</u>. Josephus recounts, apparently with approval, an instance of physiognomy in *Jewish War*. Caesar Augustus had sent one Celadus to determine whether someone posing as a prince was an impostor. Celadus exposes the plot in language reminiscent of physiognomists' reading the features of the face and body. Josephus writes, "Celadus had no sooner set eyes on him than he detected the points of difference in the face, and noting that his whole person had a coarser and servile appearance, penetrated the whole plot" (*B.J.* 2.107).[56]

Early Christian

<u>*Papias' account of Judas' death*</u>. Recently, Papias' account of Judas' death has been characterized as an ekphrasis.[57] Papias' account echoes and improvises on that given in Acts 1. Papias wrote:

> But Judas wandered around the world as a prominent example of impiety. His flesh was so bloated that he couldn't go through where a chariot could easily do so—not even the massiveness of his head! For they say that his eyelids were so swollen that he couldn't see any light at all and that his eyes couldn't be seen even with a doctor's lens, because they were buried too deep from the surface. And his penis looked larger and more disgusting than all such members but pus and worms flowed from each part of his body through into his genitals [lit. 'to his shame'], causing such alone to be brought through it with pain. And they say after many tortures and torments that he died on his own land. This land has been deserted due to its stench and is now uninhabited—why, even to this day no one can go past that place unless they remember to plug their nose. (*Frag.* 3.4–13 [Zeichmann])

Papias has followed ekphrastic conventions by describing Judas' body, beginning from the head and working his way down (see Aphthonius, *Prog.* 12.1). Papias begins by describing his body as a whole, then his head, eyes, privates, and finally his bodily emissions. "The image is unified by the fantastic swelling that affects each body part, while the comments on particular organs contribute additional invective to the literary portraits."[58] Furthermore, his vocabulary matches the description: "Hilariously, he employed no less that twelve sibilants when insinuating Judas' enuresis."[59] Most importantly, the ekphrasis of Judas' death matches the impiety of his act of betrayal—that is, the punishment fit the crime! Of particular relevance is the story of Nadan, who betrayed his uncle Ahiqar and implicates him in a plot to kill the king, a tradition that dates back as early as the fifth century BCE.[60] Nadan's treachery is exposed and his grisly death is recorded in explicitly ekphrastic terms: "He (Nadan) swelled up immediately and became like a blown-out bladder. And his limbs swelled and his feet and his side, and he was torn and his belly burst asunder and his entrails were scattered, and he perished, and died. And his latter end was destruction, and he went to hell" (Ahiqar 8:38). As Jesse Robertson has observed:

> It is apparent that in Greco-Roman, Jewish, and Christian literature, death-accounts that describe the putrefaction of living flesh, worms, foul stench, and (in some cases) dropsy are typically associated with impious persons who commit acts of excessive violence against their defeated enemies, their own countrymen, the innocent, or the people of God. Authors seem to relish the ekphrastic presentation of the most lurid details in these cases, including the description of affected genitals and bodily excretions. A sympathetic reader would find these shocking images as morbidly satisfying demonstrations of divine justice, an implication frequently made explicit in these accounts. Heard in relation to these types of deaths, Papias' account of the death of Judas would characterize Judas as one who commits gross violence against innocent persons, lives a dissolute life, and who, as a result, suffers a hideously shameful death under divine judgment.[61]

The ekphrasis of Judas' death was so effective that it served as a model for later writers to describe the punitive death of an opponent. Judas' death is echoed in the description of the death of Arius by Socrates Scholasticus (c. 380–439):

> Soon after a faintness came over him [Arius], and together with the evacuations his bowels protruded, followed by a copious hemorrhage, and the descent of the smaller intestines: moreover portions of his spleen and liver were brought off in the effusion of blood, so that he almost immediately died. The scene of this catastrophe still is shown at Constantinople, as I have said, behind the shambles in the colonnade: and by persons going by pointing the finger at the place, there is a perpetual remembrance preserved of this extraordinary kind of death. (*Eccl. hist.* 37)[62]

Places and Events

Graeco-Roman

Clitophon's garden. The ancient novels have proven "fertile ground for exploring the form and function of ekphrasis."[63] Longus' novel *Daphnis and Chloe* is a book-length ekphrastic narrative of a painting, and ekphrases also feature prominently in other novels (e.g., Petronius 89 and Heliodorus, *Aethiopica* 4.8). Many of these ekphrases are employed in such a way as to advance the narrative's plot. Achilles Tatius' tale of the star-crossed lovers Leucippe and Clitophon provides "a striking example of the way the novel creates visual analogues in order to convey meaning can be found in the ekphraseis of Clitophon's garden (1.15) and Leucippe's face."[64]

Clitophon describes a formal garden adjacent to his home:

> It was in fact a grove of very pleasant aspect. . . . Protected with the columns stood a populous assembly of trees. A network of sturdy branches interlaced to form an intricate pattern wherein petals gently embraced their neighbours, leaves wound round other leaves, and fruits rubbed softly on other fruits. Thus far the world of plants knows intercourse.
>
> Ivy and bindweed raveled their way around some of the massy trunks: the bindweed clung to the plane tree by a soft reticulation of tendrils, while the ivy spiraled intimately among the pine boughs. This symbiosis provided support for the ivy and ivy wreaths of honor for the tree. (*Leucippe and Clitophon* 1.15 [Winkler])

He then goes on to describe the flowers in the garden:

> The flowers of various colors displayed their beauty in turn—violet, narcissus, rose—the earth's dyed stuffs. The calyx of the rose has the same contour as that of the narcissus—a natural drinking cup. . . . The violet's calyx is nowhere to be seen; its color is like that of sunlight flashing on a still sea. (1.15 [Winkler])

For Leucippe's benefit, Clitophon then describes the various erotic desires found in nature including those of a peacock, a stone, a plant, a stream, and the mating practice of a viper and an eel (1.16–18). Next Clitophon describes his beloved in a way that parallels the elaborate and erotic description of the garden:

> I was looking at the young lady to see how she reacted to my erotic lesson. She discreetly indicated that she had not been displeased by my discourse. . . . The beauty of her body challenged the flowers of the field: her face was the essence of pale jonquil; roses arose on her cheeks; her glance was a revelation of violet; her hair had more natural curls than spiral ivy. Such was the meadow of Leukippe's face. (1.19 [Winkler])

This analogy between the garden and the "meadow of Leucippe's face" "serves not only to emphasize Leucippe's beauty, but also her ability to arouse Clitophon. The garden is a highly erotic space, whose appearance compels Clitophon to perceive the plants as amorously clinging to one another (1.15) in sexual intercourse and whose contents allow for Clitophon to wax sensual about the mating habits of plants and animals in an attempt to seduce Leucippe (1.16–18). Thus, Leucippe's beauty arouses Clitophon in a similarly erotic way. . . . Here, *ekphrasis* operates by presenting to the reader images that are linked through their descriptive elements."[65]

Jewish

The Jerusalem temple. In *Jewish War* Josephus gives an extended ekphrasis of the Jerusalem temple on the eve of the Roman conquest (*B.J.* 5.184–247; cf. *Ant.* 8.95–98). His larger description of Jerusalem along with the temple in book 5 is the most detailed description in all of *Jewish War*. Here we cite only a part that describes the brilliance of the temple's exterior:

> Now the outward face of the temple in its front wanted nothing that was likely to surprise either men's minds or their eyes; for it was covered all over with plates of gold of great weight, and, at the first rising of the sun, reflected back a very fiery splendor, and made those who forced themselves to look upon it to turn their eyes away, just as they would have done at the sun's own rays. But this temple appeared to strangers, when they were coming to it at a distance, like a mountain covered with snow; for as to those parts of it that were not gilt, they were exceeding white. On its top it had spikes with sharp points, to prevent any pollution of it by birds sitting upon it. (*B.J.* 5.222–223)

Unlike his other descriptions of cities in *Jewish War*, the description of Jerusalem and the temple in book 5 appears in the past tense, indicating the place as he describes it no longer exists:[66]

> The elaborate description of Jerusalem and Temple in War 5 serves several narrative functions. It indicates what is at stake when the siege of Jerusalem begins, and of what was lost when the Temple burnt down because of a fire started by the Jews themselves (6.249–253). It also enhances the readers' awareness of

> the crimes of the Jewish insurgents defiling the Temple. . . . The details of the description in Book 5 imply that his ambitions went even further. Whilst his own memories were still relatively fresh, he apparently wanted to preserve the memory of Jerusalem and its Temple as a visualized monument in writing. Even after city's actual destruction, Jerusalem and God's Temple form the centre of Josephus' universe.[67]

And we may add, with the use of ekphrasis, Josephus sought also to stir his audience's emotions and plant the image also in their hearts and minds.

Early Christian

Pontus. Tertullian employs an ekphrasis of Pontus (and its inhabitants), the birthplace of Marcion, in order to paint a scathing invective against his opponent:

> The sea called Euxine, or hospitable, is belied by its nature and put to ridicule by its name. Even its situation would prevent you from reckoning Pontus hospitable: as though ashamed of its own barbarism it has set itself at a distance from our more civilized waters. Strange tribes inhabit it—if indeed living in a wagon can be called inhabiting. . . . There is sternness also in the climate—never broad daylight, the sun always niggardly, the only air they have is fog, the whole year is winter, every wind that blows is the north wind. Water becomes water only by heating: rivers are no rivers, only ice: mountains are piled high up with snow: all is torpid, everything stark. Savagery is there the only thing warm—such savagery as has provided the theatre with tales of Tauric sacrifices, Colchian love-affairs, and Caucasian crucifixions.
>
> Even so, the most barbarous and melancholy thing about Pontus is that Marcion was born there, more uncouth than a Scythian, more unsettled than a Wagon-dweller, more uncivilized than a Massagete, with more effrontery than an Amazon, darker than fog, colder than winter, more brittle than ice, more treacherous than the Danube, more precipitous than Caucasus. (*Marc.* 1.1)

Like Achilles Tatius, Tertullian draws on the physical description of a place to underscore the (in this case, very unflattering) character of Marcion.

Examples from the New Testament

Persons/Animate Characters

Ethiopian eunuch. There are very few physical descriptions of persons in the Gospels and Acts. Descriptions where they do exist are often in miracle stories in which the malady of the recipient of healing is described, albeit usually in very brief terms. There are several notable exceptions to this observation, and the exceptions generally occur in passages that employ ekphrasis to subvert existing physiognomic conventions that equate outer physical attributes with (usually negative) inner moral qualities. One is the case of the Ethiopian eunuch in Acts 8.[68] Although the physical description is limited to the word "eunuch," the word occurs four times in the narrative and is heavily freighted with cultural and ideological layers of meaning.

The description of the official as a eunuch evoked a thoroughly negative image in antiquity.[69] Eunuchs in antiquity "belonged to the most despised and derided group of men."[70] This claim would certainly find support in the writings of Polemo, author of one of the extant physiognomic handbooks.[71] Polemo notes that a certain kind of eye is reflective of a lack of sexual control. He goes on to claim, "This nature is in the eyes of men who are not like the other men, like the eunuch who is not a [castrated] eunuch but who was born without testicles. . . . Eunuchs are an evil people, and in them is greed and an assembly of various (evil) qualities" (1.162F).[72]

This negative assessment was not limited to the physiognomic handbooks, however.[73] Lucian of Samosata claimed that it was "an ill-omened, ill-met sight if on first leaving home in the morning, one should set eyes on any such person" (*Eunuch.* 6 [Harmon, LCL]). We see this ostracism among Greek-speaking Jews of the first century as well. Josephus wrote:

> Shun eunuchs and flee all dealings with those who have deprived themselves of their virility and of those fruits of generation, which God has given to men for the increase of our race; expel them even as infanticides who withal have destroyed the means of procreation. (*Ant.* 4.290–291)

Why were eunuchs thus demonized and ostracized in antiquity? In part, the answer lies in their ambiguous sexual identity. To quote Lucian again, a eunuch "was an ambiguous sort of creature like a crow, which cannot be reckoned either with doves or with ravens . . . neither man nor woman but something composite, hybrid and monstrous, alien to human nature" (*Eunuch.* 9-11 [Harmon, LCL]).[74] In a culture where honor was gender based, to be sexually ambiguous was to blur clear-cut gender roles and expectations and thus to bring shame upon oneself and one's community.[75] Nevertheless, this physical "deformity" for Luke does not indicate a social or sexual flaw so severe that it disqualifies him from entrance into the eschatological community.[76]

Places and Events

Jesus' baptism. Jesus' baptism is a key moment in the narrative plot(s) of the Synoptics, and the story reflects several rhetorical strategies all aimed at the same theological point. The omen (opening of heaven, voice from heaven, descent of the Spirit) provides divine confirmation of Jesus' identity (cf. Cicero, *Top.* 20.76–77) and is a rhetorical convention typical of bios literature to underscore the greatness of the protagonist. These marvelous signs are also often associated with the birth of the hero (Ps.-Hermogenes, *Prog.* 15; Nicolaus, *Prog.* 51–52, 59–60), and the account here does highlight Jesus' origins as God's "beloved son" (Luke 3:22).

The accounts of Jesus' baptism also contain visual elements that may count as ekphrastic language. Mark reports that as Jesus "was coming up out of the water, he saw the heavens torn apart and the Spirit descending like a dove on him" (Mark 1:10). There is some ambiguity as to whether "like a dove" modifies "the Spirit" or functions adverbially to describe the motion of the Spirit's descent (echoing perhaps Gen 1:1). Luke, however, removes any ambiguity and highlights the visual aspect by adding the phrase *sōmatikō eidei* to describe the Spirit: "The Holy Spirit descended upon him *in bodily form* like a dove, and a voice came from heaven: 'You are my beloved son; I am very pleased with you'" (3:22). The language appeals to the eye and not just the ear (Theon, *Prog.* 118; *Rhet. Her.* 4.50.68), inviting the audience to enter the story and imaginatively "see" the Spirit's descent upon Jesus. Thus, the audience's imagination is stoked with the mental image of the Spirit as a dove, even if the symbolism of the dove has proven elusive over the course of interpretive history![77]

Jesus' transfiguration. The transfiguration is in the form of a dream-vision (cf. Luke 1:5-25; Matthew explicitly refers to the transfiguration as a "vision" [*horama*] 17:9).[78] Luke's version includes these elements of a dream-vision: scene setting (9:28), dream-vision proper (9:29-31, 34-36a), reaction/response (9:32-33, 36b).

The dream-vision proper occurs in two parts with two corresponding reactions. In the first part of the dream-vision, Luke reports: "And it happened that while he was praying the appearance of his face became different and his clothes became gleaming white" (9:29). While colors are relatively rare in the Gospels, they were often employed in ekphrases with symbolic functions that shed light on the narrative's characterization or plot, or both.[79] For example, later in Luke's passion narrative we learn that "after Herod had [also] treated him with contempt, along with his soldiers, and made fun of him, he put elegant clothes on him and sent him back to Pilate" (23:11). Commentators are divided as to whether or not Jesus' robing was part of the mockery or indicated something else. But here the color of the garment is decisive. Influenced by Mark 15:17 (in which the soldiers clothe Jesus in a purple robe and crown of thorns, later removing the robe [15:20]), some see the "elegant" clothes as a way of ridiculing Jesus' purported kingship.[80] More likely, Herod, frustrated that Jesus refuses to perform any signs, creates a "sign" himself; the robe is a sign of Jesus' innocence.[81] At least that is evidently the way in which Pilate will interpret it (23:15). Given the "carnivalesque" context of Herod's interrogation, however, it is fair to conclude that Herod also intended to humiliate Jesus with the act.[82] So here, too, in the transfiguration story, the description of Jesus' changing countenance and transformed garments uses the rhetorical device of *ekphrasis* or *oracular demonstration* (*Rhet. Her.* 4.55.68) to indicate the glory.[83]

The ekphrasis of Jesus' clothing both anticipates and explains Peter's subsequent action. The first reaction/response is recorded in 9:32: "Now, Peter and those with him were extremely sleepy, but when they were fully awake, they saw his glory and two men standing with him." The authorial audience familiar with the rest of Luke's story may hear in the reference to Peter, James, and John being "extremely sleepy" an echo of their inability to watch and pray during Jesus' ordeal in Gethsemane (22:39-46).[84] Peter suggests building a monument to commemorate the event: "And it happened that as they were leaving him, Peter said to Jesus, 'Master, it is good for us to be here. Let us make three shelters, one for you and one for Moses and one for Elijah,' not knowing what he was saying" (9:33). Peter's impulse to build three shelters is puzzling but may be understandable in light of contemporary Jewish interpretation of Psalm 43.[85] Within Luke's narrative, Peter's response both echoes (cf. 5:1-11) and anticipates (22:33, 54-62) similar outbursts in Luke.

Pentecost. As we have noted, the function of ekphrasis or ekphrastic language in a narrative is often to draw attention to the significance of the event thus described for the overarching argument of the narrative. The ekphrastic language in the Pentecost scene underscores the continuity between the founder of the "Way" and his followers. As significant events in Jesus' life and ministry (baptism, transfiguration, resurrection/ascension) were depicted in language that appealed to the "eye and not the ear," so also is the beginning of the disciples' "public ministry" described in vivid language, marking the disciples' reception of the Holy Spirit. The Spirit descended in "bodily form" on Jesus, and the Spirit manifested itself "like the rush of a violent wind" and "as tongues of fire." Thus, for Luke, the beginning of the follower's public ministry paralleled and echoed the beginning of the founder's public ministry. Furthermore, in describing the event as accompanied by these natural and visible phenomena, Luke is echoing the theophany scenes of the OT, in which God's presence is accompanied by similar signs (Exod 19:16; Judg 5:4-5; cf. Pss 18:7-15; 29:3-9). Again, the audience is invited to participate in the event as witnesses.

Christ's crucifixion (Gal 3:1). Ekphrasis can also be used in epistolary material to highlight key moments in the "story" being narrated by the author.[86] Along these lines, recent studies have underscored the use of ekphrasis by Paul (and Pauline circles).[87] In his letter to the Galatians, Paul reminds his audience that "it was before your eyes that Jesus Christ was publicly exhibited (*proegraphē*) as crucified!" (Gal 3:1). To re-present the crucifixion, Paul employs the rhetorical device of ekphrasis.[88] John Chrysostom has captured the force of Paul's ekphrasis: "Since Christ was crucified not in the Galatian's territory but in Jerusalem, what does he [Paul] mean by this phrase 'before your eyes'? . . . He said not 'crucified' but 'portrayed as crucified,' showing that with eyes of faith they [the Galatians] saw more accurately than those who were there and witnessed the events. . . . He blames them because, having seen Christ stripped, crucified, nailed, spat upon, mocked . . . they have forsaken this man and run back to the law, showing no awareness of Christ's sufferings" (*Hom. Gal.* 3.1).[89] Thus, according to Chrysostom, "'seeing' with the eyes of faith" what Paul has publicly displayed before their eyes causes the Galatians to participate in the event of Christ's crucifixion.[90] And even though the Galatians were not present at Jesus' crucifixion there was plenty in their visual culture to allow them to create a mental image (*phantasia*) of the event.[91] Paul's claim is forcefully captured in this translation of Galatians 3:1b: "Who has cast a spell on you, doing so in spite of the fact that in my sermons a picture of Jesus Christ marked by crucifixion was painted before your eyes?"[92] In his notes on 3:1, J. Louis Martyn offers this explanation:

> The verb *prographō* can have either of two major accents: to proclaim publicly, or to proclaim by providing a vivid portrait. Here we see a combination of the two. Paul told the Galatians the hideous story of Jesus' death by crucifixion, not, to be sure, as to bring them to cheap tears, but as to bring them face-to-face with three facts: (a) Jesus died as a condemned criminal. (b) His death is the event in which God has begun to free the whole of the cosmos from bondage to the powers of evil (1:4). (c) The Galatians were grasped by God in the realistic message of this death, and their being so grasped was signified in the baptism by which they participated in the death of that condemned criminal (3:13, 26-29).[93]

Paul had already made the claim that *he* had been crucified with Christ (Gal 2:19-20), and now, via ekphrastic language, he reminds the Galatians that they, too, have participated in Christ's crucifixion and that they, like he, have died to the law (Gal 2:19), despite the temptation to begin practicing Torah obedience, abandoning Paul's gospel (1:6) and turning from God (4:9-10).[94]

<u>*Defeating the powers through the cross*</u> (*Col 2:15*). Paul's use of ekphrastic language inspired his followers to emulate this strategy. The author of Colossians, presumably a follower of Paul, offers this ekphrasis of Christ's defeat of the powers and principalities: "He disarmed the principalities and powers and made a public example of them, triumphing over them in it" (Col 2:15). The author presumably has in mind here the Roman *triumphus*, the triumphal procession of a victorious Roman military conquest, in which the defeated army is led through the streets in shame and humiliation (cf. Josephus, *B.J.* 7.123–157; Dio Cassius, *Hist. Rom.* 6).[95] Plutarch described the scene after Romulus had defeated his foe, Acron, outside the village of Caenina: "Then he himself [Romulus], girding his raiment about him and wreathing his flowing locks with laurel . . . began a triumphal march, singing songs of victory, with the whole army marching after him; and being received by the citizens with joyful amazement. This procession was the origin and model of all subsequent triumphs" (Plutarch, *Rom.* 16.6).

The triumphal procession of a victorious Roman general was institutionalized, with certain prescribed rules and regulations established by the Roman Senate. Polybius wrote, "For the processions they call triumphs, in which the generals bring the actual spectacle of their achievements before the eyes of their fellow-citizens, cannot be properly organized and sometimes even cannot be held at all, unless the senate consents and provides the requisite funds" (Polybius, *Hist.* 6.15.8). "The triumph metaphor here is again evocative; the author could rely upon listeners to draw on the recurring experience of military iconography, if not the experience of mini-triumphs, to picture in their minds the image prompted by the text. Arguably the author chose the image precisely for that end, as with it he believed a series of emotional responses would be triggered, that would help in the task of persuasion."[96] It is this sense of humiliation and shame that underlies the picture painted in the author's use of ekphrasis in Colossians 2:15: "Here the paradox would lie in the affirmation that when Christ hung naked on the cross, exposed to public ridicule, it was in reality the hostile powers that God was exposing and holding up to ridicule."[97] The author of Colossians uses vivid, ekphrastic language to set before the audiences' eyes (and create in their minds) the mental image that through the cross God has defeated the cosmic, anti-God powers.

<u>*Sinai and Zion in Hebrews 12*</u>. Two particularly vivid displays of ekphrasis are seen in Hebrews 12:18-25. The first is a depiction of Sinai, as approached by the wilderness generation:

> You have not come to something that can be touched, a blazing fire, and darkness, and gloom, and a tempest, and the sound of a trumpet, and a voice whose words made the hearers beg that not another word be spoken to them. (For they could not endure the order that was given, "If even an animal touches the mountain, it shall be stoned to death." Indeed, so terrifying was the sight that Moses said, "I tremble with fear.") (12:18-21)

As the writer depicts it, Sinai is a place of approach that stands under the shadow of fear and death. Appeal to the senses of touch, sight, and hearing bring the mountain before the audience in vivid detail. Items not found in the Deuteronomic account, but added by the writer, enhance the appeal: "something touched" underscores the this-worldly physicality of the mountain, in anticipation of the otherworldly, heavenly mountain of the next scene; and "gloom" (*zophos*, used by the writer in replacement of *gnophos*, "darkness"; LXX Deut 4:11; 5:22) contributes the darkest note to an already dark portrait, as the term conjures for the audience the "gloom of the underworld."[98]

A second ekphrasis, which follows immediately on the first, is of a very different mountain of approach, the heavenly Zion:

> But you have come to Mount Zion and to the city of the living God, the heavenly Jerusalem, and to innumerable angels in festal gathering, and to the assembly of the firstborn who are enrolled in heaven, and to God the judge of all, and to the spirits of the righteous made perfect, and to Jesus, the mediator of a new covenant, and to the sprinkled blood that speaks a better word than the blood of Abel. (12:22-24)

In contrast to Sinai, Zion in the author's depiction is characterized by the joyful sights and sounds of eschatological festal ascent. Together, the two contrasting portraits form what in the speech is yet another syncrisis or comparison of old and new covenant subjects. As such, these ecphrases are more than mere ornament; rather, they contribute to the larger pattern of argumentation at work in the speech. Repeatedly, the author has compared various old and new covenant subjects and presented the new as even greater than the old; and repeatedly, the author has followed the comparison with a deliberative argument "from the lesser to the greater"—namely, that if faithfulness was advantageous, or apostasy disadvantageous, in the case of old covenant experience, then *how much more* will it be so in the case of new covenant experience.[99] Here the author returns to the pattern, following the comparison of mountains of approach with the usual *how-much-more* deliberative argument against apostasy:

> See that you do not refuse the one who is speaking; for if they did not escape when they refused the one who warned them on earth, *how much more* will we not escape if we reject the one who warns from heaven. (12:25 NRSV [adapted])

All that is new in this final comparison of the speech is the incorporation of ekphrasis into the syncritical argument. On the one hand, the ekphrasis of Sinai serves to bring the fearful mountain and its voice of warning before the hearers vividly, so that they are gripped by reverence for its voice of warning. On the other hand, the ekphrasis of Zion as a place of joyful ascent heightens the desire for heavenly city, even as it brings before the audience a heavenly voice of warning that deserves even greater reverence.

Conclusion

Like others in their literary environment, early Christian writers employed the rhetorical device of ekphrasis to draw their audience into the stories they were telling and to identify with their point of view on both emotional and intellectual levels.[100] Setting the story before the eyes of the audience does more than simply adorn the literary landscape with interesting word pictures. Ekphrasis allowed the author to develop the characterization of the protagonists (and antagonists) of his "story" (whether writing in the genre of narrative or epistle), "showing" the audience through physical description whether the character should be judged "good" or "bad." Ekphrasis also assisted the author and audience in moving the plot forward, often foreshadowing through description important events about to unfold. Attending to the form and function of the visual language employed in the New Testament (and its literary environs) can reward the reader with deeper and more nuanced understandings of its message.

Notes

1 Traces of those variant traditions are found (among others) in Nicolaus, who observes that "*some* . . . put ecphrasis right after comparison" (*Prog.* 67; our emphasis) and "this is what *some* have said, but following the prevailing custom, we put ethopoeia after syncrisis and ecphrasis after that" (*Prog.* 68; our emphasis).

2 Ruth Webb, *Ekphrasis, Imagination and Persuasion in Ancient Rhetorical Theory and Practice* (Surrey, England: Ashgate, 2009), 17, 18.

3 On Achilles' shield, see Andrew Sprague Becker, *The Shield of Achilles and the Poetics of Ekphrasis* (London: Rowman & Littlefield, 1995).

4 On Aeneas' shield, see Michael J. Putnam, *Virgil's Epic Designs: Ekphrasis in the* Aeneid (New Haven: Yale University Press, 1998), 119–88.

5 See Webb, *Ekphrasis, Imagination and Persuasion*, 7–9.

6 Webb, *Ekphrasis, Imagination and Persuasion*, 54.

7 Webb, *Ekphrasis, Imagination and Persuasion*, 54.

8 Not all of the instances cited by A. T. Robertson in his six-volume *Word Pictures in the New Testament* (Nashville: Broadman, 1929) would qualify as ekphrastic language by the progymnasmatists' definition, but many do evoke mental images as Robertson demonstrates.

9 Apthonius, *Prog.* 67, reports that some theorists place ekphrasis immediately after synkrisis or comparison, although this is not true of any of the extant progymnasmata.

10 Apparently, by "persons," Theon means animate or living creatures (as opposed to inanimate objects), since under "persons" he includes not only Eurybates and Thersites (from the *Odyssey* and *Iliad*, respectively) but also the ibis, the hippopotami, and crocodiles. Cf. James Butts ("The Progymnasmata of Theon: A New Text with Translation and Commentary" [Ph.D. diss., Claremont Graduate School, 1986], 437n6), who translated *prosōpa* as "characters."

11 Webb, *Ekphrasis, Imagination and Persuasion*, 63.

12 About Ps.-Hermogenes' statement, Webb, *Ekphrasis, Imagination and Persuasion*, 50, observed: "Such comments remind us both how interconnected various exercises were and how flexible ekphrasis was: the techniques it taught could be put to use in a variety of contexts."

13 Modified from Webb, *Ekphrasis, Imagination and Persuasion*, 64.

14 Angela Holzmeister, "Ekphrasis in the Ancient Novel," in *A Companion to the Ancient Novel*, ed. Edmund P. Cueva and Shannon N. Byrne (Oxford: Wiley Blackwell's, 2014), 411–23, here 414.

15 Adapted from Webb, *Ekphrasis, Imagination and Persuasion*, 42.

16 Robyn J. Whitaker, *Ekphrasis, Vision, and Persuasion in the Book of Revelation*, WUNT 2/410 (Tübingen: Mohr Siebeck, 2015), 45–52.

17 To these three, Whitaker (*Ekphrasis, Vision, and Persuasion*, 52–53) adds verisimilitude or "lifelikeness." Undoubtedly presenting a literary visualization that conforms to cultural conventions and audience expectations was critical, and although plausibility is mentioned as a virtue of narrative by Theon (*Prog.* 79) and others (cf. also Cicero, *De or.* 1.70; *Top.* 73), it is not specified in the exercises on ekphrasis in the *Progymnasmata* and therefore is not included in the discussion here.

18 This example is discussed later on pp. 123–24. Whitaker, *Ekphrasis, Vision, and Persuasion*, 52, cites a passage from Lucian (*Am.* 12), in which a temple of Aphrodite is described, as a contrast in style to Demosthenes.

19 Waltz, *Rhetores graeci*, 3:579–90 (1.10; 1.29). Cited by Webb, *Ekphrasis, Imagination and Persuasion*, 57n73. Whitaker, *Ekphrasis, Vision, and Persuasion*, 51n54, also cites as an example of style fitting subject Ovid, *Metam.* 6.70–128, in which Ovid describes Arachne's web with language that weaves and threads "in a way that parallels Arachne weaving her web" and describing "his own work here as drawing a thread from the ancients to the present."

20 Walz, *Rhetores graeci*, 2:652. Cited by Webb, *Ekphrasis, Imagination and Persuasion*, 57n73.

21 See, e.g., Dionysius of Halicarnassus' charges of "unclarity" against Plato for abandoning a plain and simple style (which he praises) for metaphors and figures of speech that produce a style that "is less pleasing than the other, since it lacks its purity of dialect and transparency of texture. It darkens what is clear and reduces it almost to obscurity" (*Dem.* 5 [Usher, LCL]). See Margaret Mitchell, "Le style, c'est l'homme: Aesthetics and Apologetics in the Stylistic Analysis of the New Testament," *NovT* 51 (2009): 385–86.

22 Whitaker, *Ekphrasis, Vision, and Persuasion*, 50. Here Theon sounds a bit like Dionysius in his warnings to avoid ambiguous language. Perhaps it is a difference in degree, not kind. Despite the call for clarity, fitting style with substance may occasionally require more ornate language; recall Ps.-Hermogenes' admonition (above): "If the subject is flowery, let the style be so too" (*Prog.* 23).

23 Whitaker, *Ekphrasis, Vision, and Persuasion*, 45.

24 Of course, this ability to "see" is itself an illusion. The progymnasmata speak of "*all-but-seeing* what is described" (Theon, *Prog.* 119); "the expression should *almost* create seeing through hearing" (Ps.-Hermogenes, *Prog.* 23); "what is elaborated in ecphrasis . . . *all but* makes spectators" (Nicolaus, *Prog.* 69).

25 Quintilian's discussion of what corresponds to ekphrasis is not in his discussion of the progymnasmata but rather in his section on figures and tropes; on the relationship of Quintilian and the progymnastic tradition, see Ian H. Henderson, "Quintilian and the Progymnasmata," *Antike und Abendland* 37 (1991): 82–99.

26 Quintilian does not here refer to ekphrasis, but Sopatros the Rhetor refers to an account of a sacked city, similar to the one offered by Quintilian above, as an ekphrasis; cf. *On the Division of Questions* 1.20 (cited by Webb, *Ekphrasis, Imagination and Persuasion*, 74).

27 Webb, *Ekphrasis, Imagination and Persuasion*, 88. Webb notes here that Quintilian mentions *enargeia* as a strategy for eliciting emotional response from the audience in book 6 and as way to persuade the listener of the speaker's point of view in book 8.

28 Webb, *Ekphrasis, Imagination and Persuasion*, 88.

29 Cited by Webb, *Ekphrasis, Imagination and Persuasion*, 25. For more on *enargeia* and *phantasia*, cf. Webb chs. 4 and 5; also Gerard Watson, *Phantasia in Classical Thought* (Galway: Galway University Press, 1988); idem, "The Concept of 'Phantasia' from the Late Hellenistic Period to Early Neoplatonism," *ANRW* 36.7:4765–810.

30 Simon Goldhill, "What Is Ekphrasis For?" *CP* 102 (2007): 6. This point is made throughout the rhetorical tradition about *pathos*: Aristotle, *Rhet.* 1.2.5; Quintilian, *Inst.* 5.14.29; and Cicero, *De or.* 2.42.178, who says it well: "For men decide far more problems by hate, or love, or lust, or rage, or sorrow, or joy, or hope, or fear, or illusion, or some other inward emotion, than by reality, or authority, or any legal standard, or judicial precedent, or statute" (Sutton and Rackham, LCL).

31 The difference may be that topoi appeal to logos while ekphrases appeal to pathos, and ancient rhetoricians knew that the emotions can only be affected indirectly, but logos can be appealed to directly. Thus, there are two different forms, reason and emotion, of inducing the audience to make judgments about someone or something. We owe this insight to Greg Barnhill.

32 Kennedy, *Progymnasmata*, 46n148.
33 See ch. 6 on encomium/invective.
34 See Mikeal C. Parsons, *Body and Character in Luke and Acts* (Waco: Baylor University Press, 2011), 127–28. For ancient critiques of physiognomy, see *Body and Character*, 34–36, 61–65.
35 The relationship is further complicated by the fact that in many literary traditions, influenced by zoological physiognomy, human characters were often assigned animallike traits.
36 For other descriptions of persons in the ancient novel tradition, see *Leuc. Clit.* 1.19.1–2 (of Leucippe); Heliodorus, *Aethiopica* 2.21.2 (of Calasiris); 1.2.1–2; 3.4.2–6 (of Charicleia); and 2.35.1; 3.3.5–7 (of Theagenes).
37 Patillon, 67n326, attributes the slight change in text from Homer to Theon to the probability that Theon is citing Homer from memory. The pervasive use of Homer in rhetorical education in antiquity is well documented. See especially Raffaella Cribiore, *Writing, Teachers, and Students in Graeco-Roman Egypt* (Atlanta: Scholars Press, 1996); Ronald F. Hock, "Homer in Greco-Roman Education," in *Mimesis and Intertextuality in Antiquity and Christianity*, ed. Dennis R. MacDonald (Harrisburg, Pa.: Trinity Press International, 2001), 56–77.
38 On this, see Philip DeLacy, "Review of Physiognomics in the Ancient World by Elizabeth C. Evans," *AJP* 92 (1971): 508–10.
39 Dio Chrysostom praised Homer for his economy of portraiture (see *Or.* 21.16–17). While it is true to say that Homer, the author of the "Greek Bible," "refrained from detailed portraiture of his characters," it would be inaccurate to say such literary depictions are altogether missing from Homer's work (DeLacy, "Physiognomics," 58). See especially on this passage, Geneva Misener, "Iconistic Portraits," *CP* 19 (1924): 103–4.
40 Liddell and Scott translate this phrase as "sugar loaf head"!
41 Andrea Kouklanakis comes to a similar conclusion without appeal to physiognomy: "The character of Thersites represents dissent and rebellion on a social level, and this dissent is magnified into a caricature of both his verbal style and his physical appearance"; see "Thersites, Odysseus, and the Social Order," in *Nine Essays on Homer*, ed. Miriam Carlisle and Olga Levaniouk (Lanham, Md.: Rowman & Littlefield, 1999), 35–54, esp. 45.
42 In Phaedo the Socratic's dialogue, Zopyrus is mentioned by Theon at 75 (Kennedy, 25).
43 Putnam, *Virgil's Epic Designs*, 97. In contrast, several ekphrases appear in the early Christian apocryphal Acts: lion (*Acts of Paul and Thecla* 7); obedient bedbugs (*Acts of John* 60–61); serpent (*Acts of John* 70–86); talking dog (*Acts of Peter* 4.9–5.12). David G. Horrell, Bradley Arnold, and Travis B. Williams, "Visuality, Vivid Description, and the Message of 1 Peter: The Significance of the Roaring Lion (1 Peter 5:8)," *JBL* 132 (2013): 697–716, have argued that the "roaring lion" in 1 Peter 5:8 represents a brief ekphrasis that "most likely would have called to mind the concrete setting of the arena and the terrifying scenario of *ad bestias*" (715–16).
44 Putnam, *Virgil's Epic Designs*, 99.
45 Putnam, *Virgil's Epic Designs*, 118. Putnam (109) points to Silvia's weaving the stag's hard antlers with soft garlands as another sign of its metamorphosis into a civilized being, lacking only the "use of words to keep from expressing human emotion by human means" (101). Putnam also contrasts the stage with the virgin warrior Camilla (11.537–584):

> The complementarity with the stag episode can be succinctly put. Whereas the animal becomes anthropomorphic, leaving the wild for domesticity and a form of marriage, the opposite happens to Camilla. Humans foster the stage to become one with them, whereas Camilla's father "nourishes her on the milk of wild creatures" (*lacte ferino/nutribat*), suitable enough accompaniment to his own *feritas*. She is brought up to choose the country over the city, the feral over the human, virginity over a girl's normal course toward marriage, a man's pursuits over those of a woman, pursuits that soon lead her into the violence and bestialization of war. (116)

46 The translation is taken from Florentino García Martínez, *The Dead Sea Scrolls Translated: The Qumran Texts in English*, trans. Wilfred G. E. Watson (Leiden: Brill, 1992), 456. For the original text (and a slightly different English translation), see Florentino García Martínez and Eibert J. C. Tigchelaar, eds., *The Dead Sea Scrolls Study Edition: Volume One IQI-4Q273* (Leiden: Brill, 1997), 380–84.

47 Philip S. Alexander, "Physiognomy, Initiation, and Rank in the Qumran Community," in *Geschichte—Tradition—Reflexion: Festschrift für Martin Hengel zum 70. Geburtstag. Band I. Judentum*, ed. Hubert Cancik, Hermann Lichtenberger, and Peter Schäfer (Tübingen: J.C.B. Mohr, 1996), 385. Alexander goes on to argue that 4Q186 should be renamed "4QAstrological Physiognomy" to replace its persistent misnomer "4QHoroscopes." Even Lawrence Schiffman who continues to refer to 4Q186 as a "horoscope" admits that "physiognomy and chiromancy played an important role in the sect's thought and practice" (*Reclaiming the Dead Sea Scrolls: The History of Judaism, the Background of Christianity, the Lost Library of Qumran* [Philadelphia: Jewish Publication Society, 1994], 364).

48 Alexander, "Physiognomy," 386–87.

49 Alexander, "Physiognomy," 390. Which of these forces and to what degree one is ruled by them "appears to be totally predestined and beyond one's control" (390).

50 Alexander, "Physiognomy," 388.

51 Alexander, "Physiognomy," 387. This approach stands in contrast to some forms of physiognomy that focused on a particular part of the body: chiromancy (palm-reading), metoposcopy (reading the lines of the forehead), or phrenology (reading the shape of the cranium).

52 Alexander, "Physiognomy," 387.

53 Alexander, "Physiognomy," 392.

54 On the Christian interpolations, see H. C. Kee, "Testament of the Twelve Patriarchs: A New Translation and Introduction," in *The Old Testament Pseudepigrapha*, ed. James Charlesworth, 2 vols. (London: Darton, Longman & Todd, 1983), 1:777, 781.

55 See Kee, "Testament of the Twelve Patriarchs," *OTP* 1:811n2a. Elsewhere Kee speaks of the relationship of human organs to human behavior as "a kind of somatic psychology" and lists T. Sim. 2:4; T. Zeb. 2:4; T. Gad. 5:11; and T. Jos. 15:3 as examples (1:778–79).

56 The parallel passage (*Ant.* 17.333–334) is not as explicitly "physiognomic."

57 Christopher B. Zeichmann, "Papias as Rhetorician: Ekphrasis in the Bishop's Account of Judas' Death," *NTS* 56 (2010): 427–29; cf. Jesse E. Robertson, *The Death of Judas: The Characterization of Judas Iscariot in Three Early Christian Accounts of His Death* (Sheffield: Sheffield Phoenix, 2012). In addition to the examples cited below, see also the discussion of the physical description of Paul in the *Acts of Paul and Thecla* in Parsons, *Body and Character*, 51–56 (and the bibliography).

58 Robertson, *The Death of Judas*, 128. See 129–33 on reading Judas' bodily ailments in light of ancient medical, philosophical, and physiognomic treatises.

59 Zeichmann, "Papias as Rhetorician," 429n7, cites Papias, *Frag.* 3.10.

60 See J. M. Lindenberger, "Ahiqar: A New Translation and Introduction," *OTP* 2:479–80.

61 Robertson, *The Death of Judas*, 138. In support of this assessment, Robertson cites the examples of Pheretime (Herodotus, *Hist.* 4.205), Cassander (Pausanias, *Description of Greece*, 7.7.2–3), Sulla (Plutarch, *Sull.* 36.2–3), Antiochus IV (2 Macc 9.9–12), Herod the Great (Josephus, *Ant.* 17.168–171; *B.J.* 1.656; Eusebius *Hist. eccl.* 1.8.6–10), Herod Agrippa I (Acts 12:23; Eusebius, *Hist. eccl.* 2.10.1–9), and Galerius (Eusebius, *Hist. eccl.* 8.16.3–5; Lactantius, *Mort.* 33.1–8).

62 See also Athanasius, fourth-century anti-Arian Bishop of Alexandria, whose description of Arius' death in his letter to Serapion is also similar to Papias (and Acts; cf. *Letter* 54; *NPNF*[2] 2:4).

63 Holzmeister, "Ekphrasis in the Ancient Novel," 413.

64 Holzmeister, "Ekphrasis in the Ancient Novel," 413. Shadi Bartsch has also drawn attention to the parallels between Clitophon's garden and the meadow in the painting of Europa at the beginning of the novel (1.1). This link confirms the painting of Europa as "foreshadower" of the garden's role as the place where "the first successful steps" to Clitophon and Leucippe's "love affair are taken"; cf. Shadi Bartsch, *Decoding the Ancient Novel: The Reader and the Role of Description in Heliodorus and Achilles Tatius* (Princeton: Princeton University Press, 1989), 52. For other parallels between the painting of Europa and the plot of *Leucippe and Clitophon*, see Bridget T. Reeves, "The Role of the Ekphrasis in Plot Development: The Painting of Europa and the Bull in Achilles Tatius' *Leucippe and Clitophon*," *Mnemosyne* 60 (2007): 87–101.

65 Holzmeister, "Ekphrasis in the Ancient Novel," 413–14. For more on ekphrasis in Achilles Tatius, see Helen Morales, *Vision and Narrative in Achilles Tatius' Leucippe and Clitophon* (New York: Cambridge University Press, 2004), 184–99.

66 Jan Willem van Henten, "Josephus, Fifth Evangelist, and Jesus on the Temple," *HTS* 71 (2015): 1–11.

67 van Henton, "Josephus," 4–5.

68 For what follows, see Parsons, *Body and Character*, 123–41. See also Sean D. Burke, *Queering the Ethiopian Eunuch: Strategies of Ambiguity in Acts* (Minneapolis: Fortress, 2013); Brittany E. Wilson, *Unmanly Men: Refigurations of Masculinity in Luke-Acts* (Oxford: Oxford University Press, 2015), 118–49.

69 Ethiopians, because of their dark skin, were also often the subject of ridicule and negative characterization; see Parsons, *Body and Character*, 132.

70 Scott Spencer, "The Ethiopian Eunuch and His Bible: A Social Science Analysis," *BTB* 22 (1992): 156. While some evidence for the view that eunuch is simply a royal title does exist, that does not seem to be the overriding emphasis in Acts 8. Genesis 39:1 reports that "Joseph was brought down to Egypt; and Potiphar an officer (LXX, *euneuchos*) of Pharaoh . . ." Potiphar was of course married, and the NRSV is probably correct in understanding eunuch here simply to refer to his standing in Pharoah's court. Some early Christian writings developed the notion of eunuch as a reference to those who remain celibate; see Athenagoras, *A Plea for the Christians* 33.3; Clement of Alexandria, *Strom.* 3.1.

71 The relevant passage is found in Foerster's edition of Polemo, 1.160–164. Richard Foerster, ed., *Scriptores Physiognomonici Graeci et Latini*, 2 vols. (Leipzig: Teubner, 1893).

72 Polemo is evidently thinking of one eunuch in particular. He says, "I do not know if I have seen any of this description [congenital eunuch] except for one man. He was from a land called Celtas" (1.160F; for the translation, see Simon Swain, *Seeing the Face, Seeing the Soul: Polemon's* Physiognomy *from Classical Antiquity to Medieval Islam* [New York: Oxford University Press, 2007]). This person is Polemo's archenemy, the sophist philosopher Favorinus, a congenital eunuch who lived at the end of the first century until the mid-second century CE. Philostratus says that Favorinus "used to speak in oracular riddles about the three paradoxes of his life: he was a Gaul who spoke Greek, a eunuch who was prosecuted for adultery, a man who had quarreled with the emperor and was still alive" (*Lives* 489). On Polemo and Favorinus, see Maud W. Gleason, *Making Men: Sophists and Self-Presentation in Ancient Rome* (Princeton: Princeton University Press, 1995), 131–58.

73 It is conceivable that Luke may have known about eunuchs from actual classroom exercises. Libanius, e.g., in Ethopoeia 26, considers the question "What words would a eunuch say when he falls in love?"

74 Josephus comments along similar lines: "For plainly it is by reason of the effeminacy of their soul that they changed the sex of their body also. And so with all that would be deemed a monstrosity by the beholders" (*Ant.* 4.291). Likewise, Philo of Alexandria claims that eunuchs were "men who belie their sex and are affected with effemination, who debase the currency of nature and violate it by assuming the passions and the outward form of licentious women"

(*Spec.* 1.324–325). Further, eunuchs by belonging neither to the cultural expectations of male nor female had violated purity codes (see Spencer, "Social-Science," 158–59). Like amphibians who lived in two worlds, but belonged to neither, eunuchs were considered unclean (see Lev 11:9-12; 21:19-20). In addition, the physical body was thought to mirror the corporate social body, so a physical body that was damaged or mutilated had the potential of defiling the social body (Jerome H. Neyrey, "The Symbolic Universe of Luke-Acts: 'They Turn the World Upside Down,'" in *The Social World of Luke-Acts: Models for Interpretation*, ed. Jerome H. Neyrey [Peabody, Mass.: Hendrickson, 1991], 278–85; Spencer, "Social-Science," 159). The Ethiopian eunuch, as Scott Spencer has noted, "embodied impurity as much as he exhibited shame. His ambiguous sexual identity ('neither male nor female') denied him a distinctive place on the purity map of the social body, even as his defective genital anatomy depicted his polluted map of the physical body" (159).

75 See Spencer, "Social Science," 157; Bruce J. Malina and Jerome H. Neyrey, "Honor and Shame in Luke-Acts: Pivotal Values for the Mediterranean World," in *The Social World of Luke-Acts*, 41–44. The fact that many eunuchs, despite their social stigmatization, held important offices, were literate, and had access to material wealth only made them that much more socially ambiguous (see again Lucian, *Eunuch.* 6–11). Crossing socioeconomic borders between the elite and the outcast only made the eunuch that much more of a liminal figure—trusted, yet treated with suspicion, prosperous, yet ostracized, the "powerful" whose access to power, ironically, came only through their humiliation (cf. Luke 1:48).

76 As it may have done from entrance into the temple; cf. Acts 8:27; Lev 21:20; 22:24; Josephus, *Ant.* 4.290–291; Philo, *Spec.* 1.324–325.

77 For a history of modern solutions to the presence of the dove at Jesus' baptism, see Leander E. Keck, "The Spirit and the Dove," *NTS* 17 (1970): 41–67. Keck's own solution, that the pericope originated in a Palestinian setting and the dove functioned adverbially to refer to the motion of God's Spirit and then was "objectified" in a Hellenistic setting by Luke into an adjective modifying the Spirit, is not incompatible with the focus here. In fact, this "reification into a phenomenon," as he calls it, finds further explanation in the penchant toward ekphrasis, in which it is the Spirit rather than the Spirit's motion that is more naturally visualized. Although Keck despairs in finding a compelling interpretation that explains why a dove in particular is used to indicate this divine descent, he concludes that we should "listen closely and patiently to what is said and why it is said precisely the way it is" (67). We concur with this conclusion and think the rhetorical strategy of ekphrasis contributes to our understanding especially of Luke's presentation of the Spirit's "bodily" descent.

78 Derek S. Dodson, *Reading Dreams: An Audience-Critical Approach to the Dreams in the Gospel of Matthew*, LNTS 397 (London: T&T Clark, 2009), 175–85.

79 This is especially true of the ancient novels. See Charles H. Hedrick, "Conceiving the Narrative: Colors in Achilles Tatius and the Gospel of Mark" in *Ancient Fiction and Early Christian Narrative*, ed. R. Hock, B. Chance, and J. Perkins (Atlanta: Scholars Press 1998), 177–97.

80 Here "elegant" translates *lampran* (lit. "shining" or "white"); cf. the adverbial form in Luke 16:19; also James 2:2-3. On this interpretation, see Darrell L. Bock, *Luke*, 2 vols., BECNT 3 (Grand Rapids: Baker, 1994–1996), 2:1821.

81 Joseph A. Fitzmyer, *The Gospel according to Luke*, 2 vols., AB 28–28A (Garden City, N.Y.: Doubleday, 1981–1985), 2:1480; Arthur A. Just, *Luke*, 2 vols. (St. Louis: Concordia, 1996–1997), 2:903; Raymond E. Brown, *The Death of the Messiah: From Gethsemane to the Grave: A Commentary on the Passion Narratives in the Four Gospels*, 2 vols. (New York: Doubleday, 1994), 1:776.

82 John T. Carroll, *Luke: A Commentary*, NTL (Louisville: Westminster John Knox, 2012), 458.

83 Cf. Edith M. Humphrey, *And I Turned to See the Voice: The Rhetoric of Vision in the New Testament* (Grand Rapids: Baker Academic, 2007), 141.

84 Cf. Humphrey, *Rhetoric of Vision*, 143–44.

85 Herbert W. Basser, "The Jewish Roots of the Transfiguration," *BRev* 14 (1998): 30–35. In the midrash on Ps 43, Moses and Elijah appear with the "Chosen One" of Isa 4:1 (identified in the Aramaic Targum on Isaiah as the Messiah). In Ps 43 the psalmist pleads with God: "Send your Light and your Truth" (Ps 43:2). The midrash replies that God has already sent Moses and Aaron (citing Ps 105:26) and promises now to send Elijah and the "chosen one" (quoting Mal 3:23 and Isa 42:1, respectively). Thus, the midrashist insists, "This is the interpretation of the words of Ps. 43:3: 'Send your Light' [i.e., Elijah] and 'your Truth' [i.e., the 'chosen one,' the Messiah] . . . they will bring me to your holy mountain and to your tents" (*Midr. Ps.* 43; citing Ps 43:3).

86 See Bruce W. Longenecker, ed., *Narrative Dynamics in Paul: A Critical Assessment* (Louisville, Ky.: Westminster John Knox, 2002).

87 Harry O. Maier, *Picturing Paul in Empire: Imperial Image, Text and Persuasion in Colossians, Ephesians and the Pastoral Epistles* (London: T&T Clark, 2013); Harry O. Maier, "Vision, Visualization, and Politics in the Apostle Paul," *MTSR* 27 (2015): 312–32; Steven Muir, "Vivid Imagery in Galatians 3:1—Roman Rhetoric, Street Announcing, Graffiti, and Crucifixions," *BTB* 44 (2014): 76–86

88 Hans Dieter Betz, *A Commentary on Paul's Letter to the Churches in Galatia*, Hermeneia (Philadelphia: Fortress, 1989), 131. Unfortunately, as Muir, "Vivid Imagery," 76, points out, Betz does not apparently grasp the full impact of the ekphrasis, arguing rather that Paul employs ekphrasis "in a case of self-ironic exaggeration" (*Commentary on Paul's Letter*, 131).

89 See M. J. Edwards, *Galatians, Ephesians, Philippians*, ACC 8 (Downers Grove, Ill.: InterVarsity, 1998), 35.

90 On *prographō* as "public display," see Muir, "Vivid Imagery," 78–79, which analyzes Gal 3:1 as an example of ekphrastic language via the progymnasmata and Quintilian. The NRSV reflects this nuance of the verb with its rendering of *proegraphē* as "publicly exhibited."

91 Muir, "Vivid Imagery," 81–83; cf. also John Granger Cook, "Envisioning Crucifixion: Light from Several Inscriptions and the Palatine Graffito," *NovT* 50 (2008): 262–85; idem, "Crucifixion as Spectacle in Roman Campania," *NovT* 54 (2012): 68–100.

92 J. Louis Martyn, *Galatians: A New Translation with Introduction and Commentary*, AB 33A (New York: Doubleday, 1997), 281.

93 Martyn, *Galatians*, 283. Martyn does not label the language as ekphrastic, but his description of its function fits well within the ancient ekphrastic conventions.

94 It should be noted that the canonical gospels are reserved in their presentation of Christ's crucifixion; nothing in them rises to the level of the description of Judas' death (in Acts, Matthew, or Papias); see also the description of the seven martyrs in 2 Macc 7, who are put to death for their refusal to eat pork. The first death is especially vivid:

> The king fell into a rage, and gave orders to have pans and caldrons heated. These were heated immediately, and he commanded that the tongue of their spokesman be cut out and that they scalp him and cut off his hands and feet, while the rest of the brothers and the mother looked on. When he was utterly helpless, the king ordered them to take him to the fire, still breathing, and to fry him in a pan. The smoke from the pan spread widely, but the brothers and their mother encouraged one another to die nobly, saying, "The Lord God is watching over us and in truth has compassion on us, as Moses declared in his song that bore witness against the people to their faces, when he said, 'And he will have compassion on his servants.'" (2 Macc 7:3-6)

95 See Lamar Williamson, "Led in Triumph: Paul's Use of *Thriambeuō*," *Int* 22 (1968): 317–22; H. S. Versnel, *Triumphus: An Inquiry into the Origin, Development, and Meaning of the Roman Triumph* (Leiden: Brill, 1970). Some commentators question the metaphorical use of the *triumphus* image and debate whether the formal Roman *triumphus* was at the forefront in

the author's thinking here in Colossians (cf. Markus Barth and Helmut Blanke, *Colossians: A New Translation with Introduction and Commentary*, AB 34B; trans. Astrid B. Beck [New York: Doubleday, 1994], 334), or elsewhere in 2 Cor 2:14 (cf. Victor Furnish, *2 Corinthians: A New Translation with Introduction and Commentary*, AB 32A [New York: Doubleday, 1984], 174–79). Furnish (179) concludes the allusion to the *triumphus* is present but secondary. More recently, Maier, *Picturing Paul*, 69–71, has argued that Paul (and the author of Colossians if not Paul) could have been imagining "mini-triumphs" that occurred throughout the Roman provinces and not necessarily the formal Roman *triumphus*.

96 Maier, "Vision, Visualization, and Politics in Paul," 327.

97 Williamson, "Led in Triumph," 326–27. Paul himself appears to appeal to this same imagery in 2 Cor 2:14, but there the appeal is "to identify himself with the shame and humiliation experienced by the prisoners who were put on display" (Furnish, *2 Corinthians*, 175); cf. Peter Marshall, *Enmity in Corinth: Social Conventions in Paul's Relations with the Corinthians*, WUNT 2/23 (Tübingen: Mohr, 1987). Williamson (325–26) sees in 2 Cor 2:14 a typical Pauline paradox (cf. 2 Cor 8:9): "To be sure, it is paradoxical to affirm that one is a conquered slave exposed to public ridicule, and at the same time that he is a joyful participant in Christ's victory celebration! It is, in fact, just the kind of paradox Paul loved! . . . Paul's paradoxical use of *thriambeuō* in II Corinthians 2:14 is thoroughly consistent with that understanding of Christ's victory in defeat, his glory in humiliation, his joy in suffering."

98 Cf. *Od.* 20.356; 2 Pet 2:4, 17; David A. deSilva, *Perseverence in Gratitude: A Socio-rhetorical Commentary on the Epistle to the Hebrews* (Grand Rapids: Eerdmans, 2000), 465; David Peterson, *Hebrews and Perfection: An Examination of the Concept of Perfection in the "Epistle to the Hebrews,"* SNTSMS 47 (New York: Cambridge University Press, 1982), 162.

99 See Michael W. Martin and Jason A. Whitlark, *Inventing Hebrews.*

100 Other NT examples of ekphrasis (or ekphrastic language) could be marshaled, but hopefully these few show the range of possibilities in developing characterization and plot. Revelation is particularly rich in visual imagery; cf. Whitaker, *Ekphrasis, Vision, and Persuasion*; Gregory M. Barnhill, "Seeing Christ through Hearing the Apocalypse: An Exploration of John's Use of Ekphrasis in Revelation 1 and 19," *JSNT* 39 (2017): 235–57.

5

Speech-in-Character

Conforming Speech to Character

> Speech-in-character is the introduction of a person to whom words are attributed that are suitable to the speaker and have an indisputable application to the subject discussed.
>
> Theon

Theory

Terminology and Definition

The first issue to address with this preliminary exercise is one of terminology and translation.[1] Theon refers to all kinds of attributed speech as prosopopoeia (*Prog.* 115), as does Quintilian (*Inst.* 9.2.30–31). Theon shows no awareness of the distinctions among prosopopoeia, ethopoeia, and eidolopoeia found in the later progymnasmata.[2] Aphthonius, for example, defines *ethopoeia* as inventing speech for a known person that fits the person's character. *Eidolopoeia* refers to speech again for a known person but who is dead "and no longer able to speak."[3] Finally, in *prosopopoeia* "everything is invented, both character and speaker" (Aphthonius, *Prog.* 44–45). Pseudo-Hermogenes agrees that *eidolopoeia* refers to speech attributed to the dead and clarifies that prosopopoeia refers to a thing or inanimate object that has been personified or to a nonexistent person (*Prog.* 20). For Nicolaus, "in ethopoeia real persons are specified, while prosopopoeia is that in which we invent persons and attribute words to them" (*Prog.* 65).[4] Theon, on the other hand, focuses on speech attributed to "real" persons, whether specific or representative, and tries to disaggregate speech appropriate to different kinds of speakers and expressing different kinds of emotions (see below).[5] Unlike Theon, Quintilian is aware of various terms applied to the concept of attributed speech, and although writing in Latin, Quintilian actually prefers the Greek term *prosopopoeia* to the Latin, *fictiones personarum* (9.2.29, 30, 31).[6] Like Theon, Quintilian also applies the term *prosopopoeia* to invented speech for both (living or deceased) human characters or imaginary ones (abstract or inanimate), choosing to "follow the now established usage in calling them both by the same name" (9.2.32 [Russell, LCL]). The character may be real or imagined, alive or dead (at the time of the character's speaking), specific or conventional, animate or inanimate. We will, where possible, disaggregate among these options even while using *prosopopoeia* as a flexible, umbrella term. "Speech," as we will see below, may also extend to communication in writing, e.g., epistolary prosopopoeia.[7]

Settling on the term *prosopopoeia*, however, does not settle the matter of terminology. There is next the question of how to translate the term, and there are several options in the literature. George Kennedy, whose translation of the progymnasmata we have generally followed, has used "personification" for prosopopoeia when he opts against simply transliterating the word.[8] "Personification" in English parlance, however, typically connotes the animation of an inanimate object, clearly not how Theon imagines the device functioning, and more akin to the way the later rhetoricians employed the term.[9] The rendering of *prosopopoeia* as "impersonation" by Donald Russell (Loeb translator of Quintilian's *Institutio oratoria*) founders for similar reasons (cf. *Inst.* 9.2.29).[10] James Butts offered "speech-in-character" as an alternative nomenclature that makes up in its descriptive power what it lacks in aesthetic sensibilities;[11] it communicates the "core element of speaking in another character's voice."[12] Thus, we will render the term *prosopopoeia* as "speech-in-character"; and by that terminology, we intend to designate the rhetorical strategy of inventing or attributing speech to another character.[13]

Constituent Elements of Speech-in-Character[14]

For Theon speech can be invented or attributed to a specific historical character or a representative type. In terms of the latter, Theon suggests these examples: "What would a man say to his wife when leaving on a journey? Or a general to his soldiers in time of danger?" (*Prog.* 115). For specific persons, he suggests: "What words would Cyrus say when marching against Massagetae? Or what would Datis say when he met the king after the battle of Marathon?" (*Prog.* 115).[15]

What does interest Theon is "what the personality of the speaker is like and to whom the speech is addressed," and here he specifies: "the speaker's age, the occasion, the place, the social status of the speaker; also the general subject which the projected speeches are going to discuss" (*Prog.* 115). Such a "social location" (as we might describe it in modern parlance) is important because

> different ways of speaking belong to different ages of life, not the same to an older man and a younger one; the speech of a younger man will be mingled with simplicity and modesty, that of an older man with knowledge and experience. Different ways of speaking would also be fitting by nature for a woman and for

> a man, and by status for a slave and a free man, and by activities for a soldier and a farmer, and by state of mind for a lover and a temperate man, and by their origin the words of a Laconian, sparse and clear, differs from those of a man of Attica, which are valuable. (*Prog.* 115–116)

Likewise, the attributed speech can be shaped by the places, occasions, and subjects of the speech:

> Speeches in a military camp are not the same as those in the assembly of the citizens, nor are those in peace and war the same, nor those by victors and vanquished; and whatever else applies to the persons speaking. And surely each subject has its appropriate form of expression. We become masters of this if we do not speak about great things vulgarly nor about small things loftily nor about paltry things solemnly nor about fearful things in a casual manner nor about shameful things rashly nor about pitiable things excessively, but give what is appropriate to each subject, aiming at what fits the speaker and his manner of speech and the time and his lot in life and each of the things mentioned above. (*Prog.* 116)[16]

It is possible to infer certain characteristics of the exercise as presented by Theon:[17]

1. Speech-in-character involves crafting and attributing speech to a person.[18]
2. The person for whom speech is scripted may be a specific person or a representative type of person.
3. The attributed speech may be actual or invented.
4. The attributed speech must be appropriate for
    a. the speaker's character, age, race, social status, gender, and occupation;
    b. the addressee's character; and
    c. the occasion, place, and subject of the speech.
5. The speech is most appropriate for the rhetorical species of consolation, exhortation, or letter writing.[19]

Although we can identify core, constituent elements of speech-in-character, in ancient practice there is no consistent patterning of argumentation reflecting the preliminary exercise of speech-in-character, as we sometimes find with other exercises (e.g., chreia). This is especially true of the New Testament writers, leading Craig Gibson to ask, "Why are there seemingly so few examples of attributed speech in the New Testament that show evidence of the writer's formal training in prosopopoiia?"[20] After surveying a "grab bag" of possible explanations, Gibson concludes: "The exercise in prosopopoiia was not an endpoint in ancient rhetorical training. Not only did other exercises that followed this one in the sequence incorporate prosopopoiia, but students who had completed some training in prosopopoiia were apparently supposed to go back and incorporate attributed speech into earlier exercises."[21] He then concludes:

> It is clear, then, that although prosopopoiia begins as an *exercise* with certain formal characteristics and no real rhetorical context, students take away from it a *skill* to be applied elsewhere. . . . In the hands of accomplished writers, both ancient and modern, simpler compositional forms either become identifiable component parts of more advanced forms, or are abandoned as forms, leaving only particular skills. When we look at the recommended uses of attributed speech elsewhere within the progymnasmata, it is clear that the artificial context of the original exercise drops away in actual practice. The original exercise is intended to teach the student how to convey ethos and pathos through attributed speech, and that is all.[22]

We do see clearer traces of the progymnasmata in ancient prose composition, including the New Testament, with certain exercises, but as we noted in the introduction, we should not expect in most cases to see these rhetorical exercises brought over in toto in prose composition. This is especially true with speech-in-character, which Gibson rightly notes is seen in practice most clearly "in terms of skills transference."[23]

Letter Writing as a Form of Speech-in-Character

Before turning to examples of the influence of speech-in-character as a skill practiced in ancient prose composition, let us pause for a moment on another form of speech-in-character, mentioned in passing in the progymnasmata. They suggest that, in addition to speeches, letter writing was an appropriate medium through which to explore speech-in-character (Theon, *Prog.* 115; cf. Ps.-Hermogenes, *Prog.* 20; Aphthonius, *Prog.* 34). In his chapter on speech-in-character, Nicolaus writes, "To me, it seems also to exercise us in the style of letter writing, since in that there is need of foreseeing the character of those sending letters and those to whom they are sent" (*Prog.* 67). These allusions prompted George Kennedy to conjecture that "letter-writing in character may have occasionally been practiced in schools."[24]

From the Second Sophistic period (second and third centuries CE) there exist collections of fictive letters by Alciphron, Aelian, and Philostratus. In these letter collections, letters rather than speeches were composed to answer such questions as "What did the fisherman's daughter in love say to her mother?" (see Alciphron, *Letters* 1.11.1–4).[25] Alciphron has 123 extant fictional prose letters in four books, categorized under farmers, fishermen, parasites, and courtesans.[26] These fictive letters were designed to reveal something of the "character" associated with the stock characters to whom they are attributed.[27] The effectiveness of letters for revealing the character of the author finds confirmation elsewhere in antiquity. Demetrius observed:

> The letter, just as the dialogue, should have a strong use of characterization. For everyone, more or less, writes a letter as an image of his or her own soul. It is also possible to see the character of the writer in every other form of written-communication, but in none so clearly as in the letter. (*Eloc.* 4.227; cf. Cicero, *Quint. fratr.* 1.45)

Quintus wrote to his brother Cicero that he had "seen all that is you in your letters" (Cicero, *Fam.* 44.2 [16.16.2]). About the emperor Marcus Aurelius, Philostratus argued, "In addition to his judicious speech, his steadfast character has also been carved into his letters" (*Ep.* 2.1.6–7). Of particular interest are "embedded letters," epistolary materials couched within a larger narrative context. We have included several examples of epistolary speech-in-character in what follows.

Examples from Ancient Literature

In a sense, since the speech-in-character exercise taught students the skill of attributing speech to characters that was fitting both to the character and the situation, one could reasonably argue that almost any speech in ancient composition owed its origins in part to this preliminary exercise and in part to the experience of listening to and reading speeches in antiquity. But certain speeches attributed to characters in ancient historiography, biography, and romance disclose character and contribute to plot development in particularly significant ways. Furthermore, the use of speech-in-character to personify an abstract idea or inanimate object is also a favorite rhetorical strategy. And finally, this strategy is also employed in embedded epistles. Below we present a few examples of each that have, perhaps, more obviously retained traces of progymnastic influence.

Speech-in-Character and Human Characters: Specific, Representative, Hypothetical, Living, or Deceased

Thucydides. Thucydides' eight-volume *History of the Peloponnesian War* is chock-full of speeches given in his recounting of the background and story of the conflict between Athens and Sparta. Distinctive among these many speeches are three attributed to Pericles whom Thucydides describes as "the foremost man of the Athenians at that time, wielding greatest influence both in speech and in action" (*Hist.* 1.139.4).[28] The three speeches (1.139–145; 2.34–46; 2.59–65) illustrate Pericles' persuasiveness in oratory. The peroration, or conclusion, to the first speech is representative:

> But we must realise that war is inevitable, and that the more willing we show ourselves to accept it, the less eager will our enemies be to attack us, and also that it is from the greatest dangers that the greatest honours accrue to a state as well as to an individual. Our fathers, at any rate, withstood the Persians,

> although they had no such resources as ours, and abandoned even those which they possessed, and by their resolution more than by good fortune and with a courage greater than their strength beat back the Barbarian and advanced our fortunes to their present state. And we must not fall short of their example, but must defend ourselves against our enemies in every way, and must endeavour to hand down our empire undiminished to posterity. (1.144.3–4)

Pericles here seeks to "sway his contemporary audience by deftly portraying them as the crucial link in a chain stretching from their revered ancestors who defeated the Persians to the future generations of Athenians who will similarly laud the triumph over the Peloponnesians, provided that they heed Pericles' counsel."[29] Thucydides reports that Pericles was successful in his appeal: "Such were the words of Pericles: and the Athenians, thinking that he was advising them for the best, voted as he directed, and answered the Lacedaemonians according to his bidding" (1.145.1). Pericles' other two speeches are equally, if not more, effective, and at the conclusion of the third address, Thucydides praises Pericles, who

> by his rank, ability, and known integrity, was enabled to exercise an independent control over the multitude—in short, to lead them instead of being led by them; for as he never sought power by improper means, he was never compelled to flatter them, but, on the contrary, enjoyed so high an estimation that he could afford to anger them by contradiction. Whenever he saw them unseasonably and insolently elated, he would with a word reduce them to alarm; on the other hand, if they fell victims to a panic, he could at once restore them to confidence. (2.65.8–9)

It is also noteworthy that Pericles offers "stand-alone" speeches, an unusual feature for speeches in Thucydides, which usually are delivered in the context of a debate.[30] Thus, Pericles' speeches fit his characterization, as Thucydides presents it, and answer the speech-in-character question: How would a statesman and speaker of Pericles' character (as Thucydides presents it) have addressed the Athenians in a variety of circumstances—namely, (1) at the outset of the war, (2) in the wake of the first significant wave of casualties, and (3) at a time when Athens' prospects of success looked particularly bleak?[31]

Theophrastus. Theophrastus compiled thirty brief sketches of representative types, whose behaviors, according to Theophrastus, are characteristic of the times. For most of these characters, Theophrastus has invented speech that is fitting or indicative of the behavior whose name the character bears. Below are a few examples in which the speech-in-character is mostly self-evident.

The arrogant's contempt "for anyone other than himself" is revealed in this comment: "When he sends a commission he doesn't write 'would you be so kind as to . . .' but rather 'I want this done' and 'I've sent to you to pick up . . .' and 'no deviations' and 'immediately'" (24.13).

The authoritarian who "covets power and profit" (26.1) says, "We ought to get together by ourselves and make decisions about this, and be rid of the rabble and the marketplace, and stop depending on them as we do for reward or rejection when we compete for public offices"; and "Either they must run the city or we must!" (26.3).

Slander is "a tendency of the soul toward derogatory talk" (28.1). The slanderer says, "This house practically has its legs in the air. That's not just a joke, you know, the old saying, they really copulate in the streets like dogs" (28.3).

The patron of scoundrels says about an evil man being tried in court, "You must judge the case, and not the man" (30.4a).[32]

Epictetus. Epictetus criticizes those who would deny a proposition, such as the existence of universal truths, by employing the logic and proof of the very proposition they deny. He claims: "For example, if a man should contradict the proposition that there is a universal statement which is true, it is clear that he must assert the contrary, and say: No universal statement is true" (*Disc.* 2.20.2). Later, he laments as "misfortune" the fact that a person "has received from nature measures and standards for discovering the truth, and then does not go on and take the pains to add to these to work out additional principles to supply the deficiencies, but does exactly the opposite, endeavouring to take away and destroy whatever faculty he does possess for discovering the truth" (2.20.22). He engages in a repartee with a hypothetical philosopher to prove his point:

> What do you say, philosopher? What is your opinion of piety and sanctity?
>
> "If you wish, I shall prove that it is good."
>
> By all means, prove it, that our citizens may be converted and may honour the Divine and at last cease to be indifferent about the things that are of supreme importance.
>
> "Do you, then, possess the proofs?"
>
> I do, thank heaven.
>
> "Since, then, you are quite satisfied with all this, hear the contrary: The gods do not exist, and even if they do, they pay no attention to men, nor have we any fellowship with them, and hence this piety and sanctity which the multitude talk about is a lie told by impostors and sophists, or, I swear, by legislators to frighten and restrain evildoers."
>
> Well done, philosopher! You have conferred a service upon our citizens, you have recovered our young men who were already inclining to despise things divine.
>
> "What then? Does not all this satisfy you? Learn now how righteousness is nothing, how reverence is folly, how a father is nothing, how a son is nothing."
>
> Well done, philosopher! Keep at it; persuade the young men, that we may have more who feel and speak as you do. It is from principles like these that our well-governed states have grown great! Principles like these have made Sparta what it was! (2.22–26 [Oldfather, LCL])[33]

The diatribe nature of this dialogue has long been recognized, but it also contains recognizable elements of speech-in-character.[34] By his speech, the philosopher identifies himself as one of those whom Epictetus has criticized for "destroying their naturally endowed ways of discovering and knowing truth" (2.20.21).[35] Further, the philosopher who had agreed to provide proofs for the benefits of devotion and sanctity relinquishes those proofs, arguing rather for the uselessness of devotion and sanctity. The philosopher's speech marks him as one of those (like the Academics and Epicureans) against whose logical inconsistencies Epictetus rails. Engaging the invented speech of a hypothetical character is a particularly effective rhetorical strategy for making Epictetus' point.[36]

Chariton. Chariton's ancient novel *Chaereas and Callirhoe* is replete with speeches, especially of a forensic nature. In the middle of the story, Dionysius, who first acquires beautiful Callirhoe as a slave and later marries her, accuses Mithridates (king of Caria, who has, unbeknownst to Dionysius, purchased Chaereas, Callirhoe's first husband and true love, as a slave) of planning to commit adultery with Callirhoe. As ancient fiction, all the speeches in *Chaereas and Callirhoe* could be considered invented "speech-in-character," especially if the speech in question reveals something of the character of the one speaking. Mithridates' defense speech is representative of such speech-in-character: it reveals Mithridates to be a shrewd and calculating figure, one familiar with the laws of the land and able to use them to his advantage. Even more noteworthy is the fact that in the speech, Mithridates invents speech in anticipation of what Dionysius might say in certain situations.[37] Mithridates remarks:

> Dionysius' accusation is not based on a legally valid marriage—his wife [Callirhoe] was offered for sale, and he bought her; and the law against adultery does not apply to slaves. He will have to read you the title of emancipation before he can talk of marriage. Are you actually calling her your wife—a woman sold to you by a pirate, Theron—who had snatched her from a tomb, at that? "Ah, but," he [Dionysius] will say, "it was a freeborn woman that I bought." Then you have kidnapped her. (*Chaereas and Callirhoe* 4.7)

Here Mithridates imagines what objection Dionysius might make to the charge that he has no legal ground for accusing Mithridates of premeditated adultery because Callirhoe, legally, is Dionysius' slave, not his wife.[38]

Later in the same speech, Mithridates again practices speech-in-character by attributing direct speech to Dionysius, this time anticipating Dionysius' reaction to Mithridates' hypothetical protest that Chaereas, and not Mithridates, wrote the letter:

> You produce a letter. I could say: "I did not write it. That is not my writing. It is Chaereas who is trying to find Callirhoe—he is the one you should be bringing to court." "Ah yes," he [Dionysius] will say, "but Chaereas is dead. It is you who

> used a dead man's name to try to seduce my wife." Dionysius, you are throwing down a challenge to me.... Retract this charge; it is in your interest to do so.... If you persist, you will regret it; you will be condemning yourself. I am warning you: you will lose Callirhoe! The King will find you the adulterer, not me! (4.7)[39]

Mithridates' attribution of speech to Dionysius is in keeping with Dionysius' impulsive and ultimately self-destructive behaviors, rooted in his obsession with Callirhoe, that Chariton portrays throughout the novel.[40]

4 Maccabees. There is an interesting example of speech-in-character in 4 Maccabees 5, which is a retelling of the martyrdom of Eleazar recorded also in 2 Maccabees 6 (second century BCE). In 2 Maccabees 6:18-31, an elderly Jewish scribe, Eleazar, is put to death for refusing to eat pork, as ordered by the Seleucid king, Antiochus IV Epiphanes. The author briefly summarizes the story:

> Eleazar, one of the scribes in high position, a man now advanced in age and of noble presence, was being forced to open his mouth to eat swine's flesh. But he, welcoming death with honor rather than life with pollution, went up to the rack of his own accord, spitting out the flesh, as all ought to go who have the courage to refuse things that it is not right to taste, even for the natural love of life. (2 Macc 6:18-20)[41]

The author of 4 Maccabees expands the story, first by giving an extended introduction to Antiochus Epiphanes, describing him as "an arrogant and terrible man" (4 Macc 4:15) and giving examples of his "terrible" behavior (deposing the high priest, Onias, and putting his successor, Jason, on his payroll, and seeking to force every Jew to eat swine and reject Judaism; 4:15-26). Next the author invents a speech for Antiochus when he sees the aged Eleazar:

> Before I have the tortures begun on you, old man, I would advise you to eat of the swine's flesh and save yourself. I respect your age and your gray hairs, although to have had them for so long and still cling to the religion of the Jews makes you anything but a philosopher in my eyes. Why should you abhor eating the excellent meat of this animal which nature has freely bestowed on us? Surely it is sheer folly not to enjoy harmless pleasures, and it is wrong to spurn nature's good gifts. But in my judgment it will be greater folly still if you indulge in idle conceits about truth and continue to defy me to your own cost in suffering. Will you not awaken from your preposterous philosophy, abandon your nonsensical calculations, assume a frame of mind to match your years, and accept the true philosophy of expediency. Bow to my benevolent advice and have pity on your own old age. Consider this also, that, even if there is some power that watches over this religion of yours, it would pardon you for any transgression committed under compulsion. (4 Macc 5:5-13)[42]

Antiochus' words fit the characterization the narrator has just presented. He is arrogant, assuming to know that whatever "power" watches over Eleazar's faith will pardon his transgression. He offers a backhanded compliment to Eleazar, first telling him he respects his "age and gray hair," then insulting him by wondering how, at his advanced age, he could still embrace the "religion of the Jews." He refers to Eleazar's "folly," his "preposterous philosophy," and his "nonsensical calculations." The narrator has creatively filled the gap left in the sparse storytelling of 2 Maccabees with regard to the question "What would a tyrant say to a recalcitrant person of faith to try to compel him to violate his religious traditions?" The "speech-in-character" attributed to Antiochus Epiphanes in 4 Macc 5 provides the answer, even if the speech itself fails to produce the intended results. Its failure is due to Eleazar's unrelenting resolve and not necessarily to any flaw in the tyrant's speech.[43]

Seneca. The Stoic philosopher Seneca wrote a treatise of consolation for one Marcia, daughter of the Roman historian Aulus Cremutius Cordus, who was grieving the death of her son. Near the end of the essay, Seneca employs speech-in-character to place words of comfort on the lips of Marcia's deceased father who in "the loftier tone that befits his more exalted state, speaks to you from the citadel of high heaven":

> Why, my daughter, are you held by such lengthy sorrow? Why do you live in such ignorance of the truth as to believe that your son was unfairly treated because, leaving his family fortunes whole, he himself returned to his forefathers, safe and whole? Do you not know how mighty are the storms of Fortune that demolish everything? How if she shows herself kindly and indulgent, it is only to those who have the fewest possible dealings with her? Need I name to you the kings who would have been the happiest of mortals if death had removed them sooner from the evils that were threatening? or even the Roman leaders who would lose not a tithe of greatness if you should subtract some years from their life? or those heroes of the highest birth and fame who calmly bowed their necks to receive the stroke of a soldier's sword? Look back upon your father and your grandfather. Your grandfather fell into the power of a foreign assassin; I myself suffered no man to have any power over me, and, having cut myself off from food, I proved that I was as courageous as I seemed to have been in my writings. Why should that member who has had the happiest death be longest mourned in our family? We are all together in one place, and, released from the deep night that envelops you. (*Marc.* 26.1–4)

The last lines of the essay are the last words of the father: "Happy, Marcia, is your son, who already knows these mysteries!" (*Marc.* 26.7). This example of speech-in-character would be later labeled as *eidolopoeia*, invented speech for a person deceased at the time of speaking (Ps.-Hermogenes, *Prog.* 20).[44] The speech also intersects with Theon's observation that speech-in-character was especially appropriate for addresses of consolation (*Prog.* 116–117).[45] Seneca has placed in the mouth of Aulus Cremutius Cordus what one might expect a deceased Roman patrician to say to his daughter who is grieving the death of her son.

Tertullian. In his treatise on proper dress for Christian women, Tertullian anticipates an objection to his proscription for Christian women to avoid the scandalous dress that might draw comparisons to prostitutes by inventing speech for a representative interlocutor: "Perhaps some (woman) will say: 'To me it is not necessary to be approved by men; for I do not require the testimony of men: God is the inspector of the heart'" (*Cult. fem.* 13.2.1 [Schaff]). Tertullian responds: "(That) we all know; provided, however, we remember what the same (God) has said through the apostle: 'Let your probity appear before men'" (13.2.3). It is not enough, for Tertullian, that the Christian woman be chaste; her outward appearance must show as much, the protest of his female interlocutor notwithstanding.[46]

Speech-in-Character and Personification

Plato. In Plato's *Crito*, Socrates and Crito are discussing whether Socrates should accept Crito's offer to finance Socrates' escape from prison and certain death. Crucial to the decision were the Laws (*nomoi*) of the polis. Near the end of the dialogue, Socrates introduces the Laws as an interlocutor.

SOCRATES

> Consider it in this way. If, as I was on the point of running away (or whatever it should be called), the laws and the commonwealth should come to me and ask, "Tell me, Socrates, what have you in mind to do? Are you not intending by this thing you are trying to do, to destroy us, the laws, and the entire state, so far as in you lies? Or do you think that state can exist and not be overturned, in which the decisions reached by the courts have no force but are made invalid and annulled by private persons?" What shall we say, Crito, in reply to this question and others of the same kind? For one might say many things, especially if one were an orator, about the destruction of that law which provides that the decisions reached by the courts shall be valid. Or shall we say to them, "The state wronged me and did not judge the case rightly"? Shall we say that, or what?

CRITO

> That is what we shall say, by Zeus, Socrates.

SOCRATES

> What then if the laws should say, "Socrates, is this the agreement you made with us, or did you agree to abide by the verdicts pronounced by the state?" Now if I were surprised by what they said, perhaps they would continue, "Don't be surprised at what we say, Socrates, but answer, since you are in the habit of employing the method of question and answer. Come, what fault do you find

> with us and the state, that you are trying to destroy us? In the first place, did we not bring you forth? Is it not through us that your father married your mother and begat you? Now tell us, have you any fault to find with those of us who are the laws of marriage?"
>
> "I find no fault," I should say. "Or with those that have to do with the nurture of the child after he is born and with his education which you, like others, received? Did those of us who are assigned to these matters not give good directions when we told your father to educate you in music and gymnastics?" "You did," I should say. "What shall we reply to this, Crito, that the laws speak the truth, or not?"
>
> CRITO
>
> I think they do. (*Crito* 11–12)

Socrates leads Crito to the same conclusion that the laws reach, namely, that it was necessary that Socrates stay in prison and face death. This is a case of speech-in-character attributed to an abstract/inanimate object, the Laws.[47]

Lycurgus of Athens. The ancient Greek orator Lycurgus also employs speech-in-character in the form of personification in order to prosecute a certain Leocrates for acts of treason against the state. Unable to marshal personal arguments against Leocrates, Lycurgus personifies the public space of the city itself to depict the harm Leocrates has wrought:

> If you acquit Leocrates, you vote to betray the city and the temple and the ships. But if you kill this man, you will encourage the protection and preservation of the father land and its revenues (or assemblies) and its happiness. Believe, then, Athenians, that beseeching you are the countryside and the trees, that begging you are the harbors, dockyards, and walls of the city, and that thinking it right that you help them are the temples and shrines. (*Leoc.* 150)

Lycurgus differs from other examples in presenting the personified speech-in-character as indirect, reported speech rather than direct discourse, but he is no less effective in characterizing these inanimate objects as giving voice to the offenses of Leocrates against the city.[48] Dionysius praised Lycurgus' ability to place "words in [the speakers'] mouths which suit their several conditions," including "age, family background, education, occupation, way of life."[49]

Epistolary Speech-in-Character

Sallust. The Roman historian and politician Sallust employed the rhetorical device of the embedded letter as a form of speech-in-character to develop his characterization of Catiline, a Roman patrician and politician who led a conspiracy to overthrow the Roman government in 63 BCE.

> Lucius Catilina to Quintus Catulus. Your eminent good faith, known by experience and pleasing to me in my great peril, inspires me with confidence in my putting things into your hands. For that reason I have decided not to make a formal defense in adopting a novel course of action; I have resolved out of no feeling of guilt to set forth an explanation which, so help me, you may perceive is valid. Provoked by wrongs and outrages, since I had been robbed of the fruits of my toil and exertion and was unable to maintain the position of my prestige, I took up the general cause of the unfortunate in keeping with my usual custom; not because I could not pay my personal debts from my own holdings (and the liberality of Orestilla, by means of her own and her daughter's resources, would have wiped out the obligations incurred through others), but because I saw the unworthy elevated to public office and realized that I was an outcast because of baseless suspicion. On this account I have pursued honorable enough hopes of preserving my remaining prestige in view of my situation. Though I would like to write more, word has come that violence is being prepared against me. Now I commend and entrust Orestilla to your protection. Defend her from harm, I beseech you in the name of your own children. Farewell. (*Bell. Cat.* 35.1–6 [Rolfe, LCL])

Despite the apologetic nature of the letter, certain aspects of it confirm and contribute to the negative characterization of Catiline developed by Sallust throughout his portrayal of Catiline's speeches and actions.[50] Sallust begins his essay with these words: "Lucius Catiline, born of a noble family, had great vigor of both mind and body, but an evil and depraved nature. From an early age he delighted in civil wars, bloodshed, pillage, and political dissension" (5.1). Later, Sallust describes the unsavory company Catiline kept:

> In so great and so corrupt body of citizens, Catiline gathered around himself throngs of all depraved and criminal sorts, like attendants (a thing which was very easy to do). For whatever lecher, glutton, or gambler had squandered his family's property in gaming, feasting, or lechery; anyone who had run up immense debt in order to buy his way out of a shameful deed or crime; further, absolutely everyone convicted of murder or sacrilege (or fearing prosecution for their deeds); moreover, those whose hand and tongue supported them by perjury or the murder of their fellow citizens; finally, all who were hounded by depravity, poverty, or a guilty conscience—all these were Catiline's nearest and dearest friends. And if anyone without guilt had happened to become his friend, daily intercourse and allurements easily made him just like the rest. (14.1–3; cf. 18.4)

Catiline admits in his letter that he "took up the general cause of the unfortunate in keeping with my usual custom" and because he himself "had become alienated because of false suspicion" (35.3), though he puts the best face possible on it (35.4–5). This is the very group Catiline rallies to revolution (20.1–7). Finally, before the Roman Senate Catiline, "prepared as he was to conceal all his guilt, with downcast eyes and pleading voice [he] began to beg the senators not to believe rashly anything concerning him" (31.7). So too, in his letter, Catiline refuses to admit guilt or to make a defense (35.2), choosing rather to go into self-imposed exile (34.2–3). Thus, Sallust has employed the rhetorical device of speech-in-character to confirm and extend his depiction of Catiline as an example of the kind of moral decay responsible for the decline of the Roman Republic.[51]

Chariton. We have already encountered Chariton's novel, *Chaereas and Callirhoe*, in Mithridates' *apologia* against Dionysius' accusations of plotting adultery with Callirhoe. There Mithridates invents speech in anticipation of Dionysius' hypothetical response to Mithridates' defense.[52] That conflict was sparked by a letter to Callirhoe from Chaereas, Callirhoe's first husband (whom she believes is dead). The letter (4.4), which ironically everyone except Callirhoe reads, drives the plot of the novel forward, introducing conflict and tension as a love triangle between Callirhoe, Chaereas, and Dionysius unfolds (and is further complicated by Mithridates and the Babylonian satrap, both of whom also fall in love with "beautiful Callirhoe"). Later in the novel, Callirhoe writes a letter of her own, which both brings some partial resolution to the plot and, as an example of epistolary speech-in-character, also reveals something of Callirhoe's character:

> From Callirhoe: greetings to Dionysius, my benefactor—for it was you who freed me from pirates and slavery. Please do not be angry: I am with you in spirit through the son we share; I entrust him to you to bring up and educate in a way worthy of us. Do not let him learn what a stepmother is like. You have a daughter as well as a son; two children are enough for you. Marry them to each other when he comes of age; and send him to Syracuse so that he can see grandfather too. Plangon, my greetings to you; this letter is written in my own hand. Fare you well, good Dionysius, and remember your Callirhoe. (*Chaereas and Callirhoe* 8.4)

On the one hand, with the letter, Callirhoe closes the chapter on her previous marriage to Dionysius. She refers to him as "my benefactor" and not "my husband." Dionysius is no longer Callirhoe's beloved (if he ever was); still, he deserves her respect and gratitude for rescuing her from "pirates and slavery." The change is not lost on Dionysius. When first he receives the letter in the privacy of his own quarters, he kisses the letter and "clasped it to his breast as if it were Callirhoe present in the flesh" (8.5). Kissing the name, "Callirhoe," Dionysius thinks he is receiving a love letter. That hope is dashed: "When he came to the phrase 'to Dionysius, my benefactor,' he groaned—'Ah no longer 'my husband' '" (8.5). On the other hand, Callirhoe does not extinguish the flame of Dionysius' love completely. She pleads with him not to be angry and reminds him that she is with him "in spirit." She speaks of them in the plural as though still a couple. They remain connected by "the son *we* share"; "educate [him] in a way worthy of *us*."[53] She exhorts him not to remarry ("Do not let him learn what a stepmother is like"). And her last words are also a command: "remember *your* Callirhoe." Callirhoe "uses her letter to re-inscribe the love affair, to reinforce the eternal triangle."[54] Her purpose, of course, is to insure a good future for her son.

The letter is successful. Dionysius "was pleased with the plea that the letter contained . . . for it seemed to suggest that she had left him unwillingly" (8.5).[55] He rocks the child in his arms, blames his own jealously for losing Callirhoe, and sets off to Miletus, hoping to find consolation in the many statues of Callirhoe that were erected in that city.

The persona of Callirhoe that is reflected in the letter conforms to her character as developed in the letter. She has always loved Chaereas, though reluctant to make that view public while she was with Dionysius. Without making her own preference known, she allows the queen's servants to offer their advice: "Choose the man who first loved you!" "Choose your benefactor, your savior, not the man who killed you" (6.1).[56] In fact, she had resigned herself to the fact that it was the king who would decide to whom she would be wife, Chaereas or Dionysius ("Let him [the King] release me all the sooner from my worry, I beg, by deciding the issue"; 6.5). But in private, it is clear where her loyalties lay: "Callirhoe would not have welcomed Zeus himself as a husband, or preferred immortality to one day with Chaereas" (6.8; cf. 6.6).

Yet the letter also shows development in Callirhoe's character. Previously, she saw herself as the victim of her beauty: "My beauty, my treacherous beauty, you are the cause of all my troubles. It was because of you that I was carried off and sold; because of you that I married another after Chaereas; because of you that I was taken into Babylon and brought into a courtroom. How many times have you handed me over—to pirates, to the sea, to the tomb, slavery, judgment!" (6.6). Throughout the narrative, Callirhoe has been the object acted upon, in all the ways she lists. But with the letter, she assumes agency. In fact, the narrator reports that her letter to Dionysius "was the only thing she did independently of Chaereas" (8.4). When she gives the letter to her courier, Statira, Artaxerxes' wife, Callirhoe "blushes" (8.4). While the blush may be from a sense of shame or guilt, more likely Callirhoe's blush "is a straightforward acknowledgment that simply writing the letter is a bold act under these circumstances, no matter what its actual contents are."[57]

In the letter itself, she exhorts Dionysius not to remarry and to educate "their" son. She pleads with him to insure a marriage for the boy with one of appropriate status and rank (his half sister), and she commands Dionysius to "remember your Callirhoe" and to remain faithful to her spirit even while being denied her body. Chariton effectively employs epistolary speech-in-character finally to reveal Callirhoe's essence as a character and her development from the object of the actions of others to a self-determined agent on her own.

Examples from the New Testament

We continue to assume, as we did for the examples from the larger rhetorical environment in antiquity, that we should not expect to find full-blown, formulaic expressions of speech-in-character in the New Testament but rather traces of the ways in which the practice of speech-in-character exercises are made manifest as skills transference, in which attributed speech reveals (or adds) something of the speaker's (or writer's) essence.

Speech-in-Character: Specific, Representative, Hypothetical, Living, or Deceased Characters

Parable of the Rich Fool (Luke 12:16-21). The parable of the Rich Fool in Luke 12 presents an interesting case of speech-in-character.[58] First, it is the only parable in Luke in which God functions as a speaking character.[59] And what God says in the parable fits the characterization of God elsewhere in Luke's Gospel. God speaks Scripture (see below), another confirmation that the speech fits the character of God, who is the author of the Jewish Scriptures.

> Then he told them a parable: "The land of a rich man produced abundantly. And he thought to himself, 'What should I do, for I have no place to store my crops?' Then he said, 'I will do this: I will pull down my barns and build larger ones, and there I will store all my grain and my goods. And I will say to my soul, "Soul, you have ample goods laid up for many years; relax, eat, drink, be merry."' But God said to him, 'You fool! This very night your life is being demanded of you. And the things you have prepared, whose will they be?' So it is with those who store up treasures for themselves but are not rich toward God."

The parable "reinforces the concept of the sovereignty of God, a theme that has been explored from the birth narratives and will continue to be explored as the narrative presents a new understanding of the unfolding plan of God."[60] This sovereignty in Luke is often expressed in terms of the "Great Reversal" in which God will exalt the humble and cast down the rich and powerful. In the Magnificat, Mary asserts: God "has brought down the powerful from their thrones, and lifted up the lowly; he has filled the hungry with good things, and sent the rich away empty" (Luke 1:52-53), a sentiment that the Lukan Jesus echoes in his woes in Luke 6 (esp. 6:24) and other teachings (cf. 16:19-31, etc.). In the passage just before the parable in Luke 12, Jesus warns his audience to "fear him, who, after he has killed, has authority to cast into hell" (12:5); clearly, for Luke the one with that authority is God. So one might couch the Lukan Jesus' portrayal of God as a speech-in-character designed to address this question: What would a righteous and sovereign God say to a rich man who hoarded his wealth?[61] This way of reading the parable as depicting Jesus portraying the character of God within direct discourse (in this case, a parable) is, in that sense, reminiscent of Mithridates' characterization of Dionysius in his defense speech in *Chaereas and Chariton*. It also gains traction if one reads Luke 12 as an expanded paraphrase of a briefer version of the parable, preserved in the *Gospel of Thomas*.

> Jesus said, "There was a rich man who had much money. He said, 'I shall put my money to use so that I may sow, reap, plant, and fill my storehouse with produce, with the result that I shall lack nothing.' Such were his intentions, but that same night he died. Let him who has ears hear." (Gos. Thom. 63)[62]

God is missing as a character in Thomas' version, and while one can certainly infer that the rich man's death was the result of divine judgment, that point remains implicit in Thomas. In this scenario, Luke expands (or introduces) the role of God by inventing speech appropriate to the developing characterization of God in the Third Gospel in the form of speech-in-character.[63]

But God is not the only character to whom the Lukan Jesus attributes speech in this parable. The rich man whose land "produced abundantly" (12:16) also speaks. He is not a specific person, but representative of the "rich" (see the representative characters in Theophrastus), and once again, his speech, understood as speech-in-character, fits the larger characterization in the Third Gospel regarding those who have misused their wealth. Within the immediate context of Luke 12, the rich man of the parable illustrates Jesus' warning: "Take care! Be on your guard against all kinds of greed; for one's life does not consist in the abundance of possessions" (12:15). Later in the same chapter, Jesus reiterates this point: "Sell your possessions, and give alms. Make purses for yourselves that do not wear out, an unfailing treasure in heaven, where no thief comes near and no moth destroys. For where your treasure is, there your heart will be also" (12:33-34). These comments comport well with Jesus' criticism of greed and the abuse of wealth elsewhere in the Third Gospel (in addition to the theme of reversal, which includes riches, cf. Luke 1, 6, and 16 cited above; see also 14:12; 16:1-13; 18:1-10, 25; 21:1-4).[64] The character, God, in the parable also adds to the negative characterization of this hoarding attitude by labeling the rich man a "fool." If the reference to "fool" is taken as an intertextual allusion to Psalm 14:1 ("The fool says in his heart, 'There is no God'"), then the rich man is characterized further as a kind of "functional atheist" whose refusal to "render to God what is God's" (Luke 20:25) adds to his condemnation. The implicit question here might be "What words would a (selfish, self-reliant) rich person say when his crops produced an abundant yield?"[65] Once again, speech-in-character is an effective rhetorical tool. Here, as in other places in the Gospels, the Evangelist has "composed words (or redacted written sources) to produce a speech or dialogue that was rhetorically pleasing, suitable to the speaker and listeners, coherent with his exigence and purpose, and that gave what he understood was the substance of the message."[66]

James' speech (Acts 15:13-21).[67] Following the implied speech of Paul and Barnabas, James, the representative of the Jerusalem elders, addresses the assembly. As Peter had offered a theological argument for Gentile inclusion in part on the basis of his personal experience, James offers a theological argument based on another source of authority, Scripture. James begins his speech with a reference to Peter's: "Simeon has explained how God first acted and took a people from among the Gentiles for himself" (15:14). The Greek word for "people" (*laos*) is used elsewhere in Luke and Acts exclusively for the Jews, but here it unmistakably identifies believing Gentiles with God's chosen "people." In James' opinion, circumcision is not necessary for the Gentiles to be saved. On the soteriological question, James agrees with Peter (and Paul and Barnabas). But whereas Peter makes the argument on the basis of God's gift of the Holy Spirit to the Gentiles, making no distinction between Jew and Gentile, and Paul and Barnabas appealed to the signs and wonders performed by God through them among the Gentiles, James makes his argument from Scripture.[68]

James argues that "the words of the prophets agree with this" (15:15), namely that the Gentiles are included in the people of God: "After these things I will return, and I will restore the tent of David, which had fallen. I will rebuild its ruins and restore it in order that the rest of humankind may seek the Lord, even all the nations whom I have called by my name, says the Lord who made these things known long ago" (15:16-18). James employs an exegetical method similar to the *pesharim* found at Qumran in which what "appears to be merely a quotation of a scriptural text turns out to be in fact also an interpretation of the text."[69] Depicting the Jewish Christian, James, as a skilled exegete, familiar with the intricacies of *pesharim*, is another example of speech-in-character. As we shall see, James' audience is well disposed toward his speech and ultimately follows his counsel.

James further contends that the "dwelling of David" that God will build is the eschatological temple, composed not of mortar and bricks but rather formed by the Gentiles together with Jews.[70] Several features of the cited Scriptures support this claim.[71] James offers an intricate exegesis based on Amos 9:11-12. But in the opening and closing frame of the text, he draws also on allusions to other prophetic texts (Jer 12 and Isa 45), hence the opening reference to "the words of the prophets." The first three Greek words of the quotation, "after these things, I will return," do not appear in Amos; rather, they allude to Jeremiah 12:15-16:

> And *after* I have plucked them [the Gentile nations] up, I *will again* have compassion on them. . . . And then, if they will diligently learn the ways of my people, . . . *they shall be built up* in the midst of my people.

Jeremiah refers both to the conversion of the Gentiles and "their being built up" as the eschatological temple.

The conclusion of James' citation, "who made these things known long ago," also departs from Amos, which in the Septuagint version has simply "who did these things." "Known long ago" is an allusion to Isaiah 45:21, which is in the context of another prophecy that the Gentiles will turn to God and be saved (Isa 45:20-22). Thus, these allusions "which frame the main quotation from Amos put the latter in a context of prophecies which associate the eschatological conversion of the Gentile nations with the restoration of the Temple in the Messianic age."[72]

The quotation from Amos itself, however, is necessary to support James' interpretation. Other prophetic texts that predict the inclusion of the Gentiles into God's people *could* be interpreted to mean that these Gentiles would first become proselytes to Judaism and thus undergo circumcision (Zech 2:11; Isa 19:25). But Amos (assisted by allusions to Isa 45 and especially Jer 12) states that the nations *as* nations belong to God. The phrase "all the nations whom I have called by my name" (15:17) is a literal rendering of a Hebrew idiom that elsewhere expresses ownership, especially God's ownership of the people of Israel (Deut 28:10; 2 Chron 7:14; Jer 14:9; Dan 9:19). To these now belong also the Gentiles, and there is no mention here, explicitly or implicitly, of the Gentiles being circumcised or obeying the Mosaic law in order to be called by God's name. Furthermore, in Amos, these Gentiles do not enter the eschatological temple; they *are*, along with remnant Israel, the temple! Therefore, James concludes that Scripture confirms Peter's experience that the Gentiles should not have to become Jews in order to become Christians: "We should not trouble those among the Gentiles who turn to God" (15:19). On the soteriological question, James agrees with Peter: circumcision is *not* necessary for Gentile salvation.

Festus' speech (Acts 25:13-23a). In light of the function of speech-in-character, it is helpful to attend to Festus' speech not only in terms of what it contributes to the plot of Paul's trial but also to the authorial audience's understanding of the characterization (and character) of Festus.

Festus uses the opportunity of Agrippa's presence to involve him in the proceedings against Paul, and of equal importance, to offer a public defense of his own actions. In these two speeches by Festus (25:14-22, 24-27), Luke subtly discloses Festus' hypocrisy without explicitly labeling it as such.[73] Festus' report adds details to the case missing from the narrative, and providing, from his perspective, a fuller account of the proceedings, but in the process, also attempts to put himself in the best possible light before Agrippa. He begins: "There is a man (here), whom Felix left as a prisoner, concerning whom, while I was in Jerusalem, the high priest and elders of the Jews presented charges and requested a ruling against him" (25:14b-15). This description conforms well enough to the narrator's description in 25:2-3 (although it omits any reference to the Jews asking for a "favor"). The language of Festus' claim "not to hand over/grant" (*charizesthai*), however, echoes his intention to grant a "favor" (*charis*) to Paul's accusers (25:9; cf. 25:11). "Festus cites the point in the narrative where he looked good. He guaranteed Paul a trial in Caesarea. However, his choice of words reminds us that he did not show the same commitment to justice when it came to the verdict."[74]

Festus' next statement about conducting the interrogation without delay is likewise accurate but self-serving: "So after they came (back) here with (me), I did not delay at all, but on the next day I sat on the judgment seat and ordered the man to be brought" (25:17). The next part of Festus' report is similar: "But when his accusers stood up, they brought no accusation of the horrible things that I had suspected. Instead, they had certain disagreements with him about their own religion and about a man named Jesus who had died, whom Paul claimed to be alive" (25:18-19). Festus acknowledges that the accusers brought no charges of "horrible things" worthy of the death penalty in Roman law (cf. 25:25), but rather the disagreements were of an intra-Jewish religious nature. This charge resonates with earlier Roman judgments (18:14-15; 23:29) but raises the question for the authorial audience, "If Festus perceived this to be the case, why did he not say so at the trial and acquit Paul?"[75] Why, in other words, does he allow it to get to the point where Paul must appeal to Caesar for any chance of justice?

Festus' next statement stands in direct conflict with the earlier account provided by the narrator: "Since I was baffled by the dispute over these matters, I asked if he might want to go to Jerusalem and be tried there on these charges" (25:20). Festus' confession to being "baffled by the dispute over these matters" can be taken as admission to his lack of knowledge of and experience with matters of Jewish religion (cf. also 26:24). Thus, he could be appealing for help from Agrippa, who is not only a Jew but acknowledged (later in the narrative by none other than Paul) to have expertise in Jewish matters (26:3, 26). But the authorial audience also knows that the public face of ignorance of things Judaica stands in conflict with the fact that Festus suggests Jerusalem as a venue for the trial, not because there are others there more familiar with Jewish customs who can insure a fair trial for Paul, but because he wished "to grant a favor to the Jews" (25:9). Whether ignorant or calculating, Festus, in the eyes of the authorial audience, "has ceased to be a just judge."[76]

Festus arranges for Agrippa himself to meet Paul, and the appointed time for the interview arrives (25:23a). Festus continues with his self-serving report, this time before a public audience. He exaggerates the pressure he is under. He claims "the entire Jewish populace appealed" to him "both in Jerusalem" and in Caesarea. He portrays the situation as one of near mass chaos and a people on the verge of riot, enough to disturb any Roman official. But the fact is that the disturbance with the Jewish mob at the temple occurred before Festus arrived in Jerusalem and only "the high priests and prominent men of the Jews" made appeals to him in Jerusalem (25:2-3) and later in Caesarea (25:6-7). He has magnified the extent of the disturbance and his role in quelling it.

In this imagined riot, Festus depicts the crowd shouting that Paul must die; he, however, just dispenser of Roman law that he was, decreed: "I, on the other hand, realized that he had done nothing worthy of death; but since he himself appealed to the Emperor, I decided to send him" (25:25). The authorial audience is left to wonder: if Festus is the great model of Roman justice, why does Paul invoke the *provocatio*, a provision usually reserved for Roman citizens who fear justice will not otherwise be served for them? If one takes Festus' remarks at face value, then Paul's request is incomprehensible. If, however, his speeches are understood as a cover-up, then Paul's appeal to Caesar to escape the incompetence if not corruption of this "judge" is understandable.

Festus ends his speech with an appeal for aid: "I do not have anything definite to write to our Master about him. Therefore, I have brought him before you all, and especially before you, King Agrippa, so that after a hearing has occurred I will have something to write. For it seems ridiculous to me to send a prisoner without indicating the charges against him" (25:26-27). The mention of Festus writing to the emperor refers to a "letter of report" (*dimissoria littera*), similar to the one Lysias had sent Felix. Such letters were sent when a judge or official determined to send a prisoner to a higher court. The letter was intended to present the results of previous inquiries and interrogations along with reasons justifying the remission of the prisoner to a higher court (see Ulpianus, *Digest* 49.6.1; cf. also Acts 23:26-30). Festus, however, cannot justify charges against Paul and therefore cannot pen the letter. The decision to send Paul to Rome relieves one problem but creates another. Festus is no longer responsible for rendering a judgment in Paul's case, but he must specify the charges against Paul in a letter to the emperor. Perhaps his motivation to include Agrippa is grounded in the desire to have someone share the responsibility should the authorities at Rome determine that the charges against Paul are of no substance but rather are due to the incompetence of the local administration.

As we have seen, speeches allow for the writer to explore the character of the speaker through the rhetorical convention of speech-in-character. In the case of Festus, that personality is complex, even duplicitous. The actions and motives for actions shown to the audience by the narrator do not mesh with the public persona that Felix gives himself before Agrippa and Bernice and later their entourage. He seeks to portray himself as a competent Roman administrator, capable of meting out justice, but this portrayal stands in contrast to Luke's presentation in which Festus' actions are, partially at least, "tainted by favoritism."[77] With literary finesse, Luke uses the rhetorical strategy of the speech-in-character to characterize the ambiguous, conflicting, and even hypocritical responses of Roman authority to Paul and his message.

1 Thessalonians.[78] In the context of his discussion of the "times and the seasons," Paul employs a form of speech-in-character, speech attributed to an unspecified "they":

> Now concerning the times and the seasons, brothers and sisters, you do not need to have anything written to you. For you yourselves know very well that the day of the Lord will come like a thief in the night. When they say, "There is peace and security," then sudden destruction will come upon them, as labor pains come upon a pregnant woman, and there will be no escape! (5:1-3)

In order to depict the suddenness with which the "day of the Lord" will arrive, Paul first uses the dominical image of a "thief in the night" (cf. Matt 24:43-44/ Luke 12:39-40). Then he introduces unspecified speakers: "When they say, 'There is peace and security,' then sudden destruction will come upon them." He adds a third image comparing the coming of that day with labor pains coming upon a pregnant woman, from which "there will be no escape." Those making this statement, "there is peace and security," stand in contrast with Paul's audience, the Thessalonian Christians: unlike the saying's speakers, they (Thessalonian Christians) are "not in darkness" but are "children of light and of the day" (5:4-5).[79] But who are "they"? In a sense, their identity is problematic for the modern interpreter, but not for Paul's original audience, who, presumably, would have known their identity.[80] The speakers have been viewed as representing false prophets, who, like their counterparts in the Jewish scriptures, cry, "Peace, peace, where there is no peace" (Jer 6:14).[81] Others think Paul is offering a critique of those who, through these words, are expressing a pro-Roman imperialism. They have mistakenly placed their trust in the Roman authorities to provide "peace and security."[82]

Justin King has combined these two views to argue that Paul has modified Jeremiah 6 (which also includes a reference to birth pangs, cf. 6:24) by replacing "Peace, Peace," with "Peace and Security," thus extending Jeremiah's critique of false prophets to include those in Thessalonica who were depending on Rome to provide what it could not, eschatological security: "As Jeremiah's false prophets were claiming peace in its absence, so also those proclaiming the Roman values of peace and security were advocating the present reality of Roman peace and security in ignorance of the eschatological peace that was yet to come."[83] The attributed speech, assigned now to an unspecified group, fits the characterization of nonbelievers who have misplaced their trust for their well-being and now are unprepared for the sudden destruction which will fall upon those "in the darkness" when the day of the Lord comes.[84]

Hebrews.[85] The author of Hebrews attributes three Scripture passages to Jesus in Hebrews 2:11b-13 in a form of speech-in-character:

> For this reason Jesus is not ashamed to call them brothers and sisters, saying, "I will proclaim your name to my brothers and sisters, in the midst of the congregation I will praise you." And again, "I will put my trust in him." And again, "Here am I and the children whom God has given me."

The first citation (2:12) comes from Psalm (LXX) 21:23 ("I will proclaim your name to my brothers and sisters, in the midst of the congregation I will praise you"), a psalm that begins with the familiar lament uttered by Jesus, "My God, my God, why have you forsaken me?" (Mark 15:34; Matt 27:46). The author of Hebrews had just asserted that God had made Jesus, the pioneer of salvation, "perfect through suffering" (2:10) and just after the speech-in-character affirms the solidarity Christ shared "in flesh and blood" so that "through death he might destroy him who has the power of death, that is, the devil" (2:14). Thus, here Jesus is "not ashamed" to identify fellow human beings as "brothers and sisters" (2:11; cf. 2:7; 5:1-3). This citation also underscores Jesus' relationship to God (cf. 1:5-8; 3:3; 5:5); Jesus, through the psalm, proclaims (*apangelō*) God's name to his siblings; Jesus also sings hymns (*hymnēsō*) to God in the midst of the congregation (*ekklēsia*). "The fact that Jesus leads the congregation in the worship and praise of God . . . hints at Christ's role as high priest" (cf. Heb 1:3; 4:14–5:5; 7:15-28; 8:1-7; 9:11-14; 10:11-12).[86]

The next two quotations attributed to Jesus in Hebrews 2 appear to derive from Isaiah (LXX) 8:17-18;[87] however, all three Scripture citations are separated by the words "and again" (*kai palin*). Splitting the Isaiah passage suggests the two halves are intended to make different points. The second of the three citations ("I will put my trust in him") is taken from the second half of Isaiah (LXX) 8:17. The author slightly modifies the quotation by adding the emphatic pronoun *egō*, clarifying that Jesus is still the speaker. The quotation, originally spoken by Isaiah, is now attributed to Jesus and through it Jesus declares his ultimate trust in God. This characterization fits the depiction found later of Jesus in which he "offered up prayers and supplications . . . to him who was able to save him from death" (5:7) and was obedient to God (5:8; 10:7-9).

In its original context, the final quotation ("Here am I and the children whom God has given me") referred to Isaiah and his children. Here on Jesus' lips, the children are not Jesus' biological children but refer to his family of faith: "The one who exemplified trust in God is now in turn entrusted with God's children to care for them."[88] The kinship imagery shifts from siblings to children. Jesus stands in egalitarian solidarity with humanity as a brother, but he also been made benefactor of those same believers, who are dependent upon him for their salvation as children are dependent on parents for their well-being. Once again, this depiction fits well with Jesus' characterization elsewhere in Hebrews: everything is "in subjection to him" (1:8). Christ is "pioneer of their ['the many sons and daughters'] salvation" (2:10; cf. 5:9; 7:25). He has delivered "all those who through fear of death were subject to lifelong bondage" (2:16). "Christ was faithful over God's house" (3:6). By attributing scriptural citations to Jesus through the rhetorical device of speech-in-character in Hebrews 2:12-13, the author of Hebrews is able to enrich the characterization of Jesus found throughout the remainder of the argument.[89]

Speech-in-Character and Personification[90]

Galatians. In Galatians 3:8, Paul employs personification as a form of speech-in-character: "And the scripture, foreseeing that God would justify the Gentiles by faith, declared the gospel beforehand to Abraham, saying, 'All the Gentiles shall be blessed in you'" (3:8).[91] The Scripture is depicted as having foreknowledge of God's justification of the Gentiles and of declaring that good news to Abraham. Paul attributes direct speech to personified Scripture,[92] a point underscored by the shift from the third person singular pronoun *auto* (in LXX Gen 18:18) to the second person singular pronoun *soi* (in LXX Gen 12:3). This use of personified speech-in-character allows Paul to present the continuing relevance of the divine directive given to Abraham not only for the Jews but for "all the Gentiles."[93] Thus, Galatians 3:8 meets the expectations of speech-in-character developed in the rhetorical tradition:

> (1) Paul shapes and attributes speech to another speaker. (2) The assigned speech is appropriate to the character of the imagined speaker. (3) The assigned speech is actual speech that is recorded within scripture itself. (4) All three accompanying elements are present: Paul first identifies a new speaker, characterizes the newly introduced speaker, and assigns appropriate speech-in-character. Finally, (5) Paul's attribution of speech to an inanimate object is sufficiently supported in the discussions of the rhetorical figure in the primary literature.[94]

Romans. There is another example of personified speech by Paul in Romans 10:6-8:[95]

> But the righteousness that comes from faith says, "Do not say in your heart, 'Who will ascend into heaven?'" (that is, to bring Christ down) "or 'Who will descend into the abyss?'" (that is, to bring Christ up from the dead). But what does it say? "The word is near you, on your lips and in your heart" (that is, the word of faith that we proclaim).

Paul attributes speech to an "abstract" concept, "righteousness that comes from faith," to bolster his argument that righteousness based on faith "has nothing to do with 'doing' by 'ascending' or 'descending' (i.e., 'chasing'); rather the proclaimed word about πίστις is already nearby in one's mouth and heart and requires no one to retrieve it."[96] As such, the personified righteousness provides additional support from scripture itself (LXX Deut 9:4, 30:11-14; LXX Ps 106:26) of

Paul's claim in Romans 10:4 that the telos of the law is Christ, which results in righteousness for all those characterized by faith (and not works).[97] The work of Christ's descent and ascent has already been accomplished; what remains is the word of faith proclaimed "on your lips and in your heart" (10:8). Once again, speech-in-character is an effective rhetorical device employed by Paul in his theological argument. It is attributed speech to an abstract concept, appropriate to the context, that conforms to the characterization of the concept of righteousness, based on faith, found before this point in Romans (cf. Rom 1:17; 3:21-22; 4:3-13, 22; 6:16-20; 9:30-31).

Epistolary Speech-in-Character

Given what we learned above about speech-in-character being practiced in the context of fictive letter writing, we should not be surprised to find that the letters in Acts 15 and 23 also reveal something about the character of their senders.[98]

Apostolic decree (Acts 15).[99] Following their deliberations regarding the inclusion of Gentiles in the fledgling Christian communities (Acts 15:1-21), attendees at the so-called Jerusalem Council came to the following decision.

> Then the apostles and the elders, with the consent of the whole church, decided to choose men from among their members and to send them to Antioch with Paul and Barnabas. They sent Judas called Barsabbas, and Silas, leaders among the brothers, with the following letter:
>
> "The brothers, both the apostles and the elders, to the believers of Gentile origin in Antioch and Syria and Cilicia, greetings. Since we have heard that certain persons who have gone out from us, though with no instructions from us, have said things to disturb you and have unsettled your minds, we have decided unanimously to choose representatives and send them to you, along with our beloved Barnabas and Paul, who have risked their lives for the sake of our Lord Jesus Christ. We have therefore sent Judas and Silas, who themselves will tell you the same things by word of mouth. For it has seemed good to the Holy Spirit and to us to impose on you no further burden than these essentials: that you abstain from what has been sacrificed to idols and from blood and from what is strangled and from fornication. If you keep yourselves from these, you will do well. Farewell." (15:22-29)

When placed in the larger context of Acts 15, the "apostolic decree" contributes to the characterization of its senders, especially James.[100] The prohibitions listed in the decree echo James' conclusion in 15:20 and solidify his position not only as a competent messianic exegete of Scripture but also as the acknowledged leader not only of the elders but of "the apostles and and elders," indeed, of all the fellow believers (15:23). This position as leader of the Jerusalem church is reiterated when Paul visits Jerusalem and presents himself to James, along with the elders of the church (21:18); once again, Paul is reminded of the contents of the letter (21:25). But the letter does more than contribute to James' characterization.

The letter also amplifies the decision-making process to include the Holy Spirit: "It seemed best to the Holy Spirit and to us" (15:28). Not explicitly mentioned in the deliberations of 15:1-21 (though see 15:8), the Holy Spirit's inclusion in the letter contributes to the characterization of the Holy Spirit's pivotal role in the Gentile mission. The Spirit directs Philip to the Ethiopian eunuch (8:29) and Peter to Cornelius (11:12). The gift of the Spirit to Cornelius and his household provides the testimony Peter needs to baptize them (10:44, 46). After the council the Holy Spirit continues to guide the mission; in fact, Paul gives his final words in Acts over to the Holy Spirit who through the prophet Isaiah proclaims, "Therefore, let it be known to you that this salvation from God has been sent to the Gentiles; and they will listen!" (28:28). Thus, the addition of the Holy Spirit adds authoritative weight to the church's decision.

Lysias' letter (Acts 23). The second embedded letter in Acts is by the Roman military tribune, Lysias, who extracted Paul from a dispute with the Jewish leaders that had turned violent and placed him under house arrest (23:1-11); he also thwarted an effort to ambush and kill Paul, being warned by Paul's nephew (23:12-24, 31-32).

> Claudius Lysias to his Excellency the governor Felix, greetings. This man was seized by the Jews and was about to be killed by them, but when I had learned that he was a Roman citizen, I came with the guard and rescued him. Since I wanted to know the charge for which they accused him, I had him brought to their council. I found that he was accused concerning questions of their law, but was charged with nothing deserving death or imprisonment. When I was informed that there would be a plot against the man, I sent him to you at once, ordering his accusers also to state before you what they have against him. (23:26-30)

Lysias' letter not only recapitulates the events leading up to and including Paul's arrest (with the requisite amplifications and omissions, cf. *Rhet. Alex.* 28.2–4) but also reveals something of the character of Claudius Lysias (and perhaps more than Lysias himself would have preferred). Lysias is a complex figure. He has acted decisively in Paul's behalf, thrice intervening in life-threatening situations (21:31-36; 23:10; 23:23-25). He has also been persistent in his investigations to learn the facts about Paul, and he has been willing to change previous impressions about Paul (that he was an Egyptian insurrectionist; to accept that he was a Roman citizen; and now to believe the reports of Jewish conspiracy to kill Paul). Thus, he accurately reports that his conclusion that the conflict between Paul and his opponents was an intra-Jewish dispute "with respect to matters of their law." And he rightly concludes that Paul "was charged with nothing deserving death or imprisonment" (Acts 23:29).

But in this letter, the audience also learns that Lysias is willing to rearrange and suppress the facts to put himself in a better light. In the letter to Felix, Lysias suggests that he intervened in Paul's behalf *because* he was a Roman citizen (23:27); from this account Paul presumably would not have been bound or imprisoned (underscored by the fact that Lysias found no charge worthy "of imprisonment"). But the audience knows that Lysias had at first thought Paul was a revolutionary and learns of Paul's citizenship only *after* he had placed him in chains and nearly had him flogged, a point Lysias conveniently omits. "In both instances, the discrepancies suggest that Roman officials need to present a public image that partially conceals the truth about their actions and motives."[101] Lysias' self-assurance in decision-making is marred with interests of self-protection.[102]

Conclusion

The preliminary exercise on speech-in-character is not often imported as an identifiable genre in ancient prose composition. Nevertheless, speeches—recorded, reported, attributed, and invented—permeated ancient culture, and the skills developed in practicing speech-in-character and then employed by writers attributing speeches to characters in their compositions are unmistakable. These speeches, when well formed, contribute to the disclosure and development of the speaker's character and, in the case of narrative texts, often contribute to the plot's development and resolution.

Notes

1 See Justin King, "Speech-in-Character, Diatribe, and Romans 3:1-9: Who's Speaking When and Why It Matters" (Ph.D. diss., Baylor University, 2016), 16n1.

2 Further on the distinctions, see Brian C. Small, *The Characterization of Jesus in the Book of Hebrews*, BibInt 128 (Leiden: Brill, 2014), 140–44. Theon is also distinctive in placing this exercise after ekphrasis; the others all place it after the exercise on synkrisis. Nicolaus (*Prog.* 63–64) justifies placing "ethopoeia" (as he calls it) after comparison since both exercises require addressing the "'proposed situations' since it is necessary to take account of the speaker and the one to whom he is speaking; 'ethos or pathos or both' since one looks either to the universal or to what came from the circumstance; for this is how ethos differs from pathos."

3 George A. Kennedy, *Progymnasmata: Greek Textbooks of Prose Composition and Rhetoric* (Atlanta: Society of Biblical Literature, 2003), 115n70, clarifies: "The status of the speaker at the time the speech is imagined as being given is what determines whether it is ethopoeia or eidolopoeia. A speech Heracles might have given while alive is an example of ethopoeia, a speech he might have given after death is an eidolopoeia."

4 In a similar way, the anonymous author of *Rhetorica ad Herennium* (4.66) distinguishes between *sermocinatio* (attributing real or invented speech to human characters, named or representative) and *conformatio* (attributing speech to mute and inanimate objects [or ideas]).

5 Nicolaus also focuses on the arrangement of ethopoeia, suggesting the rhetorical movement should be from the present to the past, back to the present, and then to the future (*Prog.* 65–66;

see also Ps.-Hermogenes, *Prog.* 21–22; Aphthonius, *Prog.* 35). He also asserts (66–67) that ethopoeia is best suited for "speaking an encomium and prosecuting and giving counsel."

6 Quintilian also introduces the notion of ethopoeia in a convoluted way that does not impact our discussion (9.2.58). See King, "Speech-in-Character," 32n19.

7 Nicolaus (*Prog.* 65) notes it is usually the poets who practice personification of inanimate objects or abstract ideas because they have "the privilege of changing lifeless things into persons and giving them things to say."

8 See Kennedy's translation of *prosopopoeia* in Theon, *Prog.* 115, in *Progymnasmata: Greek Textbooks of Prose Composition and Rhetoric*, 47. Harry Caplan, in his Loeb translation of *Rhetorica ad Herennium* (which we also use in this work), also uses "personification." For more on the various options for translation of these terms, see King, "Speech-in-Character," 16n1.

9 On personification in antiquity, see Emma Stafford and Judith Herrin, eds., *Personification in the Greek World: From Antiquity to Byzantium* (Aldershot: Ashgate, 2005).

10 In addition, "'impersonation' potentially suggests the kind of mimicry and sarcasm Quintilian specifically wishes to avoid (*Inst.* 1.8.3)" (King, "Speech-in-Character," 16n1).

11 James R. Butts, "The *Progymnasmata* of Theon: A New Text with Translation and Commentary" (Ph.D. diss., Claremont Graduate School, 1987), 459–60.

12 King, "Speech-in-character," 16n1.

13 See also Emma Stafford, *Worshipping Virtues: Personification and the Divine in Ancient Greece* (London: Duckworth, 2000), 5–9.

14 Our focus will be on Theon's presentation of speech-in-character. As we proceed, we will explore the other progymnasmata and handbooks in light of his comments.

15 Interestingly, at none of these points does Theon give examples of what such speech might look like. One must wait for Aphthonius to give the example of "what words Niobe might say when her children lie dead" (*Prog.* 45–46).

16 Theon also asserts that the exercise of speech-in-character is appropriate for the rhetorical species of consolation, exhortation, and letter writing. We will return to letter writing momentarily (which Theon himself does not pursue), but first let us explore what Theon calls the "special materials" for exhortation and consolation, to which he also adds the activity of dissuading and seeking forgiveness (*Prog.* 116). These "special materials" are important especially if the speech-in-character includes pathos and aims at eliciting an emotional response (in addition to fitting the character of the speaker). If the purpose of the speech-in-character is to exhort, then the speech should be "beneficial, just reverent . . . [and] pleasant." Any prior relationship between the exhorter and exhorted should be specified. If the purpose is to dissuade, then the opposite kind of arguments should be in play (*Prog.* 117). In consolation, the speaker should indicate "that what has happened was unavoidable and common to all [hu]mankind and was unintentional" (*Prog.* 117).

17 The following is taken (with modifications) from King, "Speech-in-Character," 53–54.

18 Unlike Quintilian and later theorists, for whom speech may be attributed to an idea, inanimate object, or animal. We will include samples of such speech-in-character (what resemble "personification") in our examples section below.

19 King has a similar, but distinctive, list of core elements of speech-in-character, derived from a comparison and synthesis of common elements in the progymnasmata, Quintilian, and *Rhetorica ad Herennium*; see 65–70.

20 Craig A. Gibson, "*Prosopopoeia* in the New Testament: Where Should We Look, and What Should We Expect to Find?" (paper presented at the Annual Meeting of the Society of Biblical Literature, Philadelphia, November, 2005), 5. Cited by permission of the author.

21 We generally agree with Gibson's conclusion, but because he follows Heath in dating Theon to the fifth century CE, Gibson's analysis is somewhat skewed. His six-point pattern of speech-in-character is drawn exclusively on evidence from Aphthonius and Nicolaus and

creates expectations regarding the length and form of speech-in-character that may set the bar unreasonably high for any ancient authors, and not just the NT writers. He cites the example of Nikephorus, a twelfth-century Christian teacher of Greek rhetoric, who used NT examples in teaching the progymnasmata. But Nikephorus shares with the earlier progymnasmatists a pedagogical focus on instructing students in particular rhetorical skills and conventions. For a critique of Gibson's argument, see King, "Speech-in-Character," 64n31.

22 Gibson, "*Prosopopoeia* in the New Testament," 9 (emphasis in original).

23 Gibson, "*Prosopopoeia* in the New Testament," 11. Gibson continues, "We might learn more about the New Testament's use of attributed speech by studying how other progymnasmata, declamations, and contemporary Greek literature outside the New Testament, absorbed, dismembered, or redirected the original exercise, stripping it of the formal markers that would make it easier for us to identify its origin" (11).

24 Kennedy, *Progymnasmata: Greek Textbooks of Prose Composition and Rhetoric*, 48n149.

25 Patricia A. Rosenmeyer, *Ancient Epistolary Fictions: The Letter in Greek Literature* (Cambridge: Cambridge University Press, 2001), 260. See also Patricia A. Rosenmeyer, *Ancient Greek Literary Letters: Selections in Translation* (London: Routledge, 2006), 130–60.

26 Rosenmeyer, *Ancient Epistolary Fictions*, 260.

27 Any Pauline letter deemed to be a pseudonym (e.g., the Pastoral Epistles) might be considered an example of a letter form of speech-in-character in which the author writes in the character of Paul addressing a question something like, "What would Paul say to this particular situation?" See Harry O. Maier, *Picturing Paul in Empire: Imperial Image, Text and Persuasion in Colossians, Ephesians and the Pastoral Epistles* (London: Bloomsbury, 2013).

28 Plutarch (*Per.* 8.4) also recognized Pericles' reputation as a skilled orator.

29 John D. Duncan, "Adaptation and Alienation: Speakers' Sensitivity to Audiences in the Rhetorical Handbooks, Ancient Greek Narrative Works, and the Book of Acts" (Ph.D. diss., Baylor University, forthcoming), 34–35.

30 See Duncan, "Adaptation and Alienation," 33. Duncan (33n85) notes: "Pericles' first speech (1.139–45) does effectively function for Thucydides' authorial audience as a response to the Corinthian speech at 1.119–25 . . . , but the two speeches are nonetheless addressed to different narrative audiences so that no characters in the narrative are able to weigh the competing claims of the two speeches as in more typical Thucydidean debates."

31 Our thanks to John Duncan for suggesting this example and providing interpretive insights on it.

32 For other examples of speech-in-character in Theophrastus, see 1.6 (dissembly); 2 (flattery, occurs throughout); 3.3 (idle chatter); 4.12 (boorishness); 5.5, 10 (obsequiousness); 7.2, 7, 8 (garrulity); 8.2, 3, 6, 8, 9 (rumor-mongering); 13.11 (overzealousness); 14.2, 6, 12, 13 (absent-mindedness); 15.2, 4 (grouchiness); 17.2, 3, 5, 6, 7, 9 (griping); 19.9 (mistrust); 20.5, 7, 10 (bad taste); 21.11 (petty ambition); 22.11 (miserliness); 23.4 (fraudulence). Thanks to Amanda Brobst-Renaud for suggesting these examples.

33 The editors of the Loeb edition have marked the philosopher's response with quotation marks. We have retained the quotation marks for the philosopher and set the text into the form of a dialogue.

34 On Epictetus' exchange with the "philosopher" as an example of both diatribe and speech-in-character, see King, "Speech-in-Character," 199–203.

35 King, "Speech-in-Character," 202.

36 King, "Speech-in-Character," 202.

37 Mithridates had Chaereas write a letter to Callirhoe telling her he was still alive. The letter was intercepted by Dionysius, and thinking it was forged by Mithridates and taking it as evidence that Mithridates intended to begin an adulterous affair with Callirhoe, he initiated legal proceedings against Mithridates.

38 And, as Mithridates points out, if Dionysius asserts that Callirhoe was freeborn, then Mithridates is innocent and Dionysius is guilty of kidnapping.
39 The king does, in fact, dismiss the case against Mithridates for "he had produced a brilliant defense" (4.8), and moves on to decide who, in fact, was Callirhoe's legal husband, a judgment complicated by the fact that the king himself had fallen in love with Callirhoe!
40 See also the discussion of Callirhoe's letter below.
41 The story continues in 2 Macc 6 to record the last words of Eleazar before he succumbs to death.
42 The narrator also invents a speech by Eleazar in response to Antiochus (4 Macc 5:16-38), which is another example of speech-in-character that answers the implicit question, "What would a pious Jew say to a tyrant threatening him with martyrdom if he did not participate in acts that repudiated his faith?"
43 On this example, see Hans-Josef Klauck, *Ancient Letters and the New Testament: A Guide to Context and Exegesis* (Waco: Baylor University Press, 2006), 178–79.
44 See also Cicero's speech-in-character invented for the spirit of Appius Claudius Caelio (*Cael.* 33–34); cited by Kennedy, *Progymnasmata: Greek Textbooks of Prose Composition*, 85n44.
45 See note 16 above.
46 Jerome (*Epist.* 22.13.2) echoes Tertullian's argument; see Neil Adkin, "'Istae sunt, quae solent dicere': Three Roman Vignettes in Jerome's 'Libellus de virginitate servanda' (*Epist.* 22)," *MH* 39 (1992): 131–40.
47 Later progymnasmatists would label this prosopopoeia (cf. e.g., Ps.-Hermogenes, *Prog.* 20).
48 Danielle S. Allen, "Changing the Authoritative Voice: Lycurgus' 'Against Leocrates,'" *ClAnt* 19 (2000): 5–33.
49 Cited in Kristine S. Bruss, "Persuasive Ethopoeia in Dionysius' *Lysias*," *Rhetorica: A Journal of the History of Rhetoric* 31 (2013): 34–57, here 36.
50 See Ann Thomas Wilkins, *Villain or Hero: Sallust's Portrayal of Catiline* (New York: Peter Lang, 1994), 29–70. Wilkins argues for a more complex characterization of Catiline than is typically found in the secondary literature.
51 On the example of Catiline's letter in Sallust as speech-in-character, see Justin Howell, "Embedded Letters and Rhetorical αὔξησις," in *Contemporary Studies in Acts*, ed. Thomas E. Philips (Macon, Ga.: Mercer University Press, 2009), 160–62.
52 See above, pp. 148–49.
53 The audience knows that Chaereas is father of the child, but Dionysius still thinks the child is his.
54 Rosenmeyer, *Ancient Epistolary Fictions*, 145.
55 The narrator makes transparent his evaluation of Dionysius' misreading of the letter: "Love is such an irresponsible thing and can easily persuade a lover that he is loved in return!"
56 In a fit of jealousy, Chaereas had kicked Callirhoe and, thinking he had killed her, had her buried.
57 Rosenmeyer, *Ancient Epistolary Fictions*, 144. Callirhoe confides to Statira that she fears that "now that he [Dionysius] is separated from me he may kill himself" (8.4). Given that the purpose of the letter is to secure her son's future, which is dependent on Dionysius' benevolence toward him, her concern for his safety is clearly not limited simply to her continuing affection for Dionysius.
58 For much of what follows, see Josh Stigall, "The Progymnasmata and Characterization in Luke's Parables: The Parable of the Rich Fool as a Test Case," *PRSt* 39 (2012): 349–60.
59 Certainly, there are parables in which a main character is easily allegorized as a God figure, for example the Father in the parable of the Prodigal Son in Luke 15, but none of the Lukan parables names God as a character other than this one in Luke 12.
60 Charles Wade Bibb, "The Characterization of God in Luke-Acts" (Ph.D. diss., Southern Baptist Theological Seminary, 1996), 115; cited by Stigall, "Progymnasmata and

Characterization" 359. See also John T. Squires, *The Plan of God in Luke-Acts* (Cambridge: Cambridge University Press, 1993).

61 Slightly modifying Stigall, "Progymnasmata and Characterization," 359.

62 The translation is taken from Helmut Koester, *The Gospel of Thomas*, in *The Nag Hammadi Library in English*, ed. James M. Robinson (San Francisco: Harper, 1990), 133.

63 The reference to Thomas' version is purely for illustrative purposes. We are not suggesting that Luke had direct knowledge of Thomas (or even an earlier version of the parable), but Thomas does have the heuristic value of highlighting the speech of God. The parable certainly could have achieved the same purpose(s) without introducing God as a character or attributing speech to God, and, of course, it is entirely plausible that the Gos. Thom. does not have the interest in the characterization of God that Luke does and has condensed a longer version reflected in the Third Gospel (see ch. 2 on fables).

64 See Stigall, "Progymnasmata and Characterization," 358. On Luke's view of wealth, see, inter alia, Luke Timothy Johnson, *The Literary Function of Possessions in Luke-Acts*, SBLDS 39 (Missoula, Mont.: Scholars Press, 1977); Christopher M. Hays, *Luke's Wealth Ethics: A Study in Their Coherence and Characterization*, WUNT 2/275 (Tübingen: Mohr Siebeck, 2010).

65 Once again modifying Stigall, "Progymnasmata and Characterization," 357. In the Gos. Thom. version, the rich man does speak (unlike God whose explicit mention, as we noted, is missing). Still, it is instructive to notice the expansions in Luke in light of the rhetorical device of speech-in-character.

66 Robert Simons, "The Magnificat: Cento, Psalm or Imitatio?" *TynBul* 60 (2009): 33. Simons (esp. 42–45) examines the Magnificat (Luke 1:46-55) as an example of speech-in-character.

67 For what follows, see Parsons, *Acts*, Paideia (Grand Rapids: Baker Academic), 212–15.

68 Richard Bauckham, "James and the Jerusalem Church," in *The Book of Acts in its Palestinian Setting*, ed. Richard Bauckham (Grand Rapids: Eerdmans, 1995), 452.

69 Bauckham, "James and the Jerusalem Church," 453.

70 Bauckham, "James and the Jerusalem Church," 454–55.

71 For what follows, see Bauckham, "James and the Jerusalem Church," 454–58.

72 Bauckham, "James and the Jerusalem Church," 455.

73 Robert C. Tannehill, *The Narrative Unity of Luke-Acts: A Literary Interpretation*, 2 vols. (Philadelphia: Fortress, 1986–1990), 2:310–15.

74 Tannehill, *Narrative Unity*, 2:311.

75 Tannehill, *Narrative Unity*, 2:311.

76 Tannehill, *Narrative Unity*, 2:313.

77 Tannehill, *Narrative Unity*, 2:314.

78 For what follows, see King, "Speech-in-Character," 78–85.

79 King, "Speech-in-Character," 78.

80 Abraham Malherbe, *The Letters to the Thessalonians: A New Translation with Introduction and Commentary*, AB 32B (New York: Doubleday, 2000), 291.

81 Malherbe, *Thessalonians*, 291–304; cited by King, "Speech-in-Character," 80.

82 Peter Oakes, "Re-mapping the Universe: Paul and the Emperor in 1 Thessalonians and Philippians," *JSNT* 27 (2005): 317; Jeffrey A. D. Weima, "'Peace and Security' (1 Thess 5:3): Prophetic Warning or Political Propaganda?" *NTS* 58 (2012): 331. Joel R. White, "'Peace and Security' (1 Thessalonians 5:3): Is It Really a Roman Slogan?" *NTS* 59 (2013): 382–95, has argued that "peace and security" cannot be established as a slogan of imperial propaganda (as Oakes and Weima suggest). That does not mean that Paul did not intend to evoke the concept or notion of imperial propaganda with the phrase; cf. King, "Speech-in-Character," 81–82.

83 King, "Speech-in-Character," 83.

84 And, as King, "Speech-in-Character," 83, points out, the fact that the speech-in-character of 1 Thess 5:3 is within a hortatory context comports well with Theon's observation that

exhortation was especially well-suited for speech-in-character (see *Prog.* 115.20–22; 116.27–117.4).

85 See Small, *Characterization of Jesus in Hebrews*, 197–201; also Matthew W. Bates, *The Hermeneutics of the Apostolic Proclamation: The Center of Paul's Method of Scriptural Interpretation* (Waco: Baylor University Press, 2012), 296–97; 315.

86 Small, *Characterization of Jesus in Hebrews*, 197–98.

87 See Small, *Characterization of Jesus in Hebrews*, 198, who nonetheless recognizes that other texts (Isa 12:2; 2 Sam 22:3) have also been suggested as intertextual echoes of Heb 2:13.

88 Small, *Characterization of Jesus in Hebrews*, 201.

89 The Fourth Gospel also uses speech-in-character in which Scripture citations are attributed to Jesus to contribute to his characterization; see Alicia D. Myers, *Characterizing Jesus: A Rhetorical Analysis on the Fourth Gospel's Use of Scripture in its Presentation of Jesus*, LNTS 458 (London: T&T Clark, 2012). Since the Gospel of John is a narrative in which Jesus' speech has a narrative audience, Myers has noted that Jesus' speech, while appropriate to the rhetorical characterization of Jesus developed by the narrator, is frequently deemed inappropriate by the narrative audience, especially when that audience comprised Jesus' antagonists in the story, the religious authorities. Thus, the authorial audience of John view Jesus' Scripture saturated speech-in-character as appropriate to both context and speaker, in contrast to the audience in the narrative, who often misunderstand Jesus' comments. See, e.g., Myers' comments (*Characterizing Jesus*, 112–20) on Jesus' speech-in-character in the story of the Feast of Tabernacles (John 7:1-52; 8:12-59).

90 There are a number of personifications also in Jewish literature (Prov 8; Sir 24; Bar 3–4; Wis 7–9; *Community Rule*; see Joseph R. Dodson, *The "Powers" of Personification: Rhetorical Purpose in the "Book of Wisdom" and the Letter to the Romans* [Berlin: Walter de Gruyter, 2008]), suggesting that the rhetorical device of personification was a transcultural phenomenon and not necessarily evidence that the authors had been exposed to the specific rhetorical exercise of speech-in-character. The examples marshaled here from the New Testament likewise need not necessarily be viewed as deriving directly from exposure to the preliminary exercises, but given their close resemblance to the prescriptions of the rhetorical tradition, and from what we know about ancient education (see introduction, p. 3), it is reasonable to assume their presence is due, at least in part, to awareness of these rhetorical practices in antiquity. And, if the author already gives evidence elsewhere of progymnastic influence, the author is more likely to have been influenced by the practice of "speech-in-character."

91 R. Dean Anderson Jr., *Ancient Rhetorical Theory and Paul*, rev. ed. (Leuven: Peeters, 1998), 162, who argues that "such personification is not elsewhere found in the New Testament." Anderson (162n73) cites Philo, *Leg.* 3.118ff., as parallel to Gal 3:8, in which Philo personifies *ho ieros logos*.

92 See J. Louis Martyn, *Galatians*, AB 33A (New York: Doubleday, 1997), 300.

93 King, "Speech-in-Character," 87.

94 King, "Speech-in-Character," 88.

95 See Anderson, *Ancient Rhetorical Theory and Paul*, 236–37. Paul employs personified speech-in-character at Gal 4:6. Paul also frequently personifies death, sin, and the powers (but not necessarily accompanied by speech); see, e.g., Paul W. Meyer's comments on personified sin in Rom 7:7-25 in "The Worm at the Core of the Apple: Exegetical Reflections on Romans 7," in *The Conversation Continues: Studies in Paul and John in Honor of J. Louis Martyn*, ed. Robert T. Fortna and Beverly Roberts Gaventa (Nashville: Abingdon, 1990), 72–78. For further discussion on personified righteousness in Romans, see David J. Southall, *Rediscovering Righteousness in Romans: Personified* dikaiosynē *within Metaphoric and Narratorial Settings*, WUNT 2/240 (Tübingen: Mohr Siebeck, 2008).

96 King, "Speech-in-Character," 113. See also Robert Jewett, *Romans: A Commentary*, Hermeneia (Minneapolis: Fortress, 2007), 625.

97 King, "Speech-in-Character," 114n89. King (114) assigns the parenthetical commentary to Paul (Rom 10:6a, 6d, 7c, 8a, 8c) and the remaining (mostly) Scripture quotations to personified Righteousness. For a different reading, also based on speech-in-character, see Bates, *The Hermeneutics of the Apostolic Proclamation*, 225–40, who sees yet another speaker, the presumptuous person, posing the questions of 10:6c, 7b; cf. Bates *Hermeneutics*, 232–38. For a rebuttal of Bates' view, see King, "Speech-in-Character," 114n89 and 117n97.

98 Reading Acts 15 and 23 in the context of speech-in-character and fictive letter writing is not to suggest the apostolic decree was necessarily invented speech, but neither does it provide much comfort to those who argue that Luke draws on an earlier source in presenting it. Whether invented or quoted (perhaps from an "Antiochene source") or "something in between" (Rosenmeyer, *Ancient Epistolary Fictions*, 60) is most likely beyond our ability to resolve conclusively.

99 For what follows, see Parsons, *Acts*, 216–17.

100 For a brief comparison of the decree's content in Acts 15 and 21, see Parsons, *Acts*, 219–20. On the text-critical difficulties, see esp. W. A. Strange, *The Problem of the Text of Acts* (Cambridge: Cambridge University Press, 1992).

101 Tannehill, *Narrative Unity*, 2:295.

102 One might also consider some variants in the textual tradition from the perspective of speech-in-character. E.g., Acts 8:37 is missing from the best manuscripts of Acts: "And Philip said, 'If you believe with all your heart, you may.' And he replied, 'I believe that Jesus Christ is the Son of God.'" One might view its addition as a response to the question: "What would the Eunuch (or any baptismal candidate) confess before receiving baptism?" The answer is perhaps supplied by a scribe anxious to ensure that the Ethiopian Eunuch was not baptized without making an appropriate baptismal confession.

6

Encomium

Crafting Words of Praise and Critique

> *Encomion* is language expressive of inherent excellences.
>
> Aphthonius

Unlike most of the progymnastic forms, which were literary "building blocks" used to create all genres of Graeco-Roman literature and oratory, the encomium was a fully formed genre unto itself. It belonged to the epideictic species of oratory, which was taught in declamation as one of the three classes of speeches (alongside judicial and deliberative) that an orator might give in the course of his public life. Encomium thus receives further treatment beyond the progymnasmata not only in the rhetorical handbooks (e.g., Aristotle's *Rhetorica* and Quintilian's *Institutio oratoria*) but also in treatises devoted solely to it (e.g., the two treatises attributed to Menander Rhetor, and that of Ps.-Dionysius).

Why, then, the inclusion of encomium among the progymnasmata? Nicolaus, addressing this very question, states that encomium is both a "part" and a "whole"—that, unlike judicial and deliberative speeches, the encomium may appear as a piece within the other species of oratory, as, for example, when an orator needs to praise someone or something related to the case (*Prog.* 47–48). The *Rhetorica ad Herennium*, moreover, suggests that this auxiliary function of epideictic—its use as a "part" rather than a "whole"—is its most common function:

> And if epideictic is only seldom employed by itself independently, still in judicial and deliberative causes extensive sections are often devoted to praise or blame. Therefore, let us believe that this kind of cause must also claim some measure of our industry. (*Rhet. Her.* 3.15 [Caplan, LCL])[1]

Encomiastic materials, too, were commonly incorporated into written narratives of every kind—both fictive and nonfictive. Thus, it was appropriate for students to learn the form before graduating to declamation, and in the exercises designed to equip students with the literary forms basic to every manner of composition.

In this chapter, we are interested to examine encomium from the perspective of the progymnasmata primarily as a microstructure, or a "part" appearing within other "wholes." After surveying progymnastic theory, we explore the auxiliary use of encomium within other genres in the Mediterranean milieu generally, and then within the various genres of the New Testament specifically. Treatment of encomium as a macrostructure—the primary concern of the handbooks—we reserve for another study.

Theory

Definition

In introducing encomium to young students, the theorists offer etymological explanations of the term that speak to its purpose.[2] Theon says it "derives from the ancient custom of eulogies of the gods at a revel (*kōmos*) or game (*paidia*)" (*Prog.* 109). Pseudo-Hermogenes says the term "comes from the fact that poets sang hymns praising the gods in *kōmai* (villages) in ancient times" (*Prog.* 15)—a view echoed by Aphthonius (*Prog.* 35). Modern opinion, however, is that the term "derives from *kōmos,* a song escorting home a victor in athletic games."[3]

Whatever its etymology, the theorists agree that the term signified the genre of praise—a matter reflected in their varying definitions:

> *Encomion* is language revealing the greatness of virtuous actions and other good qualities belonging to a particular person. (Theon, *Prog.* 109)
>
> *Encomion* is exposition of the good qualities of a person or thing, in general or individually. (Ps.-Hermogenes, *Prog.* 14)
>
> *Encomion* is language expressive of inherent excellences. (Aphthonius, *Prog.* 35)
>
> *Encomion* is speaking well of some specified person or thing in a discursive way on the basis of acknowledged merits. (Nicolaus, *Prog.* 48).

Related to the encomium genre was a number of other epideictic forms that the progymnasmata introduce in connection with the main form: *invective,* encomium's opposite, defined by the theorists as "language expressive of inherent evils" (Aphthonius, *Prog.* 40);[4] *epitaphios,* the encomium of the dead or "funeral oration";[5] *epainos* (praise), a brief sentence of general laudation;[6] and *hymnos,* the form of encomium devoted to the gods.[7]

In the Roman period, a proliferation of encomiastic genres beyond these occurred, and these were made the subject of treatises covering their varying forms (e.g., the two treatises attributed to Menander Rhetor).[8] Nicolaus, the latest of the Greek progymnasmata, attests the development and resultant multiplicity of forms: "The account of encomium is complicated, no longer limited to a single form (like descriptions of earlier exercises), and divided among many kinds. For speeches of arrival (*epibatērioi*) and addresses to officials (*prosphōnêtikoi*) and wedding speeches (*epithalamioi*) and funeral orations (*epitaphioi*), and, of course, also hymns to gods and every kind of speech of praise are listed under this species" (*Prog.* 47). But for Nicolaus, however, the progymnasmatists still imagine a single essential form common to encomium, invective, *epitaphios*, and *hymnos*, one that could be used regardless of whether the subject were praiseworthy or blameworthy, living or dead, mortal or divine.[9] As Theon observes, "whether one praises the living or the dead or heroes or gods, the method of speaking is one and the same" (*Prog.* 109).

Subjects of Encomium

Each of the theorists devotes a portion of the exercise to the kinds of subjects encomium proper may praise. Generally, the theorists agree that encomium may praise persons or things but disagree on the range of the latter. Theon defines encomium as the praise of "persons" but in his concluding comments allows that encomia may also be "of inanimate things such as honey, health, virtue, and the like" (*Prog.* 112). Pseudo-Hermogenes includes mention of persons and things in his definition of the genre. His ensuing comments suggest categories of things both animate and inanimate, in contrast to Theon: "We also praise things; for example, justice, and dumb animals, for example, a horse; and there have even been encomia of plants and mountains and rivers" (*Prog.* 14–15). Pseudo-Hermogenes also notes that encomia may be general, as in "an *encomion* of man," and individual, as in "an *encomion* of Socrates" (*Prog.* 14). Aphthonius is similarly broad in his understanding, observing that encomia may be of persons "like Thucydides or Demosthenes," things "like justice or self-control," occasions "like summer or winter," places "like harbors and gardens," "dumb animals" "like a horse or ox," or plants "like olive or vine" (*Prog.* 36). Aphthonius observes, too, that encomia may be collective, as in "an *encomion* of all Athenians," or individual, as in "an *encomion* of one Athenian" (*Prog.* 36). Last, Nicolaus joins Theon against the other two in restricting encomia to persons and inanimate things, dividing the latter somewhat pedantically between "corporeal" and "incorporeal" (*Prog.* 57). From these discussions, one gathers that in addition to persons virtually anything *could* be encomionized, but that some preferred limiting encomium to worthy *inanimate* subjects out of good taste.

Topoi of Encomium

More important to encomiastic theory is the recurring discussion of the topoi (literally, "places") of encomium.[10] These were, in essence, search headings that Hellenistic education prescribed for finding praiseworthy or blameworthy qualities of a subject. Armed with a conventional list of topoi, a student could conduct a thorough investigation of a subject's praise- or blameworthiness. Topos lists thus functioned, too, as compositional templates for encomium, guiding not only the selection, but also the order, of materials in the writing process. Thus they shed valuable light on the content, structure, and meaning of all ancient encomiastic writing.

Hellenistic education did not invent the topoi but rather borrowed them from the culture generally, classical Greek literature specifically, and classical Greek encomium especially, where they regularly are featured, sometimes by name. The topoi reflected long-established, culture-specific ways of apprehending the human personality. We may think of them as an ancient Mediterranean anatomy of honorable personhood, born of an honor-and-shame culture.

They frequently reflect, too, the values of the aristocratic classes responsible for ancient Mediterranean culture, literature, education, and the like. Certain qualities generally exclusive to these classes—coming from the right places, the right ancestry, the right families, receiving a quality education, having inherited wealth or power, attaining positions of power or esteem, living to an old age—were institutionalized in Hellenistic education as marks of honor, even as the absence of the same was associated, by implication, with shame.

Because the topos lists typically encouraged comment on the praise- or blameworthiness of a subject's *ethnos* (race, ethnicity, or nation), they tended as well to reinforce various ethnic and racial stereotypes endemic to the Graeco-Roman world. Though it is beyond the scope of an introductory study such as this, the ancient Mediterranean world could be mapped fairly comprehensively in terms of these stereotypes. Generally speaking, the Mediterranean West (Greece and Rome) was more highly regarded than the East; "Greeks" (peoples at the power centers of the Graeco-Roman world) were esteemed more than "barbarians" (usually, northern European peoples beyond the borders of the empire, but also all peoples beyond the empire).[11] All major ethnic groups within these ranges, moreover, had certain agreed-upon qualities, honorable or otherwise, that in histories were made to account for their successes or failures.

The topoi were also reflective of the ancient Mediterranean religious milieu from which they emerged. Though religiously diverse, Graeco-Roman peoples generally imagined a world in which the divine and human interacted in various ways. Signs of praiseworthiness derivative of this interaction thus are fixtures in the topos lists. A subject could be praised, for example, because of divine ancestry or parentage, divine signs attending birth, deeds normally associated with the gods, oracles concerning death or beyond, or postmortem divinization.

Pseudo-Hermogenes' exercise, because it provides helpful concrete illustrations of the topoi, offers the modern reader an excellent introduction:

> Encomiastic topics are (the subject's) national origin, such as Greek, city, such as Athenian, family, such as Alcmaeonid. You will mention also any marvelous occurrences at birth, for example from dreams or signs or things like that. After this, nurture; for example in the case of Achilles, that he was nurtured on lions' marrow and by Cheiron; then upbringing, how he was trained or how educated. Of course, the nature of mind and body will be examined and each of these divided into several qualities. You will say about his body that it was beautiful, large, swift, strong; about his mind that it was just, temperate, wise, brave. After this you will draw on his pursuits; for example, what sort of life he led: Was he a philosopher or an orator or a general? Most important are deeds; for deeds are included among pursuits; for example, having chosen a soldier's life, what did he accomplish in it? As for externals, they include relatives, friends, possessions, servants, luck, and the like. Moreover, from the topic of time comes how long he lived, much or little. Each provides the starting point of encomia; for you will praise one who had long life because of that fact and one who did not in that "he had no share of the diseases of old age." Further, from the manner of his death (for example,) how he died fighting for his country; and if there was anything unusual about it, as in the case of Callimachus, because his corpse remained standing. And you will praise him because of who killed him, for example, that Achilles died at the hand of the god Apollo. You will examine also events after death: if they held games in his honor, as for Patroclus (*Iliad* 23); if there was an oracle about his bones, as with Orestes; if he had famous children, as did Neoptolemus. The best source of argument in encomia is derived from comparisons, which you will utilize as the occasion may suggest. (*Prog.* 15–17)

Though the topos lists vary greatly from one theorist to the next, there is nonetheless a good deal of agreement among them. We may illustrate the matter by listing the progymnastic topoi in the order the theorists discuss them. We include Theon's and Pseudo-Hermogenes' syncrisis exercise lists, which are summative, shorter re-presentations of their encomium lists and thus lend insight into what the theorists thought were the most essential topoi:

Theon (Encomium Exercise, *Prog.* 109–112)[12]

- External goods
    - High descent
        - City, tribe, constitution
        - Ancestors and other relatives
    - Education
    - Friendship
    - Reputation
    - Official position
    - Wealth

- Good children
- Good death

Bodily goods

- Health
- Strength
- Beauty
- Acuteness of sense

Ethical virtues (goods of the mind) and resultant actions

- Goods of the mind
- Prudent
- Temperate
- Courageous
- Just
- Pious
- Generous
- Magnanimous
- And the like

Fine actions

- Those praised after death
- Those we praise when we are alive
- Done for others rather than ourselves
- Done for the sake of the honorable, not the expedient or pleasant
- With common benefit
  - For the populace
  - For benefactors
  - For the dead
- Braving retributions and dangers for friends
- On basis of occasion
- Done alone
- Done first
- Done when no one else acted
- Done more than others
- Done with few helpers
- Beyond what is characteristic of age
- Done contrary to expectation
- Done with toils
- Done very easily
- Done quickly

- Judgment of the famous
- Done conjecturally on basis of past actions

Comparison

Names, homonyms, nicknames

Theon (Syncrisis Exercise, *Prog.* 112–115)

Bodily and external goods

- High descent
- Education
- Excellence of offspring
- Offices
- Reputation
- Condition of bodies
- Any other bodily and external goods

Actions

- More beautiful
- Good qualities
  - More numerous
  - Greater
  - More steadfast
  - More lasting
- Done at a more critical time
- If not done there would have been great harm
- Done by choice, not necessity or chance
- Which few did more than what many did
- Done with toil rather than easily
- Accomplished beyond (expectations of) age and (apparent) ability more than when (such actions are ordinarily) possible

Ps.-Hermogenes (Encomium Exercise, *Prog.* 14–18)

National origin, city, family

Marvelous occurrences at birth

Nurture

Upbringing (how he was trained or educated)

Nature of mind and body

- Body: beautiful, large, swift, strong
- Mind: just, temperate, wise, brave

Pursuits and deeds

Externals: relatives, friends, possessions, servants, luck, and the like

Time: how long he lived

Manner of death

Because of who killed him

Events after death

Comparison

Ps.-Hermogenes (Syncrisis Exercise, *Prog.* 18–20)

City

Family

Nurture

Pursuits

Deeds

Externals

Manner of death

Events after death

Aphthonius (Encomium, Invective, and Syncrisis Exercises, *Prog.* 35–44)

- Prooemion
- Origin
    - Nation
    - Homeland
    - Ancestors
    - Parents
- Upbringing
    - Habits
    - Acquired skill
    - Principles of conduct
- Deeds
    - Mind
        - Courage
        - Prudence

- Body
  - Beauty
  - Swiftness
  - Strength
- Fortune
  - Power
  - Wealth
  - Friends
- Comparison
- Epilogue

Nicolaus (Encomium, Invective, and Syncrisis Exercises, *Prog.* 47–63)

["The form used in ancient times by Plato" (*Phaedrus* 270b):]

- Goods of the mind
  - Prudence
  - Justice
  - Temperance
  - Courage
- Goods of the body
  - Beauty
  - Strength
  - Size
  - Speed
- External goods
  - Origin
  - Friends
  - Wealth
  - And such

["The prevailing form":]

- Prooemion
- Origin
  - Nationality
  - Native city
  - Ancestors
- Birth

Circumstances of upbringing
Activities in youth
Deeds
  Refer his action to virtues
  Introduce comparisons

One observes from these lists two patterns of organization. Theon attests arrangement by the three traditional goods of Greek philosophy—that is, goods of the mind, goods of the body, and goods external to the person. The remaining three theorists commend a chronological ordering of topoi more reflective of actual composition. Nicolaus actually discusses the two patterns, noting that the former is the "ancient" and the latter the "prevailing" method.

> The godlike Plato in *Phaedrus* (270b) and others of ancient times divided subjects of praise into goods of the mind, goods of the body, and external goods. Those of the mind are divided into prudence, justice, temperance, and courage; those of body into beauty, strength, size, and speed; external goods are divided into origin, friends, wealth, and such. We, however, shall not follow this division but the prevailing one. (*Prog.* 50)

We may observe from these lists, too, those topoi that are multiply attested and those that by contrast are idiosyncratic. The former may be viewed as the conventional, core topoi of encomium: origin (includes geography [city, homeland] and generation [family, ancestors, parents, relatives, tribe, *ethnos*]), birth, upbringing and training, deeds, manner of death, and events after death.

One theme in particular that emerges from the theorists' discussion of topoi is the significance of the topos of deeds. Pseudo-Hermogenes calls it the "most important" topos (*Prog.* 16). Apthonius commends quite an extensive treatment, referring deeds to all three goods. Theon and Nicolaus, by contrast, recommend a similarly thorough referring of deeds to the various virtues they display. From these discussions, it is clear that treatment of deeds typically constitutes the heart of the encomium. Theon's lengthy set of sub-topoi of fine actions provides an especially illuminating description of the kinds of deeds ancients thought praiseworthy.

Another important theme that emerges from these discussions concerns the nature of the topoi as search headings. The theorists agree that one does not have to use all the topoi in the composition of an encomium. Indeed, the theorists *discourage* the use of all topoi, saying that one should pass over those that do not serve the laudatory interests of the writer/orator well. The lists, then, function more as suggestions for topoi or "places" to look for sources of praise, rather than checklists to be treated thoroughly.

Because encomium was taught beyond the progymnasmata in rhetorical handbooks and treatises devoted solely to epideictic oratory, we may supplement the progymnastic lists above with lists from the latter. In these lists, too, we see a similar set of core topoi common to all, as well as less attested and idiosyncratic topoi. We also witness the older arrangement by goods giving way to the newer chronological ordering (beginning with the first-century CE list of Quintilian).

Rhetorica ad Alexandrum (35 [1440b.14–1441b.28])

- Goods external to virtue
  - High birth
  - Strength
  - Beauty
  - Wealth
- Goods inherent in virtue
  - Wisdom
  - Justice
  - Courage
  - Creditable habits

Rhetorica ad Herennium (3.6.10–11)

[Introduces topoi by three goods:]

- External circumstances
  - Descent
  - Education
  - Wealth
  - Kinds of power
  - Titles to fame
  - Citizenship
  - Friendships
- Physical attributes
  - Agility
  - Strength
  - Beauty
  - Health
- Qualities of character
  - Wisdom
  - Justice
  - Courage
  - Temperance

[Prescribes chronological arrangement of topoi for an epideictic speech:]

- Externals
  - Descent
  - Education
- Physical advantages
- Externals and virtues evinced with respect to these
  - Wealth
  - Kinds of power
  - Titles to fame
  - Friendships/feuds
  - Death
  - Consequences following death

Cicero (*Inv.* 2.177–178; cf. 2.159–165)

- Mind
  - Wisdom
  - Justice
  - Courage
  - Temperance
- Body
  - Health
  - Beauty
  - Strength
  - Speed
- External circumstances
  - Public office
  - Money
  - Marriage
  - High birth
  - Friends
  - Country
  - Power
  - Other things

Cicero (*Inv.* 1.34–36)[13]

- Name
- Nature: Divine or mortal
  - Mortal: human or animal?

- Human
  - Sex: male or female
  - Race: Greek or Barbarian
  - Place of birth ("patria"): Athenian or Lacedaemonian
  - Family: ancestors and kin
  - Age: boy, youth, middle age, or old man
- Mind: bright or dull; retentive or forgetful; affable or unmannerly; modest, long-suffering, or the contrary
- Body: strong or weak, tall or short, handsome or ugly, swift or slow

Manner of life

- Rearing: in what tradition, under what direction
- Teachers in liberal arts
- Instructors in art of living
- Friendships
- Occupation, trade, or profession
- Management of private fortune
- Character of home life

Fortune

- Slave or free
- Rich or poor
- Private citizen or official with authority
- If official, whether he acquired position justly or unjustly
- Whether he is successful or famous or the opposite
- What sort of children he has
- Nature of his death

Habit

- Acquisition of some capacity or of some art
- Special knowledge
- Some bodily dexterity not given by nature but won by training and practice

Feeling

- Temporary change in mind or body due to some cause: joy, desire, fear, vexation, illness, weakness, etc.

Interest: unrelenting mental activity ardently devoted to some subject and accompanied by intense pleasure: e.g., philosophy, poetry, geometry, literature

Purposes: deliberate plan for doing or not doing something

Achievements: what he did

Accidents: what happened to him

Speech: what he said

Cicero (*Part. or.* 74–75)

- External goods
    - Family
    - Fortune
    - Estate
- Goods of the body
- Goods of the mind/achievements (three methods)
    - (1) Chronological
    - (2) Most recent first
    - (3) Actions under the virtues

Quintilian (*Inst.* 3.7.10–18)

- Before birth
    - Country
    - Parents
    - Ancestors
    - Prophecies/omens before birth
- During lifetime
    - Body
    - External goods
    - Mind (two methods)
        - (1) Chronological
            - Natural abilities
            - Education
            - Whole series of works: deeds and sayings
        - (2) By virtues
- After death
    - Divine honors
    - Decrees
    - Public statues
    - Monuments of genius
    - Children
    - Cities founded

- Laws proposed
- Arts invented
- Institutions initiated

Menander Rhetor (*Imperial Oration*, 2.368–377)

- Origin
  - Nation
  - City
  - Family
- Birth
- Nature
- Nurture/education
- Accomplishments
- Actions (two methods)
  - (1) By war/peace
  - (2) By the four virtues
- Fortune
- Comparison
- Epilogue

Menander Rhetor (*Epitaphios*, 2.420)

- Family
- Birth
- Nature
  - Physical beauty
  - Mental endowment
- Nurture
- Education
- Accomplishments
- Actions
- Fortune
  - Wealth
  - Happiness of children
  - Love of friends
  - Honor from emperors
  - Honor from cities

Pseudo-Dionysius (*Epideiktikos, Ars. rhet.* 278)

Country

Family

Nature

Upbringing

Actions

An important tenet of encomiastic composition frequently attested among the progymnastic theorists concerns topoi used in the praise of things. The theorists agree that the conventional topos lists, though designed for praise of persons, may be adapted for the praise of all manner of subjects.[14] Theon thus states, "Encomia of inanimate things such as honey, health, virtue, and the like we shall compose analogously from the same topics, arguing from whatever is possible" (*Prog.* 112). Nicolaus echoes Theon, offering some helpful illustrations:

We said above that encomium also busies itself with praise of things. Things are either

> lifeless but corporeal, like a shield or spear or stone or something of that sort, or incorporeal, like rhetoric and features of human activity generally. It is reasonable, therefore, to ask how we shall make an *encomion* of these things and if it is possible to use the same headings as when we praise a man. One should, then, understand that we shall use for them the topics available in *encomion*; for example, to take the case of activities, taking up those who invented or first used the activity instead of their origin, and instead of rearing, the training involved in them, and instead of their deeds, their uses in the life of humans and their benefits, and in each of the others similarly. (*Prog.* 57–58)

Pseudo-Hermogenes also exemplifies the method with regard to "dumb animals," "activities," "growing things," and a "city" (*Prog.* 17–18). We cite his discussion of how to encomionize a city in illustration:

> And surely you will undertake an *encomion* of a city without difficulty from these topics; for you will speak about its origin, (saying) that its people are autochthonous, and about its growth, how it was nurtured by gods, and about education, how the people have been taught by the gods. And you will examine, as in the case of a man, what sort of manners the city has, what sort of institutions, what pursuits it follows, what it has accomplished. (*Prog.* 18)

These topoi were, of course, similarly adaptable to the other genres of epideictic—invective, *epitaphios, hymnos,* and the like. This was the point of Theon's aforementioned observation that "the method is the same" regardless of whether one praised the living, the dead, heroes, or gods. Increasingly, though, topos lists specific to these and other epideictic forms began to be taught in Hellenistic education, particularly in treatises devoted to declamation. This was largely, however, a development beyond the first century CE. Until that point, single lists learned as adaptable templates were evidently the norm of Hellenistic education.

The one exception to the rule, however, is *hymnos*.[15] Already in Quintilian (late first century CE) a specialized topos list tailored specifically for praise of the gods is attested. It may be compared with similar lists from later centuries:

Quintilian (*Inst.* 3.7.7–9)
Majesty of nature
Power
Inventions benefiting humanity
Actions
Parents
Age
Offspring
Born immortal / earned immortality by virtue

Alexander Numenius (558–560)
Origin
Age
Identity with others
Universality of worship
Power
Favorite haunts
Skills
Inventions
Sacred plants or trees
Places he visits
Other gods with whom he is associated

Menander Rhetor (2.438–446)
Address
Birth myth
Place of birth
Country

Powers
- Archery
- Prophecy
- Music
- Healing

City

Festival

Temple

Statue

Names

These lists suggest that, at least with regard to *hymnos*, theorists as early as the first century CE were not in agreement as to how adaptable the normal encomium list was for use in praising the gods. The situation is likely attributable to the more variable form of *hymnos* itself, which (as we will see) was more flexible with regard to the topoi treated. In any case, we may summarize the state of *hymnos* theory in our period by stating that whereas some theorists prescribed adapting the standard lists used in praise of persons, others offered somewhat idiosyncratic lists likely based on observed practice.

Examples from Ancient Literature

Encomium and its related forms are widely attested in the ancient Mediterranean world, both as microstructures within other literature and as macrostructures encompassing complete orations and other encomiastic forms ("parts" and "wholes," respectively, in the terminology of Nicolaus). The concern of the present section is to note examples of the former in ancient literature, taking progymnastic theory as our guide. Though innumerable occurrences of generalized- or single-topos praise (i.e., *epainos* and brief encomium) could be mentioned in this connection, our focus will be on literary pieces more developed in form, and with a complexity that progymnastic theory may enlighten. All occurrences, however, and not just the more developed forms we discuss here, may be viewed as belonging to encomium as described in theory.

Examples that correspond to this theory may be in the form of oratory or written narration (as is true generally of progymnastic forms). They must have in view the kinds of subjects named by the theorists—that is, persons or things (encomium, invective), or gods (*hymnos*). They also ideally must take up topoi prescribed by the theorists—and preferably, as a clear indication of encomiastic intent, multiple topoi, and in a traditional order.

Of course, slavish correspondence to the encomium progymnasmata and other related treatises should not be expected. As D. A. Russell and N. G. Wilson observe, "Even in this very banal and conventionalized branch of literature, the relation between teaching and practice is less close than is sometimes thought." Concerning Menander's treatises on encomium, which are merely expansions on the theory surveyed above, Russell and Wilson state:

> Menander's partial "fair copies" are of course meant as hints, not as models to be copied out, though doubtless the indifferent student will have treated them as just that. And if we look at any respectable epideictic piece—say the *Panathenaicus* or a monody or hymns of Aristides—it is clear that the writer's sophistication and sensitivity to the particular circumstances (καιρός) is of far greater importance in the successful execution of the commission than the application of rules and formulas. Every ancient rhetor knew this, even if some of his pupils never grasped it.[16]

Such cautions remind us that the clearest examples of encomium—that is, those that correspond most closely to progymnastic theory—may not be the best. They do serve, however, to illustrate the close application of the method, much as Aphthonius' original, model compositions do, and so have an introductory value useful in a study such as this.

In the survey that follows, we give attention first to encomiastic forms that follow a standard topical template (i.e., encomium, invective, and *epitaphios*). We divide these by nonfiction and fiction—or, what the theorists in the narrative exercise call "historical" and "dramatic" narrative, respectively. We include examples from Graeco-Roman, Jewish, and Christian writers. Second, we give attention to the one encomiastic genre that by the first century CE was being granted by some theorists its own topical form, *hymnos*. Considered neither "historical" nor "dramatic," *hymnos* by virtue of its focus on the gods belongs to what the theorists regarded as a third class of narrative, the "mythic." We include two kinds of *hymnos*, those that follow standard encomiastic form, and those that take up topoi specific to the gods. We also cite examples, again, from Graeco-Roman, Jewish, and Christian writers.

Nonfictional Encomiastic Forms

Thucydides. Among the most famous occurrences of encomium is Pericles' Funeral Oration, which is embedded within Thucydides' *History of the Peloponnesian War* (2.35–46).[17] The speech is commonly cited by the theorists as a model of the encomiastic form. Theon, for example, lists it among a few select examples that teachers should commend to students for imitation (*Prog.* 68). As a complete oration recorded in a history, the speech occupies a middle ground in Nicolaus' "part"/"whole" polarity and thus makes for an excellent entrée into extant encomiastic writing.

Though nominally an *epitaphios* of the Athenian dead, the speech is, in fact, an encomium of the city of Athens itself. (The theorists who mention "cities" as examples of things that might be praised very likely have this speech in mind.) As an encomium of a "thing," the speech employs the topoi normally used for the praise of persons, adapting them for the subject at hand. Multiple topoi are treated, and in a traditional order. We may outline the speech as follows in the light of progymnastic theory:

Prooemion	(2.35)
Origin	
Ancestors	I shall speak first of our ancestors, for it is right and at the same time fitting, on an occasion like this, to give them this place of honour in recalling what they did. . . .
Fathers	Not only are they worthy of our praise, but our fathers still more; for they, adding to the inheritance which they received, acquired the empire. . . .
Present Generation	And we ourselves here assembled, who are now for the most part still in the prime of life, have further strengthened the empire . . . (2.36)
Deeds	The military deeds whereby our several possessions were acquired, whether in any case it were we ourselves or our fathers that valiantly repelled the onset of was, Barbarian or Hellenic, I will not recall, for I have no desire to speak at length among those who know. (2.36)
Pursuits	But I shall first set forth by what sort of pursuits we have come to our present position, and with what political institutions and as the result of what manner of life our empire became great, and afterwards proceed to the praise of these men. . . .
	"Form of government" (2.37)
	"Relaxations from toil" (2.38)
	"System of training for warfare" (2.39)
	Miscellaneous qualities (2.40)
	"Power" (2.41)
Death	And then when the moment of combat came, thinking it better to defend themselves and suffer death rather than to yield and save their lives, they fled, indeed, from the shameful word of dishonour, but with life and limb stood stoutly to their task, and in the brief instant ordained by fate, at the crowning moment not of fear but of glory, they passed away. (2.42 [Smith, LCL, with adaptation])
Exhortation/epilogue	(2.43–46)

The speech begins with a prooemion (compare Aphthonius and Nicolaus on this point) and then proceeds to the first topos, origins. Here the speaker addresses something analogous in the life of a city to a person's familial origins—in this case, the city's "ancestors" and "fathers." Indeed, the opening unit functions much like a brief genealogy in the life of person, tracing three praiseworthy generations of Athenian citizenship. The speech concludes, too, with something analogous to death in the life of a city—in this case, the praiseworthy Athenians who died on the battlefields. The heart of the speech explicitly mentions, but forgoes, "deeds" of the citizenry—evidence that such treatment was conventional—and focuses instead on "pursuits" and analogous materials. The kinds of materials covered in this section may very well be the inspiration for Pseudo-Hermogenes' suggestion that praise of cities give consideration to "what sort of institutions [it possesses], what pursuits it follows, what it has accomplished." The close correspondence to the theory espoused in the progymnasmata is undoubtedly why the theorists pointed to this speech with regularity as a model example of the form.

Invective against Sallust. As an example of invective we may cite the speech against Sallust.[18] Though a free-standing speech purportedly by Cicero, the form was likely created as a school exercise by an anonymous writer—hence its consideration here in connection with progymnastic theory. Whatever its origins, the speech illustrates how invective was written following the same topical template as encomium:

Proemion	Whither shall I turn first, Fathers of the Senate, where shall I begin? . . . (1)
	Cicero's Self-Defense
Origin	Well then, to begin with, since Gaius Sallustius weights and measures the ancestors of all men according to the same standard and rule. . . . I have outshone my ancestors in merit, so that if they were not known before, I would give them fame for the first time; but you by the base life which you have led have enveloped yours in thick darkness, so that even if they were once eminent citizens, they assuredly have fallen into oblivion. (2)
Office/deeds	It is not just, Fathers of the Senate, to compare me with those who have already passed away, and who are free from all hatred or envy; I should rather be matched against those who have been associated with me in public life. If I have been too ambitious in seeking preferment (I do not refer to the ambition which aims at the good of the people, in which I admit that I have always been among the foremost, but to that ruinous and lawless kind in which Sallust is a leader), or if I have been so strict in administering the offices which I have held or in punishing evil-doing, or so vigorous in the defence of our country, that you, Sallust, call it a proscription . . . (2)

	Are you not ashamed, most inconsistent of men, to censure conduct for which you glorify me in your own histories? . . . (3)
Words	But why should I make further complaint of your calumnies? For what falsehood would you consider shameful, when you have dared to make my eloquence an accusation against me, that eloquence whose protection you have always required because of your guilt? . . . (3)
External goods	
Relatives	As for the unheard of virulence of your attacks upon my wife and daughter . . . (3)
Wealth	You are greatly mistaken, I think, if you hoped to rouse enmity against me because of the amount of my property . . . (3)
Other things	Am I a runaway, Gaius Sallustius? . . . (3)
Friends	And by Heaven! it is small wonder if I have always thought that I merited the friendship of all mankind; . . . (4)
Attack on Sallust	
Origin	I shall now return to you, Sallust, saying nothing of your father; for even if he never committed a sin in all his life, he could not have inflicted a greater injury upon his country than in begetting such a son. (5)
Activities in youth	Nor shall I inquire into any sins of your boyhood, lest I may seem to criticize your father, who had full control of you at that time, but how you spent your youth. For if this be shown, it will readily be understood how vicious was the childhood which led up to a manhood so shameless and lawless. . . . (5)
Office/deeds	When he obtained the quaestorship as his first office, he brought contempt upon this place and upon this assembly . . . (5)
	Be content, Sallust, with having lived as you pleased, and with having acted as you wished; . . . (6)
	"But perhaps he conducted himself with moderation and integrity after he became a praetor." Not so; he so pillaged . . . (7)
Words	One ought oneself to be wholly free from fault who is making ready to speak against another. He only has a right to utter reproaches who cannot hear a just reproach from another's lips. . . . Cease, then, to assail good men with your most wanton tongue. . . . (8)
Epilogue	I shall cease speaking, Fathers of the Senate, for . . . (8 [Rolfe, LCL])

That the speech follows a standard set of topoi in a standard order is evident enough from the outline above. This speech is exceptional only in charting a self-defense first by the same topoi, before proceeding to the invective proper.

Dionysius of Halicarnassus. While Thucydides offers an example of a complete oration quoted beginning to end within historical writing, more common is the use of encomiastic narration as part of the historical narrative itself. This is in keeping with the nature of encomium as a preliminary exercise. Students learned encomium and other progymnastic forms as literary building blocks to be employed in all manner of composition, both written and oral. Ancient Mediterranean history, accordingly, regularly depicts major historical figures via the topoi of praise and blame systematized in the encomium progymnasma. A good example is seen in Dionysius' account of Numa Pompilius.[19] The piece is clearly encomiastic, in that it praises a person in multiple sentences, taking up a standard set of encomiastic topoi, and in their conventional order:

Prooemion	This man, therefore, I should take no shame in placing among the foremost of those who have been celebrated for their felicity in life.
Origin	For he was of royal birth
Body	and of royal appearance;
Training	and he pursued an education which was not the kind of useless training that deals only with words, but a discipline that taught him to practise piety and every other virtue.
Activities in youth	When he was young he was thought worthy to assume the sovereignty over the Romans, who had invited him to that dignity upon the reputation of his virtue;
Pursuits and deeds	and he continued to command the obedience of his subjects during his whole life.
Fortune	He lived to a very advanced age without any impairment of his faculties and without suffering any blow at Fortune's hands;
Death	and he died the easiest of all deaths, being withered by age, the genius who had been allotted to him from his birth having continued the same favour to him till he disappeared from among men.
Time	He lived more than eighty years and reigned forty-three,
Events after death	
Children	leaving behind him, according to most historians, four sons and one daughter, whose posterity remain to this day; but according to Gnaeus Gellius he left only one daughter, who was the mother of Ancus Marcius, the second king of the Romans after him.

Honors	His death was greatly lamented by the state, which gave him a most splendid funeral. He lies buried upon the Janiculum, on the other side of the river Tiber.
Epilogue	Such is the account we have received concerning Numa Pompilius. (2.76.3–6 [Cary and Spelman, LCL])

That the piece may be described as encomiastic is evident too from its conventional handling of individual topoi. Throughout there is an uncritical privileging, typical of ancient encomium, of aristocratic characteristics as praiseworthy. The subject has a birth and appearance that is counted "royal." He receives an education that is exclusive. Even in youth he assumes offices of power. His career is praised summarily because he "commanded obedience" of others. He lives a long life, enjoys an easy death, is outlived by well-established children, and receives a state funeral. Conformity to theory specific to individual topoi is also occasionally evident. Pseudo-Hermogenes and Quintilian, for example, both mention "children" as material specific to the topos of events after death. This piece, accordingly, introduces mention of Numa's children in connection with other posthumous honors. Pseudo-Hermogenes, too, states, "You will praise one who had a long life because of that fact and one who did not in that 'he had no share of the diseases of old age.'" One may compare this to the line, "He lived to a very advanced age without any impairment of his faculties and without suffering any blow at Fortune's hands." Though this particular piece is one of several excellent specimens of encomiastic narration found in Diodorus' history, there are at least as many lines devoted to persons that take up briefly one or two topoi (e.g., X, son of Y)—a fact suggestive of the pervasiveness of encomiastic standards throughout the work in its characterization of persons.

Josephus. In Jewish historiography, one may cite a number of texts from Josephus' writings as examples of embedded encomium.[20] Josephus' account in *Jewish War* of Sabinus, the first man to surrender after Titus' speech, may be mentioned in illustration.[21] The passage, which is clearly laudatory in intent, may be arranged in accordance with the topoi it takes up:

Name	But there was one whose name was Sabinus,
Pursuits	a soldier that served among the cohorts,
Origin	and a Syrian by birth,
Deeds	who appeared to be of very great fortitude, both in the actions he had done,
Virtue	and the courage of his soul he had shown;
Body	although anyone would have thought, before he came to his work, that he was of such a weak constitution of body that he was not fit to be a soldier; for his colour was black, his flesh was lean and thin, and lay close together;

Mind	but there was a certain heroic soul that dwelt in this small body, which body was indeed much too narrow for that peculiar courage which was in him.
Words	Accordingly, he was the first that rose up; when he thus spoke: "I readily surrender up myself to you, O Caesar: I will first ascend the wall, and I heartily wish that my fortune may follow my courage and my resolution. And if some ill fortune begrudge me the success of my undertaking, take notice that my ill success will not be unexpected, but that I choose death voluntarily for your sake."
Deeds	When he had said this, and had spread out his shield over his head with his left hand, and had, with his right hand, drawn his sword, he marched up to the wall just about the sixth hour of the day. There followed him eleven others, and no more, that resolved to imitate his bravery; but still this was the principal person of them all, and went first, as excited by a divine fury. (*B.J.* 6.54–59 [Whiston])

Much is conventional in this text's handling of individual topoi. One sees ethnic stereotyping at work in the portrayal of Sabinus overcoming the negative qualities ancients would normally associate with the color of his skin. Courage, which Josephus attributes to the man's actions, is regularly named by the theorists among the "ethical virtues" or "goods of the mind illustrated by deeds"; indeed, it was widely counted one of the four cardinal virtues alongside wisdom, justice, and temperance. Josephus repeatedly stresses, too, that Sabinus acted first ("the first that rose up"; "I will first ascend the wall"; "but still this was the principal person of them all, and went first . . ."). Such an emphasis accords with the Theonic doctrine that "fine actions" to be narrated include "actions done first."

Another clear example from Josephus of embedded, historical encomium is seen in his autobiographical *Life* (which itself follows an encomiastic outline).[22] Josephus' brief depiction of his wife touches in order on three of the most essential topoi (they are three of the four Aphthonius mentions in what is the shortest of all topos lists)—and in the traditional order:

Origin	
Ethnicity	After this I married a wife who had lived at Crete, but a Jewess by birth:
Parents/comparison	a woman she was of eminent parents, and such as were the most illustrious in all the country,
Virtue/comparison	and whose character was beyond that of most other women, as her future life did demonstrate. (*Life* 1.427 [Whiston])

Josephus is quick to clarify that though his wife was from Crete, she was not a Cretan but rather of the Jewish *ethnos*. Here we see him distancing her from the negative ethnic stereotype that attended the people of Crete (Epimenides, *Cretica*; Callimachus 1.4–9; Titus 1:12). One sees, too, the ancient concern for derivation from "good stock"—as well as the concern, reinforced by an exercise fully devoted to it (see the next chapter), for evaluative comparison with others. Josephus, in essence, is drawing on conventional, aristocratic standards to say that he married well.

Eusebius of Caesarea. Eusebius of Caesarea's *Ecclesiastical History* provides us with many examples of Christian nonfiction encomium.[23] A good example is Eusebius' interesting account of another famous figure in religious history, Philo of Alexandria. The passage, which is clearly laudatory, follows a conventional encomiastic template:

Prooemion	Under this emperor, Philo became known; a man most celebrated not only among many of our own, but also among many scholars without the Church.
Origin/comparison	He was a Hebrew by birth, but was inferior to none of those who held high dignities in Alexandria.
Training	How exceedingly he labored in the Scriptures and in the studies of his nation is plain to all
Deeds/comparison	from the work which he has done. How familiar he was with philosophy and with the liberal studies of foreign nations, it is not necessary to say, since he is reported to have surpassed all his contemporaries in the study of Platonic and Pythagorean philosophy, to which he particularly devoted his attention. (*Eccl. hist.* 2.4.2 [*NPNF*[2] 179–80])

Under the topos of origin, Eusebius identifies Philo as Hebrew and compares him favorably to the best-born Alexandrians, who had a reputation for learning. The move in the next line from Philo's ethnic origins to his "studies" shows that Eusebius is following encomiastic convention. Though brief, the account follows precisely the trim four-topos outline of Aphthonius.

Another example from Eusebius is his depiction of a bishop by the name of Anatolius. The account is explicitly laudatory and follows an obvious topical template:

Prooemion	Anatolius was appointed his successor; one good man, as they say, following another.
Origin	He also was an Alexandrian by birth.
Training/ comparison	In learning and skill in Greek philosophy, such as arithmetic and geometry, astronomy, and dialectics in general, as well as in the theory of physics, he stood first among the ablest men of our time, and he was also at the head in rhetorical science.

Deeds/ comparison	It is reported that for this reason he was requested by the citizens of Alexandria to establish there a school of Aristotelian philosophy. They relate of him many other eminent deeds during the siege of the Pyrucheium in Alexandria, on account of which he was especially honored by all those in high office; but I will give the following only as an example. . . . [*Gives account of Anatolius' successful efforts to save a multitude during the siege*]
Words	Anatolius did not write very many works; but in such as have come down to us we can discern his eloquence and erudition. In these he states particularly his opinions on the passover. It seems important to give here the following extracts from them. . . . [*Excerpts follow from the Paschal Canons of Anatolius*] The same writer has also left the Institutes of Arithmetic, in ten books, and other evidences of his experience and proficiency in divine things.
Office	Theotecnus, bishop of Caesarea in Palestine, first ordained him as bishop, designing to make him his successor in his own parish after his death. And for a short time both of them presided over the same church. But the synod which was held to consider Paul's case called him to Antioch, and as he passed through the city of Laodicea, Eusebius being dead, he was detained by the brethren there.
Death	And after Anatolius had departed this life,
Events after death	the last bishop of that parish before the persecution was Stephen, who was amired by many for his knowledge of philosophy and other Greek learning. (7.32.6–22 [*NPNF*² 822–27])

As in other examples from the milieu, one sees in this Christian occurrence conventional handling of various topoi. The naming of Anatolius' Alexandrian origins draws on the reputation of the city for higher learning. The progression of origin, training, and deeds is a telltale sign of encomiastic composition. The setting aside of a distinct section devoted to words is anticipated by the occasional topic list that names "words" or "speech" alongside "deeds" as a distinct topos, and the practice of the same by others (see Josephus above).

Fictional Encomiastic Forms

Xenophon. The use of the encomiastic form as a building block of fictional narration, or drama, is no less widely attested in the ancient world. A good example of Graeco-Roman origin is found in the introduction of Xenophon's *An Ephesian Tale*, where the writer introduces his main character, Habrocomes, in laudatory terms via a highly conventional encomiastic template:[24]

Origin	
City	Among the most influential citizens of Ephesus
Father	was a man called Lycomedes. He
Mother	and his wife, Themisto, who also belonged to the city, had a son
Name	Habrocomes;
Body/ comparison	his good looks were phenomenal, and neither in Ionia nor anywhere else had there ever been anything like them. This Habrocomes grew more handsome every day;
Mind	and his mental qualities developed along with his physical ones.
Training	For he acquired culture of all kinds and practiced a variety of arts; he trained in hunting, riding, and fighting under arms.
Friends	Everyone in Ephesus sought his company, and in the rest of Asia as well;
Official position	and they had great hopes that he would have a distinguished position in the city.
Comparison	They treated the boy *like a god*, and some even prostrated themselves and prayed at the sight of him.
	He had a high opinion of himself, taking pride in his attainments, and a great deal more in his appearance. Everything that was regarded as beautiful he *despised as inferior*, and nothing he saw or heard seemed up to his standard.
	And when he heard a boy or girl praised for their good looks, he laughed at the people making such claims for not knowing that *only he* himself was handsome.
	He did not even recognize Eros as a god; he rejected him totally and considered him of no importance, saying that no one would ever fall in love or submit to the god except of his own accord. And whenever he saw a temple or statue of Eros, he used to laugh and claimed that he was *more handsome and powerful* than any Eros. And that was the case: for whenever Habrocomes appeared, no one admired any statue or praised any picture. (*An Ephesian Tale* 1.1 [Anderson])

Judged in the light of encomiastic theory, the piece is thoroughly conventional. The progression of origin, body, mind, and training corresponds to the order attested in Quintilian's topos list. One sees the usual handling of origin in terms of both geography and generation. The treatment of body and mind as a couplet is reflective of the same pairing in progymnastic theory—for example, Pseudo-Hermogenes' list, "nature of body and mind." The topos of body is considered under "beauty," one of the qualities, alongside strength, size, and speed, listed as sub-topoi of body. Habrocomes' youthful acquisition of culture, practicing of arts, and training in hunting, riding, and fighting under arms is standard fare for upbringing and training (Ps.-Hermogenes: "upbringing, how he was trained or educated"; Nicolaus: "activities in youth; for example, did he practice rhetoric or poetry or anything of that sort") and specifically recalls Aphthonius' sub-topos, "acquired skills." The less common topos of "friends," which is attested in only a few lists among the theorists, is nonetheless consistently counted among the external goods. One sees in this piece, too, the unexamined association of aristocratic privilege with the praiseworthy reflected in the content under nearly every topos. Also, the importance of the Graeco-Roman religious milieu as background for ancient drama is reflected in the comparisons—made from the point of view of the citizens and Habrocomes himself—with Eros.

That Xenophon is working with a conventional template of encomiastic topoi may be seen from his account not a few paragraphs later of the other major character of his story, Anthia:

Name	Anthia led the line of girls;
Origin	
Parents	she was the daughter of Megamedes and Euippe,
City	both of Ephesus.
Body/comparison	Anthia's beauty was an object of wonder, far surpassing the other girls'.
Age	She was fourteen;
Body	her beauty was burgeoning, still more enhanced by the adornment of her dress. Her hair was golden—a little of it plaited, but most hanging loose and blowing in the wind. Her eyes were quick; she had the bright glance of a young girl, and yet the austere look of a virgin. She wore a purple tunic down to the knee, fastened with a girdle and falling loose over her arms, with a fawnskin over it, a quiver attached, and arrows for weapons; she carried javelins and was followed by dogs.
Comparison	Often as they saw her in the sacred enclosure the Ephesians would worship her as Artemis. And so on this occasion too the crowd gave a cheer when they saw her, and there was a whole clamor of exclamations from the spectators: some were amazed and said it was the goddess in person; some that it was someone else made by the goddess in her own image. But all prayed and prostrated themselves and congratulated her parents. "The beautiful Anthia!" was the cry on all the spectators' lips. (1.2 [Anderson])

Here the topos list, though shorter, follows closely the pattern used to depict Habrocomes. There is treatment first of origin in terms of both geography and generation, extensive praise of the body via the sub-topos of *beauty*, and comparison with a god. Conspicuously absent, however, are the topoi of mind, training, and official position—an absence reflective of the male, aristocratic values inherent encomiastic convention.

Tobit. A good example of encomium embedded within Jewish dramatic narrative is found in the novel Tobit.[25] Like Xenophon's Ephesian tale, the story begins with the introduction of the main character via standard encomiastic topoi and in a conventional order:

Name	This book tells the story of Tobit
Origin	
Parents	son of Tobiel
Ancestors	son of Hananiel son of Aduel son of Gabael son of Raphael son of Raguel of the descendants of Asiel,
Tribe	of the tribe of Naphtali,
Age	who in the days of King Shalmaneser of the Assyrians
Accidents	was taken into captivity from Thisbe, which is to the south of Kedesh Naphtali in Upper Galilee, above Asher toward the west, and north of Phogor.
Deeds	I, Tobit, walked in the ways of truth and righteousness all the days of my life. I performed many acts of charity for my kindred and my people who had gone with me in exile to Nineveh in the land of the Assyrians. (1:1-4)

From this brief sketch, one witnesses a handling of topoi that is highly conventional. The passage begins with the topos of name, which appears first or last in the theorist's lists who think to mention it. It treats origin in terms of three common sub-topoi, *parents*, *ancestors*, and *tribe*. The introductory genealogy may strike modern readers as unimportant minutia, but genealogies were standard fair in accounts of origins and served to establish for ancient readers the credentials of the "stock" from which a subject derived. The topos "age" (like the English word used to translate it) had two interpretations: the years of age of an individual, or the epoch or time—usually measured by the reigns of kings—in which a subject lived.[26] Tobit clearly is following the latter interpretation of the topos in naming the "days of King Shalmaneser of the Assyrians" as the time in which Tobit lived. Last, most theoretical models would locate "was taken into captivity" under the topos of deeds together with the actions subsequently attributed to Tobit; only

Cicero helpfully distinguishes the topos of "accidents" ("what happened to him") from "achievements" ("what he did").

What is interesting about this account is the manner in which this Jewish novel subverts some of the aristocratic values inherent in the topos lists. Tobit has no office or position that is laudatory by traditional standards; he is merely a captive in exile in Assyria. Nor is he praised for the cardinal virtue one traditionally displays toward an enemy in Graeco-Roman encomium: courage. Instead, he is praised for virtues inculcated by the Jewish faith and crucial to the cohesion of the Jewish community in its captive state, namely, his faithfulness to Torah and his charity toward captive neighbors. The piece illustrates how the experience of suffering in the exile reshaped notions of the "laudatory" for some ancient Jews.

Judith. Another example of Jewish dramatic encomium, with a remarkably similar subversive streak, is the novel Judith.[27] The main character and namesake of the book is first introduced to the reader in chapter 8, and like the novels surveyed above, the book follows an obvious encomiastic template:

Name	Now in those days Judith heard about these things:
Origin	
Parents	she was the daughter of Merari
Ancestors	son of Ox son of Joseph son of Oziel son of Elkiah son of Ananias son of Gideon son of Raphain son of Ahitub son of Elijah son of Hilkiah son of Eliab son of Nathanael son of Salamiel son of Sarasadai
Nation	son of Israel.
Relatives	Her husband Manasseh, who belonged to her tribe and family, had died during the barley harvest. For as he stood overseeing those who were binding sheaves in the field, he was overcome by the burning heat, and took to his bed and died in his town Bethulia. So they buried him with his ancestors in the field between Dothan and Balamon. Judith remained as a widow for three years and four months at home where she set up a tent for herself on the roof of her house. She put sackcloth around her waist and dressed in widow's clothing. She fasted all the days of her widowhood, except the day before the sabbath and the sabbath itself, the day before the new moon and the day of the new moon, and the festivals and days of rejoicing of the house of Israel.
Body	Her husband Manasseh had left her gold and silver, men and women slaves, livestock, and fields; and she maintained this estate.
Reputation	No one spoke ill of her, for she feared God with great devotion.

Deeds	When Judith heard the harsh words spoken by the people against the ruler, because they were faint for lack of water, and when she heard all that Uzziah said to them, and how he promised them under oath to surrender the town to the Assyrians after five days, she sent her maid, who was in charge of all she possessed, to summon Uzziah and Chabris and Charmis, the elders of her town. They came to her, and she said to them, "Listen to me, rulers of the people of Bethulia! What you have said to the people today is not right; you have even sworn and pronounced this oath . . ." (8:1-11)

The extended treatment, furthermore, of Judith's husband, Mannasseh, in the section devoted to the topos of relatives may be mapped according to the topoi it takes up:

Name	Her husband Manasseh,
Origin	
Tribe	who belonged to her tribe
Family	and family,
Manner of death	had died during the barley harvest. For as he stood overseeing those who were binding sheaves in the field, he was overcome by the burning heat, and took to his bed and died in his town Bethulia.
Events after death	So they buried him with his ancestors in the field between Dothan and Balamon. Judith remained as a widow for three years and four months at home where she set up a tent for herself on the roof of her house. She put sackcloth around her waist and dressed in widow's clothing. She fasted all the days of her widowhood, except the day before the sabbath and the sabbath itself, the day before the new moon and the day of the new moon, and the festivals and days of rejoicing of the house of Israel. (8:2-6)

Clearly evident in the pieces above is conventional handling of topoi; for example, origins, by the sub-topoi of fathers, ancestors, tribe, and nation, and via genealogy; body, by the sub-topos of beauty; external goods, via the topoi of origins, wealth, reputation, death, and manner of death. In both pieces, too, the topoi are arranged in a conventional order.

Also striking is the manner in which the conventional male, aristocratic notions of female honor are overturned. Whereas in Gorgias' *Helen*, the main subject's deeds are passive (they are "accidents," to use Cicero's idiosyncratic topos) and defended in the encomium as unavoidable, in Judith the main character has agency, and her deeds clearly evidence, per progymnastic theory, her virtue (or goods of the mind). Whereas in the former Helen does not speak, in the latter Judith not only speaks but summons the male elders of her city and engages in a brief invective of their actions. And whereas in Xenophon's *An Ephesian Tale* the only external good for which Anthia is explicitly praised is her body, in Judith the protagonist is predominately praised via male-centric external goods: her origins are traced to the founder of her nation, she possesses and oversees wealth, and she has a reputation of sufficient status that city elders respond to her summons obediently.

Joseph and Aseneth. As a final example of dramatic encomium, we turn to *Joseph and Aseneth*, a novel of either Jewish or Christian origin, and one that in any case enjoyed a readership among both religious groups.[28] One recognizes in the opening paragraphs of the story what surely must be labeled a convention of ancient novels, the laudatory use of an encomiastic template to introduce a protagonist:

Origin	
City	Now there was in that city
Parent	a man, satrap of Pharaoh; and this *man* was the chief of all Pharaoh's satraps and lords. And he was very rich, and wise, and generous, and he was Pharaoh's counsellor, and his name was Pentephres; and he was the priest of Heliopolis.
Sex	And Pentephres had a virgin daughter
Age	of about eighteen years of age,
Body	tall and beautiful and graceful,
Comparison	more beautiful than any other virgin in the land. And she was quite unlike the daughters of the Egyptians, but in every respect like the daughters of the Hebrews. And she was as tall as Sarah, and as beautiful as Rebecca, and as fair as Rachel;
Name	and this virgin's name was Aseneth.
Fame	And the fame of her beauty spread through all that land, even to its remotest corners;
Friendships and feuds	and all the sons of the lords and of the satraps and of the kings sought her hand in marriage, young men *all of them*. And there was great rivalry between them because of her, and they began to fight among themselves because of Aseneth. And Pharaoh's eldest son heard about her, and he begged his father to give her to him as *his* wife. And he said to him, "Give me Aseneth the daughter of Pentephres the priest of Heliopolis as *my* wife." And his father Pharaoh said to him, "Why should you want a wife of lower station than yourself? Are you not king of all the earth? No! See now, the daughter of King Joakim is betrothed to you, and she is a queen and very beautiful indeed: take her as your wife." (1.3–14 [Cook])

Though employing a number of standard topoi in conventional ways, this introduction also takes up topoi less commonly attested among the theorists but nonetheless taught as external goods (fame, friendships, feuds). One sees, too, the attribution of traditionally female goods to the protagonist. She does not act or speak (at least not yet) but is prized for her beauty and suitability as a bride. In contrast to her father—who is himself praised in a mini-encomium divisible by severable topoi—she is not assigned praiseworthy official positions, wealth, or even virtues such as wisdom and generosity (the two named for her father). Rather, she is praised strictly on account of the virtues of her body: strength, height, and grace. The introduction thus provides insight into the standards of ancient encomium as they relate to gender (though the story itself arguably departs in meaningful ways from those standards).

Hymnos

The last category of encomiastic narration that concerns us occupies a middle, or perhaps transcendent, space between/above history and drama. We are speaking of the genre of encomium devoted to mythic subjects, *hymnos*. The examples we cite here are mythic "parts" embedded either within larger nonmythic narratives or within collections of other hymns or psalms.[29] These include both prose and poetic examples, as the genre was not limited either in theory or in practice to one mode or the other.[30] As a reflection of the division of opinion attested among the theorists, two topical forms are attested. The first follows the same template of topoi used to encomionize persons or things, and the second, a template developed specifically for praise of the gods.

Hymn to Aphrodite. An example of the first form is seen in the Homeric hymn to Aphrodite, the outline of which resembles the historical and dramatic encomiastic pieces above:[31]

Name	Of Cytherea,
Origin	born in Cyprus, I will sing.
Deeds	She gives kindly gifts to men:
Body	smiles are ever on her lovely face, and lovely is the brightness that plays over it.
Office	Hail, goddess, queen of well-built Salamis and sea-girt Cyprus;
Prayer	grant me a cheerful song. And now I will remember you and another song also. (10.1–5 [Evelyn-White, LCL])

The hymn is characteristic both in length and in content of the anonymously authored Greek "Homeric Hymn" collection as a whole. Like the rest of the collection, the hymn is poetic, written in the same meter as Homer's *Iliad* and *Odyssey*, dactylic hexameter. The opening sentence is at once a prooemion and a treatment of name and origin. The body of the hymn is devoted to the characteristic most notable about the divinity—in this case, her famed beauty. Here the tendencies of ancient encomium with regard to gender are projected even onto the gods, though divinity does afford Aphrodite a degree of agency that her mortal, female counterparts may lack. The epilogue includes a closing petition, which is common in Homeric and other Greek hymns. The address in the epilogue of Aphrodite as "queen of well-built Salamis and sea-girt Cyprus"—here interpreted under the topos of office (royal office being subject matter typical of the heading)—might as readily be read as treatment of the topos mentioned by Alexander Numenius, "Favorite Haunts."

Hymn to Zeus. Callimachus' first hymn to Zeus is another example of Greek *hymnos* that follows a standard encomiastic template of topoi:

Names and titles	Zeus, "mighty for ever, king for evermore, router of the Pelagonians, dealer of justice to the sons of Heaven" (1–3 [Mair, LCL]).
Origin	The poem considers the rival claims concerning Zeus' place of origin. Arcadia is preferred to Crete, as all Cretans are liars. (4–9)
Birth	The story of Zeus' birth. Rheia gives birth to Zeus; place of birth holy, so that animals and humans do not approach it to give birth. Rheia commands the earth to give birth, striking the mountain with her staff, rending it in two, so that a flood pours forth in which she washes Zeus' body. (10–32)
Upbringing	Rheia gives Zeus to Neda, the oldest of tree nymphs to rear him secretly in Crete. There he is "cradled by Adrasteia, attended by the Dictaean Meliae, suckled by the she-goat Amaltheia, and fed on honey by the Panacrian bees, while the Curetes danced round him to protect him from Cronus."* (33–53)
Pursuits/deeds	Zeus is granted sovereignty over other gods in the heavens "not by casting of lots but by the deeds of thy hands, thy might and that strength which thou has set beside thy throne" (65–66 [Mair, LCL]). Makes the birds his messengers; distributes men of lesser skills—seafaring, warring, minstreling—to other gods; chooses kings who rule for himself. Accomplishes by evening whatever he plans by morning. (53–86)
Comparison	Other gods accomplish some things in a year, and some not in one; Zeus frustrates the accomplishments and thwarts the desires of other gods. (87–89)
Epilogue/prayer	(90–95)

* *The summary of Mair,* Callimachus, *19.*

Also written in the Homeric dactylic hexameter, the hymn is typical of Callimachus' other hymns in its handling of epideictic topoi. It begins conventionally with "origin," mentioning the topos by name. Its rejection of the Cretan claim is dependent on the aforementioned negative ethnic stereotype attached to Cretans as "liars." The hymn's treatment of birth accords with Pseudo-Hermogenes' instruction that attention be given especially to any attendant "marvelous occurrences." The account of Zeus' miraculous nurture by a she-goat and bees recalls Pseudo-Hermogenes' example of the topos, that Achilles "was nurtured on lion's marrow and by Cheiron"; Zeus' protection from threats while young is also a recurring motif under this topos.

The hymn's treatment of Zeus' kingship is conventional material for the topos of "pursuits" (or "office" of "official position"). The hymn devotes most attention to deeds, "the most important" topos (so Ps.-Hermogenes). Actions praised include what Theon would call those "done with toil" (he earns sovereignty rather than receiving it by luck) and those "done quickly" (he completes by evening what he plans by morning).

The Isis and Osiris steles. Diodorus Siculus provides examples of hymns that display the second form, one that takes up a template of topoi specific to the gods.[32] Describing the tombs of the gods in Nysa of Arabia, Diodorus mentions steles erected to the Isis and Osiris, each bearing an inscription written in hieroglyphs. Though Egyptian in origin, they conform to the theoretical parameters of the Graeco-Roman *hymnos*. Each reflects the same topoi taught in Hellenistic education for use in praise of gods.

Name	I am Isis,
Origin	queen of every land,
*Training**	she who was instructed of Hermes,
Deeds	and whatsoever laws I have established, these can no man make void.
Parents	I am the eldest daughter of the youngest god Cronos;
Relatives	I am the wife and sister of the king Osiris;
Inventions benefiting humanity	I am she who first discovered fruits for mankind;
Offspring	I am the mother of Horus the king;
Powers	
City	by me was the city of Bubastus built.
Place of birth	Farewell, farewell, O Egypt that nurtured me. (Diod. Sic. 1.27.4–5 [Oldfather, LCL])

* *Or, perhaps, "Other gods with which . . . associated," a topos mentioned by Alexander Numenius (558–560).*

The hymn on the Isis stele reflects a mixture of topoi characteristic of encomium generally (pursuits, training, deeds, parents, relatives, offspring) and some prescribed specifically for the gods (inventions benefiting humanity, identity with others, powers). The final line, here interpreted as treatment of place of birth, might as easily be read as a treatment of nurture, and in any case is most certainly an epilogue.

Parents	My father is Cronus, the youngest of all the gods,
Name	and I am Osiris
Title/pursuit	the king,
Deeds	who campaigned over every country as far as the uninhabited regions of India and the lands to the north, even to the sources of the river Ister, and again to the remaining parts of the world as far as Oceanus.
Parents	I am the eldest son of Cronus,
Birth myth	and being sprung from a fair and noble egg I was begotten a seed of kindred birth to Day.
Places he visits	There is no region of the inhabited world to which I have not come,
Inventions benefiting humanity	dispensing to all men the things of which I was the discoverer. (1.27.5–6 [Oldfather, LCL])

The Osiris hymn is similar in content to its counterpart. The opening topoi are characteristic of epideictic generally (parents, name, pursuits, parents), while the final topoi typify *hymnos* (birth myth, places he visits, inventions benefiting humanity). Such material in hymns of Egyptian origin suggests the topoi were pan-Mediterranean in usage.

Psalm 23. Generally speaking, Jewish psalms display a form and content that is more diverse and complex than the Graeco-Roman *hymnos*.[33] Those that have a purely epideictic thrust, however, may display a correspondence close enough to *hymnos* that they may be said to meet the theoretical parameters of the form.[34] For example, Psalm 23—one of the better-known psalms—praises God in multiple sentences that correspond to the topoi of *hymnos*. It thus may be cited as an example of *hymnos* that is Jewish in origin and both Jewish and Christian in readership.

Name	The Lord
Pursuits	is my shepherd,
Deeds	I shall not want.
	He makes me lie down in green pastures; he leads me beside still waters; he restores my soul.
	He leads me in right paths for his name's sake.
	Even though I walk through the darkest valley, I fear no evil; for you are with me; your rod and your staff—they comfort me.
	You prepare a table before me in the presence of my enemies; you anoint my head with oil; my cup overflows.
Epilogue	Surely goodness and mercy shall follow me all the days of my life, and I shall dwell in the house of the Lord my whole life long.

Viewed from the perspective of Graeco-Roman theory, the psalm may be seen as taking up a template of topoi typical of praise of persons—a factor likely owing to the analogy of God as shepherd. The piece begins, as some theoretical models suggest, with the name of the subject.[35] The psalm closely associates the divine deeds that it praises with what the Greeks would describe as the divine pursuits—here, his position as divine shepherd. The association is reminiscent of Pseudo-Hermogenes' instruction: "After this you will draw on his pursuits; for example, what sort of life he led: Was he a philosopher or an orator or a general? Most important are deeds; for deeds are included among pursuits; for example, having chosen a soldier's life, what did he accomplish in it?"

Odes of Solomon. Similar comments could be made about early Christian psalmody, which is indebted in obvious ways to Jewish psalmody. As with the latter, so early Christian psalmody is more diverse and complex in form and content than Graeco-Roman *hymnos*. Nevertheless, those early psalms that are strictly epideictic in nature do tend to conform rather well like their Jewish counterparts with Graeco-Roman theory of *hymnos*. Ode 29 of the Syriac *Odes of Solomon* is a good example.[36] The psalm invokes throughout the same kinds of topoi as Graeco-Roman *hymnos*. Given their appearance in Greek, Egyptian, Jewish, and Syriac Christian hymns, we may conclude that such topoi belonged as much to the ancient Mediterranean world generally as to the ancient Greeks and Romans specifically. We may outline Ode 29 as follows:

Proemion	The Lord is my hope: in Him I shall not be confounded.
Deeds	For according to His praise He made me,
	and according to His goodness even so He gave unto me:
	And according to His mercies He exalted me:
	and according to His excellent beauty He set me on high:
	And brought me up out of the depths of Sheol:
	and from the mouth of death He drew me:
	And thou didst lay my enemies low,
	and He justified me by His grace.
	For I believed in the Lord's Messiah: and it appeared to me that He is the Lord;
	And He showed him His sign: and He led me by His light, and gave me the rod of His power;
	That I might subdue the imaginations of the peoples; and the power of the men of might to bring them low:
	To make war by His word, and to take victory by His power.
	And the Lord overthrew my enemy by His word:
Comparison	and he became like the stubble which the wind carries away;
Epilogue	And I gave praise to the Most High because He exalted me His servant and the son of His handmaid. Hallelujah. (Platt)

In form, this psalm displays perfect conformity to the Aphthonion model of *hymnos*, taking up four of Aphthonius' six topoi, and in the exact order he prescribes them. It begins with proemion and ends with epilogue (which Aphthonius, in contrast to the other theorists, lists as topoi). Its body begins with deeds, referring them to virtues and other goods such as praise, goodness, mercies, excellent beauty, and grace. This is in keeping with Aphthonius' instruction that deeds be referred to the goods of the mind, body, and/or fortune. The ode closes with a concluding comparison, too, just as Aphthnonius both requires and displays in all three of his model encomiastic pieces. Whether or not the hymn is actually constructed with Aphthonian or similar doctrine in view, is difficult to say; clearly, though, it is drawing at the very least on similar streams of rhetorical design.

Examples from the New Testament

As in the larger ancient Mediterranean milieu, so too in the New Testament is encomium regularly employed as a "part" within larger narrative "wholes." New Testament examples are generally limited to nonfictional and mythic narrative, as there are no fictional genres within the canon. Conformity in such cases to progymnastic theory is evident, once again, from the kinds of subjects praised, the topoi treated, and their order.

Nonfictional Encomiastic Forms

Acts. An excellent example of nonfictional encomiastic oratory is seen in Paul's speech before the violent mob in Jerusalem (Acts 22:3-21).[37] As an epideictic "part" within a judicial "whole" (Paul calls the speech a "defense," and it certainly has that function), the piece displays the auxiliary function that Nicolaus, *Rhetorica ad Herenium,* and Quintilian say is typical of encomium. The encomiastic portion of the speech belongs to the *narratio,* and in it the Lukan Paul brilliantly depicts himself in terms that the angry mob would initially consider laudatory. Of course, Paul's subsequent defense ultimately serves to disavow his "laudatory" opposition to the Way, so that the "encomium" is transformed, ironically, into a narration of what Paul considers his own crime. Like other encomiastic pieces surveyed from the Mediterranean milieu, this one follows a fairly standard encomiastic template:

Origin	
Ethnicity	I am a Jew,
City	born in Tarsus
Homeland	in Cilicia,
Upbringing	but brought up in this city at the feet of Gamaliel,
Training	educated strictly according to our ancestral law,
Virtue	being zealous for God,
Comparison	just as all of you are today.
Deeds	I persecuted this Way up to the point of death by binding both men and women and putting them in prison, as the high priest and the whole council of elders can testify about me. (22:3-5)

Much in this encomiastic narration is conventional. It treats origin via three sub-topoi mentioned by the theorists, ethnicity/nation, city, and homeland. In each case, Paul cites origins his audience would have judged honorable. Obviously, a Jewish crowd would count Paul's Jewish ethnicity as praiseworthy, even if Romans might not have. Tarsus as a Roman city, and Cilicia as a Roman province, would have enjoyed wide esteem. The accounts of upbringing and training remind one especially of Cicero's counsel to say in what tradition, or under what direction, the person was reared, and to mention any teachers in liberal arts or instructors in the art of living (*Inv.* 1.34–36). Zeal, however, is a virtue specific to the Jewish religious milieu and may be contrasted with the four cardinal virtues prescribed in Hellenistic education.

A remarkably similar self-encomium is seen in Paul's subsequent defense before Agrippa, again in the opening *narratio* of the speech:

Origin	My life from youth from my origin
Ethnicity	among my race
City	and in Jerusalem is known by all the Jews.
Pursuits and deeds	They have known for a long time, if they are willing to testify, that I have belonged to the strictest sect of our religion and lived as a Pharisee. (26:4-5)

As in the earlier speech, Paul's origins here are treated via multiple standard sub-topoi. The use of ethnicity and city specifically reflect the common practice of touching on both geography and generation. The topos here label "pursuits" goes by several names among the theorists (e.g., "occupation, trade, or profession"; Cicero, *Inv.* 1.34–36) and is generally associated with deeds accomplished in connection with one's occupation.

Philippians. If Paul is remembered in Acts as someone occasionally given to self-encomium of his former pre-Christian life, his own letters lend credence to the memory. Philippians 3 contains a self-encomium of Paul's own life apart from Christ, and in comparison with his Judaizing opponents, whom Paul criticizes for putting "confidence in the flesh." The initial point Paul makes is that, for all the pride his opponents put in their "Jewishness" as a mark of their superiority, Paul has cause for more in that his Jewish credentials are unsurpassed. After a prooemion that makes just this claim, Paul lists seven marks of his own superior greatness in this regard (seven being a number symbolic of perfection among the ancients), and these follow a conventional encomiastic template:[38]

Proemion	For it is we who are the circumcision, who worship in the Spirit of God and boast in Christ Jesus and have no confidence in the flesh—even though I, too, have reason for confidence in the flesh. If anyone else has reason to be confident in the flesh, I have more:
Origin	circumcised on the eighth day,
Nation	a member of the people of Israel, of the
Tribe	tribe of Benjamin,
Birth	a Hebrew born of Hebrews;
Pursuits	as to the law, a Pharisee;
Deeds/virtues	as to zeal, a persecutor of the church; as to righteousness under the law, blameless. (3:3-6)

Until this point the self-encomium is thoroughly conventional. The treatment of origins considers sub-topoi prescribed for the heading, *nation* and *tribe*; but it also adapts the topos to the particular subject at hand in treating circumcision as origins specific to *Jewish* life (one's life in Judaism begins with the rite). The treatment of birth reveals nothing new (he has already said he is an Israelite) and is merely rhetorical in effect. The final three items, a subgroup bound together by a common parallel form, treats Paul's pursuits (he is a Pharisee) and deeds (he persecutes the church and keeps the law blamelessly) together, as in progymnastic theory. The deeds, moreover, are referred to specific virtues (zeal, righteousness) as many theorists require.

It is in the discussion that follows, however, where Paul departs from convention and rejects the traditional topoi of praise he has cited as legitimate measures of honor. That Paul is still following encomiastic form is evident from the topoi guiding the departure, death and events after death, which naturally follow the topoi already addressed:

Death / events after death	Yet whatever gains I had, these I have come to regard as loss because of Christ. More than that, I regard everything as loss because of the surpassing value of knowing Christ Jesus my Lord. For his sake I have suffered the loss of all things, and I regard them as rubbish, in order that I may gain Christ and be found in him, not having a righteousness of my own that comes from the law, but one that comes by way of Christ's faithfulness—a righteousness from God that is in fact based on Christ's faithfulness.
Comparison	I want to know Christ and the power of his resurrection and the sharing of his sufferings by becoming like him in his death, if somehow I may attain the resurrection from the dead. (3:7-11)

In these reflections Paul cites his union with Christ in his suffering, death, and resurrection as the reason he has come to regard these seven aforementioned "gains" as "loss."[39] He thus moves beyond the topoi under which he formerly considered himself praiseworthy, to the only topoi he presently counts as having any value in an accounting of his honor: death and events after death. All that is of value to Paul, he argues, is his sharing in Christ's death and resurrection.

The final sentence of the unit continues the reflection on Paul's participatory dying and rising with Christ, only in an explicitly comparative fashion. The sentence thus completes the encomiastic piece by reflecting on what most theorists count the final topos, comparison. Theorists would describe this as a rare syncrisis from the lesser to the greater (see the next chapter).

1 Corinthians. The theorists' discussions regularly mention virtues among the inanimate things that may be made the subject of encomium. Aphthonius even

provides for his students a model encomium of wisdom that adapts the topoi normally used in praise of a person for the subject at hand. Paul's laudation of love in 1 Corinthians 13 may be seen as an example of just such an encomium and outlined via the personal topoi it employs in adapted form:[40]

Prooemion	If I speak in the tongues of mortals and of angels, but do not have love, I am a noisy gong or a clanging cymbal. And if I have prophetic powers, and understand all mysteries and all knowledge, and if I have all faith, so as to remove mountains, but do not have love, I am nothing. If I give away all my possessions, and if I hand over my body so that I may boast, but do not have love, I gain nothing.
Deeds/virtues	Love is patient; love is kind; love is not envious or boastful or arrogant or rude. It does not insist on its own way; it is not irritable or resentful; it does not rejoice in wrongdoing, but rejoices in the truth. It bears all things, believes all things, hopes all things, endures all things.
Death/ comparison	Love never ends. [*With prophecies, tongues, and knowledge*] But as for prophecies, they will come to an end; as for tongues, they will cease; as for knowledge, it will come to an end. For we know only in part, and we prophesy only in part; but when the complete comes, the partial will come to an end. When I was a child, I spoke like a child, I thought like a child, I reasoned like a child; when I became an adult, I put an end to childish ways. For now we see in a mirror, dimly, but then we will see face to face. Now I know only in part; then I will know fully, even as I have been fully known.
Comparison	[*With faith and hope*] And now faith, hope, and love abide, these three; and the greatest of these is love. (13:1-13)

What we have interpreted here as the prooemion introduces the thesis—that all Christian activity is worthless if devoid of love—that the subsequent encomium of love is enlisted to support. The body of the encomium opens with consideration to deeds and virtues together (several theorists tie the two together). Next, the piece considers something analogous in the "life" of love to the topos of death, asserting that love "never ends." In amplification of love's praise in this regard, a supporting comparison of love with prophesies, tongues, and knowledge points out that the latter three do in fact, by contrast, "come to an end"; hence, love is superior. The encomium closes with a comparison of love with two other Christian virtues, faith and hope, declaring that love is "the greatest of these." Once again, Paul has closed his encomium with what several theorists commend as the final topos, comparison. The conclusion is reminiscent of Aphthonius' model encomium of wisdom, which ends with a comparison of wisdom with another virtue, courage, asserting the superiority of the former. Because Paul elsewhere displays a propensity for topically ordered encomiastic composition, and especially that which ends conventionally in comparison, the form of this piece may be viewed as an important clue favoring Pauline authorship and against the belief commonly held among scholars that it is a pre- or non-Pauline interpolation.[41]

Galatians. There is some scholarly debate as to whether the autobiographical Galatians 1:13–2:14 should be interpreted as encomium.[42] Progymnastic theory, however, appears to commend the identification. Throughout the piece, Paul is certainly intent to frame himself in a laudatory light, and against potential or real accusations that might detract from his honor. The piece, moreover, employs multiple encomiastic topoi throughout. Previous analysis may be criticized for failing to identify the treatment of topoi in a conventional order. Such criticism, however, is mitigated when it is recognized that Paul has in view two lives, his former life in Judaism, and his new life in Christ. Once the division is recognized, a conventional order with respect to both is apparent.

Paul's former life in Judaism. The sentences devoted to Paul's "earlier life in Judaism" are brief but nonetheless take up standard topoi in a conventional order. Paul begins with fame, an external good—and one of some concern to Paul given the challenges he is addressing to his reputation. He then moves to his pursuits and deeds as a persecutor who sought to destroy the church. Finally, he concludes with comparison, which (a) several theorists prescribe as a concluding topos; (b) is widely employed as such in the milieu (see several examples above); (c) is regularly employed by Paul as a concluding topos in his other encomiastic pieces (see additional Pauline examples of encomium and *hymnos* below in this chapter, and of syncrisis in the next chapter); and (d) is the concluding topos of the encomium of his new life in Christ in the very next section. The point of the piece is not unlike the similar encomiastic pieces in Acts and Philippians 3 above, that Paul's "earlier life" in Judaism was demonstrably praiseworthy by fleshly standards at least, even if he now views it with little regard.

Fame	You have heard, no doubt, of my earlier life in Judaism.
Pursuits/deeds	I was violently persecuting the church of God and was trying to destroy it.
Comparison	I advanced in Judaism beyond many among my people of the same age, for I was far more zealous for the traditions of my ancestors. (Gal 1:13-14)

Paul's new life in Christ. The transition to praise of Paul's second, new life in Christ is signaled not only by Paul's explicit contrasting of his "earlier life" with his present one, and not only by his use of comparison as a *concluding topos* in the praise of the former, but also by his use of conventionally *introductory topoi* in praise of the latter: origin, birth, and training. We may sketch the narration topically as follows, drawing especially on Theon's sub-topoi of "fine actions" to account for the piece's lengthy section devoted to Paul's pursuits and deeds as an apostle to the Gentiles:

Origin/birth	But when God, who had set me apart from my mother's womb and called me through his grace,
Training	was pleased to reveal* his Son to me,
Pursuits/deeds	
Done with common benefit	so that I might proclaim him among the Gentiles,
Done alone	I did not confer with any human being, nor did I go up to Jerusalem to those who were already apostles before me,
Done quickly	but I went away at once into Arabia, and afterwards I returned to Damascus.
Judgment of the famous / done with few helpers	Then after three years I did go up to Jerusalem to visit Cephas and stayed with him for fifteen days; but I did not see any other apostle except James the Lord's brother. In what I am writing to you, before God, I do not lie!
Judgment of the famous	Then after fourteen years I went up again to Jerusalem with Barnabas, taking Titus along with me. I went up in response to a revelation. Then I laid before them (though only in a private meeting with the acknowledged leaders) the gospel that I proclaim among the Gentiles, in order to make sure that I was not running, or had not run, in vain. But even Titus, who was with me, was not compelled to be circumcised, though he was a Greek.
Braving retribution and dangers for friends	But because of false believers secretly brought in, who slipped in to spy on the freedom we have in Christ Jesus, so that they might enslave us—we did not submit to them even for a moment, so that the truth of the gospel might always remain with you.

Judgment of the famous / done alone	And from those who were supposed to be acknowledged leaders (what they actually were makes no difference to me; God shows no partiality)—those leaders contributed nothing to me. On the contrary, when they saw that I had been entrusted with the gospel for the uncircumcised, just as Peter had been entrusted with the gospel for the circumcised (for he who worked through Peter making him an apostle to the circumcised also worked through me in sending me to the Gentiles), and when James and Cephas and John, who were acknowledged pillars, recognized the grace that had been given to me, they gave to Barnabas and me the right hand of fellowship, agreeing that we should go to the Gentiles and they to the circumcised. They asked only one thing, that we remember the poor, which was actually what I was eager to do.
Comparison	But when Cephas came to Antioch, I opposed him to his face, because he stood self-condemned; for until certain people came from James, he used to eat with the Gentiles. But after they came, he drew back and kept himself separate for fear of the circumcision faction. And the other Jews joined him in this hypocrisy, so that even Barnabas was led astray by their hypocrisy. But when I saw that they were not acting consistently with the truth of the gospel, I said to Cephas before them all, "If you, though a Jew, live like a Gentile and not like a Jew, how can you compel the Gentiles to live like Jews?" (Gal 1:15–2:14)

* *Paul in the thesis sentence (1:11-12) of chapters 1–2 has already framed this "revealing" as a kind of divine education to be contrasted with human teaching: "For I did not receive [my gospel] from a human source, nor was I taught it, but I received it through a revelation of Jesus Christ" (Gal 1:12).*

It is important to recognize that Paul here is encomionizing not his life generally or his old life in "Judaism" but his new life "in Christ." Such a unique subject of praise requires, per progymnastic theory, the *adaptation* of the topoi to the particular nature of the subject. Paul accordingly begins with origins, just as he does in other encomiastic pieces (see, e.g., Rom 1:3; Phil 2:6; 3:5; 2 Cor 11:22). But he must point to the origins not of his life generally as he does in Philippians 3:5 or 2 Corinthians 11:22 but of his new life in Christ specifically and in contrast to the old. One sees the results: his new life in Christ has its origins not with his mother and father but rather *with God*, who set him apart *when* his mother gave birth to him and who called him through divine grace. Here we see simultaneously what some theorists distinguish as a second topos, marvelous occurrences at birth. Paul claims his birth was attended by nothing less than the signs of divine sanctification and calling.

Similar adaptation of topical content, too, is seen in the treatment of training. In accordance with encomiastic theory, Paul must ask what training or education prepared him not for life generally but for his new life in Christ specifically. Paul's answer: the revelation of the Son that he received from God (presumably on the road to Damascus; cf. Acts 9:3-19). What must be noted is that Paul in his earlier introductory remarks (1:11-12) has already framed this "revealing" in pedagogical terms as the divine counterpart to human "teaching": "for I did not receive [my Gospel] from a human source, nor was I taught it, but I received it through a revelation of Jesus Christ" (1:12).

Having touched on the origin, birth, and training of his new life in Christ, Paul naturally proceeds to the pursuits and deeds specific to it. The entire section concerns Paul's apostleship (= pursuits) and associated evangelistic actions (= deeds). Throughout, Paul is concerned to show that his apostleship and preaching are on par with, and not derivative of (i.e., lesser than), that of the leaders in Jerusalem. This is a thoroughly encomiastic concern. Theon's sub-topoi of "fine actions" help us to see the particular contours of Paul's self-laudatory agenda. Because Paul received his revelation directly from God and was not taught it by others, he begins his evangelizing immediately (= actions done quickly) and without the commissioning of other apostles (= actions done alone). Only after three years (well after he had been preaching) is he received in hospitality by other apostles and thereby tacitly approved in his ministry (= judgment of the famous), and even then, it was only Peter and James who received him; otherwise, his ministry carried on without the official sanction of other apostles (= actions done with few helpers). Only after fourteen additional years do the three primary Jerusalem apostles for the first time formally sanction Paul's apostleship and ministry to the Gentiles (albeit privately), in that they do not require Titus to be circumcised (= judgment of the famous). Paul mentions, too, his resistance to the Judaizers—described as a threat to freedom—on behalf of the Galatians and all Gentiles (= braving retributions and dangers for friends). Paul then returns to the formal sanction that the three "pillars" of the Jerusalem community extended to Paul. On the one hand, he insists their standing meant nothing to him and that they added nothing to his ministry (again = actions done alone). On the other hand, he notes that these "acknowledged pillars" approved his ministry to the Gentiles and recognized him as an apostle of equivalent standing with Peter (= judgment of the famous).

Paul concludes his self-encomium with a comparison in narrative form. Having established himself in the preceding section as Peter's equivalent, he now tells a story in which he displays a superiority to Peter with regard to moral authority, rebuking Peter publicly for equivocating on the Gentile question. Paul thus ends his piece conventionally via attention to what most theorists count the final topos.

Hebrews. Hebrews, which employs encomiastic forms everywhere (see *hymnos* below and syncrisis in the next chapter), offers a brief encomium of Melchizedek in the seventh chapter.[43] The piece, which is intended to paint Melchizedek as typological progenitor of Christ's priestly tribe, shapes Melchizedek into the image of the divine Christ—so much so that the piece might well be classified as a *hymnos*:[44]

Proemion	This "King Melchizedek of Salem, priest of the Most High God, met Abraham as he was returning from defeating the kings and blessed him"; and to him Abraham apportioned "one-tenth of everything."
Name	His name, in the first place, means "king of righteousness";
Title	next he is also king of Salem, that is, "king of peace."
Origins	
Father	Without father,
Mother	without mother,
Ancestors	without genealogy,
Birth	having neither beginning of days
Death	nor end of life,
Comparison	but resembling the Son of God,
Events after death	he remains a priest forever.
Epilogue	See how great he is! (7:1-4)

In the light of encomiastic theory, the encomium appears to be a nearly perfect specimen of topical composition. The proemion introduces the proof text from Genesis 14:17-20 as the basis for the topical analysis. The latter begins with names and titles—a topos some theorists place at the head of their lists as a kind of prefatory subject. The treatment of all subsequent topoi that follows depends upon the silence of the text as to Melchizedek's father, mother, ancestors, birth, and death. The phrase "but resembling the Son of God" introduces explicit comparison with Jesus—though it is possible, given that every topos is intended to suggest the resemblance, to interpret the piece as a syncrisis. Last, the phrase "he remains a priest forever" (cf. Ps. 110:4) speaks at once to Melchizedek's priestly pursuits and his immortality. The reasons for praising Melchizedek in this fashion we explore in the next chapter on syncrisis.

Hymnos

Hymnos, the mythical form of encomium devoted to the gods, is commonly attested in the New Testament, with most occurrences taking Jesus/Christ or God as the subject of praise.[45] Though our focus here is on more topically developed pieces, virtually all sentences of praise of God, Jesus, Christ, the divine Word, the Holy Spirit, and the like in the New Testament may be classed as *hymnos*, as ancient theory makes no distinction in genre between shorter and more developed forms (as it does, e.g., in distinguishing epainos from encomium). In nearly every case surveyed, scholarship has proposed and debated hymnic status, albeit apart from any extended consideration of progymnastic theory, and usually on the shared assumption that hymnic identification implies interpolation of a foreign text from an original liturgical context. In each case here examined, analysis in the light of progymnastic theory vindicates the identification but also calls into question the *necessity* of an associated interpolation theory, as *hymnos* and other progymnastic forms were taught primarily as "parts" to be composed for and incorporated into larger "wholes." Finally, as in the larger literary milieu, so in the New Testament, both theoretical forms of *hymnos* are attested—namely, those that adapt the topoi normally employed in praise of persons and those that employ topoi specific to the gods.

1 Peter. A brief *hymnos* of the first variety, framed as an exemplum serving the larger argumentation for faithful endurance, appears in 1 Peter.[46] The piece is in praise of Christ, whom it regards as then in a resurrected and exalted state (see the final sentence); thus, it is squarely in the realm of *hymnos* rather than encomium. The topical template it follows is standard both in content and order:

Prooemion	For to this you have been called, because Christ also suffered for you, leaving you an example, so that you should follow in his steps.
Deeds	"He committed no sin,
Words	and no deceit was found in his mouth."
Comparison	When he was abused, he did not return abuse; when he suffered, he did not threaten; but he entrusted himself to the one who judges justly.
Death	He himself bore our sins in his body on the cross, so that, free from sins, we might live for righteousness; by his wounds you have been healed.
Epilogue	For you were going astray like sheep, but now you have returned to the shepherd and guardian of your souls. (2:21-25)

The divisions of the hymn are fairly straightforward. The comparison juxtaposes not persons as wholes but rather the words and deeds of Jesus with those of his persecutors, hence its location immediately after the lines devoted to deeds and words, rather than at the end of the piece per convention. The epilogue might also be viewed as treatment of events after death, in that it pictures Jesus in his postmortem exalted status. It could be interpreted further, perhaps, as treatment of pursuits, insofar as it names Christ's vocation as a shepherd and guardian. We have interpreted it as epilogue, however, because of the shift back to the readers ("you") as the subject, as in the prooemion.

1 Timothy. A brief hymn of the first type is seen in the first pastoral epistle to Timothy.[47] Its encomiastic outline may be represented as follows:

Proemion	Without any doubt, the mystery of our religion is great:
Birth	He was revealed in flesh,
Accidents / events after death	vindicated in spirit,
	seen by angels,
	proclaimed among Gentiles,
	believed in throughout the world,
	taken up in glory. (3:16)

The proemion puts forward an explicitly laudatory thesis concerning Jesus (= "the mystery of our religion"), that he is "great." Though the topical outline might be framed a number of different ways, it is clear the piece begins conventionally with a common introductory topos, birth, and ends conventionally with events after death. The intervening lines of praise might be grasped in connection with several topoi. They are here labeled "accidents" (Cicero's idiosyncratic topos, *Inv.* 1.34–36) because they are expressed consistently in the passive voice; besides Cicero, however, the other theorists do not distinguish active "deeds" from passive "accidents" and so would likely interpret these items as "deeds." Most if not all four of the middle items are also possibly "events after death," though it is not clear that each is strictly posthumous.

Philippians. Until recent years, the consensus view of New Testament scholarship was that Philippians 2:6-11 was a hymn—and in all likelihood, one Paul was quoting from early Christian liturgy.[48] Progymnastic theory vindicates the identification of genre but also highlights features that, because they are found in Pauline encomiastic composition generally, cast some doubt on the interpolation thesis.[49] Most notably, the piece follows a topical outline that is characteristic of Pauline encomium, beginning as it does with origin and birth, ending with comparison, and giving consideration in between to deeds, manner of death, and posthumous events.[50]

Origin/comparison	Who being in the form of God considered not as something to seize upon equality with God, but emptied himself
	taking the form of a slave,
Birth	being born in the likeness of humans,
Body	and being found in appearance as a human,

Mind/virtues	he humbled himself,
Deeds	becoming obedient to the point of death,
Manner of death	even death on a cross.
Posthumous events	Therefore God also highly exalted him
Names and titles/ comparison	and gave to him the name that is above every name that at the name of Jesus every knee should bow in heaven and on earth and under the earth and every tongue confess that Jesus Christ is Lord to the glory of God the father.* (2:6-11)

* *It is possible to describe some of the Christ hymns via topoi prescribed for praise of gods. Quintilian's list, e.g., begins with "majesty of nature" and ends with "earned immortality through virtue"—headings that are apt for the first and final lines the Christ hymn. Alexander Numenius' topos, universality of worship, is similarly well suited as a descriptor of the hymn's conclusion.*

More important, the piece displays a highly subversive streak with regard to traditional encomiastic standards that is typical of Paul. Just as Paul in his self-encomia rejects the standards by which his former life might have been viewed as laudatory and instead embraces topoi adapted to and transformed by the Christ event as alternative measures of honor, so too in this hymn to Christ does Paul reject the traditional standards by which a god is lauded and instead embrace standards that this side of the Christ event are the very opposite of the traditional. That is, the hymn praises Christ in the case of nearly every topos for taking up stations of *shame*, rather than stations of *honor*, out of service to the world.

Origin/comparison	Though Christ's origin is in the "form of God," he is praised for taking the "form of a servant"—a transportation from the highest station of the divine household to the lowest.
Birth	Though gods were commonly praised for being born immortal, Christ is praised for being born in the likeness of humans.
Body	Though gods were normally lauded for having bodies of exquisite divine form, Christ is praised for taking on human appearance.
Mind/virtues	Though gods and humans alike were typically hailed for displaying the virtues of justice, temperance, wisdom, or bravery, Christ is praised for his humility—a quality the Graeco-Roman world counted a shameful vice associated with the servile.

Deeds	Though gods were typically praised for the arena of human life they commanded, Christ is praised for obedience that leads to the point of death.
Manner of death	Though gods were commonly praised for their immortality, and humans for honorable deaths, Christ is praised for his death on a cross—a torturous death so shameful that it was generally reserved only for criminal slaves or aliens.
Posthumous events	Though divinized men were commonly praised for achieving immortality through traditional acts of virtue, Christ is praised as exalted by God *because* of all the stations of shame he willingly occupied ("*Therefore* God exalted him . . .").
Name	Similarly, his superior name and title are granted *because* of his self-humbling.

Whatever its authorship, the hymn is certainly remarkable for its radical subversion of traditional Graeco-Roman measures of divine honor. The hymn may be viewed as the first occurrence of ancient Mediterranean *hymnos* that lauds its god for standing in solidarity with, rather distancing itself from, humanity in all its shameful aspects of existence.

Romans. Though long considered a pre-Pauline interpolation, the *hymnos* of Jesus in Romans 1:3-4 fits the pattern of Pauline encomiastic composition well.[51]

Origin and birth	. . . concerning his son who was born a descendant of David[52] according to the flesh
Events after death	and was declared to be Son of God with power according to the spirit of holiness by resurrection from the dead,
Names and Titles	Jesus Christ our Lord.

In beginning with origins and birth, the piece takes up topoi regularly found at the opening of other Pauline encomiastic pieces (see above Gal 1:15-2:14; Phil 2:6-11; 3:3-11; see in the next chapter on syncrisis Gal 4:21-31; 1 Cor 15:45-49; 2 Cor 3:7-11; 11:21-12:11; Rom 5:12-21). The use of the Greek verb *ginomai* (translated here "was born") in connection with these topoi is also characteristically Pauline (cf. Phil 2:7; 1 Cor 15:45; 2 Cor 3:7). The treatment of the exaltation in connection with events after death is attested in the other Pauline hymn surveyed here, Philippians 2:6-11. The hymnic conclusion under names and titles, with explicit mention of "Jesus" and "Lord," is likewise attested in Philippians 2:6-11. This evidence, together with the invocation of "flesh"/"spirit" polarity that is so characteristic of Pauline thought, suggests the piece is written by Paul.

Hebrews. An excellent example of the second type of *hymnos*, that which employs topoi specially tailored for the gods, is found in the exordium of Hebrews.[53]

The piece has long been proposed as a *hymnos*, albeit in connection, again, with the assumption that the identification necessarily implies interpolation.[54] In point of fact, the writer of Hebrews shows himself everywhere to be a master of epideictic composition, and so it is most natural to view the piece as original to him.

We may represent the topical form of the hymn as follows:

Majesty of nature	Who being the radiance of his glory and the imprint of his nature,
Power	and bearing all things by the word of his power,
Actions	having accomplished purification of sins,
Immortality by virtue	he sat down at the right hand of the majesty on high,
Comparison	having become so much greater than the angels,
Name	as much as he has inherited a name more excellent than they. (1:3-4)

Evidently the writer is following a hymnic topos list very similar to that of Quintilian (*Inst.* 3.7.7–9). The hymn begins by employing four of Quintilian's eight topoi, addressing them in the same order as Quintilian, and by name in several cases. It closes with treatment of comparison and name, two addenda topoi widely treated as concluding headings beyond the standard topoi.[55] These are the same two addenda topoi found at the conclusion of the Philippians Christ-hymn, too (see above). Thus, the *hymnos*, though more conventional in its approach than its Pauline counterparts, ends on the same notes, reflecting on the exaltation of Christ and the consequential comparative greatness of his name.

Notes

1 Cf. also Quintilian, *Inst.* 3.7.1–6; and Michael W. Martin and Jason A. Whitlark, *Inventing Hebrews: Design and Purpose in Ancient Rhetoric* (Cambridge: Cambridge University Press, forthcoming in 2018), ch. 6.

2 For the following discussion of theory see the encomium exercises of Theon, *Prog.* 109–112; Ps.-Hermogenes, *Prog.* 14–18; Aphthonius, *Prog.* 35–42; Nicolaus, *Prog.* 47–58; cf. Quintilian, *Inst.* 1.9.1–3.

3 George A. Kennedy, *Progymnasmata: Greek Textbooks of Prose Composition and Rhetoric* (Atlanta: Society of Biblical Literature, 2003), 50n155.

4 Theon, Ps.-Hermogenes, and Nicolaus treat invective within the encomium exercise. Aphthonius reserves it as a separate exercise but agrees with the others that the method of composition (see below) is the same as with encomium.

5 Theon distinguishes encomium, "praise of living persons," from *epitaphios*, "praise of the dead." Nicolaus, by contrast, treats *epitaphios* as a subspecies of encomium. Ps.-Hermogenes and Aphthonius do not mention *epitaphios*.

6 Theon does not mention *epainos*. Aphthonius states that "an epainos is brief but an *encomion* is artistically developed"; similarly, Ps.-Hermogenes, "*encomion* differs from *epainos* (praise) in that *epainos* can be short; e.g., 'Socrates is wise,' while *encomion* is found in longer passages."

Kennedy observes, "Aristotle (*Eth. eud.* 2.1.12) says that *epainos* is praise of the subject's general character, *enkōmion* of particular deeds" (*Progymnasamata*, 81n30).

7 Theon and Apthonius distinguish *hymnos* from the encomium. Nicolaus, by contrast, treats *hymnos* as a subspecies of encomium.

8 See the discussions in George A. Kennedy, *New Testament Interpretation through Rhetorical Criticism* (Chapel Hill: University of North Carolina Press, 1984), 73–85; D. A. Russell and N. G. Wilson, *Menander Rhetor* (Oxford: Clarendon, 1981), xiii–xviii.

9 *Epainos*, because of its brevity, is exceptional among the forms mentioned in the progymnasmata; as a single sentence of general praise, it did not require the elaborate form taught for use with the others.

10 For the following, see especially Russell and Wilson, *Menander Rhetor*, xviii–xxxiv; Jerome H. Neyrey, "Encomion versus Vituperation: Contrasting Portraits of Jesus in the Fourth Gospel," *JBL* 126 (2007): 529–52; and Michael W. Martin, "Progymnastic Topic Lists: A Compositional Template for Luke and Other *Bioi?*," *NTS* 54 (2008): 18–41.

11 Furthermore, these topoi, indeed the overall thrust of the progymnasmata, serve also to reinforce male over female, free over slave, and able-bodied over disabled, as well as Graeco-Roman peoples over other ethnic groups; see Maud Gleason, *Making Men: Sophists and Self-Presentation in Ancient Rome* (Princeton: Princeton University Press, 2008); Mikeal C. Parsons, *Body and Character in Luke and Acts: The Subversion of Physiognomy in Early Christianity* (Grand Rapids: Eerdmans, 2006), 25–26.

12 In contrast to this list, Theon's topos list in the narrative exercise ("origin, nature, training, disposition, age, fortune, morality, action, speech, death, what followed death"; *Prog.* 78) is arranged chronologically and includes treatment of the topos "events after death."

13 Attributes of a person, listed by Cicero for use in *confirmatio*. In 1.2.127–128, Cicero refers to this list and states that these same attributes are to be used for encomium, only his summation differs in some respects and is arranged by the three goods.

14 See the discussion in Michael W. Martin and Jason A. Whitlark, "The Encomiastic Topics of Syncrisis as the Key to the Structure and Argument of Hebrews," *NTS* 57 (2011): 415–39.

15 For the following, see Michael W. Martin and Bryan A. Nash, "Philippians 2:6-11 as Subversive *Hymnos*: A Study in the Light of Ancient Rhetorical Theory," *JTS* 66 (2015): 90–138.

16 Russell and Wilson, *Menander Rhetor*, xviii–xix.

17 On the *History*, see Charles Forster Smith, *Thucydides: History of the Peloponnesian War*, LCL (Cambridge, Mass.: Harvard University Press, 2003), 1:vii–xxiii.

18 Cf. also the *Invective against Cicero*. On both works, see J. C. Rolfe, *Sallust*, LCL (Cambridge, Mass.: Harvard University Press, 2001), 2:xix–xx.

19 On Dionysius' *Roman Antiquities*, see Earnest Cary, *Dionysius of Halicarnassus*, LCL (Cambridge, Mass.: Harvard University Press, 2001), 1:vii–xlviii.

20 That Josephus was familiar with encomiastic composition is clear from the study of Jerome H. Neyrey, "Josephus' *Vita* and the Encomium: A Native Model of Personality," *JSJ* 25 (1994): 177–206; cf. Michael W. Martin, "Progymnastic Topic Lists: A Compositional Template for Luke and Other *Bioi*," *NTS* 54 (2008): 18–41.

21 On the *Jewish War*, see H. St. J. Thackerey, *Josephus*, LCL (Cambridge, Mass.: Harvard University Press, 2004), 2:vii–xxxi.

22 On the *Vita*, see H. St. J. Thackeray, *Josephus*, LCL (Cambridge, Mass.: Harvard University Press, 2008), 2:vii–xx. On the *Vita's* encomiastic content, Neyrey, "Josephus' *Vita* and the Encomium," 177–206; and Martin, "Progymnastic Topic Lists," 18–41.

23 On Eusebius' Ecclesiastical History, see the introduction of Kirsopp Lake, *Eusebius: The Ecclesiastical History*, LCL (Cambridge, Mass.: Harvard University Press, 1998), 1:vii–lvi.

24 For an introduction to *An Ephesian Tale*, see B. P. Reardon, ed., *Collected Ancient Greek Novels* (Berkeley: University of California Press, 2008), 125–28; and on ancient Greek novels generally, 1–16.

25 On Tobit as an ancient novel, see Lawrence M. Wills, ed. and trans., *Ancient Jewish Novels: An Anthology* (Oxford: Oxford University Press, 2002), 62–65.

26 Cf. *Aesopic Romance*, which takes up origin, body, mind, age, and fortune in the opening paragraphs (1–2), treating age by name as follows: "As to the age he lived in . . . it was when Croesus governed Lydia . . ." (1).

27 On Judith as an ancient Jewish novel, see Wills, *Ancient Jewish Novels*, 89–92.

28 On the debate concerning the authorship of the book, see John J. Collins, "Joseph and Aseneth: Jewish or Christian?" *JSP* 14 (2005): 97–112; cf. also Mills, *Ancient Jewish Novels*, 121–24. Collins argues for Egyptian Jewish origins, observing that the favorable reception among Christian copyists does not prove Christian authorship.

29 The latter type thus has characteristics of both "parts" and "wholes," to use Nicolaus' distinction. On the one hand, they are generally brief and were not circulated independently; on the other hand, they are fully formed orations and thus belong not only to the mythic but also to the political species of narrative.

30 On this point, see Martin and Nash, "Philippians 2:6-11 as Subversive *Hymnos*," 90–138. The point is most relevant to the study of hymnic forms in biblical scholarship, which has a long history of identification based on the presence or absence of poetic, rather than topical, form.

31 On this hymn, and the diverse "Homeric" collection generally, see A. W. Mair, *Callimachus: Hymns and Epigrams*, LCL (Cambridge, Mass.: Harvard University Press, 2006), 1–34.

32 On the inscriptions as *hymnoi*, see Martin and Nash, "Philippians 2:6-11 as Subversive *Hymnos*," 290–311.

33 On the diverse range of psalmic genres, see, e.g., Hermann Gunkel, *Psalms: A Form-Critical Introduction*, trans. Thomas M. Horner, FBBS 19 (Philadelphia: Fortress, 1967).

34 That is, the class biblical scholarship calls "psalms of praise"; see, e.g., Claus Westermann, *The Psalms: Structure, Content, and Message*, trans. Ralph D. Gehrke (Minneapolis: Augsburg, 1980), 25–28.

35 The psalm actually employs the divine name "Yahweh," which is traditionally rendered "Lord" in English translation.

36 On the *Odes of Solomon*, see the excellent introduction in James H. Charlesworth, trans., *Earliest Christian Psalmbook: The Odes of Solomon* (Eugene, Oreg.: Cascade, 2009), xiii–xxxvii.

37 See esp. the analysis of Mikeal C. Parsons, *Acts*, PCNT (Grand Rapids: Baker Academic, 2008), 308–9.

38 The following analysis is an adaptation, with significant modification, of the thesis of Bryan A. Nash, "Philippians 3:4-11 as Subversive Encomium," *Stone-Campbell Journal* 19 (2016): 85–94.

39 Paul's theology, evident from the full corpus of his writings, illuminates these sentences. Paul has in mind here a metaphorical death and new life beyond: a dying to the former self enslaved to sin in Adam, and a rising to newness of life, enslaved to righteousness, in Christ (see, e.g., Rom 5–8). "Suffering the loss of all things" here refers to this dying to the old self and to a participatory union with Christ in his suffering and death. Similarly, "gaining Christ," "being found in him," and "having a righteousness that comes by way of Christ's faithfulness" (faithfulness = Paul's shorthand for the fidelity Christ displayed in his death on the cross) refers to participatory union with Christ in new righteous life that follows the participatory death to self.

40 Others have previously interpreted the passage as an encomium, though apart from an analysis of topical form; see, e.g., Raymond F. Collins, *First Corinthians*, SacPag 7 (Collegeville, Minn.: Liturgical Press, 1999), 478–79.

41 On the latter view, see, e.g., the literature surveyed approvingly in William Walker Jr., *Interpolations in the Pauline Letters* (New York: Sheffield Academic, 2001), 147–65.

42 The case has been persuasively argued by Bruce J. Malina and Jerome H. Neyrey, *Portraits of Paul: An Archaeology of Ancient Personality* (Louisville, Ky.: Westminster John Knox, 1996), 23–51; but see the criticisms of Ronald F. Hock, "Paul and Greco-Roman Education," in *Paul and the Greco-Roman World: A Handbook*, ed. J. Paul Sampley (Harrisburg, Pa.: Trinity Press International, 2003), 198–227, esp. 213.

43 On the passage as encomium, see the analysis—followed below—of Martin and Whitlark, *Inventing Hebrews*, ch. 6.

44 For the question of whether Melchizedek is human or divine, see the discussion in Craig R. Koester, *Hebrews: A New Translation with Introduction and Commentary*, AB 36 (New York: Doubleday, 2001), 24–25, 338–41, and esp. 349.

45 Pieces devoted to Jesus do not have to display a high christology to be classed as *hymnos*. Ancient convention allowed that even divinized emperors may be hymned. The pieces cited herein arguably have a higher view of Jesus' divinity, and in any case meet this low threshold.

46 Scholarly debate on this passage has typically pitted hymnic identification against authorship by the letter writer, with opinion increasingly against the former; see, e.g., John H. Elliot, *1 Peter*, AB 37B (New York: Doubleday, 2000), 548–60.

47 Cf. the hymnoi in Eph 1:3-10 and Col 1:15-20. On the function of 1 Tim 3:16 as a hymn in its present literary context, see Philip H. Towner, *The Letters to Timothy and Titus*, NICNT (Grand Rapids: Eerdmans, 2006), 276–85.

48 See the survey of literature in Ralph P. Martin, *A Hymn of Christ: Philippians 2:5-11 in Recent Interpretation & in the Setting of Early Christian Worship* (Downer's Grove, Ill.: InterVarsity, 1997), 1–62; and more recently Michael W. Martin and Bryan A. Nash, "Philippians 2:6-11 as Subversive *Hymnos*: A Study in the Light of Ancient Rhetorical Theory," *JTS* 66 (2015): 90–138.

49 For the first part of this claim, we follow the analysis of Martin and Nash, "Philippians 2:6-11 as Subversive *Hymnos*," 90–138.

50 As Martin and Nash observe, *hymnos* occurred in both poetic and prose forms; thus, Phil 2:6-11's topical form, not its poetic form, is the evidence crucial to hymnic identification.

51 On the piece as original to Paul, see N. T. Wright, "Paul and Caesar: A New Reading of Romans," in *A Royal Priesthood? The Use of the Bible Ethically and Politically: A Dialogue with Oliver O'Donovan*, ed. Craig Bartholemew et al. (Carlisle, U.K.: Paternoster, 2002), 173–93.

52 We depart from the NRSV here in preserving the verb "born" in translation.

53 For the following analysis, see Martin and Whitlark, *Inventing Hebrews*, ch. 7.

54 See, e.g., Günther Bornkamm, "Das Bekenntnis im Hebräerbrief," in *Studien zu Antike und Urchristentum: Gesammelte Aufsätze*, ed. Günther Bornkamm, BEvT28 (Munich: Kaiser, 1963), 2:188–203, esp. 197–200; Reinhard Deichgräber, *Gotteshymnus und Christushymnus in der frühen Christenheit*, SUNT 5 (Göttingen: Vandenhoeck & Ruprecht, 1967), 137–40. Because of its ties to interpolation theories, the hymnic thesis has been questioned by many; e.g., Koester, *Hebrews*, 178–79; James W. Thompson, *Hebrews*, PCNT (Grand Rapids: Baker Academic, 2008), 33.

55 For comparison as a final topos, see Theon, *Prog.* 112–115; Ps.-Hermogenes, *Prog.* 18–20; Menander Rhetor, 2.368–377; Aphthonius, *Prog.* 35–44; and Nicolaus, *Prog.* 47–63; for "names, homonymns, and nicknames" as a final, additional topos, see Theon, *Prog.* 109–112; for "name" as a concluding topos, see Menander Rhetor 2.438–446; for "name" as a prefatory topos, see Cicero, *Inv.* 1.34–36.

7

Syncrisis

Evaluating Relative Honor

Syncrisis is language setting the better or the worse side by side.

Theon

In the ancient Mediterranean world, comparative evaluation of subjects in terms of praise or blame was commonplace. Such evaluation, known as "syncrisis," was employed in literature of every kind, beginning with the classics, and regularly used in oratory in amplification of any number of subjects. Thus, syncrisis came to be taught in the schools as a basic literary form essential to all manner of composition. In this chapter we explore the conventions of the device, which by the New Testament period had become fairly standardized, and illustrate its use in accordance with those conventions both within and without the New Testament.

Theory

Definition

The theorists define syncrisis simply as language that "compares" subjects or "sets them beside" one another.[1] By this definition, any and all comparison is meant, though as we shall see, the form of comparison actually practiced in the exercises featured a specific pattern of organization and content that does not appear in all comparisons.

Like encomium and invective, syncrisis was considered a form of epideictic rhetoric, as it was fundamentally concerned with relative honor. Some theorists describe it simply as "double encomium" or "double invective" since it entails praising or blaming two subjects using the same procedures as employed in those exercises. All theorists encourage, too, the transference of skills learned in the encomium and invective exercises to the practice of syncrisis, in that they locate the syncrisis exercise immediately after the encomium and/or invective exercises and in many cases refer summarily to instructions therein rather than repeat them at length. Syncrisis thus trafficked in the same categories of honor and shame as encomium and invective in the appraisal of its subjects, and it tended to reinforce the same gender, class, regional, and ethnic stereotypes as encomium and invective.

Subjects

Like encomium and invective, syncrisis developed as a form devoted primarily to human subjects but came to be adapted for use with other subjects as well. The theorists speak of "persons and things" as the two main classes of subjects one may compare in a syncrisis. There may be some disagreement among them, however, as to the range of "things" that can properly be considered. Though Theon does not explicitly limit syncritical subjects to "inanimate things" as in the encomium exercise, his examples—wisdom and bravery—suggest he is still operating with such an understanding. The other theorists, by contrast, do not so delimit the "things" that may be compared, so that for them syncrisis may take up virtually *anything* as its subject. Pseudo-Hermogenes, for example, mentions comparisons of men, cities, plants, activities, justice, and wealth as examples. Aphthonius similarly writes, "It is appropriate for us to compare as many things as we blame and celebrate: both persons and things, occasions and places, dumb animals, and in addition, plants." Nicolaus says syncrisis is "parallel scrutiny of goods or evils or persons or things," and in the course of the exercises mentions persons, activities, and plants as examples.

Classifications

The theorists, always given to the creation of taxonomies, describe a variety of classifications of syncrisis, sometimes differing on what kinds are and are not allowed.[2] Frequently attested is the *classification by relative honor / by argument*. A writer or speaker, the theorists say, may amplify a subject via three possible means: (1) *comparison to the lesser*—by far the most common form of syncrisis, this form demonstrates that a subject surpasses the selected comparison partner (the "lesser") in praise- or blameworthiness; (2) *comparison to the greater*, which amplifies a subject by showing it to be nearly as praise- or blameworthy as another who is typically acknowledged as such—the form is less common and is only explicitly discussed among the later theorists; and (3) *comparison to the equal*, which amplifies a subject by demonstrating it to be the equal of a comparison partner in praise- or blameworthiness—the form is mentioned by all but Theon, who seems to require that a verdict of superiority be given in every case.[3]

The theorists also attest a system of *classification by absolute honor* found in all theorists after Theon. One may engage in: (1) a "double encomium" comparison of two praiseworthy subjects, usually with the goal of demonstrating which is greatest; (2) a "double-invective" comparison juxtaposing two blame-worthy subjects, and usually with the goal of amplifying censure; and (3) a comparison consisting of "encomium and invective," where the stark contrast between two subjects is generally the point. Theon's discussion, which almost exclusively has in view the "double encomium" form without naming it as such, does allow in an aside that the "procedure is the opposite whenever we seek to discover the worse of two things to be avoided"—an allusion, obviously, to what later theorists term the "double-invective" form. Theon seems opposed, however—at least on the surface—to the encomium-invective class in his insistence that "comparison should be of likes and where we are in doubt which should be preferred because of no evident superiority of one to the other."[4] The rule, however, does not absolutely exclude the possibility of an encomium–invective syncrisis. It is possible, for example, to juxtapose two subjects commonly *perceived* to be similarly praiseworthy—for example, money and wisdom—and ultimately censure one and praise the other. The most that can be said, then, is that Theon makes no mention of the encomium-invective class.[5]

Theon's rule does point, however, to a theoretical disagreement as it pertains to a third taxonomy, one we may call the *classification by similarity*. Two possibilities are acknowledged among the theorists: (1) *comparison of similar subjects* and (2) *comparison of dissimilar subjects*. In Theon's view, the latter is to be avoided for reasons of taste: "First let it be specified that syncrises are not comparisons of things having a great difference between them; for someone wondering whether Achilles or Thersites was braver would be laughable." Later theorists, however, offer no such proscriptions, and generally allow greater literary license with regard to syncritical pairings.[6] Further, Pseudo-Hermogenes directly contradicts Theon in his opening sentence and definition of the device: "Syncrisis is a comparison of similar or dissimilar things."[7]

Such systems of classification, though pedantic, provided writers and orators helpful models for selecting syncritical partners appropriate for a subject's amplification. Further, they provided the better educated a common lens through which to view syncritical pairings and apprehend their essential form. For these reasons, the taxonomies lend valuable insight into the design and reception of syncrisis in ancient literature.

Topoi

The theorists commonly distinguish between comparisons that are "whole to whole" and "part to part." The former kind of syncrisis typically consists of a single comparative sentence and, as the name suggests, sets subjects in their entirety beside one another: "The man who fled in front was good, but by far a better man pursued" (Homer, *Il.* 20.158 [Murray/Wyatt, LCL]). Though the theorists prescribe this type for use within other forms—for example, narrative, common-place, encomium, or invective—they are consistent in affirming that syncrisis proper, as a fully formed literary unit unto itself, is to be conducted more thoroughly via corresponding constituent elements of the subjects, or "part-to-part."

Guiding the selection of the "parts" are the same topoi of praise and blame learned in the encomium and invective exercises and used for the construction of those forms. As compositional search headings, the topoi guided the selection and order of materials in a syncrisis and lent a general uniformity to the procedure evident across a wide range of literature in the Mediterranean world (see below). As in encomium and invective, the topoi also inculcated largely male, aristocratic notions of what was and was not considered praiseworthy. One may consult the previous chapter for extant lists of topoi appearing in the progymnasmata and handbooks. Though the lists vary, they commonly attest a core set of standard topoi used widely in epideictic generally and syncrisis specifically. Pseudo-Hermogenes' list is fairly typical: "Well then, [syncrisis] proceeds by use of encomiastic topics; for we compare the cities from which the men came, and family with family, and nurture with nurture, and pursuits and deeds and external factors and manner of death and what follows death."

As with encomium, so with syncrisis do the theorists advise adapting and using these same topoi in the comparison of *things*. One simply finds something analogous to origin, deeds, and the like in the "lives" of the things being compared and uses that as the subject matter of the comparison. Thus, Pseudo-Hermogenes, continuing from the sentence above, states,

> Similarly, if you compare plants you will evaluate against each other the gods who gave them [= familial origin], the places where they grow [= geographical origin], their cultivation [= nurture], the utility of their fruits [= deeds], and so on. Similarly, if you compare activities, you will mention those who first took up the activities [= origin] and you will set those engaged in them side by side with each other in terms of the quality of mind and body [= nature of body and mind].[8] You should apply the same principle in all cases. (*Prog.* 19)

Genus Syncrisis

Though Theon is alone (at least among extant progymnasmata) in describing how to set one group or "genus" beside another in a syncrisis, his discussion is worth noting because the methodology that he prescribes is commonplace in extant composition. Theon, in essence, proposes two methods: (1) *by "extreme" or "outstanding" members* and (2) *by numbers of great members.*

The former method takes a praiseworthy member of a group and compares him or her with a similarly praiseworthy member of a second group. The verdict of superiority in the case of the individuals is then applied to the groups as a whole—a procedure generally consistent with "part-to-part" comparison as taught by all the theorists. Theon illustrates the method as follows:

> For example, if we wanted to compare the genus of males to that of females (to find) which of them is braver, by comparing the bravest man to the bravest woman; whichever we find better, we would conclude that the whole of that genus is better than the other. If, then, we wanted to prefer the genus of males to that of females we shall compose as follows. We shall propose that Themistocles was greater than the genus of males in bravery and Artemisia greater than the genus of females; if then Themistocles was braver that Artemisia, the genus of males is also braver than that of females. But if we wanted to prefer the female genus we would propose Tomyris as the bravest of women and Cyrus of men; therefore, if Tomyris was braver than Cyrus, the genus of females is also braver than that of men. (*Prog.* 114)

The second method of genus syncrisis, comparison by numbers, simply counts the number of praiseworthy members in each group and gives preference to that with the greater numbers. As Theon puts it,

> we prefer that genus in which there are more distinguished members; for example, if there are more brave males than women, the genus of males is braver than that of women. For if Tomyris the Massagete or Sparethra, the wife of Amorges, king of the Sacae, is better than Cyrus, or by Zeus, even Semiramis, wife of Zoraster of Bactria, still one should not grant that the female is braver than the male, there being one or two very brave women but many, many males. (114–115)

Arrangement

Theon also offers a brief but noteworthy discussion of syncritical arrangement, observing that a comparison may be ordered in one of two ways: (1) *separate arrangement*, wherein one gives a full account of the first subject before proceeding to the second; and (2) *combined arrangement*, in which both subjects are treated simultaneously in a single account. Both methods, as we shall observe, are commonly employed in ancient Mediterranean literature.

Examples from Ancient Literature

Examples of syncrisis are widely attested in the ancient Mediterranean world, across a variety of genres, and from Graeco-Roman, Jewish, and Christian writers alike. In the present section we are concerned to note occurrences of extended, part-to-part comparisons, as opposed to single sentences of whole-to-whole comparison, though all would be judged "syncrisis" by progymnastic standards.[9] Such lengthier comparisons illustrate well the conventions of syncrisis highlighted in textbooks and practiced by the educated.

Graeco-Roman Syncrisis

Homer. Graeco-Roman rhetoricians and educators alike generally looked to Homer as a model of good rhetorical form.[10] In the syncrisis exercises, the theorists cite examples from Homer (cf. Nicolaus' citation above of the syncrisis of Achilles and Hector from *Il.* 20.158: "The man who fled in front was good, but by far a better man pursued"); and they make Homeric characters the subject of original model compositions (cf. Aphthonius' own model syncrisis of Achilles and Hector; *Prog.* 43–44).[11] Homeric composition itself is replete with syncrisis. In the *Iliad*, major Greek characters, or gods aligned with them, are frequently juxtaposed with Trojan counterparts and evaluated comparatively via the same topoi later standardized in the progymnasmata.[12] Thus, for example, in book 20 of the epic, the god Apollo in encouraging the Trojan Aeneas to war compares Aeneas to Achilles on the basis of origin (specifically, the sup-topoi of parents and ancestors), arguing that Aeneas is the better born of the warriors and, therefore, sure to prevail:

> But come, warrior, pray yourself also to the gods who are for ever; for men say that you were born of Aphrodite, daughter of Zeus, while he is sprung from a lesser goddess [Thetis]. For your mother is daughter of Zeus, and his of the old man of the sea [Nereus]. But carry straight against him your stubborn bronze, and do not let him turn you back with words of contempt and threats. (*Il.* 20.104–105 [Murray/Wyatt, LCL])

The passage introduces a syncritical theme that will be developed further in the book. The warriors not long after compare themselves in a series of taunts—Achilles on the basis of deeds ("Do you not remember when you were alone and I made you run from the cattle with swift steps down quickly from Ida's hills?" [20.187–190 (Murray/Wyatt, LCL)]) and Aeneas on the basis of origin:

> We know each other's lineage, we know each other's parents, for we have heard the words told of old by mortal men; but with sight of eyes you have never seen my parents nor I yours. Men say that you are son of incomparable Peleus and that your mother is fair-tressed Thetis, a daughter of the sea; but for me, I can boast that I am son of great-hearted Anchises and my mother is Aphrodite. Of these will one pair or the other mourn a dear son this day; for surely not with childish words, I say, will we two thus part from one another and return from the battle. But if you want, hear this also, so that you may know well my lineage; and many men know it: Zeus, the cloud-gatherer, first begot Dardanus, and he founded Dardania, since not yet was sacred Ilios built in the plain to be a city of mortal men, but they still dwelt on the slopes of many-fountained Ida. Dardanus in turn begot a son, king Erichthonius, who became richest of mortal men. His three thousand steeds pastured in the marshland, mares rejoicing in their tender foals . . . (20.199–254 [Murray/Wyatt, LCL])

Such comparisons are everywhere in the *Iliad*, and undoubtedly influenced syncritical theory as it developed in the last centuries BCE. They may be classified as "double encomium" comparisons to the lesser that feature mostly similar subjects (i.e., warriors of similar ability). They also function as genus syncrises, in that per the first method described by Theon, they consistently set outstanding Greek beside outstanding Trojan with a view to showing ultimately the superior greatness of the Greek peoples. Indeed, a major aim of Homeric epic, the *Iliad* included, may be said to be syncritical. As Mark W. Edwards observes, Homer wrote during "a period of great self-confidence, of renewed national pride, and of curiosity about cities and minds of other peoples (*Od.* 1.3)."[13] The poetry of this period was nationalistic in nature and was recited by bards like Homer at nationalistic festivals that celebrated the Ionic tribes (cf. *Hymn to Apollos* 146–155). Depictions of Greek victory in individual battles, and in the war generally, thus asserted a fundamentally comparative claim concerning the superiority of the Greeks. That claim was not lost on Greece's enemies, either. When Cleisthenes, tyrant of Sicycon (650–600 BCE), went to war against the Greeks, he banned the poetry contests (which by this time featured Homer) because of their pro-Ionic apologetic. As he put it, Homer's poems were "all about Argos and the Argives" (Herodotus 5.67).

Polybius. Graeco-Roman historiography quite often reflects the same nationalistic-syncritical interests of Homeric poetry. That is, historians commonly introduce their histories as comparative works setting their national subject against counterparts from history, and with the explicit goal of demonstrating that their native nation is the "greatest."[14] Polybius' *Histories* is fairly typical.[15] Polybius states in the introduction, "We shall best show how marvellous and vast our subject is by comparing the most famous Empires which preceded, and which have been the favourite themes of historians, and measuring them with the superior greatness of Rome" (1.2).[16] He then proceeds to name "the three that deserve even to be so compared and measured," the Persians, the Lacedaemonians, and the Macedonians; and in each case, he puts forward a summative argument in the form of a syncrisis for Roman superiority:

> The Persians for a certain length of time were possessed of a great empire and dominion. But every time they ventured beyond the limits of Asia, they found not only their empire, but their own existence also in danger. The Lacedaemonians, after contending for supremacy in Greece for many generations, when they did get it, held it without dispute for barely twelve years. The Macedonians obtained dominion in Europe from the lands bordering on the Adriatic to the Danube,—which after all is but a small fraction of this continent,—and, by the destruction of the Persian Empire, they afterwards added to that the dominion of Asia. And yet, though they had the credit of having made themselves masters of a larger number of countries and states than any people had ever done, they still left the greater half of the inhabited world in the hands of others. They never

> so much as thought of attempting Sicily, Sardinia, or Libya: and as to Europe, to speak the plain truth, they never even knew of the most warlike tribes of the West. The Roman conquest, on the other hand, was not partial. Nearly the whole inhabited world was reduced by them to obedience: and they left behind them an empire not to be paralleled in the past or rivalled in the future. Students will gain from my narrative a clearer view of the whole story, and of the numerous and important advantages which such exact record of events offers. (*Hist.* 1.2)

Syncritical introductions such as this obviously set a syncritical tone and agenda for the works they introduce. Often within the works, too, explicit syncrisis is employed to reinforce the comparative thesis. For example, in book 18, Polybius engages in a "syncrisis of the arms of the Romans and Macedonians, and their respective system of tactics" (18.1). Though not topically ordered, the comparison does examine its subject "part-by-part," examining various aspects of the subject one at a time. It may be considered a "double encomium" syncrisis to the lesser that shows the greatness of Roman arms and tactics by comparison with a similarly great militaristic nation. The writer concludes the syncrisis in explicitly laudatory tones, assigning superiority to Rome not because of fortune or good luck but rather because of their "leaders" who merit "the tribute of praise and admiration." As in Homer, here the military men of both nations ultimately stand for their genus, with the verdict of superiority applied accordingly.

Aristophanes. Aristophanes demonstrates how to put syncrisis to use in the genre of comedy. In his *Thesmophoriazusae*, a fairly persuasive syncritical claim is put forward by a particular group of characters for their own superiority:

> It is thus clear that we are better than you, and the proof of this is easy. Let us find out which is the worse of the two sexes. We say, "It's you," while you aver, "it's we." Come, let us compare them in detail, each individual man with a woman. Charminus is not equal to Nausimache, that's certain. Cleophon is in every respect inferior to Salabaccho. It's a long time now since any of you has dared to contest the prize with Aristomache, the heroine of Marathon, or with Stratonice. Among the last year's Senators, who have just yielded their office to other citizens, is there one who equals Eubule? Not even Anytus would say that. Therefore we maintain that men are greatly our inferiors. (799–810)[17]

The comparison operates in remarkable conformity with Theon's teaching concerning how to compare genera or groups. Theon himself uses the example of men and women to illustrate genus comparison, and commends in particular the method of setting "outstanding members" of each genus against one another in order to determine which genus is superior—clearly the method employed in this text.

Dionysius of Halicarnassus. Like Polybius, Dionysius of Halicarnassus begins his *Roman Antiquities* by putting forward an explicitly syncritical thesis concerning the superiority of Rome in comparison with other nations (1.2); and like Polybius, he introduces individual syncrises that support the larger claim.[18] For example, in telling the story of Romulus' coronation, Dionysius recounts the people's affirmation of the king in syncritical form. The piece is thoroughly conventional, in that it affirms Romulus' comparative honor via multiple topoi of comparison, and in a standard order:

Prooemion	Concerning the form of government, then, this is our decision;
Title	and to this honour we conceive none has so good a title as you yourself
Origin	by reason both of your royal origin
Virtue	and of your virtue,
Pursuits	but above all because we have had you as the leader of our colony and recognize in you great ability and great wisdom,
Deeds	which we have seen displayed quite as much in your actions
Words	as in your words. (*Ant. rom.* 2.4.2 [adapted from Gary, LCL])

Shortly thereafter, another syncrisis appears that makes the government Romulus establishes the subject of its praise. Again, many of the same syncritical topoi are employed in the comparison, and in conventional order:

Origin	He distinguished those who were eminent for their origin,
Virtue	approved for their virtue
Wealth	and wealthy for those times,
Children	provided they already had children, from the obscure, the lowly and the poor.
Title	Those of the lower rank he called "plebeians" (the Greeks would call them *demotikoi* or "men of the people"), and those of the higher rank "fathers," either because they were older than the others or because they had children or from their distinguished origin or for all these reasons. (2.8.1 [adapted from Gary, LCL])

Such comparisons may be classed as double encomium genus syncrises to the lesser demonstrating the relative greatness of Romulus and his appointed governors—and, by implication, the larger thesis concerning Rome's relative greatness. Indeed, in focusing first on Rome's founder and original governors, Dionysius may be seen to be taking up the subject of Rome itself, beginning with the topos of origin.

Tacitus. In Tacitus' *Annals* one finds a good specimen of topically ordered syncrisis in the second book, where upon the death of Germanicus mourners are depicted comparing the man to Alexander.[19] The memory leads Tacitus himself, in turn, to offer a more thorough syncrisis of the two. Both comparisons feature combined arrangement and take up a fairly conventional template of topoi. One sees throughout, too, the unexamined equation of aristocratic privilege with honor:[20]

Mourners Compare Deaths of Germanicus and Alexander	
	His funeral, though it lacked the family statues and procession, was honoured by panegyrics and a commemoration of his virtues.
Body	Some there were who, as they thought of his beauty,
Age	his age,
Manner	and the manner of his death,
Country	the vicinity too of the country where he died, likened his end to that of Alexander the Great.
Tacitus' Own Comparison of Germanicus and Alexander	
Body	Both had a graceful person
Origin	and were of noble birth;
Age	neither had much exceeded thirty years of age,
Manner of death	and both fell by the treachery of their own people in strange lands.
Virtue	
Generous	But Germanicus was gracious to his friends,
Temperate	temperate in his pleasures, the husband of one wife, with only legitimate children.
Pursuits and deeds	He was too no less a warrior, though rashness he had none, and, though after having cowed Germany by his many victories, he was hindered from crushing it into subjection. Had he had the sole control of affairs, had he possessed the power and title of a king, he would have attained military glory as much more easily as he had excelled Alexander in clemency, in self-restraint, and in all other virtues. (*Ann.* 2.72)

These comparisons clearly have a genus syncritical dimension, too, as a great Greek general has been chosen as the counterpart for the Roman Germanicus, with the implication that Rome is the new imperial counterpart to Alexander's Greece. Unlike most comparisons, which demonstrate the superiority of their main subjects (comparison to the lesser), these comparisons are examples of comparison to an equal, in which a subject is shown to be as great as a subject whose praiseworthiness is well-established.

Plutarch. No body of work illustrates as well the use of syncrisis in the genre of ancient biography, or employs syncrisis on so grand a scale, as Plutarch's *Parallel Lives*.[21] The multivolume project comprises a series of biography pairs, each devoted respectively to a famous Greek politician or general and a Roman selected by Plutarch as a counterpart. The pairs usually, but not always, have an attached "syncrisis" that weighs the relative merit of the two men in conclusion. Further, the biographies themselves are constructed in a parallel fashion with each life narrated as a mirror of the other; thus, syncrisis is fundamental to the biographies themselves and is not limited to the formal comparison attached at the end.[22]

Viewed in its entirety, the project may be judged to be a genus syncrisis showing Plutarch's native Greece to be the equal of Rome in the arena of political and military greatness. As such, the project engages in what may be classed as a syncrisis from equality, in that it shows its subject to be the equal of an acknowledged great. (Plutarch may be seen as countering the historians discussed above whose histories argue for Rome's superiority to Greece.) The project also features, depending on the pairing, either double encomium (which is most common) or double invective (e.g., in the case of Greek and Roman tyrants) comparison that, in any case, is always in conformity with the Theonic teaching that similar subjects, and never dissimilar ones, be compared.[23]

While the attached concluding syncrises tend to focus on the topos of deeds, the biographies themselves may be seen as comparing their subjects via a full set of topoi in a traditional order, and with the usual privileging of male aristocratic experience. *Alcibiades* and *Marcius Coriolanus* are typical in this regard. These parallel biographies may be outlined beginning to end via the progymnastic topoi of syncrisis as follows:

Origins	*Alc.* 1.1	*Cor.* 1.1–2
Nurture and training	*Alc.* 1.2–7.4	*Cor.* 1.2–4.2
Body	*Alc.* 1.3–4	*Cor.* 2.2b
Externals	*Alc.* 8–9	*Cor.* 4.3–4
Pursuits and deeds	*Alc.* 10–36	*Cor.* 5.1–38.4
Manner of death	*Alc.* 37.1–39.3, 4b–5	*Cor.* 39.1–4
Events after death	*Alc.* 39.4a	*Cor.* 39.5–6

The treatment of individual topoi, too, is in general conformity everywhere to progymnastic doctrine. For example, the parallel accounts of origin give consideration to two standard sub-topoi, relatives (*Alc.* 1.1a; *Cor.* 1.1) and father (*Alc.* 1.1b; *Cor.* 1.2). The sections on nurture and training focus on conventional sub-topoi such as upbringing (*Alc.* 1.2; *Cor.* 1.2) and youthful exploits (*Alc.* 1.2–7.4; *Cor.* 1.2–3.3), with a good deal of obviously parallel material under each. The brief accounts of body mention the respective bodily good of each man, beauty (*Alc.* 1.3–4) and strength (*Cor.* 2.2b). Under external goods, standard sub-topoi such as marriage and children are treated (*Alc.* 8; *Cor.* 4.3–4)—and less conventionally in Alcibiades' case, the subject of his beautiful dog (*Alc.* 9). The main body of each biography is devoted to actions in connection with the subject's role as statesman and general and so is in conformity with Pseudo-Hermogenes' counsel that "deeds [be] included among the pursuits" (16). The sections thereafter devoted to manner of death narrate, per Pseudo-Hermogenes' teaching, some "unusual" related occurrences: the conspiracy against each man (*Alc.* 37.1–39.3; *Cor.* 39.1–4; cf. *Alc.* 39.4b-5) and, in Alcibiades' case, his premonition of his own death (39.1–2). Last, the concluding sections devoted to events after death feature materials typical of the topos: the reclamation of the body after death and its "honourable burial" (*Alc.* 39.4a; *Cor.* 39.5–6) and, in Coriolanus' case, the account of his public mourning (*Cor.* 39.5–6).

Jewish Syncrisis

Genesis. In Jewish literature, syncrisis is frequently employed in ways similar to those of the Greeks and Romans. In the Pentateuch, comparisons of ancestral figures occur frequently, and with the genus they represent—usually, their descendant nations—in view. Philo, a graduate of the Hellenistic education, reads such comparisons as "syncrisis," and indeed, many of the conventions taught in connection with the Graeco-Roman device are at work in these ancient Jewish comparisons.[24] A good example is the introductory narrative devoted to Jacob and Esau, which takes up the same topoi of syncrisis as employed in Hellenistic composition, and in the same general order:

Prooemion	These are the descendants of Isaac, Abraham's son:
Origin	
Family	Abraham was the father of Isaac, and Isaac was forty years old when he married Rebekah, daughter of Bethuel the Aramean of Paddan-aram, sister of Laban the Aramean.

Marvelous occurrences at birth	[*Miracle*] Isaac prayed to the LORD for his wife, because she was barren; and the LORD granted his prayer, and his wife Rebekah conceived.
	[*Omen*] The children struggled together within her; and she said, "If it is to be this way, why do I live?"
	[*Oracle*] So she went to inquire of the LORD. And the LORD said to her, "Two nations are in your womb, and two peoples born of you shall be divided; the one shall be stronger than the other, the elder shall serve the younger."
	[*Omen*] When her time to give birth was at hand, there were twins in her womb. The first came out red, all his body like a hairy mantle; so they named him Esau.
	[*Omen*] Afterward his brother came out, with his hand gripping Esau's heel; so he was named Jacob.
	[*Miracle*] Isaac was sixty years old when she bore them.
Pursuits	When the boys grew up, Esau was a skillful hunter, a man of the field, while Jacob was a quiet man, living in tents.
External goods	Isaac loved Esau, because he was fond of game; but Rebekah loved Jacob.
Deeds	Once when Jacob was cooking a stew, Esau came in from the field, and he was famished. Esau said to Jacob, "Let me eat some of that red stuff, for I am famished!" (Therefore he was called Edom.) Jacob said, "First sell me your birthright." Esau said, "I am about to die; of what use is a birthright to me?" Jacob said, "Swear to me first." So he swore to him, and sold his birthright to Jacob. Then Jacob gave Esau bread and lentil stew, and he ate and drank, and rose and went his way. Thus Esau despised his birthright. (25:19-34)

Viewed through the lens of progymnastic theory, the text is thoroughly conventional. A comparison to the lesser, the passage functions as a genus syncrisis, with the two brothers representing the nations that bear their names, Israel and Edom respectively. Their representative value is made explicit in the oracle attending their birth: "Two nations are in your womb, and two peoples born of you shall be divided; the one shall be stronger than the other, the elder shall serve the younger." As the oracle suggests, the entire Jacob and Esau cycle functions as an etymological account of how Jacob displaced Esau—and by extension, how the nation of Israel displaced Edom—as the heir of the Abrahamic blessing. The topoi employed in the comparison are handled in a thoroughly conventional manner. In connection with origin, a full genealogy of both subjects is given; it includes father, mother, paternal and maternal ancestors—standard material for the topos. Under marvelous occurrences at birth, the kind of conventional materials prescribed by Pseudo-Hermogenes ("for example, from dreams or signs or things like that") are found: (1) miraculous conception, despite Rebekah's barrenness, in answer to a prayer; (2) the oracle concerning the nations each with father; (3) the omen of Esau's appearance at birth—he is red (foreshadowing the story of the selling of his birthright for red stew) and hairy (foreshadowing the story of his stolen blessing, wherein he deceives his blind father by placing furry skins upon his arms); (4) the omen of Jacob's appearance at birth—he grasps the heel of his brother ("grasping the heal" being a Hebrew idiom for deceitfulness—the image foreshadows Jacob's deceitful theft of both the birthright and blessing); (5) the miracle of the birth occurring despite Isaac's advanced age. The subsequent treatment of the respective occupations of each (25:27) is standard material for the topos of pursuits. The love of each parent, respectively, for the boys belongs to the topos of external goods (which includes such topoi as friendships, familial connections, and alliance). Under the topos of deeds, we have included only the initial deeds of each; in fact, the entire Jacob cycle could be construed as a syncrisis of deeds, a marvelously constructed account that ends with both brothers—and by implication, both nations—made recipients of blessing.[25] Such close conformity of Hebrew rhetoric to (later) Greek rhetorical standards suggests that such standards were pervasive in the Mediterranean world and not exclusively Greek.

Wisdom. The book of Wisdom employs syncrisis extensively in chapters 11 through 19, juxtaposing the wilderness generation and its fate with that of the Egyptians.[26] The comparison underscores the larger theme of the book, the respective fate of the wicked and the righteous. Viewed in the light of progymnastic theory, the comparison may be classed as an encomium-invective comparison to the lesser that, *contra* Theonic doctrine, juxtaposes greatly dissimilar subjects. The comparison functions as a genus syncrisis, too, with the wilderness generation and the Egyptians representing at once both moral and national genera. The ethics inculcated by the comparison, too, belong to the Jewish wisdom tradition and cut against Graeco-Roman notions of honor at every turn. Though not topically ordered, the comparison does examine its subjects part-by-part per progymnastic theory. The syncrisis consists of a series of seven comparisons, each showing how an element used to punish the Egyptians is shown to have blessed the Hebrews.

Philo. In the laudatory *Life of Moses*, Philo repeatedly compares Moses to ancient counterparts among the Greeks and other peoples, arguing in every case for Moses' superiority.[27] As in similar comparisons in Graeco-Roman histories and biographies, these comparisons function as genus syncrises demonstrating somewhat apologetically the greatness of the Jewish people.[28] They may be classed usually as double encomium comparisons to the lesser, and typically take up similar subjects. Further, they follow the topical structure of the biography itself and thus collectively constitute what by ancient standards would be considered a thorough comparative inquiry. Of particular note are those topoi that cut against the usual syncritical privileging of aristocratic qualities as honorable—for example, the praise of slave parents under origin, and the praise of King Moses under pursuits for *not* acquiring wealth, estates, slaves, and the like, though it was in his power to do so. One witnesses in the handling of these topoi a subversion of traditional Graeco-Roman values that is rooted in the more egalitarian social and economic ideals of the Torah:[29]

Origin	[*Superior parents*] He had for his father and mother the best of their contemporaries. (1.7)
Training	[*Superior in training*] Teachers at once arrived from different parts, some unbidden from the neighboring countries. . . . But in short time he advanced beyond their capacities. (1.21)
Mind	[*Superior mind*] Naturally, therefore, his associates and everyone else, struck with amazement at what they felt was a novel spectacle, considered earnestly what the mind which dwelt in his body like an image in its shrine could be, whether it was human or divine or a mixture of both, so utterly unlike was it to the majority, soaring above them and exalted to a grander height. (1.27)
Pursuits and deeds	[*Superior shepherd*] He became more skilled than any of his time in managing flocks. (1.63)
	[*Superior king*] In solitary contrast to those who had hitherto held the same authority, he did not treasure up gold and silver, did not levy tributes, did not possess houses or chattels or livestock or a staff of slaves or revenues or any other accompaniment of costly and opulent living, though he might have had all in abundance. (1.152)
	[*Superior legislator*] That Moses himself was the best of all lawgivers in all countries, better in fact than any that have ever arisen among either the Greeks or the barbarians, and that his laws are most excellent and needful, is shewn most clearly by the following proof. (2.12)
	[*Superior priest*] Thus he came to love God and be loved by Him as have been few others. (2.67)
	[*Superior king, priest, and prophet*] I have discussed the first three, and shewn that Moses was the best of kings, of lawgivers and of high priests, and will go on to shew in conclusion that he was a prophet of the highest quality. (2.187)
	[*Superior prophet*] Moses, the holiest of men ever yet born (2.192).
Events after death	[*Superior burial*] He was not laid to rest in the tomb of his forefathers but was given a monument of special dignity which no man has ever seen. (*Mos.* 2.291 [Colson, LCL])

Josephus. If Philo illustrates well the use of syncrisis in Jewish biography, Josephus attests to its use in Jewish historiography. His *Jewish Antiquities*, for example, is intended like so many Roman histories to demonstrate the superiority of the writer's own race.[30] Indeed, Josephus models the work on Dionysius of Halicarnassus' *Roman Antiquities*, adopting its twenty-book structure and overarching syncritical aim.[31] Throughout the work, Josephus repeatedly praises various Jewish subjects and compares them favorably to counterparts from other nations. For example, in the prooemion of the work, he praises Moses in comparison with the legislators of other nations, drawing on a similar syncritical piece by Philo in *On the Creation of the World*.[32] He juxtaposes Moses' death, too, with that of Aeneas and Romulus, the founders of Rome (4.326), as reported by Dionysius in the *Roman Antiquities*.[33] Thus, the project as a whole may be seen to introduce its syncritical theme by taking up the topos of origins, in that it reflects on the founders or "fathers" of the nations in view. Similar comments could be made about the use of other topoi (e.g., education—when Josephus sets the learning of great figures such as Solomon against the learning of other nations' wisest men).

On a smaller scale, one also witnesses a close conformity to syncritical theory in comparative passages within the *Jewish Antiquities*. A couple of examples will suffice to illustrate the matter. In chapter 7 of book 8, where Josephus praises Solomon as the greatest of kings, the writer employs syncrisis to amplify his subject. Though brief, the comparison runs through a series of standard syncritical topoi, many of which reflect the close connection drawn in the ancient world between male aristocracy and honor:

Pursuits	But although Solomon was become the most glorious of kings,
External goods	and the best beloved by God,
Virtue	and had exceeded in wisdom
Wealth	and riches those who had been rulers of the Hebrews before him,
Death	yet did not he persevere in this happy state till he died. Nay, he forsook the observation of the laws of his fathers, and came to an end no way suitable to our foregoing history of him. (*Ant.* 8.190 [Whiston])

Similarly, Josephus in the same chapter extols the greatness of Solomon's cavalry, taking up the major-sub-topoi Graeco-Roman education taught in connection with the topos of bodily goods—first with regard to the horses, and then with regard to their riders:

Beauty and swiftness	These horses also were so well exercised, in order to their making a fine appearance, and running swiftly, that no others could, upon the comparison, appear either finer or swifter; but they were at once the most beautiful of all others, and their swiftness was incomparable also.
Beauty and size	Their riders also were a further ornament to them, being, in the first place, young men in the most delightful flower of their age, and being eminent for their size, and far taller than other men. They had also very long heads of hair hanging down, and were clothed in garments of Tyrian purple. They had also dust of gold every day sprinkled on their hair, so that their heads sparkled with the reflection of the sunbeams from the gold. (8.184–185 [Whiston])

Syncrisis plays an important role in Josephus' other major works, too. Like the *Antiquities*, Josephus' *Jewish War* similarly pursues a syncritical agenda that serves Jewish apologetic.[34] The work tells the history of the Roman conquest of the Jewish nation in the late 60s CE. In the proem (1.1–12), Josephus complains about previous accounts that, either out of sycophancy or anti-Semitism, provide an "encomium" of the Romans and an "invective" of Jews: "For they have a mind to demonstrate the greatness of the Romans, while they still diminish and lessen the actions of the Jews, as not discerning how it cannot be that those must appear to be great who have only conquered those that were little" (1.7). Josephus' argument is recognizably Theonic, insisting as it does on pairing subjects similar in honor. Of course, it also allows Josephus to pursue his pro-Jewish apologetic without offending Rome. We may classify the syncrisis of the work as a rare double encomium to the *greater*, insofar as it praises the defeated Jewish nation for being nearly as great as the nation that conquered it.

Josephus' *Against Apion*, which is also explicitly apologetic in its aims, may be seen as pursuing a syncritical agenda in defense of the Jewish people.[35] In the introduction, Josephus states his intention "to refute Greek critics of the *Antiquities* who claim greater antiquity for the Greeks and who slander the Jewish people by insisting on their comparative modernity" (1.1–6). The work features two major syncritical sections. In the first (1.15–56), Josephus argues at length for the superiority of Moses, Jewish priests, and Jewish prophets in comparison with Greek historians and record keepers. In the second (2.151–286), Josephus responds with great detail to Greek critics who "claim that our laws are, by comparison, inferior to their own" (2.150). In these sections, Josephus engages both in double-encomium and encomium-invective syncrisis, depending on whether he praises or censures the Greek counterparts in view. Overall, the syncrisis may be classed as a comparison to the lesser that exonerates the honor of the Jewish people generally.

Christian Syncrisis

Justin Martyr. One of the earliest noncanonical examples of Christian syncrisis occurs in Justin Martyr's *First Apology*, where the writer compares Jesus Christ to the Greek gods to demonstrate both that Christ is "superior" and that Christian beliefs about Christ have pagan parallels and so are not as incredible or far-fetched as often alleged. The syncrisis is thoroughly conventional by progymnastic standards. The piece may be classified as a rare "encomium-invective" syncrisis to the lesser, in that it censures the deeds of the Greek gods while praising Christ's. It is also quite obviously a genus syncrisis, in that it takes extreme representatives of paganism and sets them against the ultimate representative of the Christian faith, Christ himself. The piece displays separate arrangement, examining the lives of the Greek gods in the first major section, and the life of Christ in the second. Justin also employs conventional topoi of syncrisis at every turn in the composition of his argument, as illustrated in the following outline:

Prologue	
Origin/birth	And when we say also that the Word, who is the first-birth of God, was produced without sexual union,
Manner of death / posthumous events	and that He, Jesus Christ, our Teacher, was crucified and died, and again, and ascended into heaven, we propound nothing different from what you believe regarding those whom you esteem sons of Jupiter.
Section 1: The Greek Gods	
Origin	For you know how many sons your esteemed writers ascribed to Jupiter: Mercury, the interpreting word and teacher of all;
Death / events after death	Aesculapius, who, though he was a great physician, was struck by a thunderbolt, and so ascended to heaven; and Bacchus too, after he had been torn limb from limb; and Hercules, when he had committed himself to the flames to escape his toils; and the sons of Leda, and Dioscuri; and Perseus, son of Danae; and Bellerophon, who, though sprung from mortals, rose to heaven on the horse Pegasus. For what shall I say of Ariadne, and those who, like her, have been declared to be set among the stars? And what of the emperors who die among yourselves, whom you deem worthy of deification, and in whose behalf you produce some one who swears he has seen the burning Caesar rise to heaven from the funeral pyre?

Deeds	And what kind of deeds are recorded of each of these reputed sons of Jupiter, it is needless to tell to those who already know. This only shall be said, that they are written for the advantage and encouragement of youthful scholars; for all reckon it an honourable thing to imitate the gods. But far be such a thought concerning the gods from every well-conditioned soul, as to believe that Jupiter himself, the governor and creator of all things, was both a parricide and the son of a parricide, and that being overcome by the love of base and shameful pleasures, he came in to Ganymede and those many women whom he had violated and that his sons did like actions. But, as we said above, wicked devils perpetrated these things. And we have learned that those only are deified who have lived near to God in holiness and virtue; and we believe that those who live wickedly and do not repent are punished in everlasting fire.
Section 2: Christ	
Origin	Moreover, the Son of God called Jesus, even if only a man by ordinary generation, yet, on account of His wisdom, is worthy to be called the Son of God; for all writers call God the Father of men and gods.
Birth	And if we assert that the Word of God was born of God in a peculiar manner, different from ordinary generation, let this, as said above, be no extraordinary thing to you, who say that Mercury is the angelic word of God.
Manner of death	But if any one objects that He was crucified, in this also He is on a par with those reputed sons of Jupiter of yours, who suffered as we have now enumerated. For their sufferings at death are recorded to have been not all alike, but diverse; so that not even by the peculiarity of His sufferings does He seem to be inferior to them; but, on the contrary, as we promised in the preceding part of this discourse, we will now prove Him superior—or rather have already proved Him to be so—for the superior is revealed by His actions.
Birth	And if we even affirm that He was born of a virgin, accept this in common with what you accept of Perseus.
Deeds	And in that we say that He made whole the lame, the paralytic, and those born blind, we seem to say what is very similar to the deeds said to have been done by Aesculapius. (*1 Apol.* 21–22 [*ANF* 1:170])

<u>*Homilies*</u>. The Pseudo-Clementine *Homilies* engages in a lengthy narrative comparison of Peter and Simon Magus that in the light of progymnastic theory may be described as a double encomium comparison to the lesser.[36] The work frames the two men as leaders of rival sects—one devoted to Christ, and the other to John the Baptist. The syncrisis of the two men, then, functions as a genus syncrisis commenting on the respective greatness of two rival sects. The comparison primarily gives consideration to the topos of deeds. Throughout the story, Peter is repeatedly depicted defeating Simon in a series of confrontations. A major concern of the comparison, too, is to address the potential preference for Simon as Peter's predecessor in preaching to the Gentiles. Syncritical theory conventionally preferred actions done first ("Actions are praised on the basis of the occasion and whether someone did them alone or was the first . . ."; Theon, *Prog.* 110). The author addresses the problem by appeal to the "doctrine of syzygies," which states, "For as with him [God] the first is the stronger and the second the weaker, so with men we find the opposite, first the weaker and then the stronger" (*Hom.* 2.16). On this basis, the writer is able to draw the desired conclusion regarding Peter's—and by implication, the Christian sect's—superiority: "He who follows this order can discern by whom Simon, who as the first came before me to the Gentiles, was sent forth, and to whom I [Peter] belong who appeared later than he did and came in upon him as light upon darkness, as knowledge upon ignorance, as healing upon sickness" (2.17).[37]

A second comparison in the work, that of Jesus and John the Baptist, functions much the same way, with the preference given to Jesus having implications for which sect is superior. The doctrine of syzygies functions, too, to vindicate Jesus despite appearing after John:

> There appeared a certain John the Baptist, who according to the disposition of the syzygies was at the same time the forerunner of our Lord Jesus. And as the Lord had twelve apostles according to the number of the solar months, so also there gathered about John thirty eminent persons according to the reckoning of the lunar month. (2.23)

Early Christian texts like the *Homilies* show how comparisons of Jesus with others, or Jesus' disciples with others, may function as genus syncrises that entail a "two-level drama" (to borrow a phrase from Gospel scholarship) that has in view not only the contest between the characters themselves but also the religious communities they represent.[38]

<u>*Recognitions*</u>. In the *Recognitions* we find an account of a public debate at the temple where speakers representing several Jewish sects—Christians, Sadducees, Samaritans, scribes and Pharisees, and disciples of John the Baptist—rise in defense of their order.[39] Included is an account of an exchange between a Pharisee and a Christian wherein the two speakers engage in syncritical oratory:

> Then a certain Pharisee, hearing this, chid Philip because he put Jesus on a level with Moses. To whom Bartholomew, answering, boldly declared that we do not only say that Jesus was equal to Moses, but that He was greater than he, because Moses was indeed a prophet, as Jesus was also, but that Moses was not the Christ, as Jesus was, and therefore He is doubtless greater who is both a prophet and the Christ, than he who is only the prophet. (1.59 [*ANF* 8.92–93])

Clearly both speakers engage in double encomium comparison to the lesser, and with implications for the superiority of the genus each man represents. Bartholomew is presented as winning the debate (it is a Christian writing, after all) on the basis of the topos of pursuits: both are prophets, but Jesus alone is Christ (i.e., the messianic king).

Later in the story, a similar debate is recounted featuring a three-way comparison of John, Jesus, and Moses:

> And, behold, one of the disciples of John asserted that John was the Christ, and not Jesus, inasmuch as Jesus Himself declared that John was greater than all men and all prophets [Matt 11:9, 11]. "If, then," said he, "he be greater than all, he must be held to be greater than Moses, and than Jesus himself. But if he be the greatest of all, then must he be the Christ." To this Simon the Canaanite, answering, asserted that John was indeed greater than all the prophets, and all who are born of women, yet that he is not greater than the Son of Man. Accordingly Jesus is also the Christ, whereas John is only a prophet: and there is as much difference between him and Jesus, as between the forerunner and Him whose forerunner he is; or as between Him who gives the law, and him who keeps the law. (1.60 [*ANF* 8.93])

Here again, the passage functions as a genus syncrisis speaking to the relative greatness of Christianity in comparison with other sects—in this case, the Pharisees and John the Baptist messianists. The Christian speaker is again presented as winning the debate—this time not only on the basis of pursuits, but also deeds. One sees in these comparisons the same two-level drama inherent in early Christian syncrises of Jesus and Moses or Jesus and John. Such comparisons have stakes not only for the men in view, but also the sects associated with them.

Eusebius of Caesarea. A good example of syncrisis in Christian historiography is found in the Eusebian passage concerning Maximinus in the *Ecclesiastical History*.[40] This passage is an encomium-invective syncrisis to the greater in which Eusebius declares the governor to be the inferior of his colleagues "in every respect." Eusebius' list of these specific respects (italicized below) corresponds, not surprisingly, to syncritical topoi in a standard order:

> Being no longer able to sustain the magnitude of the government which had been undeservedly committed to him, in consequence of his want of prudence and imperial understanding, he managed affairs in a base manner, and with

> his mind unreasonably exalted in all things with boastful pride, even toward his colleagues in the empire who were in every respect his superiors, *in birth, in training, in education, in worth and intelligence, and, greatest of all, in temperance and piety toward the true God, he began to venture to act* audaciously and to arrogate to himself the first rank. (*Eccl. hist.* 9.10.1 [*NPNF*[2] 1:366])

Interestingly, the piece distinguishes the acquisition of social rank from the possession of true virtue and greatness and in this respect continues a Christian syncritical practice seen first in the letters of Paul among extant Christian writings (see, e.g., the examples below).

Eusebius also attests the use of syncrisis in Christian biography in his glowing account of the youthful Constantine in *Life of Constantine*. The historian compares the young emperor to his contemporaries via the topoi of body and mind, and under multiple sub-topoi belonging to each:

Body	
Beauty	For no one was comparable to him for grace and beauty of person,
Size	or height of stature;
Strength	and he so far surpassed his compeers in personal strength as to be a terror to them.
Mind	He was, however, even more conspicuous for the excellence of his mental qualities than for his superior physical endowments;
Judgment	being gifted in the first place with a sound judgment,
Training	and having also reaped the advantages of a liberal education.
Intelligence	He was also distinguished in no ordinary degree by natural intelligence
Wisdom	and divinely imparted wisdom. (*Life of Constantine* 1.19 [*NPNF*[2] 1:487–488])

The piece may be classed as a double encomium comparison to the lesser featuring combined arrangement. It illustrates well, too, how syncrisis as a literary device may be employed in service of a composition's major ideological aims—in this case, encomium of the emperor.

John Chrysostom. In *Homilies against the Jews* 5, an early example of Christian oratory, Chrysostom offers what he himself terms a syncrisis juxtaposing Christ with various Greek and Jewish "leaders and chiefs" on the basis of the topos of deeds:[41]

> To help you see the truth of this, consider how many men wished to introduce their teachings among the Greeks and to establish a new commonwealth and

> way of life. Think of such men as Zeno, Plato, Socrates, Diagoras, Pythagoras, and countless others. Yet they fell so far short of success that many people do not even now know them by name. But Christ not only wrote a constitution but even brought a new way of life to the whole world. How many miracles do they say that Apollonius of Tyana worked? But all his deeds were a fraud, a vain show, and devoid of truth. And you may learn this from the fact that, in an instant, they vanished and disappeared. (*Adv. Jud.* 5.3.1)[42]

In a subsequent comparison Chrysostom juxtaposes Jesus with other leaders such as Judas the Galilean and Theudas:

> Comparison makes facts especially clear. You Jews make this comparison, then, and learn how the truth has prevailed. What deceiver has gotten for himself so many churches all over the world, what rogue extended his worship to the ends of the earth, what imposter has every man bowing down before him, and this in the face of ten thousand obstacles? No one did. (5.3.9)

Such comparisons may be classed as encomium-invective genus syncrises demonstrating the superiority of Jesus to other philosophers and religious leaders, and with the obvious implication that the philosophy/religion he represents is superior to other philosophical and religious sects. Chrysostom makes a habit of this kind of genus syncrisis in other sermons, too, comparing John the Baptist to Greek Cynic philosophers (*Matt.* 10.4), Christian apostles to Greek philosophers and the generals Themistocles and Pericles (*Matt.* 33.5), the Samaritan woman to Nicodemus (*John* 32.1), Christian martyrs to Socrates (*1 Cor.* 4.4), and Christian apostles to Greek philosophers such as Plato, Pythagorus, Stoics, Dion, and Aristippus (*1 Cor.* 35.5).[43] All these function as polemic vindicating the Christian faith in comparison with other ways of life.

Examples from the New Testament

Many examples of syncrisis are found in the New Testament, and these no less than other occurrences in the Mediterranean world conform to the conventions of syncrisis as taught in the preliminary exercises. Though again we could cite any number of single sentence, whole-to-whole comparisons as examples, our concern is to highlight more extensive part-to-part comparisons that by virtue of their comparative detail are better illuminated by progymnastic theory.

1 Corinthians. Some of the most interesting examples of syncrisis in the New Testament occur in the letters of Paul, who repeatedly shows himself well versed in the conventions of the device.[44] Near the end of his first letter to the Corinthians, for example, Paul engages in a brief comparison of "the first and last Adam" that is conventional in nearly every regard. The piece is a double encomium comparison

to the lesser that employs combined arrangement, moving back and forth as it does between its two subjects.

Birth	Thus it is written, "The first man, Adam, became a living being"; the last Adam became a life-giving spirit. But it is not the spiritual that is first, but the physical, and then the spiritual.
Origin	The first man was from the earth, a man of dust; the second man is from heaven.
Epilogue	As was the man of dust, so are those who are of the dust; and as is the man of heaven, so are those who are of heaven.
	Just as we have borne the image of the man of dust, we will also bear the image of the man of heaven. (15:45-49)

The comparison takes up two conventional topoi, birth and origin—albeit in an order opposite the normal custom and Paul's own customary pattern (see other examples below). The treatment of birth employs the word Paul commonly uses for the topos of birth, *ginomai*, in connection with both subjects. The contrast both establishes the basis of the last Adam's superiority ("spiritual" is generally superior to "physical" in the ancient Mediterranean world and in Paul's thought [cf. ch. 15 in its entirety]) and, on that basis, excuses a potential mark in the first Adam's favor—the fact that he came first (see the *Recognitions* above).[45] The treatment of origin then establishes the last Adam's superior derivations ("heaven" is superior to "earth" in ancient Mediterranean thought generally, and Pauline thought specifically). The conclusion clarifies that the comparison functions as a genus syncrisis, asserting that what is true of both Adams is true of the larger genus they represent (in Paul's thought, the old and new humanity/creation "in Adam" and "in Christ," respectively). The implicit point is that it is better to belong to "those who are of heaven" and "bear the image of the man of heaven."

2 Corinthians. In his seventh sermon on 2 Corinthians, John Chrysostom interprets the comparison of ministries in 2 Corinthians 3 as a "syncrisis."[46] The comparison displays combined arrangement and is tripartite, each point of contrast expressed in the phrase "how much more?"[47] The passage moves from the ministries in their beginnings through to their ends, taking up topics analogous to the topics of birth (vv. 7-8), deeds (v. 9), and death (vv. 10-11). The premise of the argument is that the "ministry of death" displayed glory in every stage of life—in being "born" (*ginomai*) (vv. 7-8), in effecting "condemnation" (v. 9), in coming "to an end" (vv. 10-11). The deduction from this premise, made in the form of a comparison from the lesser to the greater, reasons in each case essentially, "Thus how much more glory attends the ministry of the spirit."

Birth	Now if the ministry of death, engraved in letters on stones, was born in glory, so that the children of Israel were not able to look upon the face of Moses because of the glory (which is now abolished) of his face, how will the ministry of the spirit not exist even more in glory?
Deeds	For if in the ministry of condemnation there was glory, how much more will the ministry of justification abound in glory?
Death	For indeed what once had glory has lost its glory on account of the glory that surpasses it. For if that which came to an end did so through glory, how much more will which continues to remain do so in glory? (3:7-11)

In each case, too, the ministry of the Spirit is framed via the topos at hand as surpassing the ministry of death in some specific way: (1) *Birth*. Whereas the ministry of death was "born" in glory, the spirit "will exist" in glory. The likely implication of the change in verb is that the latter ministry has no birth but is eternal in nature; this is, essentially, the classic argument under the topos of birth used to distinguish gods from humans.[48] (2) *Deeds*. Whereas the ministry of death was glorious in accomplishing condemnation, the ministry of the Spirit is obviously superior in accomplishing justification. (3) *Death*. Whereas the ministry of death "came to an end through glory", the ministry of the Spirit "continues to remain." The change in verb implies the latter ministry never dies—again, an argument under the topos at hand commonly used to distinguish gods from humans, and here transferred to the ministries in view.[49]

In 2 Corinthians 11, Paul brings up the subject of "false apostles" who have evidently persuaded at least some of the Corinthians of a "different Gospel," and one that, as Paul puts it, "makes slaves of you" (i.e., keeping the Mosaic law; cf. Gal 5:1-4). In response, evidently, to disparagement of Paul on a variety of grounds, Paul engages in a syncrisis of himself and these apostles that at once defends his honor and has implications for which version of Christianity is superior. In other words, the comparison functions as a genus syncrisis vindicating Paul along with his law-free Christianity.[50]

The passage in its entirety may be sketched via the topoi of syncrisis it employs.[51] The elaboration of deeds, the concern of the majority of the passage, may also be explicated via the Theonic sub-topoi of "fine actions."

Prooemion	But whatever anyone dares to boast of—I am speaking as a fool—I also dare to boast of that.
Origin	
Race	Are they Hebrews? So am I.
Homeland	Are they Israelites? So am I.
Ancestors	Are they descendants of Abraham? So am I.
Pursuits	Are they ministers of Christ? I am talking like a madman—I am a better one:
Deeds	with far greater labors, far more imprisonments, with countless floggings,
Death	and often near death.
Elaboration of Deeds	
Braving retributions and dangers for friends	Five times I have received from the Jews the forty lashes minus one. Three times I was beaten with rods. Once I received a stoning. Three times I was shipwrecked; for a night and a day I was adrift at sea; on frequent journeys, in danger from rivers, danger from bandits, danger from my own people, danger from Gentiles, danger in the city, danger in the wilderness, danger at sea, danger from false brothers and sisters;
Done with toils	in toil and hardship, through many a sleepless night, hungry and thirsty, often without food, cold and naked.
Done for others rather than selves	And, besides other things, I am under daily pressure because of my anxiety for all the churches.
Virtue: weakness	Who is weak, and I am not weak? Who is made to stumble, and I am not indignant? If I must boast, I will boast of the things that show my weakness.
Judgment of the famous	The God and Father of the Lord Jesus (blessed be he forever!) knows that I do not lie.
Done contrary to expectation	In Damascus, the governor under King Aretas guarded the city of Damascus in order to seize me, but I was let down in a basket through a window in the wall, and escaped from his hands.

Which few did	It is necessary to boast; nothing is to be gained by it, but I will go on to visions and revelations of the Lord. I know a person* in Christ who fourteen years ago was caught up to the third heaven—whether in the body or out of the body I do not know; God knows. And I know that such a person—whether in the body or out of the body I do not know; God knows—was caught up into Paradise and heard things that are not to be told, that no mortal is permitted to repeat. On behalf of such a one I will boast, but on my own behalf I will not boast, except of my weaknesses. But if I wish to boast, I will not be a fool, for I will be speaking the truth. But I refrain from it, so that no one may think better of me than what is seen in me or heard from me, even considering the exceptional character of the revelations.
Condition of body	Therefore, to keep me from being too elated, a thorn was given me in the flesh, a messenger of Satan to torment me, to keep me from being too elated. Three times I appealed to the Lord about this, that it would leave me,
Weakness (= strength)	but he said to me, "My grace is sufficient for you, for power is made perfect in weakness." So I will boast all the more gladly of my weaknesses, so that the power of Christ may dwell in me. Therefore I am content with weaknesses, insults, hardships, persecutions, and calamities for the sake of Christ; for whenever I am weak, then I am strong.
Epilogue	I have been a fool! You forced me to it. Indeed you should have been the ones commending me, for I am not at all inferior to these super-apostles, even though I am nothing. (11:21–12:11)

* *Here Paul refers to himself in the third person out of rhetorical modesty.*

As this outline illustrates, Paul's handling of syncritical topoi is highly conventional. The exception to the rule, however, is seen in his treatment in two places of "weakness"—first, in the elaboration of the topos of deeds, where it is put forward as an implied virtue; then again, under the topos of bodily condition, where it is framed as a bodily good. In both cases, Paul is engaging yet again in the christological subversion of traditional topoi (see the many occurrences of encomium and syncrisis in this and the preceding chapter). Weakness, of course, is never treated in Hellenistic education as a virtue displayed in action; and its opposite, strength, is one of the four traditional "goods" commended as sub-topoi of bodily condition. Paul, however, can regard weakness as both a virtue displayed in his suffering on behalf of others, and as a bodily "good" that is the equivalent, ironically, of its opposite—strength—only because of the union he believes he experiences with

Christ. In Paul's thought, to be one with Christ in righteous suffering is also to be one with him in the power of resurrection life—both the newness of life effected by the Spirit presently and the newness of bodily resurrection yet to come (cf. Rom 6–8). Thus, Paul can say of his weakened bodily condition, "I will boast all the more gladly of my weaknesses, so that the power of Christ may dwell in me." He is thinking here, as always, of his union with Christ both in dying and rising.

Galatians. Paul's letter to the Galatians, which deals with the problem of Christian teachers persuading Gentile Christians to keep the Mosaic law, enlists syncrisis in its rhetoric opposing the practice.[52] In Galatians 4:21-31, Paul puts forward a genus syncrisis that juxtaposes Isaac and Ishmael as symbols, respectively, of those who are free children in Christ and those who become slaves by keeping the law. The comparison, which displays combined arrangement, takes up a conventional series of topoi:

Prooemion	Tell me, you who desire to be subject to the law, will you not listen to the law?
Origin	For it is written that Abraham had two sons, one by a slave woman and the other by a free woman.
Birth	One, the child of the slave, was born according to the flesh; the other, the child of the free woman, was born through the promise.
Allegorical Explication of Birth	
	Now this is an allegory: these women are two covenants. One woman, in fact, is Hagar, from Mount Sinai, bearing children for slavery. Now Hagar is Mount Sinai in Arabia and corresponds to the present Jerusalem, for she is in slavery with her children. But the other woman corresponds to the Jerusalem above; she is free, and she is our mother. For it is written, "Rejoice, you childless one, you who bear no children, burst into song and shout, you who endure no birth pangs; for the children of the desolate woman are more numerous than the children of the one who is married." Now you, my friends, are children of the promise, like Isaac.
Deeds	But just as at that time the child who was born according to the flesh persecuted the child who was born according to the Spirit, so it is now also.
External goods	But what does the scripture say? "Drive out the slave and her child; for the child of the slave will not share the inheritance with the child of the free woman."
Epilogue	So then, friends, we are children, not of the slave but of the free woman. For freedom Christ has set us free. Stand firm, therefore, and do not submit again to a yoke of slavery. (4:21–5:1)

Paul's treatment of origin in this passage takes up a standard sub-topos, parents—and in its ancient Mediterranean preference for the free person as superior to the slave. The handling of birth gives preference to Isaac for being born in accordance with the Abrahamic promise of blessing—which even in the Genesis account is a mark of superiority that trumps birth order.

Because the topos of birth is most central to Paul's main theological point (freedom and sonship in Christ vs. slavery under the law), Paul pauses to make the crucial connection between Isaac and Ishmael and their respective genera. Law followers may be said to be, like Ishmael, children of the slave woman, Hagar, once it is recognized that she is an allegory for the Sinai/earthly Jerusalem, the metaphorical mother of all law-keepers. Similarly, Christ followers may be said to be, like Isaac, children of the free woman, Sarai, once it is recognized that she is an allegory for the spiritual Jerusalem, the "mother" of all Christ followers. Having established the connection between the syncritical subjects and the genus each represents, Paul resumes the comparison, now with a view primarily for what it says about each genus. Under deeds, he argues that what was true of the sons—that the slave son persecuted the free son—remains true of the genera they represent in the present day. (Paul, of course, speaks from personal experience as a former law-keeping persecutor of Christ followers, and a present Christ follower regularly persecuted at the hands of law-keepers.) Then under external goods (to which wealth and inheritance belong as a sub-topos), Paul cites the divine command from Genesis to drive out the slave and her child since the latter will not receive the inheritance. The citation has an obvious theological implication for the genera still in view: law-keepers will not receive the inheritance of Abraham; only Christ followers will. On the basis of this implication, Paul in the epilogue concludes the comparison ("So then . . .") with the warning to "stand firm" and "not submit again to the yoke of slavery."

Romans. At a key turning point in the argument of Romans, Paul engages in a syncrisis of Adamic sin and Christ's grace/gift (5:12-21).[53] The comparison features combined arrangement. As a comparison of inanimate "things," it adapts the topoi normally used in comparisons of persons per progymnastic teaching, and in a conventional order. The first part of the comparison focuses on the origin or birth of the two: sin had its origin, or entrance into the world, through the "one man" Adam (and death through sin)—but divine grace and the free gift derived from the "one man, Jesus Christ."[54] The second part of the comparison focuses on what the two accomplish—that is, their deeds: first, Adam's sin brought judgment and condemnation, but Christ's gift brought justification; second, Adam's sin caused death to reign through the one man, Adam, but Christ's grace and gift caused their recipients to reign through the one man, Jesus Christ; third, the one man's sin led to condemnation for all, while the one man's gift led to justification and life for all; fourth, the sin made many sinners, but the gift made many righteous; fifth, sin multiplied because of law, but grace multiplied because of sin's increase. The final point of comparison moves to the topos closely related with deeds, pursuits, and takes up a motif regularly associated with pursuits in ancient praise, kingship: whereas sin reigned (*basileuō*) through death, grace reigned (*basileuō*) through justification leading to life. (It may be that Paul views this final line as a treatment of the topos of death—a concluding topos in many of encomiastic pieces. If so, he handles it somewhat unconventionally, reflecting on the death / eternal life that the two subjects *effected* rather than *experienced*.)

Origin/birth	Therefore, just as sin came into the world through one man, and death came through sin, and so death spread to all because all have sinned—sin was indeed in the world before the law, but sin is not reckoned when there is no law. Yet death exercised dominion from Adam to Moses, even over those whose sins were not like the transgression of Adam, who is a type of the one who was to come. But the free gift is not like the trespass. For if the many died through the one man's trespass, much more surely have the grace of God and the free gift in the grace of the one man, Jesus Christ, abounded for the many.
Deeds	And the free gift is not like the effect of the one man's sin. For the judgment following one trespass brought condemnation, but the free gift following many trespasses brings justification.
	If, because of the one man's trespass, death exercised dominion through that one, much more surely will those who receive the abundance of grace and the free gift of righteousness exercise dominion in life through the one man, Jesus Christ.
	Therefore just as one man's trespass led to condemnation for all, so one man's act of righteousness leads to justification and life for all.
	For just as by the one man's disobedience the many were made sinners, so by the one man's obedience the many will be made righteous.
	But law came in, with the result that the trespass multiplied; but where sin increased, grace abounded all the more,
Pursuits	so that, just as sin exercised dominion in death, so grace might also exercise dominion through justification leading to eternal life through Jesus Christ our Lord. (5:12-21)

In sum, Pauline syncrisis, like Pauline encomium, appears to be thoroughly conventional by progymnastic standards and as measured by the compositional practices evident in the ancient Mediterranean milieu. Paul does show from time to time a subversive streak, rooted in his experience of the Christ event, that undercuts much of what Hellenistic education prized as honorable; but this tendency only further suggests consciousness, not ignorance, of syncritical convention.[55] Whatever his level of education, Paul shows himself to be no less competent in his handling of syncrisis than most other writers of antiquity.

Hebrews. The book of Hebrews, an ancient Christian oration, features a recurring pattern of syncrisis throughout the composition, and to such an extent that it may be said to represent the most sophisticated use of syncrisis in the Christian canon.[56] The work features at least five major units of syncrisis, which collectively constitute roughly half of the writing in its entirety: angels versus Jesus (1:5-14), Moses versus Jesus (3:1-6), Aaronic high priests versus Jesus the high priest (5:1-10), the Levitical priestly ministry versus the Melchizedekian priestly ministry (7:1-10:18), and Sinai versus Zion (12:18-24). Most of these units are organized conventionally using standard topoi in a standard order.

We have already noted in the chapter on narrative the use of topoi of personhood as a template for the comparison of the angels and Jesus in 1:5-14.

Origin	Jesus is "begotten" as the "Son" of the "Father" on the day of his enthronement—the angels are not. (1:5)
Birth	Jesus is the "firstborn" in the coming world and worshipped by angels as such. (1:6)
Pursuits	The angels are "servants," but Jesus is the "anointed" whose "throne is forever" because he loved righteousness. (1:7-9)
Death	Jesus will have unending dominion in the coming world because he "remains," in contrast to the angels, whose dominion will "perish." (1:10-12)
Events after death	Jesus, not the angels, is exalted to God's right hand until all his enemies are subjected to him in the future. (1:13-14)

In the light of the syncrisis exercises, the unit may also be described as a syncrisis featuring combined arrangement.[57]

The comparison of Moses and Jesus (3:1-6), the second syncrisis of Hebrews, takes up a single topos—birth—in demonstration of Jesus' superior birth status, arguing that Moses is a slave *in* the house, while Jesus is a firstborn son *over* the house.

The comparison of the Aaronic high priests and Jesus the high priest (5:1-10) is organized via separate arrangement and argues that the latter undergoes the better training or *paideia*. The unit first describes the Aaronic high priests as sharing in the weakness and waywardness of the people and sacrificing sympathetically for them and for themselves (5:1-4; "weakness" and "waywardness" were considered vices that *paideia* corrected in a child—the motifs are pedagogical in nature). Then Christ is described as similarly called to his priestly profession, but as one who undergoes a course of training the Aaronic high priests lack. The description of the *paideia* Christ alone undertakes is organized topically:[58]

Origin	Jesus, not Aaronic priests, is appointed as the Father's begotten Son. (5:5)
Pursuits	Jesus, not Aaronic priests, is appointed to an eternal priesthood in the order of Melchizekek. (5:6)
Deeds	Jesus, not Aaronic priests, prays in the days of his flesh for salvation out of death and is heard because of his reverent submission. (5:7)
Death	Jesus, not Aaronic priests, learns obedience from what he suffers. (5:8)
Events after death	Jesus, not Aaronic priests, is perfected and becomes a source of eternal salvation as a Melchizedekian priest. (5:9-10)

The comparison of the Levitical priestly ministry and Melchizedekian priestly ministry (7:1–10:18), the longest and most complex comparison, displays combined arrangement and is intricately ordered using a standard set of topoi. The comparison begins in chapter 7 with a comparison of the tribes themselves via standard topoi of personhood (adapted, per convention, for the "things" being compared):

Origin	Melchizedek, the progenitor of the Melchizedekian priestly tribe, is greater than Abraham, the progenitor of the Levitical priestly tribe. (7:4-10) Whereas the Levitical priests collect tithes from the people, Melchizedek collected tithes from Abraham and blessed him. Whereas with the former tithes are received by those who are mortal, with the latter tithes are received by the one of whom it testifies that he lives.*
Birth	Jesus "arises" according to the priestly order of Melchizedek (LXX Ps 109:4). This metaphorical birth—not his literal birth into the (nonpriestly) tribe of Judah—demonstrates that the Levitical priestly tribe and the law pertaining to it has been set aside. (7:11-14) Levitical priests become priests through the law requiring that they are born into the tribe, but Christ the Melchizedekian priest "arises" through the power of indestructible life. (7:15-17) In sum, the law requiring birth in the tribe of Levi is abrogated (comparison 1), and a better hope is introduced (comparison 2). (7:18-19)

Pursuits	Levitical priests take office with no oath, but Christ the Melchizedekian priest takes office with an oath sworn by the Lord (LXX Ps 109:4b) (7:20-21). Thus, Christ has also become the guarantor of a better covenant. (7:22)
Death / events after death	Death prevents Levitical priests from continuing in office, but Christ holds priesthood permanently because he continues "forever." (7:23-24)

* *Scholars disagree as to whether the writer of Hebrews considers Melchizedek mortal (see Fred L. Horton,* The Melchizedek Tradition: A Critical Examination of the Sources to the Fifth Century A.D. and in the Epistle to the Hebrews, *SNTSMS 30 [Cambridge: Cambridge University Press, 1976], esp. 153–61) or angelic (so Eric F. Mason,* "You Are a Priest Forever": Second Temple Jewish Messianism and the Priestly Christology of the Epistle to the Hebrews, *STDJ 74 [Leiden: Brill, 2008], esp. 199–203).*

Hebrews 7:25–10:18 then juxtaposes the deeds of these priestly tribes at length. The unit features combined arrangement and is, as recent study has demonstrated, intricately arranged via sub-topoi of action.[59]

Last, Hebrews 12:18-24 juxtaposes Sinai and Zion as mountains of approach. The arrangement is separate, and the divisions are numerical rather than topical, with seven (the number of perfection or completion) items considered in each case:

You have not come

(1) to something touched
(2) and to something that has been burned with fire
(3) and to darkness
(4) and to gloom
(5) and to storm
(6) and to trumpet sound
(7) and to the voice of words, which (voice) made the hearers beg that no further word be spoken to them, for they could not endure the order that was given, "If even an animal touches the mountain, it shall be stoned to death." Indeed, so terrifying was the sight that Moses said, "I tremble with fear."

But you have come

(1) to Mount Zion and the city of the living God, to heavenly Jerusalem
(2) and to a myriad of angels in a festal gathering
(3) and to the assembly of the firstborn children enrolled in heaven
(4) and to a judge, the God of all
(5) and to the spirits of the righteous who have been made perfect

(6) and to the mediator of a new covenant, Jesus
(7) and to the sprinkled blood that speaks better than Abel's blood. (12:18-24)

Collectively, the five syncritical sections form a single genus syncritical project, as every syncrisis juxtaposes a subject associated with the old covenant with a counterpart associated with the new covenant. The effect of the project as a whole is to demonstrate the superiority of new covenant experience to that of old. That the five comparisons form a single project is clear not only from the consistent "old and new covenant" pairings, but also from the topical progression it employs. As a comparison of inanimate things (covenant experience), the syncrisis gives consideration to something analogous in the "lives" of the covenants to origin, birth, education, deeds, and death / events after death:

Old Covenant vs. New Covenant Experience	
Origin	[*Angels vs. Jesus*] The new covenant has greater origins with the superior mediator.* (1:5-14)
Birth	[*Moses vs. Jesus*] The new covenant has greater beginnings via the better born inaugurator. (3:1-6)
Education	[*Aaronic high priests vs. Jesus*] The new covenant's high priest is the better trained. (5:1-10)
Deeds	[*Levitical priestly ministry vs. Melchizedekian priestly ministry*] The deeds of the new covenant's priestly ministry are superior. (7:1–10:18)
Deaths/ events after death	[*Sinai vs. Zion*] The new covenant's mountain of eschatological access to God is superior.† (12:18-24)

* *The Mosaic/old covenant was believed in Jewish tradition to be mediated by angels. The writer of Hebrews not only expresses this view but frames Jesus as correspondingly mediating a comparatively greater "word" (2:1-4).*

† *The comparison frames Sinai as a mountain of marginal access under the threat of "death" (12:20) but Zion as a mountain of full eschatological access to the "living God" by the "spirits of the righteous made perfect" (12:22-23).*

The reason the writer engages in such comparative units is made clear in every case by what follows. Without exception, the writer moves from each syncrisis to a deliberative argument *from the lesser to the greater*: that if perseverance in faith was advantageous (or apostasy disadvantageous) in the case of old covenant experience, then how much more is perseverance advantageous (or apostasy disadvantageous) in the case of new covenant experience. In other words, the five syncrises establish the (unstated) premise upon which subsequent argumentation proceeds. By heightening or "amplifying" the importance of new covenant experience, the writer is able to encourage perseverance "all the more" in covenant faith despite the pressures to apostatize. Syncrisis is thus centrally important to the structure and argument of Hebrews in its entirety.

Luke. The opening chapters of the Gospel of Luke entail an extensive double-encomium syncrisis of John the Baptist and Jesus demonstrating the superiority of the latter (= comparison to the lesser).[60] The comparison is arranged in alternating narrative panels devoted to John and Jesus, respectively (1:5–4:30), or in what the theorists would call combined arrangement. The correspondence of these panels is established not only through many parallel narrative details that they share but also through their parallel treatment of syncritical topoi in a conventional order. Thereafter in the Gospel, the comparison of Jesus and John is resumed sporadically in brief units (5:33-35; 7:18-28, 34; 9:7-9, 18-20; 11:1-4; and 20:1-8), with additional topical points of contrast drawn. We may chart the full syncrisis as follows:

Topos of Syncrisis	John	Jesus
Origins		
Homeland	Judea (1:5a)	Galilee (1:26a)
City	Jerusalem (implied by father's status as "priest," 1:5b)	Nazareth (1:26b)—but born in Bethlehem (2:4)
Father	Zechariah (1:5b)	Joseph (1:27a)—but conceived by Holy Spirit as God's son (1:35; cf. 3:21-38)
Ancestors	Zechariah belongs to priestly division of Abijah	Joseph from the house of David (1:27b)
	Elizabeth a descendant of Aaron (1:5c)	
Mother	"Her name was Elizabeth" (1:5c)	"The virgin's name was Mary" (1:27c)
Marvelous occurrences at birth	Zechariah's vision of an angel (1:11-12)	Mary's vision of an angel (1:28-29)
	Angel's oracle to Zechariah concerning birth, name, and career (= preparer figure) of son (1:13-17)	Angel's oracle to Mary concerning birth, name, and career (= Messiah) of son (1:30-37)

Topos of Syncrisis	John	Jesus
	Zechariah does not believe oracle; receives another oracle rebuking him for his unbelief and inflicting muteness (1:18-23)	Mary believes oracle; receives another oracle—from Elizabeth—blessing her and praising her for her belief and announcing pregnancy (1:38-45)
		Signs of Jesus' superiority: Elizabeth's baby leaps at Mary's greeting; Elizabeth's oracle: "Who am I that the mother of my Lord should come and visit me?" (1:38-45)
	Oracle's fulfillment celebrated by Elizabeth: the Lord "looks favorably upon her" (= she conceives despite barrenness) (1:24-25)	Oracle's fulfillment celebrated by Mary: the Lord "looks favorably upon her" (= she conceives despite virginity) (1:46-56)
	Oracle's fulfillment: Elizabeth bears a son (1:57)	Oracle's fulfillment: Mary bears a son (2:1-7)
	Neighbors/relatives told that Lord showed great mercy to Elizabeth; they rejoice with Elizabeth (1:58)	Shepherds told of birth of "Christ the Lord"; visit Mary, Joseph, and the child (2:8-20); birth revealed through visions (2:9, 13), oracles (2:10-12, 14), and a "sign": "you will find a child wrapped in bands of cloth and lying in a manger" (2:12)
Nurture and training	Oracle concerning name fulfilled: the circumcision and naming of John (1:59-66)	Oracle concerning name fulfilled: the circumcision and naming of Jesus (2:21)
	Zechariah's oracle concerning the children, Jesus and John (1:67-79)	Jesus' presentation at the temple, and the temple oracles concerning the child, Jesus (2:25-39)

Topos of Syncrisis	John	Jesus
	The child grows and becomes strong: "The child grew and became strong in spirit" (1:80)	The child grows and becomes strong: "The child grew and became strong, filled with wisdom; and the favor of God was upon him" (2:40-52)
Pursuits and deeds	"John the son of Zechariah" begins prophetic ministry (3:1-20):	Jesus the "son of God" (so the genealogy of 3:23-29) begins prophetic ministry (3:21–4:20):
	(1) baptizes in wilderness	(1) is baptized and tested in wilderness
	(2) preaches in fulfillment of Isaianic prophecy concerning self	(2) preaches in fulfillment of Isaianic prophecy concerning self
	(3) prophetically confronts Herod	(3) prophetically confronts Nazareth synagogue
	(4) is imprisoned by Herod	(4) miraculously escapes crowd's attempt to throw him off cliff
	Who is the bridegroom? John's disciples fast and pray (5:33-35)	Who is the bridegroom? Jesus' disciples eat and drink (5:33-35)
	Who is the one to come? (7:18-20)	Who is the one to come? (7:18-20)
	John prepares Jesus' way (7:24-27)	Jesus gives sight to the blind, makes the lame walk, cleanses lepers, gives hearing to the deaf, raises the dead, and brings good news to the poor (7:21-23)
	"Among those born of women no one is greater than John" (7:28a)	"Yet the least in the kingdom of God is greater than he" (7:28b)
	"John the Baptist came eating no bread and drinking no wine, and you say he has a demon" (7:33)	"the Son of Man has come eating and drinking, and you say, 'Look, a glutton and a drunkard, a friend of tax collectors and sinners!'" (7:34)

Topos of Syncrisis	John	Jesus
	John taught disciples to pray (11:1)	Jesus taught disciples to pray (11:2-4)
	John proclaimed good news (16:16; cf. 3:18)	Jesus proclaimed good news (16:16; cf. 4:18)
	Implied: John's authority is from heaven (20:1-8)	Implied: Jesus' authority is from heaven (20:1-8)
Manner of death	John is executed (9:7-9)	Jesus is executed (22:47–23:56)
Events after death	John mistakenly thought to be resurrected	Jesus is resurrected (24:1-53)
	Herod mistakes Jesus as John resurrected (9:7-9)	
	Some of the people mistake Jesus as John resurrected (9:18-20)	

Viewed in its entirety, this syncrisis may be described as a double-encomium comparison to the lesser employing mostly separate arrangement. The detail and complexity with which the evangelist carries out the comparison is largely unrivaled in ancient historiography and biography. Only the *Parallel Lives* of Plutach with attached concluding syncrises can claim greater complexity; and even those without also fall short. Such extensive syncrisis, then, raises the question of why the evangelist has gone to such lengths to prove Jesus' superiority to John. The answer lies in syncritical theory, which would inevitably read the comparison as a genus syncrisis commenting on the relative greatness of the two religious sects known to have been associated with the two men. That is, it functions much in the same way that comparisons of Jesus and Moses (e.g., 2 Cor 3:7-11; John 1:17; 3:14; 9:28-29) in early Christian and Jewish literature function as commentary on the sects that looked to those men as leaders. That John, like Jesus and Moses, had followers that constituted a distinct religious sect that continued in various forms for centuries and rivaled factions more consciously aligned with Jesus and Moses, is evident from the evidence of early Christian literature. Charles Talbert summarizes this evidence succinctly as follows:

> It is clear that a Baptist movement continued both alongside of Jesus' ministry and after Jesus' lifetime. (a) Mark 2:18 indicates that a group of John's disciples existed alongside of Jesus and his group (cf. Lk 11:1). (b) John 3:28 ("You yourselves bear me witness that I said . . .") implies that a community of John's disciples existed alongside of Jesus and his disciples. (c) Acts 19:1-7 speaks about

a group of the Baptist's disciples at Ephesus in Paul's time. Interestingly, they are mentioned because they became realigned with the Christian movement. (d) The Pseudo-Clementines mention a Baptist movement in several places. In the *Recognitions* 1.54, we hear:

> Yea, some even of the disciples of John, who seemed to be great ones, have separated themselves from the people, and proclaimed their own master as Christ.

The *Recognitions* 1.60 say:

> And, behold, one of the disciples of John asserted that John was the Christ, and not Jesus, inasmuch as Jesus himself declared that John was greater than all men and all prophets. "If then," said he, "he be greater than all, he must be held to be greater than Moses, and than Jesus himself. But if he be the greatest of all, then must he be the Christ."

In the *Homilies* 2.23–24 (cf. *Recognitions* 2.8) reference is made to a Johannine sect that continued after John's death that was connected to the Gnostics, Dositheus and Simon Magus.[61]

In a context where such John groups existed and made rival claims to Christianity, syncrisis showing the superiority of Jesus to John would, by ancient conventions, have an obvious polemical implication: that the Jesus sect as a whole is superior to that centered around John. This is the point not only of the Lukan syncrisis of Jesus and John but of the same running comparison found commonly in other Christian literature, including Mark, Matthew, John, *Recognitions*, and *Homilies*. All these comparisons are also topically ordered and function as genus syncrises showing the superiority of Christianity to a rival sect.[62] The fact Mark, John, and *Recognitions* put forward *three-way* comparisons of Jesus, John, *and Moses*, all while positing three distinct sects devoted respectively to these three men, only further confirms the genus syncritical logic generally underlying early Christian comparisons of Jesus and John.[63]

Conclusion

Syncrisis is widely employed in ancient literature in ways that correspond closely to progymnastic theory. More intricate syncrises are typically arranged under conventional topoi of praise, and so frequently uphold conventional associations of honor with male, aristocratic, Graeco-Roman power. Occasionally, though, one sees Jewish and Christian writers subverting those associations, and often explicitly on account of the exodus experience or the Christ event, which both encouraged alternative associations between honor and powerlessness. One sees frequently, too, the use of genus syncrisis widely employed in the ancient world as a common form of polemic entailing a two-level drama that is as much commentary on the individuals compared as the genera they represent. The kinds of genera in view in these comparisons, too, are varied: nations, genders, religions, philosophies, sects, and, in Paul's case, two apocalyptically differentiated humanities.

Notes

1 See for the following discussion the syncrisis exercises of Theon, *Prog.* 112–115; Ps.-Hermogenes, *Prog.* 18–20; Aphthonius, *Prog.* 42–44; Nicolaus, *Prog.* 59–63; cf. too Quintilian, *Inst.* 2.4.20–21.

2 For the following, cf. the discussion in Michael W. Martin, *Judas and the Rhetoric of Comparison in the Fourth Gospel*, NTM 25 (Sheffield: Sheffield Phoenix, 2010), 37–77.

3 This same system of classification reappears in the handbooks in discussions of comparison as a judicial or deliberative argument requiring a decision from the audience. In such cases, the argument proceeds as follows: if X is valid in the case of a lesser (or equal, or greater), then it is certainly valid in the case of the greater (or equal, or lesser). See the discussion in Michael W. Martin and Jason A. Whitlark, "Choosing What Is Advantageous: The Relationship between Epideictic and Deliberative Syncrisis in Hebrews," *NTS* 58 (2012): 379–400.

4 See Martin, *Judas and the Rhetoric*, 37–77.

5 *Pace* Martin in his earlier analysis.

6 On this disagreement, and Plutarch's conformity to the Theonic opinion, see Friedrich Focke, "Synkrisis," *Hermes* 58 (1923): 327–68; cf. Daniel Sheerin, "Rhetorical and Hermeneutic *Synkrisis* in Patristic Typology," in *Nova & Vetera: Patristic Studies in Honor of Thomas Patrick Halton*, ed. John Petruccione (Washington, D.C.: Catholic University of America Press, 1998), 22–39; Kennedy, *Progymnasmata*, 53n166.

7 There is some question as to the authenticity of the sentence, as it appears only in Priscian's later Latin manuscript (see Kennedy, *Progymnasmata*, 83n39), and so is bracketed by Kennedy in his translation. If an interpolation, the sentence *may* attest (the scant evidence allows only for plausible hypotheses) a development in the progymnastic tradition from proscription of comparison of dissimilar subjects, to the omission of the proscription, and finally, to its prescription as one of two possible types.

8 This topos appears in Ps.-Hermogenes' encomium topos list, which is longer than the brief summative list he offers in the syncrisis exercise.

9 For many of the examples below, see Martin, *Judas and the Rhetoric*, 37–77.

10 Cf. Ronald F. Hock, "Homer in Greco-Roman Education," in *Mimesis and Intertextuality in Antiquity and Christianity*, ed. Dennis R. MacDonald, Studies in Antiquity and Christianity (Harrisburg, Pa.: Trinity Press International, 2001), 56–77.

11 Cf. Hock, "Homer in Greco-Roman Education," 56–77.

12 On the *Iliad*, see William F. Wyatt, *Homer: Iliad*, LCL (Cambridge, Mass.: Harvard University Press, 1999), 1:1–9.

13 Mark W. Edwards, *Homer: Poet of the Iliad* (Baltimore: Johns Hopkins University Press, 1987), 162.

14 See Polybius, *Histories* (Romans vs. the Persians, the Lacedaemonians, and the Macedonians); Dionysius of Halicarnassus, *Roman Antiquities* (Romans vs. Assyrians, Medes, Persians, Macedonians, Greeks); Livy, *History of Rome* (Romans vs. all nations); Appian, *Foreign Wars* (Romans vs. Assyrians, Medes, Persians, Greeks); Josephus, *Jewish Antiquities* (Jews vs. Romans).

15 On the *Histories*, see W. R. Paton, *Polybius: The Histories*, LCL (Cambridge, Mass.: Harvard University Press, 2005), 1:vii–xvi.

16 This and all subsequent citations of Polybius are from *Histories*, trans. Evelyn S. Shuckburgh, 2 vols. (New York: Macmillan, 1889).

17 For this translation and related introductory material, see Aristophanes, *Women at the Thesmophoria: The Complete Greek Drama*, trans. Eugene O'Neill Jr. (New York: Random House, 1938).

18 On the *Roman Antiquities*, see Earnest Cary, *Dionysius of Halicarnassus*, LCL (Cambridge, Mass.: Harvard University Press, 2001), 1:vii–xlviii.

19 On the *Annals*, see John Jackson, *Tacitus: Histories, Books IV–V, Annals, Books I–III*, LCL (Cambridge, Mass.: Harvard University Press, 1998), 225–42.

20 The translation is from Alfred John Church and William Jackson Brodribb, trans., *The Annals of Tacitus* (London: Macmillan, 1921).

21 On the use of syncrisis in the *Parallel Lives*, see David H. J. Larmour, "Making Parallels: *Synkrisis* and Plutarch's 'Themistocles and Camillus,'" *ANRW* 33.6:4154–200.

22 So Hartmut Erbse, who first demonstrated that the non-narrative *prooimia* and formal syncrises that "frame" each biography pair lend them their essential narrative structure ("Die Bedeutung der Synkrisis in den Parallelbiographien Plutarchs," *Hermes* [1956] 84: 398–424). As a consequence of Erbse's study, "the focus of scholarly discussion of *synkrisis* changed from the formal comparisons at the end to the broader notion of *synkrisis* as a general phenomenon of comparison throughout a pair of Lives" (see Larmour, "Making Parallels," 4159).

23 On the latter point as it pertains to Plutarch, see Focke, "Synkrisis," 327–68.

24 In *Sacr.* 11ff., Philo interprets the story of Cain and Abel as a "syncrisis," noting Moses' consideration of such syncritical topics as "birth" and "pursuits" (1.14); cf. Michael W. Martin, "Philo's Use of Syncrisis: An Examination of Philonic Composition in the Light of the Progymnasmata," *PRSt* 30 (2003): 271–97. In 16–18, Philo deals with the problematic fact that Cain is older and therefore seemingly superior in rank (syncritical logic normally prefers that which is first). Philo finds in "Moses'" comparison of Jacob and Esau proof that Esau (like Cain, an allegory for "wickedness") is indeed superior to Jacob (like Abel, an allegory for virtue) with regard to birth order but is nevertheless inferior with regard to rank, honor, and glory.

25 After Jacob steals the blessing from Esau, divine providence leads him to confer the blessing on Esau as part of their reconciliation. See Gen 33:11; cf. Jesse Long, "Wrestling with God to Win: A Literary Reading of the Story of Jacob at the Jabbok in Honor of Don Williams," *SCJ* 15 (2012): 47–61 (esp. 56 and 56n37).

26 On this section as syncrisis, see D. Winston, *The Wisdom of Solomon*, AB 43 (New York: Doubleday, 1979), 224, and the citations therein.

27 On Philo's *Life of Moses*, see F. H. Colson, *Philo*, LCL (Cambridge, Mass.: Harvard University Press, 2004), 6:vii–xx, 274–85.

28 The apologetic motive is evident from the opening sentences, where Philo complains that "the historians who have flourished among the Greeks have not chosen to think [Moses] worthy of mention" (1.1–2).

29 For the following analysis, see Martin, *Judas and the Rhetoric of Comparison*, 37–77; idem, "Progymnastic Topic Lists: A Compositional Template for Luke and Other *Bioi?*" *NTS* 54 (2008): 18–41.

30 H. St. J. Thackeray states that Josephus writes in demonstration that his "race had a history comparable, nay in antiquity far superior, to that of Rome" (introduction to *Josephus*, trans. H. St. J. Thackeray et al., 10 vols., LCL [Cambridge, Mass.: Harvard University Press, 1926–1965], 1:ix). On the *Jewish Antiquities* generally, see 5:vii–xix.

31 Thackeray et al., *Josephus*, 4:ix.

32 Thackeray et al., *Josephus*, 4:xiii.

33 Thackeray et al., *Josephus*, 4:ix, and 632–33nB.

34 On the *Jewish War*, see Thackeray et al., *Josephus*, 2:vii–xxxi.

35 On *Against Apion*, see Thackeray et al., *Josephus*, 1:vii–xx (esp. xvi–xix).

36 On the *Homilies* and other Pseudo-Clementines, see Johannes Irmscher and Georg Strecker, "The Pseudo-Clementines," in *New Testament Apocrypha*, vol. 2: *Writings Relating to the Apostles; Apocalypses and Related Subjects*, ed. Wilhelm Schneemelcher, trans. R. McL. Wilson, rev. ed. (Louisville, Ky.: Westminster John Knox, 1992), 483–541.

37 This and all subsequent citations of the *Homilies* are from Georg Strecker, "Kerygmata Petrou," in Schneemelcher, ed., and Wilson, trans., *New Testament Apocrypha* 2:531–41.

38 See the discussion in Martin, *Judas and the Rhetoric of Comparison*, 1–36 passim.

39 On the *Recognitions* and other Pseudo-Clementines, see Irmscher and Strecker, "Pseudo-Clementines," 483–541.

40 On Eusebius' *Ecclesiastical History*, see the introduction of Kirsopp Lake, *Eusebius: The Ecclesiastical History*, LCL (Cambridge, Mass.: Harvard University Press, 1998), 1:vii–lvi.

41 On syncrisis in Chrysostom, see Daniel Sheerin, "Rhetorical and Hermeneutic *Synkrisis* in Patristic Typology," 22–39.

42 Citations and translations are from John Chrysostom, *Discourses against Judaizing Christians*, trans. Paul W. Harkins, FC 68 (Washington, D.C.: Catholic University of America Press, 1979).

43 The list is from Sheerin, "Rhetorical and Hermeneutical *Synkrisis*," 26n14, with minor corrections.

44 The best study to date is that of Christopher Forbes, "Paul and Rhetorical Comparison," in *Paul in the Greco-Roman World: A Handbook*, ed. J. Paul Sampley (New York: Trinity Press International, 2003), 134–71. This chapter advances previous scholarship on Pauline syncrisis in noting the detailed topical structure that consistently characterizes Paul's more complex syncrises—which in turn vindicates those who have argued for Paul's use of the device in the technical sense, a question that is currently much debated.

45 The potential mark in Adam's favor may be why Paul has begun with birth rather than origin, as he may feel the need to address the most obvious objection to Christ's superiority immediately.

46 For a modern analysis of the passage as syncrisis, see George A. Kennedy, *New Testament Interpretation through Rhetorical Criticism* (Chapel Hill: University of North Carolina Press, 1984), 23, 89; and Forbes, "Paul and Rhetorical Comparison," 156–57.

47 On this phrase as characteristic of syncrisis, see Martin and Whitlark, "Choosing What Is Advantageous," 379–400.

48 See, e.g., Quintilian, *Inst.* 3.7.6–18.

49 Quintilian, *Inst.* 3.7.6–18.

50 For previous analysis of this passage as syncrisis, see Peter Marshall, *Enmity in Corinth: Social Conventions in Paul's Relations with the Corinthians* (Tübingen: J.C.B. Mohr, 1987), 53–55, 325–53; and Christopher Forbes, "Comparison, Self-Praise, and Irony: Paul's Boasting and the Conventions of Hellenistic Rhetoric," *NTS* 32 (1986): 1–30.

51 *Pace* Ryan S. Shellenberg, *Rethinking Paul's Rhetorical Education: Comparative Rhetoric and 2 Corinthians 10–13*, ECL (Atlanta: Society of Biblical Literature, 2013), 149–68, who rejects the interpretation of the passage as syncrisis and claims one topos at most is employed in the comparison.

52 On this passage as syncrisis, see also Christopher Forbes, "Paul and Rhetorical Comparison," 158–59.

53 For a brief reading of this passage as syncrisis, see R. Dean Anderson Jr., *Ancient Rhetorical Theory and Paul*, rev. ed. (Leuven: Peeters, 1999), 225–29; cf. Forbes, "Paul and Rhetorical Comparison," 154–55.

54 The "genitive of source" or "origin" (cf. Daniel B. Wallace, *Greek Grammar beyond the Basics: An Exegetical Syntax of the New Testament* [Grand Rapids: Zondervan, 1996], 109–10) is used here to imply a derivation from Christ that corresponds to sin's derivation from Adam.

55 As Robert Alter observes, artistic communication depends upon a "grid of conventions" that any good artist both meets and defies, working both "upon" and "against" them (*The Art of Biblical Narrative* [New York: Basic, 1981], 47–62).

56 For the following analysis and outlines (which are quoted verbatim), see Michael W. Martin and Jason A. Whitlark, *Inventing Hebrews: Design and Purpose in Ancient Rhetoric* (Cambridge: Cambridge University Press, forthcoming in 2018), esp. chs. 2 and 6; also idem, "The Encomiastic Topics of Syncrisis as the Key to the Structure and Argument of Hebrews," *NTS* 57 (2011): 415–39; idem, "Choosing What Is Advantageous," 379–400; cf. A. Vanhoye, *La structure littéraire de l'épître aux Hébreux*, 2d ed. (Paris: Desclée de Brower, 1976), 144–51, 206–7; Timothy W. Seid, "Synkrisis in Hebrews 7: The Rhetorical Structure and Strategy," in *The Rhetorical Interpretation of Scripture: Essays from the 1996 Malibu Conference*, ed. Stanley E. Porter and Dennis L. Stamps, JSNTSup 180 (Sheffield: Sheffield Academic, 1999), 322–47.

57 Epideictic materials (syncrisis included) were commonly prescribed for the *narratio* of speeches and employ the same *topoi* of personhood as *narratio*; so Martin and Whitlark, *Inventing Hebrews*, ch. 6, who on the basis of this and other evidence from rhetorical theory, argue that this section and the remaining four syncritical sections of Hebrews collectively form what the theorists call a "disjointed" *narratio* (because it is distributed piecemeal throughout the speech).

58 Moderns may miss the consistent use of ancient pedagogical motifs with each point of comparison: (1) *Origin*—*paideia* was ideally experienced as apprenticeship by a son under a father's direction; (2) *Pursuits*—*paideia* was undertaken with a particular profession or "pursuit" in view; (3) *Deeds*—*paideia* was successful if the son/apprentice practiced "submission" toward the father/pedagogue; (4) *Death*—suffering was widely viewed in the ancient world as a curriculum of learning, a view commonly expressed in the same play on Greek words used by the writer, "to learn (*math-*) from what one suffers (*path-*)"; similarly, "obedience" was seen as crucial to the advancement of the apprentice; here Jesus' death is framed as embraced out of obedience and as a curriculum of learning; (5) *Events after death*—"perfection" was widely regarded as the goal of *paideia*; here Christ is pictured graduating to perfection and therefore taking up his profession as a Melchizedekian priest. The pedagogical motifs that follow in the remainder of the chapter (see esp. 5:11-14) show the artistry of the writer in handling the theme.

59 See Martin and Whitlark, *Inventing Hebrews*, ch. 6, for an extended analysis.

60 On this comparison and the analysis below, see Michael W. Martin, *Judas and the Rhetoric*, ch. 2; idem, "Progymnastic Topic Lists," 18–41; Mikeal C. Parsons, *Luke*, PCNT (Grand Rapids: Baker Academic, 2015), 21–24; cf. A. George, "Le parallèle entre Jean-Baptiste et Jésus en Luc 1–2," in *Mélanges Béda Rigaux*, ed. A. Descamps and A. de Halleux (Gembloux: Duculot, 1970), 147–71; W. Radl, *Paulus und Jesus im lukanischen Doppelwerk. Untersuchungen zu Parallelmotiven im Lukasevangelium und in der Apostelgeschichte*, Europisch Hochschulschriften 23.49 (Frankfurt: Lang, 1975), 352–53; John A. Darr, *On Character Building: The Reader and the Rhetoric of Characterization in Luke-Acts* (Louisville, Ky.: Westminster John Knox Press, 1992), 60–84; Christoph Gregor Müller, *Mehr als ein Prophet. Die Charakterzeichnung Johannes des Täufers im lukanischen Erzählwerk*, Herders Biblische Studien 31 (Freiburg: Herder, 2001), 49–152; Fearghus O'Fearghail, *The Introduction to Luke-Acts: A Study of the Role of Luke 1,1–4,44 in the Composition of Luke's Two-Volume Work*, AnBib 126 (Rome: Pontifical Biblical Institute, 1991), 33–36.

61 Charles H. Talbert, *Reading John: A Literary and Theological Commentary on the Fourth Gospel and Johannine Epistles*, RNT 4 (Macon, Ga.: Smyth and Helwys, 2005), 109–10.

62 On the Markan and Matthean comparisons, see Martin, *Judas and the Rhetoric of Comparison*, ch. 2; see the same and above for those from the *Recognitions* and *Homilies*.

63 For examples of syncrises in the Fourth Gospel, see Alicia D. Myers, *Characterizing Jesus: A Rhetorical Analysis on the Fourth Gospel's Use of Scripture in Its Presentation of Jesus*, LNTS 458 (London: T & T Clark, 2012); and Martin, *Judas and the Rhetoric of Comparison*, 91–130.

Conclusion

> These things are, as it were, the foundation of every form of discourse, and depending on how one instills them in the mind of the young, necessarily the results make themselves felt in the same way later.
>
> Theon

Our intention in this study has been to show the pervasiveness of the progymnastic forms as building blocks of ancient Mediterranean literature, the New Testament included, and to illustrate the usefulness of progymnastic theory for the interpretation of those forms. Though an introductory survey such as this may only scratch the surface, we hope it is suggestive both of the need for additional study of individual exercises and of their value for New Testament studies (to say nothing of other fields of study). Without attempting to be exhaustive, we offer some final observations concerning how study in the light of the progymnasmata may be of benefit, in particular, to several New Testament subdisciplines. We sketch, too, some areas of needed further inquiry suggested by this study.

The Progymnasmata and New Testament Sub-Disciplines

Rhetorical Criticism

It is remarkable, but not surprising, that a book of this kind—an introductory sketch of the New Testament in the light of the progymnasmata—has not been written to date. Both within and without biblical studies, the progymnasmata have remained in relative obscurity in comparison with their better-known counterparts, the handbooks of declamation (e.g., Aristotle's *Rhetoric*, the *Rhetorica ad Herennium*, Cicero's *De inventione*, and Quintilian's *Institutio oratoria*). The latter are generally widely available in multiple modern critical editions, translated into most modern languages, and even made the subject of extensive commentaries (e.g., George Kennedy's *On Rhetoric*) and syntheses (e.g., Heinrich Lausberg's *Handbook of Literary Rhetoric*).[1] The progymnasmata, by contrast, have received far less attention. Critical editions are generally older and less numerous.[2] Commentaries are rare or, in the case of most progymnasmata, nonexistent.[3] And until relatively recently, the progymnasmata did not even exist in English translation. The first English version of Pseudo-Hermogenes did not appear until 1928 (Charles Sears

Baldwin), but it was less than literal and had no suitable replacement until George Kennedy produced his self-published translation of the four Greek progymnasmata in 1999—a work later revised and made available in wider publication by the Society of Biblical Literature in 2003.[4] Worse yet, English versions of Aphthonius and Theon did not appear until 1952 (Ray Nadeau) and 1987 (James Butts), respectively.[5] And Nicolaus remained untranslated until the turn of this century, when Kennedy's work first appeared.[6]

Despite their relative obscurity, it is our belief that the progymnasmata should be seen as the starting place, and not merely a secondary resource, for New Testament rhetorical criticism. This is owing to the nature of the New Testament as a collection of mostly nondeclamatory genres and the nature of the progymnasmata as the standard curriculum in Graeco-Roman education for prose composition. We reiterate our observations from the introduction: unlike the handbooks, which were intended for training primarily in oratory, the progymnasmata were designed for training in writing as much as oratory and therefore are the textbooks from ancient education most directly relevant for the study of most New Testament writings. As Theon observes in the introduction to his textbook, the exercises are "the foundation of every kind of discourse," and so they are "useful not only to those who are going to practice rhetoric but also if one wishes to undertake the function of poets or historians or any other writers" (Theon, *Prog.* 60). As Kennedy states in the introduction to his translation:

> The curriculum described in these works, featuring a series of set exercises of increasing difficulty, was the source of facility in written and oral expression for many persons and training for speech in public life. In addition, the compositions inculcated cultural values, as well as understanding of conventional literary forms for those who entered on literature as a career or as an elegant pastime. In classical, medieval, and renaissance literature, fable, narrative, chreia, ecphrasis, comparison, speech in character, and other progymnasmatic forms were often combined in different ways to create epics, dramas, histories, and the genres of lyric poetry. As such, they are comparable to structural features of classical architecture that were artistically utilized in the great public buildings of the Greco-Roman period and were revived in the Renaissance in the West. Not only the secular literature of the Greeks and Romans, but the writings of early Christians beginning with the gospels and continuing through the patristic age, and of some Jewish writers as well, were molded by the habits of thinking and writing learned in schools.[7]

This volume, in illustrating the use of progymnastic forms as "structural features" of ancient Mediterranean literature generally and the New Testament writings specifically, may be received as further evidence of the fundamental importance of the forms to ancient prose composition. Indeed, because the term "rhetorical criticism" is so commonly associated in New Testament research with study in the light of canons of ancient oratory, it may be better to speak of the progymnasmata as a primary resource for an ancient "compositional criticism," and perhaps as a subdiscipline primarily of literary criticism—which brings us to our next consideration.

Literary Criticism

As textbooks of composition, the progymnasmata are no less valuable to literary critical inquiry, as they speak directly to its myriad concerns, and often more directly than most other ancient textbooks of the Graeco-Roman world.[8] And it matters little whether the criticism in question is focused primarily on the author, the reader, or the text. While one cannot know the intentions of an author, the progymnasmata do shed light on the aims and ends conventionally associated with a wide spectrum of compositional decisions and thus provide a rationale for speaking objectively to the likely goals of an author rooted in the evidence of the text. The exercises also serve as an invaluable resource for criticism focused on reception by audiences both ancient and modern. For investigations into reception by the "implied," "ideal," or "authorial" audiences, the exercises may function as a primer on the culture-specific conventions governing communication of all kinds, both oral and written—and thus may greatly illuminate the reconstruction of likely responses by the audiences for which ancient compositions were originally written.[9] For inquiry focused more on reception in modernity—one thinks especially of ideological criticism of all kinds and especially the questions brought to bear upon ancient texts in cultural studies—the progymnasmata represent a conscious effort on the part of educators to inculcate the young with the values of Graeco-Roman society.[10] They thus provide a treasure trove of insight into the dominant ideologies of that society, as well as to the ways that ancient education in particular may have contributed to the marginalizing of alternative ideologies. Literary studies, meanwhile, that take narrative structure as their primary objects can hardly speak meaningfully to the organization and rhetorical design of an ancient Mediterranean narrative apart from familiarity with progymnastic compositional theory and its evident shaping of contemporary practice.[11] And we have already discussed in some detail the importance of the narrative exercise, in particular, for its outlining of what may be called an ancient Mediterranean narratology. More than any other form of literary criticism, biblical "narrative criticism" stands to benefit from this progymnasma in particular.[12]

Related literary critical fields such as genre criticism, too, may profit from study of the progymnasmata.[13] In the first place, the progymnastic forms themselves may be viewed as "subgenres" governed by their own culture-specific conventions, given the forms' aforementioned role as the "building blocks" of all ancient prose composition. An examination of each in the light of contemporary genre theory would undoubtedly prove illuminating. Further, some of the progymnastic forms—most notably, narrative and encomium—were capable of standing alone as full-fledged genres unto themselves, and so the analysis provided in the progymnasmata is often genre critical in nature. In the case of the encomium exercise, Nicolaus discusses the form, as we have seen, as both a part and a whole (i.e., subgenre and genre). And though he defers discussion of it in the latter sense for the handbooks, he first defines the form *in general* and its associated conventions, while differentiating it from other related encomiastic forms such as invective, *hymnos*, *epitaphios*, wedding speech, speech of arrival, and official address. Other theorists, too, do the same. This kind of discussion, in other words, constitutes an ancient form of genre criticism, and one granted a standardized place within Graeco-Roman education.

Editorial Criticism

Last, all inquiry into ancient Mediterranean editorial practice—in biblical studies, this would include the disciplines of source, form, and redaction criticism[14]—simply must be informed by the progymnasmata, as these were the formative textbooks of editorial theory in the ancient Mediterranean world. As discussed in several preceding chapters, biblical scholarship continues to operate in some quarters with notions of unidirectional editorial "tendencies" that characterize the transmission of tradition, when only cursory consideration of editorial training and the evident practices shaped by it would call those notions into serious question. What is needed is a more sustained inquiry into progymnastic editorial theory and its relation to editorial practice in the ancient world. Only against this backdrop can biblical studies begin to better assess the transmission and editing of the materials that eventually came to be a part of the New Testament canon.

The Progymnasmata and Further Inquiry

Though we have argued for the primacy of the progymnasmata in New Testament rhetorical criticism, this is not to say that the handbooks of declamation and other treatises on oratory should be abandoned or marginalized in any way. To the contrary, as was suggested in the introductory chapter, the progymnasmata offer a lens through which we may better apprehend the value of the handbooks for the (largely nondeclamatory) writings of the New Testament. The very division between the progymnasmata as prose compositional training *preliminary to* declamation, and the handbooks as training specific to oratory, should itself serve as a warning for how not to use the handbooks. Clearly the templates of arrangement taught in the handbooks are for speeches, not prose composition. Thus, while we may expect them potentially to illuminate the organization of speeches in the New Testament itself (such as Hebrews) or within New Testament writings (such as those within Acts), we should not expect those templates to be transferable to prose writings such as Paul's letters in any rigid way. The problems that have been documented with such rhetorical analysis in biblical studies are anticipated by this fundamental consideration.[15]

What we might more reasonably expect, however, is that compositional skills first learned in the progymnasmata as relevant for prose writing of all kinds, and then further developed in the handbooks for use especially in oratory, are the kinds of skills most likely to be found in the New Testament writings and other prose compositions—and thus the kinds of skills most likely to be illumined by the handbooks of oratory. For example, the handbooks have a good deal more to say about encomium than is said in the progymnasmata. Encomium as one of the three species of oratory not only receives extensive treatment in every handbook of declamation but is even made the subject of treatises wholly devoted to it (e.g., the two treatises attributed to Menander Rhetor and Ps.-Dionysius' treatise on epideictic speeches, *Ars. rhet.* 278). Because these higher-level materials are more substantial than the brief introductions to encomium in the progymnasmata, they provide a clearer picture of the conventions shaping encomiastic composition and so are in many cases more useful for the interpretation of the form as it appears within New Testament writings. Further, these writings may be of special value for the study of the Gospels and other ancient Mediterranean biographies.[16] Theon mentions in his introduction a number of extant encomia the teacher may point young students to as ideal examples of the genre. What is interesting is that included among these examples are longer *prose narrative* encomia—that is, "Isocrates' encomia" and "Xenophon's *Agesilaus*" (Theon, *Prog.* 68)—that modern scholarship regards as the first exemplars of the biography genre. Indeed, Richard Burridge begins his analysis of Graeco-Roman biography with Isocrates' *Evagoras* and Xenophon's *Agesilaus*, noting explicitly the "origins of βίος in Greek rhetorical encomia."[17] And while later biographies adopt goals other than encomiastic laudation, they continue to retain many of the conventions of encomiastic composition, including topical structure.[18] To be sure, many of the characteristics of bios noted on a descriptive basis in Burridge's study are named and explicated as characteristics of encomium in the treatises.

Along similar lines, we may note the place of narrative in the handbooks. Because *narratio* constituted one of the four or five parts of the speech (depending on how one counted them),[19] it receives additional and extensive treatment in the portions of the handbooks devoted to arrangement, as well as in treatises wholly dedicated to the same (e.g., Anonymous Seguerianus' *The Art of Political Speech* and Apsines' *Art of Rhetoric*). Here again, while some of what is said in these discussions is applicable only to what the progymnastic theorists call the "political" species of narrative (i.e., narrative in oratory), much of it is relevant to narrative of all kinds—and so may be used to illuminate further all ancient Mediterranean prose narrative, including that of the New Testament. Of particular interest is the role *narratio* plays in relationship to *argumentatio*. The handbooks describe a fairly standard set of ways narrative exposition may set up or be in service to argumentation, and while these accounts have in view primarily the move from *narratio* to *argumentatio* within the outline of a speech, they also reflect awareness on the part of the theorists that much of what is said applies to persuasion in general. Such materials may be of immense value for the study, especially, of New Testament letters, where one encounters persuasion that regularly moves from narrative to argument (i.e., from exposition to exhortation).

Similar comments could be made, too, about compositional skills learned across multiple preliminary exercises and further developed in the handbooks. For example, "confirmation and refutation," as we have seen, was an early form of argumentation prescribed by Theon from the earliest exercises and practiced with prose composition of all kinds in view. This same skill, however, receives far greater attention in the handbooks of declamation. Indeed, two of the five major divisions of the handbooks may be seen as devoted wholly or largely to the development of this skill—invention, where students learned established patterns or topoi of inductive and deductive proof one may summon in acts of rhetorical persuasion, and arrangement, where students learned to arrange proofs as the central feature in the organization of a speech.[20] These higher-level discussions of argumentation may not reveal much about the arrangement of, say, Cicero's letters, but they do often greatly illuminate the patterns of inductive and deductive persuasion employed in those letters. The same may be said of these materials as they relate to Paul's and other New Testament letters. Aspects of invention and arrangement are also first introduced in the common-place, thesis, and law exercises—three of the "larger and more ambitious exercises" Quintilian judges best left for the rhetors (*Inst.* 1.9.1–6)—and that we, too, have omitted from our primer (see the discussion in ch. 1). While these do offer a fruitful lens into prose argumentation as found especially in New Testament letters, they more helpfully point us to the handbooks as the more illuminating resource for analysis because of their greater depth and breadth of discussion.

One may also mention the matter of style, which receives preliminary discussion in the progymnasmata but becomes a matter of greater importance in the handbooks. Indeed, style—the third traditional division of rhetoric—receives nearly as much attention in the handbooks as invention and arrangement, and far more than the remaining two divisions, memory and deliverance (which are scarcely treated).[21] Rhetoricians also produced treatises wholly devoted to style (e.g., Demetrius' *On Style* and Dionysius of Halicarnassus' *On Literary Composition*), and with a view to literary composition of all kinds, not just oratory. All these writings typically include invaluable discussions of higher and lower styles and their suitability for various subject matter. They also catalogue, often in systematic ways, the dozens of figures of thought and speech one may employ as a feature of these styles. Examples are drawn as often from epic and history as from oratory, an indication of the value of the material for literary theory in general—and accompanying discussion sometimes includes helpful description of the literary effect of the device in view. Of particular note are the Gorgianic figures, which the theorists associate with the highly poetic (but unmetered) "periodic" style.[22] Remarkably, periodic prose of this sort bears an extremely close resemblance to ancient Jewish (both Hebrew and Greek) poetry, which is also frequently periodic and unmetered and employs most of the same devices.[23] In the New Testament, one finds the same range of styles employed in prose composition; the same range of figures used; the occasional use of periodic form and figured prose; and more poetic texts featuring purely periodic form and a concentration of Gorgianic figures.[24] Thus, in a variety of ways, the discussions of style in higher textbooks and treatises may be of immense value to the interpretation of New Testament writings.

In sum, the progymnasmata not only provide a wealth of insight into the composition, reception, editing, and transmission of the New Testament writings but also represent an important theoretical lens through which the handbooks and other higher-level rhetorical treatises may be apprehended and their value for the study of the New Testament discerned. As such, the progymnasmata are worthy of further scholarly attention and should be counted among the primary sources foundational to New Testament criticism, rhetorical and otherwise.

Notes

1 George A. Kennedy, *On Rhetoric: A Theory of Civic Discourse*, 2d ed. (Oxford: Oxford University Press, 2006); Heinrich Lausberg, *Handbook of Literary Rhetoric: A Foundation for Literary Study*, ed. David E. Orton and R. Dean Anderson, trans. Matthew T. Bliss, Annemiek Jansen, and David E. Orton (Leiden: Brill, 1998).

2 See the list of editions in the introduction.

3 A welcome exception is James R. Butts' "The 'Progymnasmata' of Theon: A New Text with Translation and Commentary" (Ph.D. diss., Claremont Graduate School, 1986).

4 Charles Sears Baldwin, *Medieval Rhetoric and Poetic* (New York: Macmillan, 1928), 23–38. George A. Kennedy, *Progymnasmata: Greek Textbooks of Prose Composition and Rhetoric* (Atlanta: Society of Biblical Literature, 2003).

5 Ray E. Nadeau, "The Progymnasmata of Aphthonius in Translation," *Speech Monographs* 19 (1952): 264–85; revised by Patricia B. Matsen in *Readings from Classical Rhetoric*, ed. Patricia B. Matsen, Philip Rollinson, and Marion Sousa (Carbondale: Southern Illinois University Press, 1999), 266–88. J. R. Butts, "*Progymnasmata* of Theon."

6 Cf. Michael W. Martin and Mikeal C. Parsons, review of *Progymnasmata: Greek Textbooks of Prose Composition and Rhetoric*, ed. and trans. George A. Kennedy, *RBL* 08/2003, repr. *JBL* 123 (2004): 180–83.

7 Kennedy, *Progymnasmata*, ix.

8 Aristotle's *Poetics* is more commonly engaged by modern literary theorists; but the progymnasmata were read by virtually all the better educated and had far more influence.

9 On the "implied" reader, see Wolfgang Iser, *The Implied Reader: Patterns of Communication in Prose Fiction from Bunyan to Beckett* (Baltimore: Johns Hopkins University Press, 1974); on the "ideal narrative reader" and "authorial audience," Peter J. Rabinowitz, "Truth in Fiction:

A Reexamination of Audiences," *Critical Inquiry* 4 (1977): 121–41, esp. 126–27; cf. idem, *Before Reading: Narrative Conventions and the Politics of Interpretation* (Ithaca: Cornell University Press, 1987); idem, "Whirl without End: Audience-Oriented Criticism," in *Contemporary Literary Theory*, ed. G. Douglas Atkins (Amherst: University of Massachusetts Press, 1989), 81–100.

10 On ideological criticism, see Sonja K. Foss, *Rhetorical Criticism: Exploration and Practice*, 4th ed. (Long Grove, Ill.: Waveland, 2009), 209–66.

11 For narratological or structuralist literary criticism, see, e.g., Seymour Chatman, *Story and Discourse: Narrative Structure in Fiction and Film* (Ithaca, N.Y.: Cornell University Press, 1978).

12 On "narrative criticism" in biblical studies, see Mark Alan Powell, *What Is Narrative Criticism?* GBSNTS (Minneapolis: Augsburg Fortress, 1990); James L. Resseguie, *Narrative Criticism of the New Testament: An Introduction* (Grand Rapids: Baker, 2005).

13 On this discipline, see E. D. Hirsch Jr., *Validity in Interpretation* (New Haven: Yale University Press, 1967), 68–126; John Frow, *Genre: The New Critical Idiom* (New York: Routledge, 2006); in biblical studies, Kenton L. Sparks, "Genre Criticism," in *Methods for Exodus*, ed. Thomas R. Dozeman (New York: Cambridge University Press, 2010), 55–94.

14 On these forms of criticism, see Charles H. Talbert, "Gospels, Critical Study of," *MDB*, 343–46.

15 See the criticisms, e.g., of R. Dean Anderson Jr., *Ancient Rhetorical Theory and Paul*, Contributions to Biblical Exegesis and Theology 18 (Kampen: Pharos, 1996), 109; cf. Jerome Murphy-O'Connor, *Paul the Letter-Writer: His World, His Options, His Skills*, Good News Studies 41 (Collegeville, Minn.: Liturgical Press, 1995), 77–86. The question remains hotly debated and can be adjudicated only with reference to the handbooks.

16 On the Gospels and Greco-Roman biography or bios, see Charles H. Talbert, *What Is a Gospel? The Genre of the Canonical Gospels* (Philadelphia: Fortress, 1977); Richard A. Burridge, *What Are the Gospels? A Comparison with Graeco-Roman Biography*, 2d ed. (Grand Rapids: Eerdmans, 2004).

17 Burridge, *What Are the Gospels?* 124–25.

18 See again ch. 3 on narrative; also, Philip L. Shuler, "The Genre(s) of the Gospels," in *Interrelations of the Gospels*, ed. David Laird Dungan (Louvain: Leuven University Press, 1990), 459–83; idem, *A Genre for the Gospels: The Biographical Character of Matthew* (Philadelphia: Fortress, 1982), 53–56, 92–98; Michael W. Martin, "Progymnastic Topic Lists: A Compositional Template for Luke and Other *Bioi?*," *NTS* 54 (2008): 18–41; Mikeal C. Parsons, *Luke*, PCNT (Grand Rapids: Baker Academic, 2015), 13–16.

19 See Lausberg, *Handbook of Literary Rhetoric*, §§260–61 (incl. the offset chart on pp. 122–23).

20 On invention and arrangement, see Lausberg, *Handbook of Literary Rhetoric*, §§260–61 (incl. pp. 122–23).

21 On style, see Lausberg, *Handbook of Literary Rhetoric*, §§453–1082; on memory and delivery respectively, §§1083–90 and §1091. The comparatively sparse discussion devoted to the latter two subjects in Lausberg is reflective of the treatment by the theorists themselves.

22 See, e.g., Aristotle, *Rhet.* 3.9.1–10; Demetrius, *Eloc.* 1–35; cf. John C. Robertson, *The Gorgianic Figures in Early Greek Prose* (Baltimore: Friedenwald, 1893).

23 See Michael W. Martin, "The Poetry of the Lord's Prayer: A Study in Poetic Device," *JBL* 134 (2015): 347–72.

24 The Lord's Prayer is but one example of the latter (see Martin, "The Poetry of the Lord's Prayer," 347–72); many texts considered poetic or hymnic display a similar periodic form.

Bibliography

Adams, Sean A. "Luke and *Progymnasmata*: Rhetorical Handbooks, Rhetorical Sophistication and Genre Selection." Pages 137–63 in *Ancient Education and Early Christianity*. Edited by Matthew Ryan Hauge and Andrew W. Pitts. London: Bloomsbury T&T Clark, 2016.

Adkin, Neil. "'Istae sunt, quae solent dicere': Three Roman Vignettes in Jerome's 'Libellus de virginitate servanda' (*Epist*. 22)." *MH* 39 (1992): 131–40.

Aletti, Jean Nöel. "James 2,14-26: The Arrangement and Its Meaning." *Bib* 95 (2014): 88–101.

Alexander, Philip S. "Physiognomy, Initiation, and Rank in the Qumran Community." Pages 385–94 in *Geschichte—Tradition—Reflexion: Festschrift für Martin Hengel zum 70. Geburtstag. Band I. Judentum*. Edited by Hubert Cancik, Hermann Lichtenberger, and Peter Schäfer. Tübingen: J.C.B. Mohr, 1996.

Allen, Danielle S. "Changing the Authoritative Voice: Lycurgus' 'Against Leocrates.'" *ClAnt* 19 (2000): 5–33.

Alter, Robert. *The Art of Biblical Narrative*. New York: Basic, 1981.

Anderson, R. Dean, Jr. *Ancient Rhetorical Theory and Paul*. Rev. ed. Leuven: Peeters, 1998.

The Ante-Nicene Fathers. Edited by Alexander Roberts and James Donaldson. 1885–1887. 10 vols. Repr. Peabody, Mass.: Hendrickson, 1994.

Aristophanes. *Women at the Thesmophoria: The Complete Greek Drama*. Translated by Eugene O'Neill Jr. New York: Random House, 1938.

Aune, David E. "Asyndeton." *WDNT* 66–67.

———. "The Use and Abuse of the Enthymeme in New Testament Scholarship." *NTS* 49 (2003): 299–320.

Avery-Peck, Alan J. "Rhetorical Argumentation in Early Rabbinic Pronouncement Stories." *Sem* 64 (1993): 49–71.

Babrius and Phaedrus. Translated by Ben Edward Perry. LCL. Cambridge, Mass.: Harvard University Press, 1965.

Baldwin, Charles Sears. *Medieval Rhetoric and Poetic (to 1400) Interpreted from Representative Works*. New York: Macmillan, 1928.

Barnhill, Gregory M. "Seeing Christ through Hearing the Apocalypse: An Exploration of John's Use of Ekphrasis in Revelation 1 and 19." *JSNT* 39 (2017): 235–57.

Barrett, C. K. "The House of Prayer and the Den of Thieves." Pages 13–20 in *Jesus und Paulus: Festschrift für Werner Georg Kümmel zum 70sten Geburtstag*. Edited by E. Earle Ellis and Erich Grässer. Göttingen: Vandenhoeck & Ruprecht, 1975.

Barth, Markus, and Helmut Blanke. *Colossians: A New Translation with Introduction and Commentary*. AB 34B. Translated by Astrid B. Beck. New York: Doubleday, 1994.

Bartsch, Shadi. *Decoding the Ancient Novel: The Reader and the Role of Description in Heliodorus and Achilles Tatius*. Princeton: Princeton University Press, 1989.

Basser, Herbert W. "The Jewish Roots of the Transfiguration." *BRev* 14 (1998): 30–35.

Bates, Matthew W. *The Hermeneutics of the Apostolic Proclamation: The Center of Paul's Method of Scriptural Interpretation*. Waco: Baylor University Press, 2012.

Bauckham, Richard. "James and the Jerusalem Church." Pages 415–80 in *The Book of Acts in Its Palestinian Setting*. Edited by Richard Bauckham. Grand Rapids: Eerdmans, 1995.

Beavis, Mary Ann. "Parable and Fable." *CBQ* 52 (1990): 473–98.

Becker, Andrew Sprague. *The Shield of Achilles and the Poetics of Ekphrasis*. London: Rowman & Littlefield, 1995.

Betz, Hans Dieter. *A Commentary on Paul's Letter to the Churches in Galatia*. Hermeneia. Philadelphia: Fortress, 1989.

Bibb, Charles Wade. "The Characterization of God in Luke-Acts." Ph.D. diss., Southern Baptist Theological Seminary, 1996.

Black, Clifton C., II. "The Rhetorical Form of the Hellenistic Jewish and Early Christian Sermon: A Response to Lawrence Wills." *HTR* 81 (1988): 1–18.

Bock, Darrell L. *Luke*. 2 vols. BECNT. Grand Rapids: Baker Academic, 1994–1996.

Bonner, S. F. *Education in Ancient Rome*. Berkeley: University of California Press, 1977.

Bornkamm, Günther. "Das Bekenntnis im Hebräerbrief." Pages 188–203 in *Studien zu Antike und Urchristentum: Gesammelte Aufsätze*. Vol. 2. Edited by Günther Bornkamm. BEvT28. Munich: Kaiser, 1963.

Boucher, Madeline. *The Mysterious Parable: A Literary Study*. CQMS 6. Washington, D.C.: Catholic Biblical Association of America, 1977.

Branham, R. Bracht. "Authorizing Humor: Lucian's Demonax and Cynic Rhetoric." *Sem* 64 (1993): 33–48.

Braun, Willi. *Feasting and Social Rhetoric in Luke 14*. SNTSMS 85. Cambridge: Cambridge University Press, 1995.

Brauw, Michael de. "The Parts of the Speech." Pages 187–202 in *A Companion to Greek Rhetoric*. Edited by Ian Worthington. Malden, Mass.: Blackwell, 2007.

Brobst-Renaud, Amanda. "The Elder Brother's Quandary and the Rich Man's Fate: Ancient Characterization, Rhetoric, and Moral Formation in Luke's Parables." Ph.D. diss., Baylor University, 2018.

Brookins, Timothy A. "Luke's Use of Mark as παράφρασις: Its Effects on Characterization in the 'Healing of Blind Bartimaeus' Pericope (Mark 10:46-52/Luke 18:35-43)." *JSNT* 34 (2011): 70–89.

Brown, Raymond E. *The Death of the Messiah: From Gethsemane to the Grave: A Commentary on the Passion Narratives in the Four Gospels*. 2 vols. New York: Doubleday, 1994.

Bruss, Kristine S. "Persuasive Ethopoeia in Dionysius' *Lysias*." *Rhetorica* 31 (2013): 34–57.

Bultmann, Rudolf. *The History of the Synoptic Tradition*. 2d ed. Translated by John Marsh. Oxford: Blackwell, 1968.

Burke, Sean D. *Queering the Ethiopian Eunuch: Strategies of Ambiguity in Acts*. Minneapolis: Fortress, 2013.

Burridge, Richard A. *What Are the Gospels? A Comparison with Graeco-Roman Biography*. 2d ed. Grand Rapids: Eerdmans, 2004.

Butts, James R. "The *Progymnasmata* of Theon: A New Text with Translation and Commentary." Ph.D. diss., Claremont Graduate School, 1986.

Callimachus. *Hymns and Epigrams*. Translated by A. W. Mair. LCL. Cambridge, Mass.: Harvard University Press, 2006.

Carroll, John T. *Luke: A Commentary*. NTL. Louisville: Westminster John Knox, 2012.

Charlesworth, James H., trans. *Earliest Christian Psalmbook: The Odes of Solomon*. Eugene, Oreg.: Cascade, 2009.

Chatman, Seymour. *Story and Discourse Narrative Structure in Fiction and Film*. Ithaca, N.Y.: Cornell University Press, 1978.

Church, Alfred John, and William Jackson Brodribb, trans. *The Annals of Tacitus*. London: Macmillan, 1921.

Cicero. Translated by Harry Caplan et al. 20 vols. LCL. Cambridge, Mass.: Harvard University Press, 2000.

Clark, D. L. *Rhetoric in Graeco-Roman Education*. New York: Columbia University Press, 1957.

Collins, John J. "Joseph and Aseneth: Jewish or Christian?" *JSP* 14 (2005): 97–112.

Collins, Raymond F. *First Corinthians*. SacPag 7. Collegeville, Minn.: Liturgical Press, 1999.

Corbett, Edward P. J., and Robert J. Connors. *Classical Rhetoric for the Modern Student*. 4th ed. New York: Oxford University Press, 1998.

Cribiore, Raffaella. *Gymnastics of the Mind: Greek Education in Hellenistic and Roman Egypt*. Princeton: Princeton University Press, 2001.

———. *Writing, Teachers, and Students in Graeco-Roman Egypt*. Atlanta: Scholars Press, 1996.

Crossan, J. D. "Seed Parables of Jesus." *JBL* 92 (1973): 244–66.

Cook, John Granger. "Crucifixion as Spectacle in Roman Campania." *NovT* 54 (2012): 68–100.

———. "Envisioning Crucifixion: Light from Several Inscriptions and the Palatine Graffito." *NovT* 50 (2008): 262–85.

Culpepper, R. Alan. "Luke." Pages 1–490 in *The New Interpreter's Bible*. Vol. 9. Nashville: Abingdon, 1995.

Danker, Frederick W. *Jesus and the New Age: A Commentary on St. Luke's Gospel*. Philadelphia: Fortress, 1988.

Darr, John A. *On Character Building: The Reader and the Rhetoric of Characterization in Luke-Acts*. Louisville, Ky.: Westminster John Knox Press, 1992.

Davies, W. D., and Dale C. Allison. *A Critical and Exegetical Commentary on the Gospel according to Saint Matthew*. 3 vols. ICC. Edinburgh: T&T Clark, 1997.

Deichgräber, Reinhard. *Gotteshymnus und Christushymnus in der frühen Christenheit*. SUNT 5. Göttingen: Vandenhoeck & Ruprecht, 1967.

DeLacy, Philip. "Review of Physiognomics in the Ancient World by Elizabeth C. Evans." *AJP* 92 (1971): 508–10.

Demosthenes. Translated by A. T. Murray et al. 7 vols. LCL. Cambridge, Mass.: Harvard University Press, 1936.

deSilva, David A. *Perseverence in Gratitude: A Socio-rhetorical Commentary on the Epistle to the Hebrews*. Grand Rapids: Eerdmans, 2000.

Dillon, John, and Tania Gergel, trans. *The Greek Sophists*. New York: Penguin, 2003.

Diogenes Laertius. *Lives of Eminent Philosophers*. Translated by R. D. Hicks. 2 vols. LCL. Cambridge, Mass.: Harvard University Press, 2006.

Dionysius of Halicarnassus. Translated by Earnest Cary and Stephen Usher. 9 vols. LCL. Cambridge, Mass.: Harvard University Press, 2001.

Dodd, C. H. *Parables of the Kingdom*. Rev. ed. New York: Scribner, 1961.

Dodson, Derek S. *Reading Dreams: An Audience-Critical Approach to the Dreams in the Gospel of Matthew*. LNTS 397. London: T&T Clark, 2009.

Dodson, Joseph R. *The "Powers" of Personification: Rhetorical Purpose in the "Book of Wisdom" and the Letter to the Romans*. Berlin: Walter de Gruyter, 2008.

Dowd, Sharyn. *Reading Mark: A Literary and Theological Commentary on the Second Gospel*. Macon, Ga.: Smyth & Helwys, 2000.

Duncan, John D. "Adaptation and Alienation: Speakers' Sensitivity to Audiences in the Rhetorical Handbooks, Ancient Greek Narrative Works, and the Book of Acts." Ph.D. diss., Baylor University, forthcoming.

Edwards, M. J. *Galatians, Ephesians, Philippians*. ACC 8. Downers Grove, Ill.: InterVarsity, 1998.

Edwards, Mark W. *Homer: Poet of the Iliad*. Baltimore: Johns Hopkins University Press, 1987.

Elliot, John H. *1 Peter*. AB 37B. New York: Doubleday, 2000.

Erbse, Hartmut. "Die Bedeutung der Synkrisis in den Parallelbiographien Plutarchs." *Hermes* 84 (1956): 398–424.

Eriksson, Anders. "Elaboration of Argument in 1 Cor 15:20-34." *Svensk exegetisk årsbok* 64 (1999): 101–14.

Eusebius. *The Ecclesiastical History*. Translated by Kirsopp Lake. 2 vols. LCL. Cambridge, Mass.: Harvard University Press, 1998.

Evans, Craig A. "Parables in Early Judaism." Pages 51–75 in *The Challenge of Jesus' Parables*. Edited by Richard N. Longenecker. Grand Rapids: Eerdmans, 2000.

Felten, J., ed. *Nicolai Progymnasmata*. Rhetores Graeci 11. Leizpig: Teubner, 1913.

Fischel, Henry A. "Studies in Cynicism and the Ancient Near East: The Transformation of a Chria." Pages 372–411 in *Religions in Antiquity: Essays in Memory of E. R. Goodenough*. Edited by Jacob Neusner. Leiden: Brill, 1968.

Fitzmyer, Joseph A. *The Gospel according to Luke*. AB 28–28A. Garden City, N.Y.: Doubleday, 1981–1985.

Focke, Friedrich. "Synkrisis." *Hermes* 58 (1923): 327–68.

Foerster, Richard, ed. *Scriptores Physiognomonici Graeci et Latini*. 2 vols. Leipzig: Teubner, 1893.

Forbes, Christopher. "Comparison, Self-Praise, and Irony: Paul's Boasting and the Conventions of Hellenistic Rhetoric." *NTS* 32 (1986): 1–30.

———. "Paul and Rhetorical Comparison." Pages 134–71 in *Paul in the Greco-Roman World: A Handbook*. Edited by J. Paul Sampley. New York: Trinity Press International, 2003.

Foss, Sonja K. *Rhetorical Criticism: Exploration and Practice*. 4th ed. Long Grove, Ill.: Waveland, 2009.

Frow, John. *Genre: The New Critical Idiom*. New York: Routledge, 2006.

Funk, Robert W., Bernard Brandon Scott, and James R. Butts. *The Parables of Jesus: Red Letter Edition: The Jesus Seminar*. Sonoma, Calif.: Polebridge, 1988.

Funk, Robert W., Row W. Hoover, and the Jesus Seminar. *The Five Gospels: The Search for the Authentic Words of Jesus*. New York: Polebridge, 1993.

Furnish, Victor. *2 Corinthians: A New Translation with Introduction and Commentary*. AB 32A. New York: Doubleday, 1984.

Frankemölle, Hubert. *Der Brief des Jakobus*. Gütersloh: Gütersloher Verlagshaus, 1994.

Garland, David E. *Luke*. Grand Rapids: Zondervan, 2011.

Garrett, Susan R. *The Demise of the Devil: Magic and the Demonic in Luke's Writings*. Minneapolis: Fortress, 1989.

Gathercole, Simon. *The Composition of the Gospel of Thomas: Original Language and Influences*. SNTSMS 151. New York: Cambridge University Press, 2012.

———. "Jesus' Eschatological Vision of the Fall of Satan: Luke 10,18 Reconsidered." *ZNW* 94 (2003): 145–58.

Geldenhuys, Norval. *Commentary on the Gospel of Luke*. Grand Rapids: Eerdmans, 1951.

George, A. "Le parallèle entre Jean-Baptiste et Jésus en Luc 1–2." Pages 147–71 in *Mélanges Béda Rigaux*. Edited by A. Descamps and A. de Halleux. Gembloux, Belgium: Duculot, 1970.

Giannontoni, Gabriele, ed. *Socratis et Socraticorum reliquiae*. 4 vols. Napoli: Bibliopolis, 1990.

Gibson, Craig. "Better Living through Prose Composition? Moral and Compositional Pedagogy in Ancient Greek and Roman Progymnasmata." *Rhetorica* 32 (2014): 1–30.

———. "*Prosopopoeia* in the New Testament: Where Should We Look, and What Should We Expect to Find?" Paper presented at the Annual Meeting of the Society of Biblical Literature, Philadelphia, November, 2005.

Gleason, Maud. *Making Men: Sophists and Self-Presentation in Ancient Rome*. Princeton: Princeton University Press, 1995.

Goldhill, Simon. "What Is Ekphrasis For?" *CP* 102 (2007): 1–19.

Goodacre, Mark. *Thomas and the Gospels: The Case for Thomas' Familiarity with the Synoptics*. Grand Rapids: Eerdmans, 2012.

Gregg, Robert C. *Athanasius: The Life of Antony and Letter to Marcellinus*. Mahway, N.J.: Paulist Press, 1980.

Gundry, Robert H. *Mark: A Commentary on His Apology for the Cross*. Grand Rapids: Eerdmans, 1993.

———. *Matthew: A Commentary on His Handbook for a Mixed Church under Persecution*. 2d ed. Grand Rapids: Eerdmans, 1994.

Gunkel, Hermann. *Psalms: A Form-Critical Introduction*. Translated by Thomas M. Horner. FBBS 19. Philadelphia: Fortress, 1967.

Güting, Eberhard W., and David L. Mealand. *Asyndeton in Paul: A Text-Critical and Stylistical Enquiry into Pauline Style*. Lewiston, Idaho: Edwyn Mellen, 1998.

Harrison, James R. "The Seven Sages, the Delphic Canon and Ethical Education in Antiquity." Pages 71–86 in *Ancient Education and Early Christianity*. Edited by Matthew Ryan Hauge and Andrew W. Pitts. London: Bloomsbury T&T Clark, 2016.

Hays, Christopher M. *Luke's Wealth Ethics: A Study in Their Coherence and Characterization*. WUNT 2/275. Tübingen: Mohr Siebeck, 2010.

Heath, Malcolm. "Theon and the History of the Progymnasmata." *GRBS* 43 (2002/2003): 129–60.

Hedrick, Charles H. "Conceiving the Narrative: Colors in Achilles Tatius and the Gospel of Mark." Pages 177–97 in *Ancient Fiction and Early Christian Narrative*. Edited by R. Hock, B. Chance, and J. Perkins. Atlanta: Scholars Press, 1998.

Henderson, Ian H. "Quintilian and the Progymnasmata." *Antike und Abendland* 37 (1991): 82–99.

Henten, Jan Willem van. "Commonplaces in Herod's Commander Speech in Josephus' *A.J.* 15.127–146." Pages 183–206 in *Josephus and Jewish History in Flavian Rome and Beyond*. Edited by Joseph Sievers and Gaia Lembi. SJSJ. Leiden: Brill, 2005.

———. "Josephus, Fifth Evangelist, and Jesus on the Temple." *HTS* 71 (2015): 1–11.

Hester, J. D. "The Use and Influence of Rhetoric in Galatians 2:1-14." *ThZ* 42 (1986): 386–408.

Hezer, Catherine. *Jewish Literacy in Roman Palestine*. WUNT 81. Tübingen: Mohr Siebeck, 2001.

———. "The Torah versus Homer: Jewish and Greco-Roman Education in Late Roman Palestine." Pages 5–24 in *Ancient Education and Early Christianity*. Edited by Matthew Ryan Hauge and Andrew W. Pitts. London: Bloomsbury T&T Clark, 2016.

Hirsch, E. D., Jr. *Validity in Interpretation*. New Haven: Yale University Press, 1967.

Hock, Ronald F. "Homer in Greco-Roman Education." Pages 56–77 in *Mimesis and Intertextuality in Antiquity and Christianity*. Edited by Dennis R. MacDonald. Harrisburg, Pa.: Trinity Press International, 2001.

———. "Observing a Teacher of *Progymnasmata*." Pages 39–70 in *Ancient Education and Early Christianity*. Edited by Matthew Ryan Hauge and Andrew W. Pitts. London: Bloomsbury T&T Clark, 2016.

———. "Paul and Greco-Roman Education." Pages 198–227 in *Paul and the Greco-Roman World: A Handbook*. Edited by J. Paul Sampley. Harrisburg, Pa.: Trinity Press International, 2003.

———, trans. and ed. *The Chreia and Ancient Rhetoric: Commentaries on Aphthonius' Progymnasmata*. WGRW 31. Atlanta: Society of Biblical Literature, 2012.

Hock, Ronald F., and Edward N. O'Neil, trans. and eds. *The Chreia and Ancient Rhetoric: Classroom Exercises*. WGRW 2. Atlanta: Society of Biblical Literature, 2002.

———, trans. and eds. *The Chreia in Ancient Rhetoric*. Vol. 1. *The Progymnasmata*. SBLTT 27. Atlanta: Scholars Press, 1986.

Hogan, Derek. "Paul's Defense: A Comparison of the Forensic Speeches in Acts, *Callirhoe*, and *Leucippe and Clitophon*." *PRSt* 29 (2002): 73–87.

Holzmeister, Angela. "Ekphrasis in the Ancient Novel." Pages 411–23 in *A Companion to the Ancient Novel*. Edited by Edmund P. Cueva and Shannon N. Byrne. Oxford: Wiley Blackwell's, 2014.

Homer. *The Iliad*. Translated by A. T. Murray. Translation revised by William F. Wyatt. 2 vols. LCL. Cambridge, Mass.: Harvard University Press, 1999.

Horrell, David G., Bradley Arnold, and Travis B. Williams. "Visuality, Vivid Description, and the Message of 1 Peter: The Significance of the Roaring Lion (1 Peter 5:8)." *JBL* 132 (2013): 697–716.

Horton, Fred L. *The Melchizedek Tradition: A Critical Examination of the Sources to the Fifth Century A.D. and in the Epistle to the Hebrews*. SNTSMS 30. Cambridge: Cambridge University Press, 1976.

Howell, Justin. "Embedded Letters and Rhetorical αὔξησις." Pages 154–80 in *Contemporary Studies in Acts*. Edited by Thomas E. Philips. Macon, Ga.: Mercer University Press, 2009.

Humphrey, Edith M. *And I Turned to See the Voice: The Rhetoric of Vision in the New Testament*. Grand Rapids: Baker Academic, 2007.

Irmscher, Johannes, and Georg Strecker. "The Pseudo-Clementines." Pages 483–541 in *New Testament Apocrypha*. Volume Two: *Writings Relating to the Apostles; Apocalypses and Related Subjects*. Edited by Wilhelm Schneemelcher. Translated by R. McL. Wilson. Rev. ed. Louisville, Ky.: Westminster John Knox, 1992.

Iser, Wolfgang. *The Implied Reader: Patterns of Communication in Prose Fiction from Bunyan to Beckett*. Baltimore: Johns Hopkins University Press, 1974.

Jeremias, Joachim. *The Parables of Jesus*. Rev. ed. Translated by S. H. Hooke. New York: Charles Scribner's Sons, 1962.

Jewett, Robert. *Romans: A Commentary*. Minneapolis: Fortress, 2007.

John Chrysostom. *Discourses against Judaizing Christians*. Translated by Paul W. Harkins. FC 68. Washington, D.C.: Catholic University of America Press, 1979.

Johnson, Luke Timothy. *The Literary Function of Possessions in Luke-Acts*. SBLDS 39. Missoula, Mont.: Scholars Press, 1977.

Josephus. Translated by H. St. J. Thackeray et al. 13 vols. LCL. Cambridge, Mass.: Harvard University Press, 2004.

Jülicher, Adolf. *Die Gleichnisreden Jesu*. 2 vols. Tübingen: J.C.B. Mohr, 1888–1899.

Just, Arthur A. *Luke*. 2 vols. St. Louis: Concordia, 1996–1997.

Karris, Robert J. *Luke: Artist and Theologian: Luke's Passion Account as Literature*. New York: Paulist, 1985.

Keck, Leander E. "The Spirit and the Dove." *NTS* 17 (1970): 41–67.

Kee, H. C. "Testament of the Twelve Patriarchs: A New Translation and Introduction." Pages 775–828 in volume 1 of *Old Testament Pseudepigrapha*. Edited by James Charlesworth. 2 vols. London: Darton, Longman & Todd, 1983.

Kennedy, George A. *New Testament Interpretation through Rhetorical Criticism*. Chapel Hill: University of North Carolina Press, 1984.

———. *On Rhetoric: A Theory of Civic Discourse*. 2d ed. Oxford: Oxford University Press, 2006.

———, trans. *Progymnasmata: Greek Textbooks of Prose Composition and Rhetoric*. Atlanta: Society of Biblical Literature, 2003.

———. "The Speeches in Acts." Pages 114–40 in *New Testament Interpretation through Rhetorical Criticism*. Chapel Hill: University of North Carolina Press, 1984.
Kindstrand, Jan Fredrik. "Diogenes Laertius and the 'Chreia' Tradition." *Elenchos* 7 (1986): 217–43.
King, Justin. "Speech-in-Character, Diatribe, and Romans 3:1-9: Who's Speaking When and Why It Matters." Ph.D. diss., Baylor University, 2016.
Klauck, Hans-Josef. *Ancient Letters and the New Testament: A Guide to Context and Exegesis*. Waco: Baylor University Press, 2006.
Kloppenborg, John S. "The Reception of the Jesus Traditions in James." Pages 94–141 in *The Catholic Epistles and the Tradition*. Edited by J. Schlosser. Leuven: Leuven University Press, 2004.
Koester, Craig R. *Hebrews: A New Translation with Introduction and Commentary*. AB 36. New York: Doubleday, 2001.
Koester, Helmut. "The Gospel of Thomas." Pages 124–26 in *The Nag Hammadi Library in English*. Edited by James M. Robinson. San Francisco: Harper, 1990.
Kouklanakis, Andrea. "Thersites, Odysseus, and the Social Order." Pages 35–54 in *Nine Essays on Homer*. Edited by Miriam Carlisle and Olga Levaniouk. Lanham, Md.: Rowman & Littlefield, 1999.
Kraus, Manfred. "Theories and Practice of the Enthymeme in the First Centuries B.C.E. and C.E." Pages 95–111 in *Rhetorical Argumentation in Biblical Texts: Essays from the Lund 2000 Conference*. Edited by Anders Eriksson, Thomas H. Olbricht, and Walter Übelacker. Harrisburg, Pa.: Trinity Press International, 2002.
Larmour, David H. J. "Making Parallels: *Synkrisis* and Plutarch's 'Themistocles and Camillus.'" *ANRW* 33.6:4154–200. Part 2: *Principat*, 33.6. Edited by Hildegard Temporini and Wolfgang Haase. New York: Walter de Gruyter, 1992.
Lausberg, Heinrich. *Handbook of Literary Rhetoric: A Foundation for Literary Study*. Leiden: Brill, 1998.
Lindenberger, J. M. "Ahiqar: A New Translation and Introduction." *OTP* 2:479–80.
Long, Jesse. "Wrestling with God to Win: A Literary Reading of the Story of Jacob at the Jabbok in Honor of Don Williams." *SCJ* 15 (2012): 47–61.
Longenecker, Bruce W., ed. *Narrative Dynamics in Paul: A Critical Assessment*. Louisville, Ky.: Westminster John Knox, 2002.
Luce, T. J. *Livy: The Composition of His History*. Princeton: Princeton University Press, 1977.
Mack, Burton L. *Anecdotes and Arguments: The Chreia in Antiquity and Early Christianity*. Claremont, Calif.: Institute for Antiquity and Christianity, 1987.
———. "Decoding the Scripture: Philo and the Rules of Rhetoric." Pages 21–115 in *Nourished with Peace: Studies in Hellenistic Judaism in Memory of Samuel Sandmel*. Edited by Frederick E. Greenspahn, Earle Hilgert, and Burton L. Mack. Chico, Calif.: Scholars Press, 1984.
———. *Rhetoric and the New Testament*. GBS. Minneapolis: Fortress, 1990.
Mack, Burton L., and Vernon K. Robbins. *Patterns of Persuasion in the Gospels*. Sonoma, Calif.: Polebridge, 1989.
Maier, Harry O. *Picturing Paul in Empire: Imperial Image, Text and Persuasion in Colossians, Ephesians and the Pastoral Epistles*. London: T&T Clark, 2013.
———. "Vision, Visualization, and Politics in the Apostle Paul." *MTSR* 27 (2015): 312–32.

Malherbe, Abraham. *The Letters to the Thessalonians: A New Translation with Introduction and Commentary*. AB 32B. New York: Doubleday, 2000.

Malina, Bruce J., and Jerome H. Neyrey. "Honor and Shame in Luke-Acts: Pivotal Values for the Mediterranean World." Pages 25–65 in *The Social World of Luke-Acts: Models for Interpretation*. Edited by Jerome H. Neyrey. Peabody, Mass.: Hendrickson, 1991.

———, and Jerome H. Neyrey. *Portraits of Paul: An Archaeology of Ancient Personality*. Louisville: Westminster John Knox, 1996.

Manson, T. W. *The Teaching of Jesus: Studies in Form and Content*. Cambridge: Cambridge University Press, 1931.

Marcus, Joel. "Jesus' Baptismal Vision." *NTS* 41 (1995): 512–21.

Marrou, H. I. *A History of Education in Antiquity*. London: Sheed & Ward, 1956.

Marshall, I. Howard. *The Gospel of Luke: A Commentary on the Greek Text*. Grand Rapids: Eerdmans, 1978.

Marshall, Peter. *Enmity in Corinth: Social Conventions in Paul's Relations with the Corinthians*. WUNT 2/23. Tübingen: Mohr, 1987.

Martin, Michael W. "Philo's Use of Syncrisis: An Examination of Philonic Composition in the Light of the Progymnasmata." *PRSt* 30 (2003): 271–97.

———. "The Poetry of the Lord's Prayer: A Study in Poetic Device." *JBL* 134 (2015): 347–72.

———. "Progymnastic Topic Lists: A Compositional Template for Luke and Other *Bioi*." *NTS* 54 (2008): 18–41.

Martin, Michael W., and Bryan A. Nash. "Philippians 2:6-11 as Subversive *Hymnos*: A Study in the Light of Ancient Rhetorical Design." *JTS* 66 (2008): 90–138.

Martin, Michael W., and Mikeal C. Parsons. Review of *Progymnasmata: Greek Textbooks of Prose Composition and Rhetoric*, ed. and trans. George A. Kennedy. *RBL* 08/2003, repr. *JBL* 123 (2004): 180–83.

Martin, Michael W., and Jason A. Whitlark. "Choosing What Is Advantageous: The Relationship between Epideictic and Deliberative Syncrisis in Hebrews." *NTS* 58 (2012): 379–400.

———. "The Encomiastic Topics of Syncrisis as the Key to the Structure and Argument of Hebrews." *NTS* 57 (2011): 415–39.

———. *Inventing Hebrews: Design and Purpose in Ancient Rhetoric*. Cambridge: Cambridge University Press, forthcoming in 2018.

Martin, Ralph P. *A Hymn of Christ: Philippians 2:5-11 in Recent Interpretation & in the Setting of Early Christian Worship*. Downer's Grove, Ill.: InterVarsity, 1997.

Martin, Troy W., ed. *Genealogies of New Testament Rhetorical Criticism*. Minneapolis: Fortress, 2014.

Martínez, Florentino García, ed. *The Dead Sea Scrolls Translated: The Qumran Texts in English*. Translated by Wilfred G. E. Watson. Leiden: Brill, 1992.

Martínez, Florentino García, and Eibert J. C. Tigchelaar, eds. *The Dead Sea Scrolls Study Edition: Volume One IQI-4Q273*. Leiden: Brill, 1997.

Martyn, J. Louis. *Galatians: A New Translation with Introduction and Commentary*. AB 33A. New York: Doubleday, 1997.

Mason, Eric F. *"You Are a Priest Forever": Second Temple Jewish Messianism and the Priestly Christology of the Epistle to the Hebrews*. STDJ 74. Leiden: Brill, 2008.

Matsen, Patricia B., Philip Rollinson, and Marion Sousa, eds. *Readings from Classical Rhetoric*. Carbondale: Southern Illinois University Press, 1999.

McArthur, Harvey K., and Robert M. Johnston. *They Also Taught in Parables*. Grand Rapids: Zondervan, 1990.

McConnell, James. *The Topos of Divine Testimony in Luke-Acts*. Eugene, Oreg.: Wipf and Stock, 2014.

McGaughy, Lane C. "Pagan Hellenistic Literature: The Babrian Fables." Pages 205–14 in *Society of Biblical Literature 1977 Seminar Papers*. SBLSPS 11. Missoula, Mont.: Scholars Press, 1977.

Mellor, Ronald. *The Roman Historians*. New York: Routledge, 1999.

Meyer, Paul W. "The Worm at the Core of the Apple: Exegetical Reflections on Romans 7." Pages 57–77 in *The Conversation Continues: Studies in Paul and John in Honor of J. Louis Martyn*. Edited by Robert T. Fortna and Beverly Roberts Gaventa. Nashville: Abingdon, 1990.

Misener, Geneva. "Iconistic Portraits." *CP* 19 (1924): 97–123.

Mitchell, Margaret. "Le style, c'est l'homme: Aesthetics and Apologetics in the Stylistic Analysis of the New Testament." *NovT* 51 (2009): 385–86.

Moeser, Marion C. *The Anecdote in Mark, the Classical World and the Rabbis*. London: Sheffield Academic, 2002.

Morales, Helen. *Vision and Narrative in Achilles Tatius' Leucippe and Clitophon*. New York: Cambridge University Press, 2004.

Morgan, Theresa. *Literate Education in the Hellenistic and Roman Worlds*. Cambridge: Cambridge University Press, 1998.

Muir, Steven. "Vivid Imagery in Galatians 3:1—Roman Rhetoric, Street Announcing, Graffiti, and Crucifixions." *BTB* 44 (2014): 76–86.

Müller, Christoph Gregor. *Mehr als ein Prophet. Die Charakterzeichnung Johannes des Täufers im lukanischen Erzählwerk*. Herders Biblische Studien 31. Freiburg: Herder, 2001.

Murphy-O'Connor, Jerome. *Paul the Letter-Writer: His World, His Options, His Skills*. GNS 41. Collegeville, Minn.: Liturgical Press, 1995.

Myers, Alicia D. *Characterizing Jesus: A Rhetorical Analysis on the Fourth Gospel's Use of Scripture in Its Presentation of Jesus*. LNTS 458. London: T&T Clark, 2012.

Nadeau, Ray E. "The *Progymnasmata* of Aphthonius in Translation." *Speech Monographs* 19 (1952): 264–85.

Nash, Bryan A. "Philippians 3:4-11 as Subversive Encomium." *SCJ* 19 (2016): 85–94.

Neyrey, Jerome H. "Encomium versus Vituperation: Contrasting Portraits in the Jesus in the Fourth Gospel." *JBL* 126 (2007): 529–52.

———. "The Forensic Defense Speech and Paul's Trial Speeches in Acts 22–26: Form and Function." Pages 210–24 in *Luke-Acts: New Perspectives from the Society of Biblical Literature Seminar*. Edited by C. H. Talbert. New York: Crossroad, 1984.

———. "Josephus' *Vita* and the Encomium: A Native Model of Personality." *JSJ* 25 (1994): 177–206.

———. "Questions, Chreiai, and Challenges to Honor: The Interface of Rhetoric and Culture in Mark's Gospel." *CBQ* 60 (1998): 657–81.

———. "The Symbolic Universe of Luke-Acts: 'They Turn the World Upside Down.' Pages 271–304 in *The Social World of Luke-Acts: Models for Interpretation*. Peabody, Mass.: Hendrickson, 1991.

The Nicene and Post-Nicene Fathers. Series 2. Edited by Philip Schaff and Henry Wace. 1890–1900. 14 vols. Repr. Peabody, Mass.: Hendrickson, 1994.

Nolland, John. *Luke*. 3 vols. WBC. Dallas: Word, 1989–1993.

Oakes, Peter. "Re-mapping the Universe: Paul and the Emperor in 1 Thessalonians and Philippians." *JSNT* 27 (2005): 301–22.

O'Fearghail, Fearghus. *The Introduction to Luke-Acts: A Study of the Role of Luke 1,1–4,44 in the Composition of Luke's Two-Volume Work*. AnBib 126. Rome: Pontifical Biblical Institute, 1991.

Padilla, Osvaldo. "Hellenistic Paideia and Luke's Education: A Critique of Recent Approaches." *NTS* 55 (2009): 416–37.

Parsons, Mikeal C. *Acts*. PCNT. Grand Rapids: Baker Academic, 2012.

———. *Body and Character in Luke and Acts: The Subversion of Physiognomy in Early Christianity*. Waco: Baylor University Press, 2010.

———. *Luke*. PCNT. Grand Rapids: Baker Academic, 2015.

———. "Luke and the Progymnasmata: A Preliminary Investigation into the Preliminary Exercises." Pages 43–63 in *Contextualizing Acts: Lukan Narrative and Greco-Roman Discourse*. Edited by Todd Penner and Caroline Vander Stichele. SBLSS 20. Atlanta: Scholars Press, 2004.

———. "Mark 2:23-28." *Int* 59 (2005): 57–60.

Parsons, P. J. "A School-Book from the Sayce Collection." *ZPE* 6 (1970): 133–49.

Patillon, Michel, ed. *Aelius Théon. Progymnasmata*. Paris: Les Belles Lettres, 1997.

Pau, David W. *Acts and the Isaianic New Exodus*. WUNT 2/130. Eugene, Oreg.: Wipf and Stock, 2000.

Pelling, Christopher. *Plutarch and History: Eighteen Studies*. London: Duckworth; Swansea: Classical Press of Wales, 2002.

Penner, Todd. "Reconfiguring the Rhetorical Study of Acts: Reflections on the Method in and Learning of a Progymnastic Poetics." *PRSt* 30 (2003): 425–39.

Peterson, David. *Hebrews and Perfection: An Examination of the Concept of Perfection in the "Epistle to the Hebrews."* SNTSMS 47. New York: Cambridge University Press, 1982.

Philo. Translated by F. H. Colson et al. 12 vols. LCL. Cambridge, Mass.: Harvard University Press, 2004.

Philostratus. Translated by Christopher P. Jones et al. 5 vols. LCL. Cambridge, Mass.: Harvard University Press, 2005.

Plutarch. Translated by Bernadotte Perrin. 11 vols. LCL. Cambridge, Mass.: Harvard University Press, 2005.

Polybius. *Histories*. Translated by Evelyn S. Shuckburgh. 2 vols. New York: Macmillan, 1889.

Polybius. *The Histories*. Translated by W. R. Paton. 6 vols. LCL. Cambridge, Mass.: Harvard University Press, 2005.

Porter, Stanley, ed. *Handbook of Classical Rhetoric in the Hellenistic Period, 330 B.C.–A.D. 400*. Leiden: Brill, 2001.

Powell, Mark Alan. *What Is Narrative Criticism?* GBSNTS. Minneapolis: Augsburg Fortress, 1990.

Putnam, Michael J. *Virgil's Epic Designs: Ekphrasis in the* Aeneid. New Haven: Yale University Press, 1998.

Quintilian. *The Orator's Education*. Translated by Donald A. Russell. 5 vols. LCL. Cambridge, Mass.: Harvard University Press, 2001.

Rabe, H., ed. *Aphthonii progymnasmata*. Rhetores Graeci 10. Leipzig: Teubner, 1926.

———, ed. *Hermogenes opera*. Rhetores Graeci 10. Leipzig: Teubner, 1913.

———, ed. *Ioannis Sardiani commentarium in Aphthonii progymnasmata*. Leipzig: Teubner, 1928.

Rabinowitz, Peter J. *Before Reading: Narrative Conventions and the Politics of Interpretation*. Ithaca: Cornell University Press, 1987.

———. "Truth in Fiction: A Reexamination of Audiences." *Critical Inquiry* 4 (1977): 121–41.

———. "Whirl without End: Audience-Oriented Criticism." Pages 81–100 in *Contemporary Literary Theory*. Edited by G. Douglas Atkins. Amherst: University of Massachusetts Press, 1989.

Radl, W. *Paulus und Jesus im lukanischen Doppelwerk. Untersuchungen zu Parallelmotiven im Lukasevangelium und in der Apostelgeschichte*. Europisch Hochschulschriften 23.49. Frankfurt: Lang, 1975.

Ramsmaran, Rollin. *Liberating Words: Paul's Use of Rhetorical Maxims in 1 Corinthians 1–10*. Valley Forge, Pa.: Trinity Press International, 1996.

Reardon, B. P., ed. *Collected Ancient Greek Novels*. Berkeley: University of California Press, 2008.

Reeves, Bridget T. "The Role of the Ekphrasis in Plot Development: The Painting of Europa and the Bull in Achilles Tatius' *Leucippe and Clitophon*." *Mnemosyne* 60 (2007): 87–101.

Reich, Keith. *Figuring Jesus: The Power of Rhetorical Figures of Speech in the Gospel of Luke*. BibInt 107. Leiden: Brill, 2011.

Resseguie, James L. *Narrative Criticism of the New Testament: An Introduction*. Grand Rapids: Baker, 2005.

Reynolds, Peter. "Miracle and Mission in Luke: A Rhetorical Analysis of Luke 5:1-11." Ph.D. diss., Baylor University, 2016.

Robbins, Vernon K. "The Chreia." Pages 1–24 in *Greco-Roman Literature and the New Testament: Selected Forms and Genres*. Edited by David E. Aune. Atlanta: Scholars Press, 1988.

———. *Exploring the Texture of the Texts: A Guide to Socio-rhetorical Interpretation*. Philadelphia: Trinity Press International, 1996.

———. "Pronouncement Stories and Jesus' Blessing of the Children: A Rhetorical Approach." *Sem* 29 (1983): 42–74.

———. *The Tapestry of Early Christian Discourse: Rhetoric, Society, and Ideology*. London: Routledge, 1996.

Robertson, A. T. *Word Pictures in the New Testament*. 6 vols. Nashville: Broadman, 1929.

Robertson, Jesse E. *The Death of Judas: The Characterization of Judas Iscariot in Three Early Christian Accounts of His Death*. Sheffield: Sheffield Phoenix, 2012.

Robertson, John C. *The Gorgianic Figures in Early Greek Prose*. Baltimore: Friedenwald, 1893.

Russell, D. A. and N. G. Wilson. *Menander Rhetor*. Oxford: Clarendon, 1981.

Rosenmeyer, Patricia A. *Ancient Epistolary Fictions: The Letter in Greek Literature*. Cambridge: Cambridge University Press, 2001.

———. *Ancient Greek Literary Letters: Selections in Translation*. London: Routledge, 2006.

Sallust. Translated by John T. Ramsey and J. C. Rolfe. 2 vols. LCL. Cambridge, Mass.: Harvard University Press, 2001.

Sanders, E. P. *The Tendencies of the Synoptic Tradition*. SNTSMS 9. New York: Cambridge University Press, 1969.

Satterthwaite, Philip E. "Acts against the Background of Classical Rhetoric." Pages 337–79 in *The Book of Acts in Its Ancient Literary Setting*. Edited by Bruce W. Winter and Andrew D. Clarke. Volume 1 of *The Book of Acts in Its First Century Setting*. Edited by Bruce W. Winter. Grand Rapids: Eerdmans, 1993.

Schiffman, Lawrence. *Reclaiming the Dead Sea Scrolls: The History of Judaism, the Background of Christianity, the Lost Library of Qumran*. Philadelphia: Jewish Publication Society, 1994.

Schneemelcher, Wilhelm, ed. *New Testament Apocrypha*. Volume 2: *Writings Relating to the Apostles; Apocalypses and Related Subjects*. Translated by R. McL. Wilson. Rev. ed. Louisville: Westminster John Knox, 1992.

Seid, Timothy W. "Synkrisis in Hebrews 7: The Rhetorical Structure and Strategy." Pages 322–47 in *The Rhetorical Interpretation of Scripture: Essays from the 1996 Malibu Conference*. Edited by Stanley E. Porter and Dennis L. Stamps. JSNTSup 180. Sheffield: Sheffield Academic Press, 1999.

Sheerin, Daniel. "Rhetorical and Hermeneutic *Synkrisis* in Patristic Typology." Pages 22–39 in *Nova & Vetera: Patristic Studies in Honor of Thomas Patrick Halton*. Edited by John Petruccione. Washington, D.C.: Catholic University of America Press, 1998.

Shellenberg, Ryan S. *Rethinking Paul's Rhetorical Education: Comparative Rhetoric and 2 Corinthians 10–13*. ECL. Atlanta: Society of Biblical Literature, 2013.

Shuler, Philip L. *A Genre for the Gospels: The Biographical Character of Matthew*. Philadelphia: Fortress, 1982.

———. "The Genre(s) of the Gospels." Pages 459–83 in *Interrelations of the Gospels*. Edited by David Laird Dungan. Louvain: Leuven University Press, 1990.

Sider, Catherine. "'His Blood Be upon Us': Innocent Blood and the Death of Jesus in Matthew." *CBQ* 70 (2008): 82–100.

Simons, Robert. "The Magnificat: Cento, Psalm or Imitatio?" *TynBul* 60 (2009): 25–46.

Sinclair, Patrick. "The Sententia in *Rhetorica ad Herennium*: A Study in the Sociology of Rhetoric." *AJP* 114, no. 4 (1993): 561–80.

Small, Brian C. *The Characterization of Jesus in the Book of Hebrews*. BibInt 128. Leiden: Brill, 2014.

Snodgrass, Klyne. *Stories with Intent: A Comprehensive Guide to the Parables of Jesus*. Grand Rapids: Eerdmans, 2008.

Soards, Marion L. "The Speeches in Acts in Relation to Other Pertinent Ancient Literature." *ETL* 70 (1994): 65–90.

———. *The Speeches in Acts: Their Content, Context, and Concerns*. Louisville: Westminster John Knox, 1994.

Southall, David J. *Rediscovering Righteousness in Romans: Personified* dikaiosynē *within Metaphoric and Narratorial Settings*. WUNT 2/240. Tübingen: Mohr Siebeck, 2008.

Sparks, Kenton L. "Genre Criticism." Pages 55–94 in *Methods for Exodus*. Edited by Thomas B. Dozeman. MBI. New York: Cambridge University Press.

Spencer, F. Scott. "The Ethiopian Eunuch and His Bible: A Social Science Analysis." *BTB* 22 (1992): 155–65.

Spengel, Leonard, ed. *Rhetores Graeci*. 3 vols. Leipzig: Teubner, 1853–1856.

Squires, John T. *The Plan of God in Luke-Acts*. Cambridge: Cambridge University Press, 1993.

Stafford, Emma. *Worshipping Virtues: Personification and the Divine in Ancient Greece*. London: Duckworth, 2000.

Stafford, Emma, and Judith Herrin, eds. *Personification in the Greek World: From Antiquity to Byzantium*. Aldershot: Ashgate, 2005.

Stegman, Thomas. "Reading Luke 12:13-34 as an Elaboration of a Chreia: How Hermogenes of Tarsus Sheds Light on Luke's Gospel." *NovT* 49 (2007): 328–52.

Stern, David. "Jesus' Parables from the Perspective of Rabbinic Literature: The Example of the Wicked Husbandman." Pages 42–82 in *Parable and Story in Judaism and Christianity*. Edited by Clemens Thoma and Michael Wyschogrod. Mahwah, N.J.: Paulist Press, 1989.

———. *Parables and Midrash*. Cambridge, Mass.: Harvard University Press, 1991.

———. "The Rabbinic Parable: From Rhetoric to Poetics." Pages 632–43 in *The Society of Biblical Literature 1986 Seminar Papers*. SBLSPS 25. Atlanta: Scholars Press, 1986.

Stern, Simon, ed. *The Life and Fables of Aesop: A Selection from the Version of Sir Roger L'Estrange*. New York: Taplinger, 1970.

Stigall, Josh. "The Progymnasmata and Characterization in Luke's Parables: The Parable of the Rich Fool as a Test Case." *PRSt* 39 (2012): 349–60.

Stott, Katherine M. *Why Did They Write This Way? Reflections on References to Written Documents in the Hebrew Bible and Ancient Literature*. New York: T&T Clark, 2008.

Strange, W. A. *The Problem of the Text of Acts*. Cambridge: Cambridge University Press, 1992.

Strecker, Georg. "Kerygmata Petrou." Pages 531–41 in *New Testament Apocrypha*. Volume 2: *Writings Relating to the Apostles; Apocalypses and Related Subjects*. Edited by Wilhelm Schneemelcher. Translated by R. McL. Wilson. Rev. ed. Louisville, Ky.: Westminster John Knox, 1992.

Suetonius. *Lives of the Caesars*. Translated by J. C. Rolfe. 2 vols. LCL. Cambridge, Mass.: Harvard University Press, 1998.

Swain, Simon. *Seeing the Face, Seeing the Soul: Polemon's* Physiognomy *from Classical Antiquity to Medieval Islam*. New York: Oxford University Press, 2007.

Tacitus. Translated by M. Hutton et al. 5 vols. LCL. Cambridge, Mass.: Harvard University Press, 2006.

Talbert, Charles H. "Gospels, Critical Study of." *MDB* 343–46.

———. *Reading John: A Literary and Theological Commentary on the Fourth Gospel and Johannine Epistles*. RNT 4. Macon, Ga.: Smyth and Helwys, 2005.

———. *What Is a Gospel? The Genre of the Canonical Gospels*. Philadelphia: Fortress, 1977.

Tannehill, Robert C. *The Narrative Unity of Luke-Acts: A Literary Interpretation*. 2 vols. Philadelphia: Fortress, 1986–1990.

Taylor, R. O. P. *The Groundwork of the Gospels*. London: Basil Blackwell, 1946.

Thompson, James W. *Hebrews*. PCNT. Grand Rapids: Baker Academic, 2008.

Thucydides. *History of the Peloponnesian War*. Translated by Charles Forster Smith. 4 vols. LCL. Cambridge, Mass.: Harvard University Press, 2003.

Towner, Philip H. *The Letters to Timothy and Titus*. NICNT. Grand Rapids: Eerdmans, 2006.

Usher, M. D. "Diogenes' Doggerel: Chreia and Quotation in Cynic Performance." *Classical Journal* 104 (2009): 207–23.

Vanhoye, A. *La structure littéraire de l'épître aux Hébreux*. 2d ed. Paris: Desclée de Brower, 1976.

Veltman, F. "The Defense Speeches of Paul in Acts." Pages 243–56 in *Perspectives on Luke-Acts*. Edited by C. H. Talbert. Perspectives in Religions Studies Special Studies Series 5. Macon, Ga.: Mercer University, 1978.

Versnel, H. S. *Triumphus: An Inquiry into the Origin, Development, and Meaning of the Roman Triumph*. Leiden: Brill, 1970.

Walker, William, Jr. *Interpolations in the Pauline Letters*. New York: Sheffield Academic, 2001.

Wallace, Daniel B. *Greek Grammar beyond the Basics: An Exegetical Syntax of the New Testament*. Grand Rapids: Zondervan, 1996.

Waltz, Christian, ed. Rhetores Graeci. 9 volumes. Tübingen: Cottae, 1823–1836.

Watson, Duane F. "Notes on History and Method." Pages 101–25 in *Rhetorical Criticism of the Bible: A Comprehensive Bibliography with Notes on History and Method*. Edited by Duane F. Watson and Alan J. Hauser. BibInt 4. Leiden: E. J. Brill, 1994.

———. "Paul's Speech to the Ephesian Elders (Acts 20.17–38): Epideictic Rhetoric of Farewell." Pages 184–208 in *Persuasive Artistry: Studies in New Testament Rhetoric in Honor of George A. Kennedy*. Edited by D. F. Watson. JSNTSup 50. Sheffield: Sheffield Academic, 1990.

Watson, Gerard. "The Concept of 'Phantasia' from the Late Hellenistic Period to Early Neoplatonism." *ANRW* 36.7:4765–810. Part 2, *Principat*, 36.7. Edited by Hildegard Temporini and Wolfgang Haase. New York: Walter de Gruyter, 1994.

———. *Phantasia in Classical Thought*. Galway: Galway University Press, 1988.

Webb, Ruth. *Ekphrasis, Imagination and Persuasion in Ancient Rhetorical Theory and Practice*. Surrey, England: Ashgate, 2009.

———. "The Progymnasmata as Practice." Pages 289–316 in *Education in Greek and Roman Antiquity*. Edited by Y. L. Too. Leiden: Brill, 2001.

Weima, Jeffrey A. D. "'Peace and Security' (1 Thess 5:3): Prophetic Warning or Political Propaganda?" *NTS* 58 (2012): 331–59.

Weiskotten, Herbert T., ed. and trans. *Sancti Augustini vita scripta a Possidio episcope*. Rev. ed. Princeton: Princeton University Press, 1919.

Westermann, Claus. *The Psalms: Structure, Content, and Message*. Translated by Ralph D. Gehrke. Minneapolis: Augsburg, 1980.

Whiston, William. *The Works of Josephus: Complete and Unabridged*. Nashville: Thomas Nelson, 1998.

Whitaker, Robyn J. *Ekphrasis, Vision, and Persuasion in the Book of Revelation*. WUNT 2/410. Tübingen: Mohr Siebeck, 2015.

White, Joel R. "'Peace and Security' (1 Thessalonians 5:3): Is It Really a Roman Slogan?" *NTS* 59 (2013): 382–95.

Whitenton, Michael R. "The Place and Scope of Composition and Rhetoric in Greco-Roman Education: A Literature Review." Seminar paper for His 4324: Ancient Rome. Dr. Kenneth R. Jones, Instructor, fall 2010.

Wiedemann, Thomas. *Adults and Children in the Roman Empire*. New Haven: Yale University Press, 1989.

Wilkins, Ann Thomas. *Villain or Hero: Sallust's Portrayal of Catiline*. New York: Peter Lang, 1994.

Williamson, Lamar. "Led in Triumph: Paul's Use of *Thriambeuō*." *Int* 22 (1968): 317–22.

Wills, Jeffrey. *Repetition in Latin Poetry: Figures of Allusion*. Oxford: Clarendon, 1996.

Wills, Lawrence M., ed. and trans. *Ancient Jewish Novels: An Anthology*. Oxford: Oxford University Press, 2002.

Wilson, Brittany E. *Unmanly Men: Refigurations of Masculinity in Luke-Acts*. Oxford: Oxford University Press, 2015.

Winston, D. *The Wisdom of Solomon*. AB 43. New York: Doubleday, 1979.

Winter, Bruce. "The Importance of the *Captatio Benevolentiae* in the Speeches of Tertullus and Paul in Acts 24:1-21." *JTS* 42 (1991): 505–31.

———. "Official Proceedings and the Forensic Speeches in Acts 24–26." Pages 305–36 in *The Book of Acts in Its Ancient Literary Setting*. Edited by Bruce W. Winter and Andrew D. Clarke. Volume 1 of *The Book of Acts in Its First Century Setting*. Edited by Bruce W. Winter. Grand Rapids: Eerdmans, 1993.

Wright, N. T. "Paul and Caesar: A New Reading of Romans." Pages 173–93 in *A Royal Priesthood? The Use of the Bible Ethically and Politically: A Dialogue with Oliver O'Donovan*. Edited by Craig Bartholemew et al. Carlisle, U.K.: Paternoster, 2002.

Wright, William M., IV. *Rhetoric and Theology: Figural Reading of John 9*. Berlin: Walter de Gruyter, 2009.

Wuellner, Wilhelm. *The Meaning of "Fishers of Men."* Philadelphia: Westminster, 1967.

Yarbro Collins, Adela. *Mark: A Commentary*. Hermeneia. Minneapolis: Fortress, 2007.

Zeichmann, Christopher B. "Papias as Rhetorician: Ekphrasis in the Bishop's Account of Judas' Death." *NTS* 56 (2010): 427–29.

Zweck, D. "The *Exordium* of the Areopagus Speech, Acts 17.22, 23." *NTS* (1989): 94–103.

Index of Scripture and Ancient Sources

Apocrypha

New Testament

Graeco-Roman Sources

Jewish Sources

Early Christian Sources

Index of Modern Authors

Index of Subjects